THE LOGIC OF CONVERSION

The Logic
OF
Conversion

The Harmony of
Heart, Will, Mind,
and Imagination
in
JOHN HENRY NEWMAN

BY ROBERT C. CHRISTIE

Angelico Press

For information, address:
Angelico Press, Ltd.
169 Monitor St.
Brooklyn, NY 11222
www.angelicopress.com

paper 978-1-62138-876-0
cloth 978-1-62138-877-7

Book and cover design
by Michael Schrauzer

To Mom and Dad

CONTENTS

PREFACE

THE LIFE AND WORK OF JOHN HENRY NEWMAN PROVIDE EVI-
dence to sustain the proposition that the work of a theologian, one's
theology and method, is an outgrowth of, and inseparably dependent
upon, the conversion-state of the theologian.

Conversion-state can be described as the multifaceted affective, aesthetic,
moral, and intellectual developments affecting the theologian.

Theology, then, is not manufactured in the vacuum of an ivory-towered
world solely of the mind, but rather is created by that mind informed by
its heart. Heart, however, is not to be misunderstood as an anti-intellectual
thrall of emotional extremism but rather as the deepest discernment of
truth, beyond conceptual expression in words. When heart and mind are
attuned and an ultimate discernment of the heart is aligned with that of
the intellect, as in true love, the validation is simply "I know that I know
that I know that I know," as Newman himself put it.

The classical definition of theology as faith seeking understanding
is another way of interpreting Newman's statement. This study probes
how he came to know what he knew. Furthermore, by doing so and
examining the documents from each period, a correlation emerges with
Newman's conversion pilgrimage and his theology and method. As the
former changed, so must the latter, inevitably.

This is a study, then, of the reality of change in the life of John Henry
Newman, a study of his conversion experiences and the determinative
role they played in shaping his theology.

INTRODUCTION

THE FOLLOWING INTRODUCTION EXPLORES MAJOR THEORIES of conversion in contemporary theology with the objective of forming a hypothesis regarding the nature of conversion.[1] This hypothesis, while not purporting to reach a definitive judgment about the nature of conversion, can serve the more modest purpose of providing terms and categories for analyzing the complex experiences of John Henry Newman as he moved through the various stages of his religious development.

The study of the sources is organized into three parts. First, the conversion theology of Bernard Lonergan is analyzed, revealing five categories into which the data is organized: conversion's source, elements (types or modes), process, function, and effects. Second, Lonergan's initial work has undergone significant development. Part two examines these contributions from the work of five theologians who have been substantially influenced by him: Walter Conn, Robert M. Doran, Donald Gelpi, Bernard Tyrrell, and Edward K. Braxton. Part three examines complementary contributions from outside the Lonergan school: the moral theology of Bernard Häring, James Fowler's theory of faith development, and lastly the theological aesthetic theory of Hans Urs von Balthasar, whose emphasis on the objective dimension of conversion experience serves to complete the study begun by Lonergan's emphasis on the subjective dimension of the experience.

1. BERNARD LONERGAN'S THEOLOGY OF CONVERSION

BERNARD LONERGAN PLACED THE EXPERIENCE OF CONVERSION and its objective of understanding the truths of faith at the heart of systematic theology, as he stated in *Method in Theology*:

> Here perhaps may be inserted brief answers to the accusations often made against systematic theology, that it is speculative,

---

1 A note on the importance of conversion: "In Christian life conversion is an indispensable foundation. Jesus in fact began the preaching of the Good News with a call for a change of heart. That conversion consists in that most personal journey of each and all Christians into the very mystery of God. The imperative of conversion is ongoing reform and remedy of life. It is expressed in the attitude of looking out from ourselves to God, in waiting on him and in obedience to his will and word in our lives." Thomas J. Norris, *Cardinal Newman for Today* (Hyde Park: New City Press, 2010), 178.

I

irreligious, fruitless, elitist, irrelevant. Now a systematic theology can be speculative, as is clear from German Idealism; but the systematic theology we advocate is really quite a homely affair. It aims at an understanding of the truths of faith, a *Glaubensverständnis*. The truths of faith envisaged are church confessions. Again, a systematic theology can become irreligious. This is particularly true when its main emphasis is, not conversion, but proof, or when positions are taken and maintained out of individual or corporate pride. But when conversion is the basis of the whole theology, when religious conversion is the event that gives the name, God, its primary and fundamental meaning, when systematic theology does not believe it can exhaust or even do justice to that meaning, not a little has been done to keep systematic theology in harmony with its religious origins and aims.[2]

An investigation of Lonergan's conversion theology will yield a better understanding of this experience and how it impacts theology. The investigation will proceed under five headings which Lonergan's analysis, upon examination, comprises: conversion's source, elements, process, function, and effects. Lonergan describes conversion as "a transformation of the subject and his world. . . . [I]t is a resultant change of course and direction,"[3] a change which can be radical: "It begins a new sequence that can keep revealing even greater depth and breadth and wealth. Such an about-face and new beginning is what is meant by a conversion."[4] The first issue, then, is the cause of this change, or the source of conversion. "So it is that in religious matters love precedes knowledge and, as that love is God's gift, the very beginning of faith is due to God's grace."[5] As a gift of grace, "Conversion is existential, intensely personal, utterly intimate."[6] Thus, conversion is inherently relational. In respect to its source, conversion has three dimensions: it is graced, personal, and relational, an invitation from God to enter into personal relationship with Him.

Next, what are its elements? In an essay written six years after the publication of *Method in Theology*, Lonergan employed Aristotle's definition of a nature as having as immanent principle of movement and of rest.[7] "The whole movement is an ongoing process of self-transcendence."[8] Thus, grace and the movement of the human spirit are linked:

---

2 Bernard J. Lonergan, *Method in Theology* (Toronto: University of Toronto Press, 1990), 350. 3 Ibid., 130. 4 Ibid., 237.
5 Ibid., 123. 6 Ibid., 130.
7 Ibid.; Bernard J. Lonergan, "Natural Right and Historical-Mindedness," in *A Third Collection* (Mahwah: Paulist Press, 1985), 172. 8 Ibid., 175.

Specifically, it would seem that God's gift of his love (Rom. 5, 5) is not something that results from or is conditioned by man's knowledge of God. Far more plausibly it would seem that the gift may precede our knowledge of God and, indeed, may be the cause of our seeking knowledge of God.[9]

Conversion gives direction to that movement: "It is an orientation to transcendent mystery."[10] In addition to ongoing movement and direction, Lonergan introduces the element of affectivity. As used in this study, affectivity refers to the affections, including feelings, emotions, and the range of sentient responses to others that are symptoms of attraction. It reaches its zenith in interpersonal love. However, affectivity can also have a negative dimension. Conversion is mediated through man's non-intentional states and intentional responses, which are distinguished by different feelings.[11] Non-intentional states are instinctive and do "not arise out of perceiving, imagining,"[12] and tend toward satisfaction as their goal. An intentional response, on the other hand:

> relates us, not just to a cause or an end, but to an object. Such feeling gives intentional consciousness its mass, momentum, drive, power. Without these feelings our knowing and deciding would be paper thin. Because of our feelings . . . we are oriented massively and dynamically in a world mediated by meaning.[13]

But while some intentional responses are directed toward satisfactions, others are toward value, which "both carries us towards self-transcendence and selects an object for the sake of whom or of which we transcend ourselves."[14] Here in man's affectivity Lonergan locates the ground of man's response to grace, which conditions his knowledge.

However, in Lonergan's Aristotelian-based anthropology, the aspects of man's nature which correlate with his three modes of conversion are grounded in a deeper, undifferentiated state:

> If what the several principles attain are only aspects of something richer and fuller, must not the several principles themselves be but aspects of a deeper and more comprehensive principle? And is that not . . . at once a principle of movement and rest, a tidal movement that begins before consciousness, unfolds through sensitivity, intelligence, rational reflection, reasonable deliberation, only to find its rest beyond all of these? I think so.

---

9 Lonergan, *Method in Theology*, 340–41. 10 Ibid., 130, 341.
11 Ibid., 30. 12 Ibid. 13 Ibid., 30–31. 14 Ibid., 31.

The point beyond is being-in-love, a dynamic state that goes before, a principle of movement at once purgative and illuminative, and a principle of rest in which union is fulfilled.[15]

Thus man moves from pre-conscious undifferentiation through conscious differentiation to conversion. In the process, man's feelings, the domain of his affectivity, condition his development toward conversion:

The handing on of development . . . begins in the affectivity of the infant, the child, the son, the pupil, the follower. On affectivity rests the apprehension of values. On the apprehension of values rests belief. On belief follows the growth in understanding of one who has found a genuine teacher. . . . Then to confirm one's growth in understanding comes experience. One now is on one's own.[16]

Thus, affectivity is the ground of knowledge and morality, and it is also mediated by interpersonal relationships. As cause and effect, understanding is conditioned by belief, which is conditioned by values, which are conditioned by affectivity, which is conditioned by development through relationships.

His insight into differentiation of consciousness led Lonergan to distinguish three related but different types of conversion: "Conversion may be intellectual or moral or religious."[17] However, at times Lonergan replaced the term religious with affective.[18] These three types of conversion correspond to the intellectual, moral, and affective dimensions of man's nature, with the religious dimension a development from within affectivity since "religious" specifies the direction of the affections to God.

Lonergan defines intellectual conversion as the clarification and elimination of a

misleading myth concerning reality, objectivity, and human knowledge. The myth is that knowing is like looking. . . . Now this myth overlooks the distinction between the world of immediacy, say, the world of the infant, and, on the other hand, the world mediated by meaning. . . . Knowing, accordingly, is not just seeing; it is experiencing, understanding, judging, and believing. . . . Intellectual conversion is to truth attained by cognitional self-transcendence.[19]

---

15   Lonergan, "Natural Right and Historical-Mindedness," in *A Third Collection*, 175.
16   Ibid., 81.   17   Lonergan, *Method in Theology*, 238.
18   Lonergan, "Natural Right and Historical-Mindedness," in *A Third Collection*, 180.
19   Lonergan, *Method in Theology*, 238, 241.

Moral conversion "changes the criterion of one's decisions and choices from satisfactions to values . . . in opting for the truly good, even for value against satisfaction when value and satisfaction conflict."[20]

Religious conversion is "being grasped by ultimate concern. It is other-worldly falling-in-love[21]. . . . Religious conversion is to a total being-in-love as the efficacious ground of all self-transcendence."[22] If religious conversion is affectivity-based, then it follows that affectivity is the ground of all self-transcendence.

More than a decade after the publication of *Method in Theology* (1973), Lonergan wrote that the problem of inauthenticity in Christian faith was due to incomplete conversion, and therefore he introduced another dimension, full conversion, which integrates the other three: "Unauthenticity is overcome by full conversion, that is, not just the initial stages of intellectual, moral, and religious conversion but also the ongoing course of development to which conversion commits one."[23] This concept of fullness complements his notion of the synthetic nature of insight written twenty-five years earlier:

> Every insight is both *à priori* and synthetic. It is *à priori*, for it goes beyond what is merely given to sense or experiential consciousness. It is synthetic, for it adds to the merely given an explanatory unification or organization. It seems to follow that insight into insight will yield a synthetic and *à priori* account of the full range of synthetic, *à priori* components in our cognitional activity.[24]

In summarizing the elements of conversion as described in Lonergan, we find that conversion is realized in three essential modes of man: the *intellectual*, the *moral*, and the *religious*, all of which are partial dimensions stemming from his previously undifferentiated consciousness and which move toward unity in differentiation, or *full* conversion.

In terms of process, the various types of conversion emanating from an undifferentiated whole are engaged in a dynamic *ongoing* process, involving the principles of *movement*, *direction*, and *rest*; the principle of *development*; and the *primacy of affectivity* in the developmental process, especially *through relationships*. In addition, Lonergan observed that conversions occur in a causal pattern beginning with the religious type, which sublates the moral, which in turn sublates the intellectual. This dimension of *sublation* is the principle of development whereby one mode exceeds the experience of

---

20   Ibid., 240.   21   Ibid.   22   Ibid., 241.

23   Lonergan, "Unity and Plurality," in *A Third Collection*, 249.

24   Bernard J. Lonergan, *Insight* (San Francisco: Harper and Row, 1957), xi.

another mode and in the process takes up into itself and transforms the other experience, making it fuller and richer. In Lonergan, religious conversion sublates moral, and both sublate intellectual, and "Then there is a new basis for all valuing and all doing good."[25] Lonergan specifically described this principle and the causal relationship of the three types:

> Though religious conversion sublates moral, and moral conversion sublates intellectual, one is not to infer that intellectual comes first and then moral and finally religious. On the contrary, from a causal viewpoint, one would say that first there is God's gift of his love. Next, the eye of this love reveals values in their splendor, while the strength of this love brings about their realization, and that is moral conversion. Finally, among the values discerned by the eye of love is the value of believing the truths taught by the religious tradition, and in such tradition and belief are the seeds of intellectual conversion.[26]

In addition to these principles affecting the process of conversion, Lonergan introduces two others, the dimensions of *complementarity* and *reciprocity*. Complementarity occurs when one conversion mode adds to another as a structural complement, tending toward a greater, more comprehensive, and fuller conversion. Reciprocity is the interaction by which the various types of conversion interpenetrate, mutually influencing one another. Lonergan describes this aspect of process through his metaphor of the horizon, which underlies his initial definition of conversion. Horizon is "the limit of one's field of vision"[27] and "the movement into a new horizon involves an about-face. . . . Such an about-face and new beginning is what is meant by a conversion."[28] Horizons are related in three possible ways: as complementary, genetic, or dialectic. When they exist as complementary, "Horizons in some measure include one another and . . . they complement one another."[29] As genetic, "They are related as successive stages in some process of development. Each later stage presupposes earlier stages, partly to include them, and partly to transform them."[30] When horizons are in opposition, they are dialectically related: "What for one is true, for another is false. What for one is good, for another is evil. Each may have some awareness of the other and so each in a manner may include the other. But such inclusion is also negation and rejection."[31] Horizons both condition and limit development.[32] Conversions, then, as changes in horizon, are

---

25 Lonergan, *Method in Theology*, 242.   26 Ibid., 243.
27 Ibid., 235.   28 Ibid., 237–38.   29 Ibid., 236.
30 Ibid.   31 Ibid.   32 Ibid., 237.

subject to the interrelated processes of complementarity, development, and, by implication of their interpenetration and mutual influence, reciprocity. The dialectical relationship can be viewed as the negation of complementarity. Thus, in Lonergan's conversion theology seven dimensions are intrinsic to the process, all of which are aspects of the major principle of *development*: *ongoing movement and rest, complementarity, reciprocity, direction,* and *sublation*.

Regarding the function of conversion, Lonergan asserts five requisite aspects, but also introduces two ambiguities. Conversion begins in the affectively grounded religious mode:

> Religious conversion is being grasped by ultimate concern. For Christians it is God's love flooding our hearts through the Holy Spirit given to us. It is the gift of grace. . . . Operative grace is the replacement of the heart of stone by a heart of flesh. Cooperative grace is the heart of flesh becoming effective in good works through human freedom. Operative grace is religious conversion. Cooperative grace is the effectiveness of conversion.[33]

First, the *change of heart* from that of stone to that of flesh is the core of the affective dimension of conversion. However, Lonergan introduces an ambiguity in his description of religious conversion as a process which occurs above and beyond man's freedom. Subsequently, he introduced a distinction clarifying man's active role, and thus his responsibility, in the process: "Religious *conversion* (occurs) when one accepts God's gift of his love bestowed through the Holy Spirit."[34] Thus, man's response to grace is essential for religious conversion.

Next, the necessity of man's response leads to the second requisite function of conversion, *faith*, which is dynamically connected to the gift of grace. But importantly, faith includes both affective and cognitive dimensions: "Faith is the knowledge born of religious love."[35] Then, interpreting Pascal's axiom regarding the primacy of the heart,[36] Lonergan synthesizes grace, faith, love, and knowledge in a dynamic interpersonal relationship:

---

33   Ibid., 241.

34   Bernard J. Lonergan, "Reality, Myth, Symbol," in *Myth, Symbol, and Reality*, ed. Alan M. Olson (Notre Dame: University of Notre Dame Press, 1980), 36.

35   Lonergan, *Method in Theology*, 115.

36   "The heart has reasons which reason does not know." Noting a similar primacy of the heart in Newman, Bouyer comments on "the motto which Newman chose for his cardinal's shield, and which perhaps provides the master key to the power, the influence, of his [*Parochial and Plain*] Sermons: *Cor ad cor loquitur*." Louis Bouyer, *Newman: An Intellectual and Spiritual Biography* (New York: Meridian Books, 1960), 181.

The meaning, then, of Pascal's remark would be that, besides the factual knowledge reached by experiencing, understanding, and verifying, there is another kind of knowledge reached through the discernment of value and the judgments of value of a person in love.

Faith, accordingly, is such further knowledge when the love is God's love flooding our hearts.... (T)here is an apprehension of transcendent value.[37]

Thus, love in the form of grace motivates faith, and faith is knowledge of being loved and then loving in return. In this respect, faith has both affective and cognitive aspects. However, faith is a dynamic dimension of the conversion process, which indicates that it too is subject to the principle of development: "But who it is we love, is neither given nor as yet understood.... Our love reveals to us values we had not appreciated.... But if we would know what is going on within us . . . we have to inquire, investigate, seek counsel."[38]

The act of faith in response to love produces a knowledge which

consists in the experienced fulfillment of our unrestricted thrust to self-transcendence, in our actuated orientation towards the mystery of love and awe... (which) may be objectified as a clouded revelation of absolute intelligence and intelligibility, absolute truth and reality, absolute goodness and holiness. With that objectification there recurs the question of God in a new form.... Such is the basic option of the existential subject once called by God.[39]

Thus, the act of faith brings us into the presence of, and into a relationship with, the *Transcendent Other*. And this presence is the third function produced by conversion, a new *vision* made possible by the act of faith: "It is as if one's eyes were opened and one's former world faded and fell away. There emerges something new."[40] Recalling Lonergan's description of horizon, we find it linked to vision: "Horizon . . . denotes . . . the limit of one's field of vision. . . . Beyond the horizon lie the objects that, at least for the moment, cannot be seen."[41] Thus, grace motivates faith, which motivates conversion, which envisions a new object of that experience as the *Transcendent Other*. Conversion "directs (man's) gaze, pervades his imagination, releases the symbols that penetrate to the depths of his psyche."[42] In respect

---

37 Lonergan, *Method in Theology*, 115.   38 Ibid, 122–23.
39 Ibid., 115–16.   40 Ibid., 130.   41 Ibid., 236.   42 Ibid., 130.

to vision, eight years prior to writing *Method in Theology*, Lonergan had written about the relationship of the imagination in regard to cognition:

> But human knowing is also formally dynamic. . . . It puts itself together, one part summoning forth the next, till the whole is reached. . . . Experience stimulates inquiry, and inquiry is intelligence bringing itself to act; it leads from experience through imagination to insight, and from insight to the concepts that combine in simple objects both what has been grasped by insight and what in experience or imagination is relevant to the insight.[43]

In summary, Lonergan's theology of the function of conversion has five essential aspects: *change of heart, faith, knowledge of being loved,* and *vision* of the *Transcendent Other.*

The effects of conversion in Lonergan's schema are threefold. "Religious conversion is . . . total and permanent self-surrender."[44] Surrender is an implicit obedience: "Then moral conversion consists in opting for the truly good, even for value against satisfaction when value and satisfaction conflict."[45] Complementing the inward encounter with grace is the outward dynamic:

> Further, religious conversion, if it is Christian, is not just a state of mind and heart. Essential to it is an intersubjective, interpersonal component. . . . There is the outward encounter with Christian witness. . . . [T]he function of church doctrines lies within the function of Christian witness. For the witness is to the mysteries revealed by God and, for Catholics, infallibly declared by the church.[46]

If witness is linked to the Church, and both are seen as two other dimensions of conversion, then conversion is also social by nature. Conversion "is not so private as to be solitary. It can happen to many, and they can form a community to sustain one another in working out the implications and fulfilling the promise of their new life."[47]

In summarizing the effects of conversion in Lonergan's theology, three are distinguishable: *obedience* (which is the ground of submission), *socialization* in the form of giving witness, and sharing and supporting the conversion experience in a communal setting, the *church.* However, these dimensions are less fully articulated than Lonergan's work on the elements and

---

43   Bernard J. Lonergan, "Cognitional Structure," in *Collection* (New York: Herder and Herder, 1967), 233.   44   Lonergan, *Method in Theology,* 240.

45   Ibid.   46   Ibid., 327.   47   Ibid., 130.

function of conversion, and other theologians have substantially developed Lonergan's initial insights and implications. An examination of the relevant developments of his thought in the work of five theologians whom he has influenced will develop further a theological understanding of conversion.[48]

2. DEVELOPMENTS OF LONERGAN'S CONVERSION THEOLOGY IN CONTEMPORARY THEOLOGY

WALTER CONN: Christian Conversion, Conversion of the Imagination, and Primacy of Type

WALTER CONN HAS BOTH ELABORATED UPON AND REVISED aspects of Lonergan's conversion theology, suggesting changes in the nature, process, and modes of conversion. In addition to affirming the primacy of affectivity in the conversion process, Conn notes an important conversion of the imagination within affectivity linked to a content shift through the vision of Jesus Christ.

For Lonergan, conversion begins with the religious mode, but Conn states:

> whatever Lonergan's intentions, his description suggests, if not perfection, at least the deepest kind of fulfillment. . . . Precisely because this radical experience is so rare, this understanding of "religious" is uncommon[49]. . . . This characterization of religious conversion does not seem to be descriptive of the ordinary religious person's experience.[50]

In respect to the elements of conversion, Conn expands the notion of conversion to include other stages prior to religious conversion in Lonergan's sense, thereby accepting but at the same time moving Lonergan's mode to the extreme end of the conversion continuum.[51] For Conn, conversions unfold through five major modes:[52] the affective mode, then the cognitive and moral, then the Christian mode as the first stage of religious conversion, and finally religious conversion in Lonergan's sense as a "special, extraordinary transformation of religious consciousness,"[53] (which is) "the surrender of absolute autonomy in the acknowledgment of one's radical

---

48 For a comprehensive examination of Newman's effect on Lonergan, see Richard L. Liddy, "John Henry Newman's Influence on Bernard Lonergan," in *Saint John Henry Newman: Preserving and Promulgating His Legacy*, ed. Robert C. Christie (Newcastle Upon Tyne: Cambridge Scholars Press, 2019), 49–71.

49 Walter Conn, *Christian Conversion* (Mahwah: Paulist Press, 1986), 194.

50 Ibid., 193.   51 Ibid., 113.   52 Ibid., 212.   53 Ibid., 197.

dependence on the power of God. And this, of course, is the core of religious conversion."[54] Conn's Christian conversion includes a key element. While religious in quality, its unique content is the image of Christ:

> Truly Christian conversion, we noted, is never merely moral, but through the response to God's love in Jesus always includes a religious quality. Love of God through love of the neighbor perceived as Jesus is the Christian version of an affective-cognitive-moral conversion[55] . . . and through the following of Jesus one begins to live this truth[56]. . . . Christian conversion is a unique integration of the three conversions in the Gospel of Jesus.[57]

However, in Conn's work, it is only at the level of Christian conversion that the image, the perception, of Jesus and its acceptance occur. This vision is not a dimension of his previous affective, cognitive, and moral modes, and so it seems that it is not an essential aspect of conversion. On that ground, it appears that these experiences of change are better described as developments. Both developments and conversions are changes, but, as James Fowler notes, a change in content is the criterion of conversion, while a change in structure is the criterion of development. Conversion in Conn has to do with changes in the *contents* of faith: "Conversion is *a significant recentering of one's previous conscious or unconscious images of value and power, and the conscious adoption of a new set of stories in the commitment to reshape one's life in a new community of interpretation and action.*"[58] Conn also states: "I specified conversion as a vertical shift in structure (in contrast to a horizontal change in content)."[59] Thus, to avoid confusion with the religious quality usually associated with conversion, the term development, rather than conversion, better expresses the changes which Conn specifies prior to Christian conversion.

Thus, incorporating but also adjusting Conn's modes, there are affective, cognitive, and moral developments up to a first-stage religious or Christian conversion, which includes an image of Jesus. This conversion may be followed by ever-deepening development into radical religious conversion in Lonergan's sense.

In Conn's system, affective conversion is the ground of all other conversions, since he holds that "the personalist drive for self-transcendence is affective at its very core."[60] Here, Conn is consistent with Lonergan. For Conn:

---

54 Ibid., 216–17. 55 Ibid., 210. 56 Ibid., 209. 57 Ibid.
58 James Fowler, *Stages of Faith* (San Francisco: Harper, 1981), 281–82.
59 Conn, *Christian Conversion*, 267. 60 Ibid., 120.

> Affective conversion is the transformation of our deepest life of
> feeling. . . . Falling-in-love, in other words, is a more or less rad-
> ical transformation of a person's life: affective conversion . . . is
> a reorientation of the whole person, but especially of those pre-
> reflective desires which must support our reflectively conscious
> decisions, choices, and loving commitments.[61]

Further, affective conversion is then the natural ground of moral conversion: "If moral conversion is the recognition of the possibility . . . of
becoming a living principle of benevolence and beneficence, affective
conversion . . . actualizes that possibility."[62]

Affectivity, however, is complex, involving not only feelings but the
imagination: "Feeling and imagination are inextricably linked in a symbolic world that recognizes no divorce."[63] As did Lonergan, Conn also
holds that affectivity has a cognitive dimension, which he develops through
the work of Robert Solomon:

> For Solomon, then, emotions are not only radically cognitive,
> but through unreflective interpretation, judgment, decision, and
> choice they are also fundamentally constitutive of our human
> world. Emotions are not essentially at odds with reason: rather,
> in reflection lies the possibility of emotional transformation[64]. . . .
> As emotion, love is not blind, it has a cognitive character. . . . Love
> can be influenced, even transformed, by reflection.[65]

In terms of process, here Conn implicitly affirms the principle of reciprocity between the affective, cognitive, and moral dimensions. Thus, they
also interact simultaneously, concurring with Charles Curran's critique
of Lonergan's developmental process: "The solution . . . cannot involve a
continuous and harmonious development . . . but rather . . . a more radical
solution which embraces at one and the same time the three aspects of
moral, religious, and Christian conversion."[66]

In addition, Conn notes a major fact — that while the process of conversion includes principles of reciprocity and simultaneity between its
various dimensions, one dimension may be primary at any given stage:

> While all the basic dimensions, including decision, are involved
> in every form of conversion, each conversion is specified by a

---

61 Ibid., 149.   62 Ibid., 135.   63 Ibid., 125.
64 Ibid., 143.   65 Ibid., 147.
66 Charles Curran, "Christian Conversion in the Writings of Bernard Lonergan,"
in *Foundations in Theology*, ed. Philip McShane (Notre Dame: University of Notre
Dame Press, 1972), 59.

particular element (e.g., as deciding is primary in moral conversion, so understanding and judging play important roles in affective conversion, but to focus on them as definitive is to miss the transformation of desire that is central to affective conversion).[67]

Another influence on Conn's conversion theology is the work of Rosemary Haughton, which not only affirms the cognitive dimension of affectivity, as did Solomon's, but also provides the basis for Conn's linking of affective conversion to the vision of Christ through an analysis of love: "Haughton's analysis of conversion in her *Transformation of Man* characterizes it precisely as a radical breakthrough of *love*."[68] But crucial interpersonal dynamics are required to accomplish this. Only the self-conscious individual person is capable of self-giving, but such self-knowledge "can only be accepted by one who has experienced himself or herself as *loved*. So loving requires self-surrender; but self-surrender requires being loved."[69] Further, the act of love is a "commitment to the unknown.... [O]nly the knowledge of *being loved* has the power to set free into faith.... Someone already transformed by love is needed.... This is the work of the community of faith."[70] The quality of genuine love is that "it opens out and gives itself.... [N]ot only the desire for the 'other' or 'beyond,' but the impulse to give oneself to that 'otherness.'"[71] In Haughton's analysis of love, it reaches beyond its human object for both its ultimate objective as well as its source.[72]

Here Conn distinguishes an important dynamic between affectivity and cognition involving symbolism and the imagination:

> Experiencing, understanding, judging, and deciding all work together through feeling to create the appropriate concrete images for discovering and communicating the deepest personal images of one's world. Cognitive conversion in this symbolic pattern might ... be appropriately called conversion of the imagination. By reason of its deeply personal and undifferentiated nature, it is closely associated with ... affective conversion ... for feeling and imagination are inextricably linked in a symbolic world that recognizes no divorce. This is why all personal conversions are so intrinsically dependent on the quality and vitality of the symbols

---

67 Conn, *Christian Conversion*, 317.   68 Ibid., 145.   69 Ibid., 147.
70 Rosemary Haughton, *The Transformation of Man* (New York: Paulist Press, 1967), 80, 174, 80, 115.
71 Rosemary Haughton, *Love* (Baltimore: Penguin, 1971), 173, 175.
72 Ibid., 176.

and stories available in one's community. . . . Conversion to the point of understanding is the point of entry into our lives of genuine mystery. The implications of cognitive conversion of the imagination for religious understanding, then, are enormous.[73]

Conversion occurs, then, when the image of Christ, mediated through the community of love, is perceived, understood, and accepted. This is Conn's stage of religiously qualified Christian conversion, requiring affective and cognitive development precipitating the conversion, which can grasp and then affirm the vision.

Conn's work is both a horizontal development through the expansion of religious conversion to include the Christian dimension, as well as a vertical development into the affective ground of conversion with its cognitive and imaginative dimensions, which make the vision of Christ not only possible but acceptable.

In summary, Conn's contribution to the study of conversion is that he expands the elements by identifying Christian conversion as a dimension within the context of religious conversion, of which Lonergan's is considered a radical form. He also further develops affectivity as the ground of all conversion.

He also develops the process of conversion in three ways. His emphasis on the cognitive dimension of affectivity and his concept of conversion of the imagination as an affective-cognitive dimension of the conversion process are both products of the process principles of reciprocity, complementarity, and simultaneity. Lastly, his insight of the primacy of one mode of conversion over the others at any given stage is an important added dimension of the process. This leads to the description of a conversion stage by that dominant type even when the other modes are operative but subordinate. In terms of function, the conversion of the imagination produces the vision of Christ which causes conversion.

In respect to the effects of conversion, his analysis of religious love in knowledge of the self as loved unconditionally is a major development, which is an effect of the Christological vision. This empowers the self to respond in kind. Since the vision is mediated through the community of love, conversion has an essential ecclesial dimension.

Conn significantly strengthens numerous implications of Lonergan's conversion theology. His unique contributions are threefold. First, the addition of the element of *Christian conversion* expands the notion of religious conversion found in Lonergan more in line with the common usage

---

73 Conn, *Christian Conversion*, 124–25.

of the term religious, and it is a more accurate reflection of common religious experience. Second, his concept of the *conversion of the imagination*, at once both cognitive and affective, is a development from within affectivity, and since it produces the Christic vision which effects conversion, it is another major insight. Third, his insight of *primacy of type or mode* at any given stage is a crucial dimension of the process of conversion. Unless and until the modes exist in a state of harmonic balance, this dissonance would appear to be an ever-present reality.

Conn, however, reverses Lonergan's cause and effect relationship of vision and conversion. For Lonergan, conversion produces the vision, whereas for Conn, the vision produced by conversion of the imagination causes Christian conversion.[74]

ROBERT M. DORAN: *Psychic Conversion, the Aesthetic Dimension, and Aesthetic Mediation*

ROBERT M. DORAN PROVIDES A FURTHER ANALYSIS OF A VERtical nature through his exploration of affectivity in relation to conversion. He proposes a mode of conversion which he calls the psychic as a complement to Lonergan's intentionality analysis.[75] Doran's work also complements Conn's in that he examines the deeper recesses of the affective dimension which he identifies as the aesthetic, or the domain of spontaneous sensitivity. Doran describes psychic conversion as

> the transformation of the psychic component of the censorship exercised by our orientation as dramatic subjects — a censorship over images for insight and over concomitant feelings — from a repressive to a constructive role, thus enabling simultaneously the participation of the psyche in the operations of intentionality, and the embodiment of intentionality through the mass and momentum of feeling.[76]

Thus, feelings, images, and insight are inextricably linked. When the psyche represses images, affectivity becomes disassociated from its "imaginal apprehensive component." The result is incoherence and breakdown of sensitive consciousness as feelings attach to non-correspondent images. Thus, psychic conversion is related to affective conversion as cause to effect: "Lonergan's affective conversion is the fruit in part of psychic conversion,"[77]

---

74   See also Walter E. Conn, *Conscience and Conversion in Newman: A Developmental Study of Self in John Henry Newman* (Milwaukee: Marquette University Press, 2010).
75   Robert M. Doran, *Theology and the Dialectics of History* (Toronto: University of Toronto Press, 1990), 8.   76   Ibid., 63.   77   Ibid., 9.

and Doran affirms both the primacy of the affective dimension as well as the need for psychic conversion, since affectivity is "the sensitive and imaginal base in aesthetic consciousness out of which there emerges all inquiry, insight, conceptualization, formulation, reflection, affirmation of the virtually unconditioned, deliberation, and decision."[78] The neglect of man's "sensitive spontaneity, the aesthetic component that permeates the narrative order of inquiry,"[79] causes psychic damage. Thus, Doran argues for restoration of this necessary dimension of consciousness: "As there is a transcendental notion of the intelligible, of the true, of the real, and of the good, so there is a transcendental notion of the beautiful."[80] This latter notion is revealed in feelings which motivate the drive for meaning, truth, and value, and thus the aesthetic dimension, or sensitive consciousness, is an essential element in the development of affectivity, which lies at the heart of the conversion process. Doran's perspective is significant in that the capacity for image formation is critical to affective conversion and therefore to all subsequent conversions. In this respect, Doran is consistent with Lonergan, who stated in *Insight* that "the image is necessary for insight."[81]

Here Doran qualifies the aesthetic dimension as not only the complement but also the ground of man's affective and cognitional activities. Man's cognitional activities do not take everything into account:

> The remainder is, I believe, best understood as the *aesthetic* dimension of the subject. It is this dimension that calls for a second mediation of immediacy by meaning, one that for subjects hitherto negligent of the aesthetic may begin as therapy but that more radically is soul-making. Soul is aesthesis. And soul-making is thus the recovery of aesthetic subjectivity. If values are primordially apprehended in feelings, then aesthetics is the foundation of existential subjectivity and thus of ethics and religion. Soul-making, as the recovery of the aesthetic dimension, is the post-therapeutic basis of morals and prayer. Lonergan's opening of a distinct level of consciousness that has to do with value, dialectic, and foundations as something distinct from, including, but more than and sublating meaning and truth is really an opening upon aesthetic consciousness as distinct from, including, but more than and sublating cognitional consciousness. Ethics is radically aesthetics; and the existential subject, concerned with character as

---

78   Robert M. Doran, *Psychic Conversion and Theological Foundations* (Chico: Scholars Press, 1981), 130.

79   Ibid., 128.   80   Ibid., 131.   81   Lonergan, *Insight*, 8.

his or her issue, is the aesthetic subject. Soul, beyond intelligence and reasonableness, is the key to character.[82]

Man's aesthetic subjectivity is inherently symbol-sensitive. Symbols evoke and are evoked by feelings.[83] Symbols and the feelings which evoke them specify one's affective capacities, dispositions, and habits.[84] Thus, "Affective development, or aberration, involves a transvaluation and transformation of symbols."[85] And so "The transformation and transvaluation of symbols, then, goes hand in hand with one's affective development. . . . Aesthetic subjectivity is the psychic correlative of our intentional existential orientation in the world mediated by meaning."[86] But a critical aspect of symbols is their content. In Doran's analysis, they mediate knowledge of being:

> Psychic conversion, initially, is the acquisition of the capacity to disengage and interpret correctly the elemental symbols of one's being and to form or transform one's existential and cognitive praxis on the basis of such a recovery of the story of one's search for direction in the movement of life.[87]

Doran expands Lonergan's theory of intentionality into the unconscious domain, noting that symbols stand in relation to affectivity as meaning does to intentionality. Thus, the aesthetic domain, through symbols, ultimately affects intentionality. Doran proposes a principle of aesthetic mediation to harmonize the aesthetic, affective, and intentional domains:

> The central thesis of psychic conversion (is) intrinsically complementary to that proposed by Lonergan[88]. . . . The opposites in the constitution of the person constitute a dialectic of desire (attaining) reconciliation only in the aesthetic mediation that shares in both poles of the opposition. . . . Through psychic conversion, the aesthetic mediation of spirit and matter is appropriated[89]. . . . Sensitive spontaneity (is) the aesthetic component that permeates the normative order of inquiry.[90]

When his conversion mode harmonizes with Lonergan's affective conversion, Doran expresses the synthesis in Lonergan's own words: "At the

---

82   Robert M. Doran, *Theological Foundations*, vol. ii (Milwaukee: Marquette University Press, 1994), 123.   83   Lonergan, *Method in Theology*, 64.
84   Ibid., 65.   85   Ibid., 66.
86   Doran, *Theological Foundations*, 315.
87   Doran, *Psychic Conversion and Theological Foundations*, 142.
88   Ibid., 163.   89   Ibid., 191.   90   Ibid., 128.

summit of the ascent (is) being in love with God. In the measure that the summit is reached, then the supreme value is God. . . . Then affectivity is of a single piece."[91]

Doran ultimately suggests, then, that psychic conversion is the base of moral and religious conversion on the cognitional level, and aesthetic subjectivity is the ground of moral and religious response as the "locus of the apprehension of values."[92] Since response conditions conversion, the capacity for aesthetic subjectivity appears to condition the psychic, religious, moral, and intellectual conversions.[93] Conversion at its most fundamental level is motivated by feelings as responses to values, and by the symbols which are evoked by, or which evoke, such feelings.

It seems that Doran's mode of psychic conversion is a cognitive dimension of development from within affectivity, as Walter Conn suggests: "It *seems* that psychic conversion would be some form of explicitly critical affective conversion — the extension of cognitive (intellectual) conversion into the domain of preconscious affectivity through the symbolic imagination."[94] Doran's analysis of aesthetic subjectivity, however, appears to go beyond the "censor," the transformation of which is the objective of psychic conversion, to the very content of affectivity, the feelings themselves and their accompanying symbolic manifestations.

Aesthetic subjectivity is the dimension of feelings and related symbols which provides the ground for development and conversion. In fact, for Doran the aesthetic is the fourth dimension of human nature, along with the affective, the intellectual, and the moral.[95] Thus, the capacity to feel and imagine conditions the capacity to know, to value, and to love. Conn's observation of psychic conversion may be accurate in that it appears to be a structural change since, in the process, the cognitive pervades the affective dimension.

However, psychic conversion is a structural alteration which makes possible and implies a change in content, but that content is not provided by the conversion of the psychic censor. Thus, the introduction of new images and feelings seems required as the positive complement to the essentially negative function of psychic conversion — the removal of an impediment. These new images and feelings provide the basis for what may be called an aesthetic conversion, and this introduction may also effect psychic conversion. This is similar to Conn's concept of the conversion of the imagination

---

91   Lonergan, *Method in Theology*, 64.   92   Doran, *Theological Foundations*, 316.
93   Ibid., 316–17.   94   Conn, *Christian Conversion*, 316–17, n. 59.
95   Doran, *Theological Foundations*, 105.

wherein all cognitive activities "work together through feeling to create the appropriate images for discovering and communicating the deepest personal meanings for our world."[96] When combined with the alteration of the psychic censor, this action can produce a conversion of the aesthetic, affective, and cognitive dimensions which can best be called an aesthetic conversion. As was the case with Conn's developments prior to religious conversion, Doran's psychic conversion is better described as a development which makes possible a conversion of aesthetic sensitivity, which requires the content of the image or symbol that effects the conversion.

In summary, Doran's contribution, which is a vertical development as a depth analysis of the conversion experience, is significant in emphasizing the aesthetic as the fourth dimension of man's nature. The establishment of aesthetic sensitivity as the ground of affectivity is a second major note, since they are related as cause and effect. Feelings respond to images and symbols, and alteration of the image censor makes new images and thus new feelings possible, which in turn can generate other new images. Doran's concept of psychic conversion, which I have suggested is a development rather than a conversion, implies the need for a complementary function which would supply the needed image or symbol. Here Doran provides the basis for what I would term an *aesthetic conversion* as the ground of affective conversion, which is an added dimension of the elements of conversion. Aesthetic conversion appears to function as *the first conversion* in the order of occurrence, effecting affective and cognitive conversions in the process.

In respect to process, his principle of *aesthetic mediation*, which harmonizes the aesthetic, affective, and cognitive domains, is a significant indication of the major function of the aesthetic dimension in the conversion process.

DONALD GELPI : *The Aesthetic Vision and Sociopolitical Conversion*

DONALD GELPI FOLLOWS LONERGAN IN REGARD TO WHAT HE distinguishes as the four modes of conversion affirmed by Lonergan: the affective, the religious, the intellectual, and the moral. While Lonergan sometimes interchanged religious and affective when addressing the various modes, it does not appear that he differentiated them into specifically separate modes as does Gelpi.

In his analysis, Gelpi also stresses the primary role of the vision of Jesus in conversion, the aesthetic element which transvalues all previous developments to the religious level in what he calls "Christian conversion"

---

96   Conn, *Christian Conversion*, 124.

(which for Gelpi is synonymous with religious conversion). This produces faith, and it occurs through the faith community, the ecclesial dimension. Gelpi sees at this point a need to move beyond the "private" nature of the four conversions to "deprivatize" conversion in social action, for which he envisions a fifth conversion mode, the sociopolitical, the absence of which he considers a deficiency in Lonergan's work.[97]

Noting the aesthetic-imaginative quality of the vision of Jesus in the process, Gelpi writes: "Affective conversion nurtures and sensitizes the heart to the divine beauty incarnate in Jesus and in people who resemble Him. We perceive beauty affectively and intuitively with the heart rather than with reason."[98] This vision, wrought by the aesthetic imagination, is the content of Christian (religious) conversion, which effects faith: "The initial consent of faith flows, I submit, from a graced, intuitive perception of divine beauty incarnate. The heart expands to the beauty made flesh in God's incarnate word and in people who resemble Him. . . . Incarnational faith demands a certain quality of the imagination."[99]

According to Gelpi, in addition to faith two other elements are produced by the vision of Christ, and both are social and relational. Gelpi's Christian conversion occurs within a community of faith and thus has a necessary ecclesial dimension, as it did in Lonergan and Conn. But Gelpi suggests a fifth mode of conversion which he sees as going beyond the "private" forms of the previous four. His sociopolitical conversion "deprivatizes" conversion and occurs when "I take responsibility for influencing, in so far as I can, the choices of others, especially of those whose decisions shape the policy and practice of large, impersonal social institutions."[100] Gelpi refers to this as a "second moment" in moral conversion, "so sufficiently distinct as to require a conversion in its own right."[101]

In summary, Gelpi's contribution is that he expands upon the elements of conversion through his insight into the function of the aesthetic dimension and seminal role of the vision of Jesus. He also expands the function of conversion when he ascribes to this vision the work of transvaluing other developments into conversions. (Gelpi uses the term conversion as Conn does to describe developments prior to religious conversion, and again these occurrences are better described as developments rather than conversions.) He also reiterates the effect of Christian conversion in the

---

97   Donald Gelpi, "Religious Conversion: A New Way of Being," in *The Human Experience of Conversion*, ed. Francis A. Eigo (Villanova: Villanova University Press, 1987), 128.   98   Ibid., 187.   99   Ibid., 187, 193.
100   Ibid., 178.   101   Ibid., 181.

act of faith, and these two dimensions of conversion, the vision of Jesus and faith, occur within the ecclesial dimension. Lastly, a second effect of Christian conversion is that of sociopolitical conversion which socializes the conversion experience. Thus, Gelpi's work expands both the elements of conversion to include the sociopolitical dimension and the function to include the transvaluation of all previous developments. All of this is effected through an aesthetic vision of Christ, which moves the affections, changes the heart, and ultimately produces faith. This is accomplished in an ecclesial setting as the locus of the vision and conversion experience, with an attendant moral effect in the expansion of personal responsibility into the social domain in sociopolitical conversion. Gelpi's theory of conversion is a horizontal expansion through his sociopolitical and ecclesial dimensions as well as a vertical expansion through the role which the vision of Jesus plays in transvaluing developments into conversions.

BERNARD TYRRELL: *The Interpersonalist-Sacramental Dimension*

ANOTHER LONERGAN FOLLOWER, BERNARD J. TYRRELL, PROposes a theologically based psychotherapeutic method called Christotherapy to promote conversion. As did Gelpi, Tyrrell follows Lonergan in respect to religious, moral, and intellectual modes of conversion but also sees the need for a psychological conversion which, in relation to affective conversion, is fundamentally the same: "A shift from a neurotic to a psychologically healthy state involves at its core a shift from an unhealthy, disturbed affectivity to a healthy, whole affectivity,"[102] which includes transformation of feelings.[103] Tyrrell's method promotes cognitive insights regarding the wounded psyche through the loving support of the therapist, who serves as the "instrument of the resurrected Christ," whereby "the power of the healing and life-giving Christ flow(s) through him or her to touch and transform the wounded psyche and spirit."[104]

At every stage of the process, two important factors are present and operative: the vision of Christ and the mediation of God's love through the therapist. In analyzing the function of image in the conversion process, Tyrrell notes that self-image tends to determine one's actions,[105] and thus, "The issues of self-image and its transformation are vital in the process of maturation in Christ, and the achievement, active reception, of, wholeness, self-transcendence . . . . Christian revelation offers the

---

102   Bernard Tyrrell, "Affective Conversion: A New Way of Feeling," in *The Human Experience of Conversion*, ed. Francis Eigo (Villanova: Villanova University Press, 1987), 128.
103   Ibid., 111.   104   Ibid., 131.
105   Bernard Tyrrell, *Christotherapy* (Mahwah: Paulist Press, 1975), 8–18.

individual a self-image which is at once realistic and yet full of hope and radically optimistic."[106] The ultimate objective of re-creating self-image is for the individual "to have as his own that self-image which was also in Christ Jesus."[107] Tyrrell has also introduced images or models of Jesus as Savior, Healer, Liberator, Brother, Friend, Beloved, and Lover to assist in this process.[108]

> The images of Jesus disclosed to us in holy scripture pro-
> vide the most basic and important revelations of the ways in
> which Jesus loves us[109].... (They) evoke powerful affective
> responses.... (F)eelings play a pivotal role ... in one's affective
> relationship with Jesus Christ and the consequent transformation
> of our affective relationships with one another in Christ.[110]

Thus, the images of Christ, which play one of the two central roles in Tyrrell's system of conversion, are more prominent in Tyrrell's conversion theology than in any previous commentator's work.

The second primary role in Christotherapy, which is linked to the image of Jesus, is that of the therapist, who serves a personalist-sacramental function. Reminiscent of Haughton's insight regarding the need not only to love but to be loved, Tyrrell's therapist is the loving mediator of Christ's love to others. Following psychologist William Glasser, Tyrrell agrees that the "quest for fulfillment in the need to love and be loved is a constant throughout life."[111] Christotherapy transforms this to the religious level: "Christotherapy sees the deepest need and desire of the human heart as the need to love and be loved by God."[112] As Tyrrell summarizes this function, "Most importantly, the human therapist experiences herself or himself as an instrument of the resurrected Christ and lets the power of the healing and life-giving Christ flow through him or her to touch and transform the wounded psyche and spirit of the person seeking wholeness and more abundant life."[113] This is not, however, an optional dimension of conversion, since, as Tyrrell says (again following Glasser), "For an individual to fulfill his basic needs, involvement with other people is necessary. At the very minimum, we must each have one person whom we care about and who cares about us.... Christotherapy ... stresses that in the ordinary purpose of providence it is only through the encounter of loving, beneficent, benevolent persons that the reality of God's love

---

106   Ibid., 77.   107   Ibid., 71.
108   Bernard Tyrrell, *Christointegration* (Mahwah: Paulist Press, 1989).
109   Ibid., 16.   110   Ibid., 16–17.   111   Tyrrell, *Christotherapy*, 36.
112   Ibid., 37.   113   Tyrrell, "Affective Conversion: A New Way of Feeling," 131.

for us becomes existentially mediated or 'really real.'"[114] Thus, Tyrrell's interpersonalist-sacramental mediator is an essential element of conversion, since it indicates the generic Christian disposition toward others.

EDWARD K. BRAXTON AND ECCLESIAL CONVERSION:
Mediation of the Vision of Jesus through the Wisdom Community

ANOTHER THEOLOGIAN WORKING WITHIN THE LONERGAN framework is Edward K. Braxton, who has developed a theory of six conversion modes: the religious, theistic, Christian, ecclesial, moral, and intellectual. His development of the ecclesial mode surpasses that of any previous commentator and moves the religious, theistic, and Christian modes into the communal sphere: "Ecclesial conversion . . . is the turn to others . . . . It is a dynamic that binds one to others who share the experience of the Jesus event."[115] Here again the image of Jesus, which is the characteristic of personal Christian conversion, is central, but now it is a shared, communal reality which, as previous commentators have noted, is an essential element of conversion. But Braxton's emphasis on the church is most notable for his understanding of the nature of this "wisdom community," which is synonymous with the Christian churches: "In its widest application, the wisdom community refers to the Christian churches . . . . More specifically, the wisdom community is a metaphor for a framework and a program for renewing understanding and communication."[116] It is in the nature of that wisdom which the church possesses that the importance of both her mission, and of the ecclesial dimension of conversion, lies: "Over and above or deep within metaphysical doctrines, ceremonies, traditions, and regulations, the Church preserves and communicates a wisdom about being."[117] We have previously seen that an understanding of being is related to the images and symbols released by Doran's psychic conversion of the censor, which promotes "the capacity to engage and interpret correctly the elemental symbols of one's being."[118]

As Braxton describes it, the wisdom that the church bears is open to all (since it is a knowledge of being) and stems from the telling and retelling of the story of Jesus of Nazareth through the centuries.[119] Thus, the ecclesial dimension of conversion supplies the wisdom of the story of Jesus, the image and symbol of Being which, we recall, is also the content of the

---

114   Tyrrell, *Christotherapy*, 35.
115   Edward K. Braxton, *The Wisdom Community* (Ramsey: Paulist Press, 1980), 80.
116   Ibid., 1.   117   Ibid.
118   Doran, *Psychic Conversion and Theological Foundations*, 142.
119   Braxton, *The Wisdom Community*, 2.

experience mediated by Tyrrell's interpersonalist-sacramental-mediator therapist. Thus, symbol, church, and person-witness engage in a tripartite dynamic of mediation to others. On this basis, the ecclesial aspect is a necessary dimension of conversion.

Braxton's general conversion theory, while derived from Lonergan, is more of a moderation between Lonergan's "total surrender" and Conn's non-religious modes of development. Braxton seems to account for the perspectives of both Lonergan and Conn in that conversion for him begins in the religious mode by which "an individual becomes explicitly aware of the religious or sacred dimension of life,"[120] with attendant symbols and feelings of awe and reverence.[121] Braxton's next stage, the theistic, "makes explicit the referent, source, or object"[122] of religious conversion with attendant "loving surrender to a loving reality that can now be explicitly named God."[123] As theistic conversion makes religious conversion more specific, Christian conversion makes theistic conversion more so: "Theistic conversion is specified as Christian conversion when the 'event' of God's self-disclosure is recognized supremely in Jesus."[124] Here the symbol is of central importance: "Christian conversion . . . is . . . also an encounter with Jesus that renders his very person as the central symbol announcing that . . . the story of the human race is going to turn out all right."[125] Ecclesial conversion is this communal experience of Christian conversion. Braxton's final modes, the moral and intellectual, follow Lonergan's pattern.

In terms of the process of conversion, Braxton holds that the various modes "are related in a compenetrating, overlapping, and sometimes dialectical manner,"[126] and "various combinations of these modes of conversion are ongoing simultaneously."[127] Braxton's analysis suggests, to a greater degree than any previous commentator, the principles of reciprocity, complementarity, simultaneity, and development which have been previously noted.

Braxton's unique contribution to conversion study is the ecclesial dimension which, as the "wisdom community," mediates knowledge of Ultimate Being to others through the image of Christ.

SUMMARY PART TWO

A SUMMARY OF THE DEVELOPMENTS OF CONVERSION PROVIDED by the work of these five theologians, following Lonergan's lead, indicates that the understanding of conversion has been significantly broadened,

---

120 Ibid., 75.	121 Ibid., 76.	122 Ibid.
123 Ibid.	124 Ibid., 79.	125 Ibid., 80.
126 Ibid., 93.	127 Ibid.	

resulting in additions and alterations to the framework of the fivefold division of source, elements, process, function, and effects.

In regard to source, all commentators follow Lonergan's lead in attributing conversion to the work of grace.

The aspect of vision is a consistently dominant theme. The human capacity for vision is improved by *psychic development*, or conversion (Doran), which is complemented by an *aesthetic conversion* or *conversion of the imagination* (Conn), which actually forms or receives the new *vision* supplied by the image of Jesus which effects *Christian conversion* (Conn) as a form of *religious conversion*, which is capable of further development. This Christian image is the content or "wisdom" (Braxton) of the community of faith (Gelpi) or love (Conn), and thus an *ecclesial conversion* (Braxton) is essential. *Sociopolitical conversion* (Gelpi), as a second moment in moral conversion, is the extension of personal responsibility into the social realm. Thus, five new aspects of conversion have been ascertained: *psychic, aesthetic, Christian, ecclesial,* and *sociopolitical*.

In terms of process, the principles of *reciprocity, simultaneity, complementarity,* and *development*, which were noted earlier, have been consistently affirmed in one form or another, as is the *primacy of affective development* in the process. However, this is now grounded in an *aesthetic conversion* critical to the apprehension of the vision of Jesus, and thus affective development is seen as part of the larger, aesthetic conversion process. Also, two new principles are introduced. There exists a *primacy* (Conn) at any given stage by that element most characteristic of that stage, and it is this primacy which causes not only development but disharmony. Secondly, the principle of *transvaluation* (Gelpi) is a helpful distinction whereby developments convert to a new level (horizon) through the community-given vision of Jesus. Thus, primacy and transvaluation are two added dimensions of the conversion process.

As for the function of conversion, all commentators point to the central role of the *vision of Christ* as the key transformative dimension of conversion, an image which functions to produce the act of *faith*, reversing Lonergan's position that conversion produces the vision. While not new dimensions, these have been broadened by the various commentators.

In respect to the effects of conversion, the role of the *interpersonal-sacramental-mediator* (Tyrrell) of the vision of Christ to others is a deepened understanding of conversion which synthesizes its aesthetic, affective, religious, moral, and intellectual dimensions. As such, it is a new and important dimension of conversion.

3. CONVERSION IN THE THEOLOGY OF HÄRING, FOWLER, AND VON BALTHASAR:
Sacramental Forgiveness, Affectivity, Faith and Imagination, and Aesthetic Vision

IN ADDITION TO THE PERSPECTIVES ON CONVERSION DEVELoped by Bernard Lonergan and his followers, significant insights are also found outside this school in the works of Bernard Häring, James Fowler, and Hans Urs von Balthasar which develop more fully these requisite conversion aspects: the ecclesial sacrament, especially penance, affectivity, faith, imagination, and aesthetics.

SACRAMENTAL FORGIVENESS IN THE CONVERSION THEOLOGY OF BERNARD HÄRING

IN BERNARD HÄRING'S WORK, CHURCH AND VISION EACH LEAD to new dimensions; respectively, the institutional sacraments, especially penance, and the act of faith. These dimensions are synthesized in Häring's moral theology and his treatment of both the social and personal consequences of sin.

> Conversion is an ever more fervent meeting with Christ (who) oriented his own sacraments to conversion. . . . Conversion is always also a gift from the fullness of grace and the apostolic spirit of the Church. . . . Conversion will only then fully mature, if one tries to become a vital, solidaric-feeling, actively cooperative member of the kingdom of God, the Church.[128]

The Church, which is the sacrament of the love of Christ, is the original and fundamental sacrament of which the seven sacraments are expressions.[129] The sacraments are the life of the church community,[130] and thus they are a "social, community-forming reality."[131] A unique dimension of the sacraments is that all "are directed toward forgiveness of sins and the healing of the consequences of sin."[132] Sin, moreover, is both a refusal of God's grace and a disruption of the harmony of God's people.[133]

---

128 Bernard Häring, *This Time of Salvation* (New York: Herder and Herder, 1966), 226–27.

129 Bernard Häring, *A Sacramental Spirituality* (New York: Sheed and Ward, 1962), 278.

130 Häring, *This Time of Salvation*, 167.   131 Ibid., 161.

132 Häring, *A Sacramental Spirituality*, 48.

133 Bernard Häring, *Shalom: Peace* (New York: Farrar, Straus, and Giroux, 1967), 21–22.

Thus, all sin has a social dimension: "He who says 'no' to God says so within the framework of the people of God."[134] Conversion, then, is a total turning away from sin and a turning to God with not only personal but social implications. Importantly, for Häring, as for several previous commentators, conversion is linked to the image of Christ, and the content of conversion is faith engendered by the image of Jesus: "Its main content is faith . . . and acceptance of him who is the Truth, the Way, and the Life . . . Faith is a total life response . . . patterned according to the Paschal mystery. . . . At the very heart of conversion is faith."[135]

For Häring, that faith, which both gains forgiveness and then must give it in return, is especially expressed in the sacrament of penance which repairs the broken or damaged relationship with God and others. In penance, Christ himself is encountered as the merciful forgiver,[136] and the penitent experiences "the forgiving love of God," which also "imposes on us the law of merciful love. . . . The best 'fruits of repentance' are works carried out for love of our neighbor."[137] Thus, conversion is linked to repentance for sin and the response of faith in the image of Jesus, who is the symbol of obedience to the Father's will, obeyed through love, or forgiveness:

> From the human point of view repentance is a response to the acts of God in his grace. And the central point of this response is *faith*. . . . The words of life, which the Lord speaks to us in the sacraments, are the image of his life; we ourselves bear his image in us. That is why our life can bear no fruit unless we respond with love to the words of the Word[138] . . . . The Paschal Mystery . . . symbolizes . . . the content and the way of conversion; victory over sin and total dedication to the will of the Father.[139]

Even though baptism is the "great sacrament of conversion," penance is the "sacrament of repeated first conversion . . . of second conversion, meaning a continual conversion."[140]

Häring's emphasis on the function of the ecclesial sacrament in conversion complements Tyrrell's interpersonalist-sacramental function through Häring's insight into the role of the priest in the sacrament of penance. In confession, the priest has "a very special obligation to present an image of the loving kindness of the Saviour by his understanding and

---

134 Ibid., 24.
135 Bernard Häring, *Free and Faithful in Christ*, vol. 1 (New York: The Seabury Press, 1978), 418–19.   136 Häring, *A Sacramental Spirituality*, 96.
137 Ibid., 274–75.   138 Ibid., 15, 6.
139 Häring, *Free and Faithful in Christ*, 418.   140 Häring, *Shalom: Peace*, 269–70.

compassion,"[141] as he is "another Christ, another image of the heavenly Father."[142] In functioning as the community of faith's mediator of forgiveness, acceptance, and love through penance, the sacrament, through the priest, serves as the ecclesial-sacramental dimension of conversion. Thus, the ecclesial-sacramental dimension of conversion, especially in the form of penance, is an important added aspect of conversion as a complement to the interpersonalist-sacramental dimension.

While the act of faith is an important aspect of Häring's theology relating to conversion, a most significant treatment of this requisite dimension of conversion appears in the work of James Fowler.

JAMES FOWLER: *Affectivity, Faith, and Imagination*

AS HÄRING EXPANDED THE ECCLESIAL DIMENSION OF CONVERsion through the sacraments, James Fowler further develops the dimension of faith, its ground in affectivity, and its related imagery.

First, even though Fowler characterizes his study of faith as focusing on the human dimension,[143] which is not always religious,[144] he considers its ultimate source to be grace, of which he distinguishes two dimensions.[145] All nature, including the processes of human development, is graced by what Fowler calls ordinary grace. This extends through the first four of his six stages of faith. The last two stages, however, are the results of "unpredictable and unexpected manifestations" of extraordinary grace, or conversions, which transcend the natural, developmental, mechanistic dynamics of earlier stages. In his developmental schema, attaining the later stages where conversion occurs is dependent upon previously successful stage developments. Fowler's analyses of the pre-stage period of infancy prior to stage one, and of stage one itself, are particularly relevant for their important connections to the development of affectivity, the imagination, and the capacity for faith. The infancy period prior to stage one "underlie(s) all that comes later in faith development"[146] because of the affective experiences of infancy. More so than any of the previous commentators, Fowler develops the importance of this affective base for faith and thus for conversion. "Our first experiences of faith and faithfulness begin with birth. . . . We all begin the pilgrimage of faith as infants."[147] This stage is preconceptual and intuitive, as one senses "whether we can be 'at home' here."[148] The relationship of parent and child forms the ground for

---

141 Häring, A Sacramental Spirituality, 275.   142 Häring, Shalom: Peace, 35.
143 Fowler, Stages of Faith, 33.   144 Ibid., 4.   145 Ibid., 302–3.
146 Ibid., 121.   147 Ibid., 16, 119.   148 Ibid., 16.

the development of Fowler's first major dimension of faith as relational, for which he provides a description of faith as a "relational enterprise, triadic or covenantal in shape,"[149] which he expresses in the image of a dynamic triad. At this time, the child begins to form "nascent images of the centers of value and power that animate the parental faith."[150] The affective relationships between the self and others form two reciprocally interactive dimensions of the triad, and their shared centers (images) of value and power form the third. Thus "faith is always *relational*; there is always an *other* in faith."[151] Secondly, since this dynamic includes images, faith is imaginative:

> Faith, as imaginative, grasps the ultimate conditions of our existence, unifying them into a comprehensive image in light of which we shape our responses and initiatives, our actions. . . . Faith as an imaginative process . . . is an active mode of knowing, of composing a felt sense or image of the condition of our lives taken as a whole. It unifies our lives' force fields.[152]

Moreover, it is affected by those rituals, concepts, images, and symbols which it experiences.[153]

Fowler's third quality of faith contained in the above description is that it is whole,[154] and here he opens a window to the transcendent:

> Faith is *response* to action and being that precedes and transcends us and our kind; faith is the forming of images of and relation to that which exerts qualitatively different initiatives in our lives than those that occur in strictly human relations. While this 'X' factor in faith is not our primary focus, it continues to impinge upon our work and to keep us modestly aware that we are encompassed in mystery.[155]

Reminiscent of the "Other" whom we encounter on Lonergan's horizon, Fowler's imaging, while straining to remain detheologized, acknowledges the presence of the Transcendent Other.

In Fowler's analysis, affectivity conditions the development of the imagination, which in turn conditions faith. Affectivity, especially through relationships, is the "stuff" of our lives which awaken and shape the imagination.[156] Fowler's grounding of faith in the imagination through affectivity has two relevant aspects. First, it is consistent with the previous

---

149 Ibid., 18.   150 Ibid., 17.   151 Ibid., 16.
152 Ibid., 25.   153 Ibid.   154 Ibid., 32.
155 Ibid., 33.   156 Ibid., 25.

commentators who noted the primacy of affectivity. But just as consistent
is his analysis of imagination as the ground of cognition: "Imagination is
a powerful force underlying all knowledge."[157] Images, as products of the
imagination, function to synthesize affectivity and knowledge in directing
our responses: "An image . . . begins as a vague, felt inner representation
of some state of affairs and our feelings about it. . . . The image unites
'information' and feeling; it holds together orientation and affectional
significance. As such, images are prior to and deeper than concepts."[158]
It is through the development of affective relationships in infancy that
the imagination is developed in Fowler's first stage of faith:

> The gift or emergent strength of this stage is the birth of imag-
> ination, the ability to unify and grasp the experience-world in
> powerful images and as presented in stories that register the
> child's intuitive understandings and feelings toward the ultimate
> conditions of existence.[159]

Affectivity and imagination combine to form the major elements in
Fowler's second major image, his "dynamic triad of faith," "wherein the
images, beliefs, and concepts we compose, with varying degrees of consciousness, affect our lives."[160] This triad is a product of faith as relational,
imaginative, and whole.

An important development regarding the relationship of faith and
imagination occurs in Fowler's analysis of the transition from his fourth
stage of faith development to the fifth stage. Recalling that stage five is the
level at which development becomes a conversion and acquires a religious
dimension, it is notable that the imagination also undergoes a significant
change at this point: "Alive to paradox and the truth in apparent contradictions, this stage strives to unify opposites in mind and experience. . . . The
new strength of this stage comes in the rise of the ironic imagination."[161]
The ironic imagination, a concept which Fowler derives from the work of
William Lynch, synthesizes Fowler's stage of faith and religious conversion
in its content — the religious vision, especially of Jesus Christ.[162]

Lynch holds that "nothing comes nearer to defining human beings than
their images of the world — than, shall we not then say, their imaginations."[163] Lynch situates the ironic dimension of the imagination at the
heart of faith, and the function of irony "is to keep opposites together in

---

157 Ibid., 30. 158 Ibid., 26. 159 Ibid., 134.

160 Ibid., 97. 161 Ibid., 198. 162 Ibid., 105.

163 William Lynch, *Images of Faith* (Notre Dame: University of Notre Dame Press,
1973), 19.

a single act of the imagination[164]. . . . (It is the) unexpected coexistence, to the point of identity, of certain contraries[165]. . . . Irony . . . is . . . a re-composing in which a fact . . . is seen within the creative presence of a contrary."[166] This leads to the dynamic interaction of intellectual, moral, and religious dimensions which promote conversion:

> The shock of irony (and of recognition) comes not only from uniting them [i.e., contraries] but also from seeing that the act of uniting them is not a mistake. . . . In Christianity . . . lowliness is the very instrument to be passed through in order to reach the high. . . . There is an actual transformation of being.[167]

The core of irony is Christ who "in his particularity is the final model (and) the basic image of faith"[168] in that "the structure of the irony of faith is . . . marked by . . . the simultaneous presence of contraries."[169]

And so, in Fowler's system affectivity, aided by the function of the ironic imagination, grounds the imagination which in turn grounds faith, and as faith develops to the fifth stage in Fowler's system, the imagination also develops into its ironic dimension.

Fowler's contribution to conversion theory is in the causal relationship he perceives between affectivity, the imagination — particularly its ironic dimension, faith — and conversion. The development of affectivity, especially during infancy and early childhood through faithful relationships with parents and other highly influential persons in one's life, is critical to the development of the imagination. When imagination develops to the level called the ironic, it can grasp the content of the religious vision of Christ, effecting religious conversion and the act of faith. Fowler's description of stage five faith, with its rise of the ironic imagination and religious conversion, is extremely relevant to the study of Newman's conversions:

> Unusual before mid-life . . . this involves a critical recognition of one's social unconscious — the myths, ideal images and preju-dices built deeply into the self-system by virtue of one's nurture within a particular social class, religious tradition, ethnic group, or the like.[170]

Thus, Fowler's principle of *affectivity-based imaginative development* is an essential dimension of the conversion process.

---

164 Ibid., 93.   165 Ibid., 84.   166 Ibid., 14.
167 Ibid., 85.   168 Ibid., 95–96.   169 Ibid., 92.
170 Fowler, *Stages of Faith*, 198.

AESTHETIC VISION IN HANS URS VON BALTHASAR[171]

ONE OF THE MOST EXPLICIT THEOLOGICAL INTERPRETATIONS of the relationship of vision and image to faith and conversion is Hans Urs von Balthasar's theological aesthetics. Von Balthasar asserts that an aesthetic principle provides both the drive and objective of conversion: "The mind sees an organized whole, with all the articulation of detail necessary for the comprehension of the basic idea manifest in its fullness."[172] He derives this anthropological notion of *Gestalt*, form, from a theological principle: "Since all are created from God, they possess the *desiderium visionis boni absoluti* (the desire to see the wholly good[173]). . . . Man's religious predisposition and desire make him strive toward a final union with God, which is God's gift to us, called Jesus Christ."[174] This movement requires the perception of Jesus as the wholly good, or the *Gehalt* within the *Gestalt*: "The content (*Gehalt*) does not lie behind the form (*Gestalt*), but within it."[175] In this process grace "fructifies" reason,[176] which enables it to see the vision, which is the heart of von Balthasar's conversion theology. As such, this perception is also the flash-point of the act of faith. As one commentator sees this aspect of von Balthasar's theory, faith's content (vision) and action (surrender to the vision) synthesize in the aesthetic act of faith:

> The contents of faith and the act of faith form a unity and come
> together in one aesthetic act whereby in the light radiating from

171 Aidan Nichols, "Littlemore from Lucerne: Newman's *Essay on Development* in Balthasarian Perspective," in *Newman and Conversion* (Edinburgh: T & T Clark, 1997), 100–116. Nichols examines Newman's influence on von Balthasar, identifying fundamental elements in our conversion hypothesis. As Balthasar explains: "The heart is the *foundation* of the intellect (as of the other particular faculties) — not its *rival*. Where the language of the heart is used more restrictively for the affective dynamism of our subjective nature rather than our intellectual capacity to reflect what is really given in objective reality, then one would have to say that Newman's theology of revelation is *not* simply cordial. . . . (T)he 'certainty of the ultimate rightness of the "true religion" does not rest,' so Balthasar remarks, 'in mere intuitions of the heart and conscience or of faith, but resides in a seeing of the rightness which in the broad sense must be called an aesthetic vision and yet which stands up to rational examination and . . . can even be made visible to the person who purifies his mind's eye'" (105). Nichols calls the two major influences "experiential holism," and "a vision, at once aesthetic and rational," and followed by "Christianity's 'rightness.'" Here we find the affective, the aesthetic, the moral, and the intellectual elements at work, as described in our conversion hypothesis below.

172 Hans Urs von Balthasar, "Theology and Aesthetic," in *Communio* 8 (Spring 1981): 63.   173 Ibid., 63.   174 Ibid., 68.

175 Hans Urs von Balthasar, "Seeing the Form," in *The Glory of the Lord*, vol. ii (San Francisco: Ignatius Press, 1989), 151.   176 Ibid., 112.

the form the subject sees the form as God in the flesh. . . . Balthasar
alludes to the approach of John Henry Newman (1801 – 1890) and
his illative sense whereby from the congruence of the evidence the
conclusion results as something suddenly seen. . . . In his analysis
of the act of faith . . . seeing and believing are complementary.[177]

Thus, the act of faith is seen as "the theological act of perception,"[178]
an aesthetic act,[179] which has several significant implications. Similar to
Doran's work, which posited a fourth dimension of human nature as
aesthetic, von Balthasar's theory notes that the "aesthetic sensibility and
its standards will come into play precisely where metaphysics and ethics
attempt to achieve a final reconciliation and harmony."[180] The essence of
the aesthetic sensibility is its capacity to grasp not only the true and the
good, but the beautiful, which constitutes von Balthasar's "first principle"
of the indissolubility of form.[181] The aesthetic capacity, or the capacity to
perceive the beautiful, is a requisite dimension of conversion because, as
Avery Dulles summarized von Balthasar's analysis, "In the pursuit of the
true and the good, theology has too often neglected the third transcendental, the beautiful, which alone can overcome the dualities (of visible
form and invisible mystery, content and form). . . . Von Balthasar appeals
to aesthetic reason in order to resurrect the category of the beautiful.
Beauty, for him, is the splendor of the true" (parenthesis added).[182] Thus,
in *Seeing the Form*, the first volume of his theory of theological aesthetics,
von Balthasar states that "what Christ brings with him is . . . the world
of creation and of redemption as a whole," and in the act of faith, "The
believer does not *believe all* of this, he *sees* it."[183] In the aesthetic act of faith,
Jesus is seen as the totality of goodness, truth, and, inseparably, beauty.

> In fact, God's Incarnation perfects the whole ontology and aes-
> thetics of created Being. The Incarnation uses created Being at a
> new depth as a language and a means of expression for the divine
> Being and essence. . . . Jesus is the Word, the Image, the Expres-
> sion, and the Exegesis of God. . . . He *is* what he expresses —
> namely, God — but he is not whom he expresses — namely, the
> Father. This incomparable paradox stands as the fountainhead

---

177 John O'Donnell, *Hans Urs von Balthasar* (Collegeville: The Liturgical Press,
1992), 23.   178 Von Balthasar, "Seeing the Form," 155.
179 O'Donnell, *Hans Urs von Balthasar*, 18 –34.
180 Von Balthasar, "Seeing the Form," 35.   181 Ibid., 26.
182 Avery Dulles, *The Assurance of Things Hoped For* (New York: Oxford University
Press, 1994), 148.   183 Von Balthasar, "Seeing the Form," 419.

of the Christian aesthetic, and therefore of all aesthetics! How greatly therefore the power of sight is demanded and presupposed at this point of origin![184]

Here vision and faith merge in von Balthasar's analysis, as he states that "the moment of faith coincides with the vision of the form."[185] But this moment requires a turning, a prerequisite "con-version," "from one's own image and to the image of God,"[186] an analysis which recalls Tyrrell's work on the reformation of self-image.

Drawing upon the work of M. J. Scheeben, whom he considers the originator of modern theological aesthetics,[187] von Balthasar holds that the vision of faith grasps certain fundamental laws of Being which "illumine faith's mystery from the standpoint of ontology,"[188] an analysis recalling the nature and function of symbols as disclosing laws of Being in the aesthetic dimension of Robert Doran's work. Here the aesthetic act of faith functions to promote what I call an aesthetic conversion, which then grounds affective, moral, and intellectual developments and conversions. As a synthesis, von Balthasar offers a summarizing statement from Scheeben, which unites many of the aspects of conversion based upon the aesthetic principle:

> The proper life of the will consists in its . . . *transformation into* the objectively good and beautiful, a transformation which, in the case of our will, appears to be partly the will and source . . . of its striving, but partly also the goal and perfection of this . . . striving. Such transformation (is) the very soul of all the will's further activity. In other words, the life of the will consists of love in so far as love, being a delight in that which is objectively good and beautiful, binds the lover to this object steeping him in it and moulding him into it.[189]

In the process of conversion according to von Balthasar, the vision moves the will to surrender to the vision in a two-part dynamic. Vision effects rapture, or conversion, which are the two phases of theological aesthetic development.[190] Here aesthetic perception effects conversion of affectivity, which then effects moral conversion. Conversion, which is the form of the will's activity, is the love of, and delight in, the good and beautiful as really an "Other," or transcendent Being. This "immanent principle" which impels the lover to act (as von Balthasar again follows

---

184 Ibid., 29. 185 Ibid., 524. 186 Ibid., 522.

187 Ibid., 104–5. 188 Ibid., 110.

189 Von Balthasar, "Seeing the Form," 111–12. 190 Ibid., 125.

Scheeben),[191] also inspires the affections and the whole interior disposition, including the will's desire for the "Other." Thus, interpreting von Balthasar, an aesthetic conversion is effected by grace's action in the revelation of God in the form of Jesus and man's seeing and acceptance of this fact, a conversion which effects a relationship to a "Transcendent Other" beyond mere subjective dimensions. This acceptance includes an affective conversion as the love and affections of the perceiver are now directed to the Transcendent Other as their primary ground. The Transcendent Other is both the source and objective of the believer's perception and affection. Simultaneously, the will is involved in the decision to act out the insights of this perception and the feelings of the affections, effecting a moral conversion by a change from an intrapersonal to an interpersonal experience. In this way, man is said to "co-effect" conversion through his will.[192]

In addition, von Balthasar, as did Braxton and Häring, emphasizes a requisite ecclesial dimension in his conversion theology:

> This perfect being becomes manifest only from the testimoni-
> als of faith. . . . Only [the Church's] eye of faith . . . could see
> the whole phenomenon of Jesus Christ. . . . Exegesis . . . can be
> practiced meaningfully only within the comprehensive view of
> the Church. . . . [A]ll roads outside of this . . . the Sancta Cathol-
> ica . . . lose some essential aspect of the perfect whole.[193]

In concluding von Balthasar's contribution regarding conversion, we note three significant facts. His theory of theological aesthetics complements the work of Häring on faith and church, and that of Fowler and Lynch on faith and imagination, by supplying a theory of the object of conversion, the Transcendental Other expressed in the image of Jesus, regarding its nature and effects. Secondly, his work complements that of Doran and Conn by supplying for the aesthetic dimension of man's nature a theory of the function of the image of Jesus: vision produces rapture, or conversion. Since this aesthetic dynamic underlies all else in the conversion process, it can be said to be the ground of all further developments and conversions: affective, moral, and intellectual. As such it appears that the development noted by previous commentators as religious or Christian, since it must include the vision of Jesus, is perhaps better expressed as an aesthetic conversion which includes the dimension of affective conversion in that affections now become religiously grounded, that is, directed to

---

191   Ibid., 112.   192   Ibid., 188.
193   Von Balthasar, "Theology and Aesthetic," 65, 67.

God. Thus, affective and religious conversions are perhaps better under-stood as developments within the aesthetic mode.

However, just as Lonergan's mode of religious conversion is a radical use of the term religious, so does von Balthasar's use of the term "faith" appear to be. In writing of faith produced by the perception of the vision of Christ, von Balthasar describes man's response as "the movement of man's whole being away from himself and towards God through Christ, a movement . . . co-effected willingly by man."[194] As Häring's work on sin points out, this movement is a constant struggle necessitating, through penance, "second conversions." Thus, as Avery Dulles has noted, "Faith is sometimes stunted. . . . It does not always lead to confident and loving self-surrender."[195] A "bare minimum" of faith may exist, which acknowledges only the existence and truthful communication of God.[196] However, this "residual faith" is a "scaffolding" for the development of faith,[197] indicating that "faith is subject to growth" with knowledge of revelation, firmer conviction, and other affective, intellectual, and moral acts directed toward God.[198]

Also, faith as an aesthetic and thus affective and religious act is cogni-tive, and, as the ground of all knowledge, is complementary to the work of Conn in this respect.

Lastly, von Balthasar's thoroughgoing analysis of faith and its contents, particularly its objective dimension in the reality of the Transcendent Other, complements the extremist misinterpretation sometimes made of Lonergan's "turn to the subject."[199] Thus, Lonergan and von Balthasar, as our opening and closing sources, respectively, complement one another's work through their detailed analysis, respectively, of the subjective and objective dimensions of conversion.

SUMMARY CRITIQUE

TOWARD THE OBJECTIVE OF DEVELOPING A CONVERSION hypothesis, the nine theologians make the following contributions:

In respect to its source, for Lonergan conversion is *graced*, *personal*, and *relational*. Lonergan develops the *religious*, *moral*, and *intellectual* modes or types as elements of conversion which tend toward a *full* integrated state uniting all three dimensions. The process of conversion has seven integral aspects: they are *ongoing*, *directed*, *movement and rest*, and the elements

---

194   Von Balthasar, "Seeing the Form," 121.
195   Dulles, *The Assurance of Things Hoped For*, 279.
196   Ibid.   197   Ibid.   198   Ibid., 278.   199   Ibid., 155.

interact and *develop complementarily* and *reciprocally* and are *sublated*: the religious sublates the moral, and the moral the intellectual. Conversion functions in five ways. It produces a *change of heart, faith,* the *knowledge of being loved,* and ultimately a *vision* with its *content* of the *Transcendent Other.* It promotes *obedience, social interaction,* and *ecclesial context.*

Walter Conn's development of conversion has four primary aspects. First, he makes two contributions to the elements of conversion. His term *Christian conversion* revises the extreme sense in which Lonergan uses the term "religious" so as to include a first-stage conversion, of which Lonergan's religious type is an exceptional development. Secondly, his concept of a *conversion of the imagination* containing the image of Jesus, which is linked to affective and Christian conversion, is a very notable development. Third, in terms of process, his identification of the *primacy of a particular element at any given stage over other elements (modes)* is a useful explanatory insight into the complexity of the conversion experience. This identification also provides a name for each stage according to its primary mode. Lastly, Conn reverses Lonergan's dynamics of cause and effect between conversion and vision. In Lonergan, conversion causes faith, which enables the vision of Christ to be seen, whereas for Conn the vision, wrought through the conversion of the imagination, effects conversion and faith.

Doran, whose psychoanalytic method probes the personal depths of the conversion experience, contributes an important insight into the aesthetic dimension of human nature as its fourth aspect along with the affective, the moral, and the intellectual. His grounding of affectivity in the aesthetic dimension is significant, and his concept of *psychic conversion (development)* implies the necessity for another element, *aesthetic conversion,* at the foundation of conversion. In regard to function, this dimension of "sensitive aesthetic spontaneity" effects an *aesthetic mediation* of this dimension with the dimensions of intentionality defined by Lonergan.

Gelpi suggests an added element of conversion, the *sociopolitical,* as a "second moment" in moral conversion, and his *transvaluation* function, whereby the vision of Christ effects conversion and faith, transforming all natural developments to the religious level, is similar to Conn's understanding of the cause-and-effect relationship of vision to conversion.

Tyrrell, also working vertically, identifies the important *interpersonalist-sacramental-mediator* effect of conversion, as the converted individual (therapist/priest) mediates to others the love and compassion present in the image of Jesus.

Braxton emphasizes the necessity of the element of *ecclesial conversion* in order to participate most fully in understanding and mediating the "wisdom" of Being found only in the vision of Jesus, the unique content of the wisdom of the church community. In a sense, ecclesial conversion is the communal correlative of Tyrrell's interpersonalist-sacramental mediator. Braxton, however, identifies a mode of Christian conversion, and in fact an entire process, similar to Conn's and less extreme that Lonergan's "religious" conversion mode, but in his system conversion always has a religious dimension, which is not the case in Conn's system. Lastly, Braxton offers perhaps the best description of the process of conversion through the interaction of the various modes as "compenetrating, overlapping, and sometimes dialectical," and "ongoing simultaneously."

Häring's *ecclesial sacrament*, especially *penance*, is an important added effect, as it crystallizes conversion's ongoing nature as a constant need for, and obligation to give, forgiveness. Complementing Tyrrell's more personal dimension through the priest's function as the mediator of the merciful vision of Jesus for the community, it also specifies the unique mission of Braxton's "wisdom community"— the promotion of ongoing conversion through ecclesial sacraments.

James Fowler's *affectivity-based imaginative development* provides a very useful theory of the importance and primacy of affective development in early life, especially through those on whom we most depend, in promoting the growth of imagination, which can develop to the level of the ironic dimension capable of perceiving the religious vision of Christ which effects faith and conversion. Fowler's dynamic also contrasts with Lonergan's: for Fowler, vision produces conversion.

Von Balthasar's contribution is fourfold. His theological aesthetic theory complements Doran's work in grounding conversion in the aesthetic domain. Secondly, his *theory of the function of the image of conversion, Jesus,* the vision which produces rapture or conversion, is further evidence in support of a concept of aesthetic conversion which is implicit in the work of Doran and Conn. Third, his *theory of the nature and object within the vision, the Transcendental Other expressed in the image of Jesus,* complements the work of Fowler and Lynch. Lastly, he also maintains, in contrast with Lonergan, that the vision produces the act of faith and conversion.

In closing this analysis of the work of major contemporary theologians on conversion, especially that of Lonergan and his school, an indication of the influence of Newman on their work will serve as a bridge from the following conversion hypothesis to the study of Newman's conversion experiences. Lonergan noted that Newman was "my fundamental mentor and guide"[200] well before the influence of Aquinas on his work. Further, F. E. Crowe documented that Lonergan found in the work of Newman "the forerunner of his own theory of rational consciousness."[201] Also, in Lonergan's *Method in Theology*, which contains his most explicit treatment of conversion, Newman is the most referenced source after Aristotle, Augustine, and Aquinas, and another study details the influence of Newman on Lonergan's development in respect to conversion:

> But if those with an interest in Newman needed another reason to be interested in Lonergan, this can be found in Lonergan's concept of conversion, of which Newman — along with Paul, Augustine, and Ignatius of Loyola — provides a classic paradigm. Moreover, Lonergan's concept of conversion as a threefold grace — intellectual, moral, and religious — as differentiated yet dynamically related, as having personal, social and historical dimensions, and as both episodic and long haul, provides in itself a hermeneutical key to the trajectory of Newman who took to heart Thomas Scott's maxim 'Growth the only evidence of life', and who himself once said, 'In a higher world it is otherwise, but here below to live is to change, and to be perfect is to have changed often.'[202]

Yet another study notes that "Lonergan cites that it was Newman, together with Augustine, Descartes, and Pascal, who revealed the possibility of a non-metaphysical, common-sense approach to self-knowledge. It seems that of this group, Newman was first in Lonergan's affection."[203] As for Von Balthasar, he repeatedly refers to Newman as standing in the same line of great conversions as Paul and Augustine.[204] "Newman perfected this tradition" of the *raisons du cœur*, from Augustine to Bernard to Pascal, wherein the heart "serves as common foundation both for the intellect and all other particular faculties."[205] And Bernard Häring refers to Newman as a "great convert" who exemplifies the ecumenical dimension of conversion, even though he "had suffered so much from traditionalists in the Church, and from parts of the institutional Church."[206]

---

200 Lonergan, "Reality, Myth, Symbol," 34.
201 Frederick E. Crowe, *Lonergan* (Collegeville: The Liturgical Press, 1992), 16.
202 Philip A. Egan, "Lonergan on Newman's Conversion," in *The Heythrop Journal* 37:4 (October 1996): 448–49.
203 Michael L. Rende, *Lonergan on Conversion: The Development of a Notion* (Lanham: University Press of America, Inc., 1991), 49, n. 113.
204 Von Balthasar, "Seeing the Form," 284.   205 Ibid., 167.
206 Häring, *Free and Faithful in Christ*, vol. i, 54–55.

In light of the preceding analysis, the following conversion hypothesis is proposed.

A CONVERSION HYPOTHESIS

I NOW OFFER A DEFINITION OF CONVERSION FOLLOWED BY A concise, systematic breakdown of its essential components. *Conversion is the ever-deepening realization that one is loved by God, a love mediated through the fact, revelation, and image of Jesus, which defines the fundamental condition of one's existence and meaning. This realization implicitly requires a loving of God in return by mediating this truth of love to all creation, especially others.* Thus, it is the communication of God as His loving Self through the medium of creation, especially that of the God-man and then those who live in His image, and the loving response of man to God through the medium of creation, especially others.

Based on the research above and its critique, the following hypothesis suggests twenty essential dimensions of the conversion experience. They are grouped according to the five-fold analysis employed during this study: conversion's source, elements, process, function, and effects. In each category, the major dimensions are enumerated, and where appropriate, subordinate aspects are specified which are dependent upon, or extensions of, the major dimensions. To the extent that these aspects are present, fulfilled, or accomplished, the conversion experience is more or less accomplished. Each dimension, as an aspect of conversion, is italicized.

SOURCE
(1) *Graced* (2) *Personal* (3) *Relational*

Conversion is a *graced* invitation to a *personal*, transforming, fulfilling, saving *relationship* with God Himself.

ELEMENTS
(1) *Aesthetic* (2) *Affective* (3) *Moral* (4) *Intellectual* (5) *Unconditional*

Conversion consists of five primary elements (modes or types): the *aesthetic*, the *affective*, the *moral*, and the *intellectual*. A fifth mode is now suggested, designated as *unconditional*, as the state of fully integrated conversion, which is attained when the following three developments occur and exist simultaneously: the four modes function in harmony, the five major functions of conversion are realized, and the three major effects of conversion are attained.

The aesthetic mode is the perception of the beauty of the paradoxical vision of Jesus as God-man and as the unity of absolute truth and goodness.

40

It also includes the dimension of *imagination* as well as the *Christian* aspects identified by some commentators. It consists of seeing the whole, the fullness, of creation in light of God's revelation.

The affective mode is the direction of feelings to the object of conversion perceived through the aesthetic mode — God. Most notably, the aesthetic and affective modes together form the *religious* dimension.

Moral conversion is acting in light of the vision of Jesus as the norm of the absolutely good. The *sociopolitical* aspect is a dimension of the major category.

Intellectual conversion is understanding truth in light of the vision of Jesus as the norm of the absolutely true, as well as the expressions of the content of that truth.

PROCESS

(1) *Developmental* (2) *Directed* (3) *Primacy of Type* (4) *Aesthetic mediation*

The *developmental* dimension is multifaceted, containing seven aspects which account for its complexity. It consists of *movement and rest*, which is *ongoing*. The elements of conversion interact *simultaneously, complementarily, reciprocally,* with the change in one affecting all others, and through *aesthetic mediation* from its ground in the aesthetic dimension, the various elements are subject to *sublation*.

Direction is the discernment of, and action to attain, the objective of ongoing movement and rest.

Primacy of type is the primacy of one element or type of conversion over others at any given stage. This causes both development and dissonance and leads to the designation of a stage by its primary element, since all other modes are simultaneously operative but subordinate.

Aesthetic mediation is the movement toward harmonization, effected through the primacy of the aesthetic dimension, of the four major dimensions of human nature: the aesthetic, the affective, the intellectual, and the moral.

FUNCTION

(1) *Vision of the Transcendent Other* (2) *Change of heart* (3) *Knowledge of being loved* (4) *Faith* (5) *Reciprocal forgiveness*

Conversion effects five primary ends. Aesthetically, it produces the *vision of the Transcendent Other in the paradoxical image of Jesus*. Affectively, it produces *a change of heart*; cognitively, it produces the *knowledge of being loved*. Then *faith* is produced as an aesthetically grounded affective act. Morally, it produces the *need for*, and *obligation of, forgiveness*, the apex of human love in the image of Jesus.

EFFECTS

(1) *Ongoing experience of the Transcendent Other* (2) *Sacramental insight and experience* (3) *Obedience*

Conversion works three primary effects: *experience of the Transcendent Other, sacrament,* and *obedience.* First, it causes the ongoing interpersonal experience of the Transcendent Other. Secondly, in response to that experience, the convert is moved to sacramental insight and experience, which is aesthetic, wherein all natural experience is transvalued to the religious level. This sacramental effect has two aspects. It is both *interpersonal* and *ecclesial*, especially in penance, as the convert is moved both personally and communally to *witness* and thus *mediate* to all others the reality of the conversion experience — the actual loving, forgiving, personal relationship with the Transcendent Other in the person of Jesus as mediated through the aesthetic vision. Thirdly, conversion effects the response of obedience, which includes the act of *submission*, in aesthetic, affective, moral, and intellectual relationship with the Transcendent Other. This is the *sine qua non* of achieving unconditional conversion.

In conclusion, the purpose of this preliminary chapter is not to settle definitively the nature of Christian conversion but rather to indicate the general features of conversion and to provide terms and categories that will make it possible to identify dimensions in the conversion experiences of John Henry Newman.

PART I

Numquàm Minus Solus, Quàm Cùm Solus

("Never less alone than when alone")

NEWMAN'S RELIGIOUS CONVERSION
1816–1827

From Human Affectivity
to Religious Faith
1816–1824

INTRODUCTION

INTERPERSONAL LOVE:
The Key to Newman's Conversions and Theological Method

JOHN HENRY NEWMAN OFTEN STRESSED THE PROBLEMATIC relationship between the seen and the unseen worlds and that of "words" versus the "ideas" they represented. His resolution of this dilemma provides a clue to how he gradually understood his experiences through the light of an ever-increasing grasp of truth. However, that intellectual evolution, which is analyzed here, was the result of a developmental process of moral discernment motivated by religious intuition.[1] The five elements of

---

1 Intuition is a faculty of perception related to, but other than, syllogistic logic. "Sense, sensation, instinct, intuition supply us with facts, and the intellect uses them." John Henry Newman, *An Essay in Aid of A Grammar of Assent* (Westminster: Christian Classics, 1973), 98. Susanne Langer, whose work Lonergan referenced positively (*Method in Theology*, 61, 64), states that "intuition is the basic intellectual function . . . in the strict sense which it was given by Locke in his *Essay*. In that sense, intuition is direct logical or semantic perception; the perception of (1) relations, (2) forms, (3) instances, or exemplifications of forms, and (4) meaning." Susanne Langer, *Mind: An Essay on Human Feeling*, vol. 1 (Baltimore: The Johns Hopkins University Press, 1970), 128. Michael Polanyi describes intuition as a mode of understanding (*Personal Knowledge* [Chicago: The University of Chicago Press, 1962], 91). For a valuable comparison of the epistemologies of Newman and Polanyi see Martin X. Molesi, *Personal Catholicism. The Theological Epistemologies of John Henry Newman and Michael Polanyi* (Washington: The Catholic University of America Press, 2000). The imagination also operates beyond the bounds of syllogistic logic as the ground of both feeling and intellect: "Imagination has the means, which pure intellect has not, of stimulating those powers of the mind from which action proceeds. . . . (I)mages have . . . power . . . upon the affections and passions" (Newman, *A Grammar of Assent*, 89). Affections are also a mode of knowledge: "Feeling includes the sensibility of . . . the whole realm of human awareness and thought . . . the perception of meaning, as well as emotion and sensation" (Langer, *Mind*, vol. i, 55). Thomas Carr,

Newman's conversion experiences—the affective, the aesthetic, the moral, and the intellectual—are major aspects leading to the fifth element, his unconditional act of submission.

However, where does this all begin? To what can we attribute Newman's religious conversion of 1816, from which his theology springs? In the answers to these questions lie the most important and revealing insights about Newman's several conversions and the theological implications he himself drew from them. When we understand Newman's "foundations," we are in a better position to interpret his work. This may serve, then, as a basic case study of the interdependence of affective and aesthetic conversions, which produce the religious dimension, their relationship to moral and intellectual, and finally unconditional conversion.

---

in his study of Newman's religious epistemology, states that "religious knowledge rests upon the cooperation of intuition and imagination, rather than ratiocination alone." Then quoting from Newman's "Fifteenth University Sermon on the Theory of Developments in Religious Doctrine," he writes, "The grist for faith's mill is that 'sacred impression,' derived from past experiences and that, lying 'prior to' propositions of faith, 'acts as a regulatory principle . . . ever present upon the reasoning.'" Thomas Carr, *Newman and Gadamer: Toward a Hermeneutics of Religious Knowledge* (Atlanta: Scholars Press, 1996), 194.

Religious intuition has both affective and aesthetic elements. Affectivity is the element of feelings which become religious when they are directed toward not only others but also to God. The aesthetic element is that dimension of perception which operates in addition to, or in ways other than, syllogistic logic. It becomes religious when it envisions the nature of the relationship between God and man and includes aspects of intuition and imagination.

Newman expressed the relationship between imagination, conception, and belief thus: "We can imagine things which we cannot conceive. . . . In like manner we can believe what we can imagine, yet cannot conceive." John Henry Newman, *Philosophical Notebook*, cited in Nicholas Lash, Introduction to *An Essay in Aid of A Grammar of Assent* (Notre Dame: University of Notre Dame Press, 1979), 14. See also Terrence Merrigan, "The Imagination in the Life and Thought of John Henry Newman," in *Cahiers victoriens et edouardiens* 70 (Autumn, 2009): "Newman's reflections on what he described as 'the theology of a religious imagination' contain considerations that are relevant to the disciplines of philosophy and literature as well as theology. Newman was convinced that all beliefs — religious, secular, or political — must first be credible to the imagination and that the religious object is only adequately appropriated *via* an imaginative process. . . . Newman portrays the imagination as the capacity to relate to an object as a 'whole', that is to say, as something with a claim on us. . . . For Newman, then, the adequate appropriation of the object of Christian faith requires both an act of the imagination and a willingness to engage in critical, historical reflection." Thus, in respect to our hypothesis, affective and aesthetic elements, including imaginative and intuitive aspects, are constituent parts of the conversion experience.

By so doing, we will arrive, to paraphrase the poet, back at where it all began, only to know that place for the first time.[2] In short, Newman's search for truth began and concluded in the realization of the mystery of being loved and the necessity of returning that love as the means to, and the fulfillment of, the quest's end. But this journey had its beginning for Newman well before 1816.

As Newman wrote in 1839, "Love [is] the safeguard of Faith."[3] He realized this upon learning that faith is the key to the grasp of revelation, and this the key to self-knowledge. He then reached the insight that self-knowledge is begotten by awareness, humility, and obedience. These insights integrate the affective, aesthetic, moral, and intellectual dimensions of the self, leading to, or preparing for, the fifth element of the unconditional, in the conversion experience.

For Newman, the lesson, or light of insight, was first kindled by the warmth of family love. It was in this milieu, with the constant support of a beleaguered father, a spiritual mother, playful brothers, and loving sisters, that young Newman's heart and soul first loved, shaping his imagination and intellect. These family experiences provided the primary paradigm for the development of his intuition, insights, and subsequent theology, leading Avery Dulles to describe it as personalist.[4] The love of Christ was mediated to Newman through loving parents. Newman was on his journey back to God from the first two sparse sentences recorded in the very first volume of his *Letters and Diaries*: "Saturday 21 February 1801 I was born Thursday 9 April baptized."[5] Through his Christian parents and his infant baptism, Newman entered the Church and the world of grace. It would take him almost three decades to synthesize this reality, to resolve intellectually this religious event. But that synthesis had its beginning in his family and through his parents as God's earthly mediators and witnesses to the truth of the Church. This "sacramental" principle played a major role in Newman's development, but the key point is that this mystery of God's love was at work through his parents

---

2   T. S. Eliot, "Little Gidding," in *The Four Quartets* (New York: Harcourt, Brace, and Company, 1943).

3   John Henry Newman, *Fifteen Sermons Preached Before the University of Oxford* (London: Rivingtons, 1872), 222.

4   "Newman remains the outstanding master of personalism in theological epistemology. His reflections on faith and reason have proved prophetic." Avery Dulles, *Newman* (New York: Continuum, 2002), 45.

5   John Henry Newman, *The Letters and Diaries of John Henry Newman*, vol. I, ed. Ian Ker and Thomas Gornall (Oxford: Clarendon Press, 1978), 3.

in cooperation with their Church long before Newman grasped it. Thus, an examination of Newman's pre-1816 conversion experience will provide valuable evidence to validate the claim that interpersonal love is the key to understanding Newman and his theology following that conversion. Overall, two major parts or phases are evident, each with six major stages. Stage one traces Newman's early home life experience where his religious intuition was quickened, and stage two examines the crisis which occurred in 1816 when that first source of love and stability was threatened by worldly pressures, resulting in his turn to evangelicalism. In stage three, this new "ultraism" clashes with home and family during the early 1820s. Then stage four examines the influences which cause Newman to turn to another extremism, liberalism,[6] in the mid 1820s. Next the loss of his father, the focus of stage five, and the subsequent correspondence on religious matters with his brother Charles, the focus of stage six, which are both very personal factors, provide the final major influences of chapter one and also underscore one of the major themes of this study: at every

---

6   We should distinguish here between two senses of liberalism. Newman opposed the excessive application of logic to religion which tends to marginalize and damage faith, as he succinctly described in his biglietto speech of 1879, but he always favored what is the open-mindedness of liberal thinking in the pursuit of truth. In that speech of 1879, Newman thus described the liberalism to which he was opposed: "I rejoice to say, to one great mischief I have from the first opposed myself. For 30, 40, 50 years I have resisted to the best of my powers the spirit of liberalism in religion. . . . Alas! It is an error overspreading, as a snare, the whole earth; and on this great occasion . . . I renew the protest against it which I have made so often. . . . Liberalism in religion is the doctrine that there is no positive truth in religion, but that one creed is as good as another, and this is the teaching which is gaining substance and force daily. It is inconsistent with any recognition of any religion as true. It teaches that all are to be tolerated, but all are matters of opinion. Revealed religion is not a truth, but a sentiment and a taste. Not an objective fact; not miraculous; and it is the right of each individual to make it say just what strikes his fancy. Devotion is not necessarily founded on faith." Speech of His Eminence Cardinal Newman on the Reception of the "Biglietto" (Rome: Liberia Spithover, 1879).

"When Newman defined liberalism as 'the anti-dogmatic principle', he meant the anti-Christian anti-dogmatic principle, for he went on to define a range of liberal dogmas, and thereby fathered Chesterton's fundamental conviction that there are only two kinds of people, 'those who accept dogmas and know it and those who accept dogmas and don't know it.' For Newman saw that there is no dogma more binding than liberal dogma, no view more deeply founded than the liberal view on unexamined preconception and prejudice, and so he was among the first to foresee and to oppose that liberal dechristianization of the Church of England which has been part of the dechristianization of England." Sheridan Gilley, "Newman and the Convert Mind," in *Newman and Conversion*, ed. Ian Ker (T&T Clark Ltd.: Edinburgh, 1997), 13.

turn Newman's intellectual and theological development was primarily influenced by the state of his interpersonal relationships. The nature of interpersonal dynamics and the accompanying mystery of love emerge as the dominant causes in each of the movements we examine. Thus a clear link existed between interpersonal relationships, conversion, and theology, the first of these forming the pattern and dynamics which govern the emergence of the last two.

Let us now examine these six major stages, beginning with the primary influence: Newman's loving home life.

STAGE ONE:
Newman's Loving Social Milieu

FERTILIZATION OF THE AFFECTIONS
AND HIS RELIGIOUS INTUITION

NEWMAN'S APOLOGIA PROVIDES SEVERAL HELPFUL DETAILS regarding this early period. We learn from its opening page that the Newman home emphasized Bible reading and the Church catechism for religious instruction. We also read of a youthful Newman possessing a vivid imagination of an "unseen" reality, and that certain religious symbolism—the cross and a rosary, although the source of these remains a mystery—made a significant impression on him. These four factors, then—the Bible, the Church catechism, his sense of a transcendent reality, and the impression of symbolism—were engendered or at least stimulated by his Christian upbringing.

When analyzing these elements, we find a common thread — an awareness of the Transcendent Other, God, and human attempts to grasp and express the reality of this encounter. These are notable influences which run throughout almost all of what Newman will later write: the reality of the "unseen" world, the problematic of "words" expressing "ideas," and ultimately the inexpressibility of the experience of the heart — love. Before he analyzed and wrote on these subjects, Newman was acquiring a storehouse of affective experience.

In keeping with his design of the *Apologia*, virtually nothing is mentioned of family members in particular or his relations with them, since Newman is "speaking there of the formation of my doctrinal opinions."[7] Yet if we turn to other sources, particularly his *Letters and Diaries* and the *Autobiographical Writings*, as well as Ward's *Young Mr. Newman*, Middleton's *Newman at Oxford*,

---

7   John Henry Newman, *The Letters and Diaries of John Henry Newman*, vol. I, 30, note 1.

Trevor's *The Pillar of the Cloud*, and Mozley's *Reminiscences Chiefly of Oriel College and the Oxford Movement*, we get to the heart of the apologist.

For example, the *Apologia* omits all mention of a pivotal problem which occurred at a crucial stage in Newman's development, at the age of fifteen — the failure of his father's bank. From our other sources, we read of how wounded young Newman was during this period: his anger when he discovered that this family-shaking catastrophe resulted from the obstinacy of one individual; that rumors spread regarding the reputation of his father despite the senior Newman's claim that "our banking-house has to-day paid everyone in full."[8] Many years later, in 1874, when recounting the history of the problems of his father during those early days, his *Letters and Diaries* record the following: "He returned to London, and after a few years his anxieties brought him to an end. For his sake who loved and wearied himself for us all with such unrequited affection, I wish all this forgotten."[9] This was the father who always fretted about his son's intellectual development, writing him in 1806 when Newman was but five years old, that "You must learn something new every day, or you will no longer be called a clever boy."[10] Even Newman's sister Harriett later wrote of, as Middleton terms it, "a very happy family circle."[11]

Thus the affective soil had been tilled and the religious seed planted during Newman's early family life. Security and happiness, established by his parents, were hallmarks of these early years. One of the parents' objectives was to direct their children toward the source of that love, God, as conceived by, and experienced through, the Church of England. However, this conception of God was largely the result of private scripture reading and interpretation, a factor which played a primary role in Newman's development. But most of all, he was to learn a much more significant principle which would play a more prominent role — the credibility of personal witness as the basis for accepting the testimony of those witnesses. In his formative years, Newman accepted the religious witness of his parents through their loving witness toward him, quickening his innate religious intuition. He accepted the God of the Church of England as he accepted and trusted his loving parents. He would return to this existential reality toward the end of the first major phase of his development in late 1827 and into 1828, after a lengthy sojourn through the emotive and intellectual attractions of evangelicalism and liberalism. But most of all it was the loving devotion his parents directed toward him that engendered his faith in

---

8   Ibid., 18.   9   Ibid., 28.   10   Ibid.

11   R. D. Middleton, *Newman at Oxford* (New York: Oxford University Press, 1950), 4.

them, causing him to embrace what they embraced. Newman learned the principle of the credibility of witness at home, long before he established it in 1825 when he asserted it as the ground for acceptance of the miracles of Scripture in his *Essay* on the subject. However, this "source experience" was jolted in 1816, which is the focus of our next stage.

STAGE TWO:
Crisis: The Threat to Religious Intuition —
Response: Evangelicalism

THE EARLY NEWMAN EVANGELICAL DOCUMENTS

THE CRISIS OF 1816 INTRODUCED A NEW FACTOR INTO THE equation, the first major extra-familial influence of Newman's young life. The personal witness of Rev. Walter Mayers, one of the classics masters at Newman's Ealing school, "was throughout this period his spiritual guide."[12] In the *Apologia*, Newman records just one, though powerful, mention of Mayers during this crisis: "The Rev. Walter Mayers . . . was the human means of this beginning of divine faith in me."[13] Here we find Newman's important distinction between the personal and the intellectual influence of Mayers, relating that "Above and beyond the conversations and sermons of the excellent man, long dead, the Rev. Walter Mayers, of Pembroke College, Oxford, [was] the effect of the books which he put into my hands, all of the school of Calvin."[14]

Newman then lists the various books which influenced his intellectual development. But let us recall Newman's statement. If we examine it carefully, we find that it was Mayers's *person* which affected Newman's faith. The ensuing intellectual development, by means of the books recommended by Mayers, followed from, and was dependent upon, the impression of Mayers the person. It was only after Newman accepted Mayers as a credible witness to truth that his recommendations were accepted. In short, a recommendation is dependent upon the credibility of its source. Further information is found in other sources, particularly the Newman-Mayers, and related, correspondence. Newman's *Letters and Diaries*, volume 1, contains an exchange of eight letters between the years 1816 – 1822. These documents reveal not only the theological depth of influence but more importantly the loving concern Mayers expressed for Newman. Even more revealing are the later

12 Ibid., 10.
13 John Henry Newman, *Apologia pro Vita Sua*, ed. Ian Ker (London: Penguin Books, 1994), 25.   14   Ibid., 25.

letters Newman exchanged with Mayers's widow, Keble, and Rev. Greaves reflecting on the personal character of Mayers, so selfless and moral, which deeply affected Newman. This was the foundation which led Newman to consider, and temporarily embrace, Mayers's Calvinism. As he had accepted the Church of England as part of the undifferentiated loving experience of his parents, so he accepted Evangelicalism as part of the undifferentiated loving experience of Mayers. Newman had not yet attained the intellectual differentiation which would distinguish the heart from the head. For this highly sensitive teenager, where the heart journeyed, the head followed, as his affections dominated this phase of his life. But symptoms of dissonance were never far removed. Let us examine the Mayers correspondence particularly for evidence of these effects; the personal and the intellectual influence of Mayers and symptoms of dissonance, or the lack of integration between the heart and the head.

The Newman–Mayers Correspondence

From December 1816 through June 1817, Mayers wrote three letters to the young evangelical convert, and Newman wrote one in reply. These occur just after Newman's conversion in late 1816 and thus offer important evidence of both Newman's state of mind and the theological positions of Rev. Mayers, his major influence of this period.

A Significant Mayers Letter: The Recommendation of Calvinist Authors and Principles[15]

This letter is noteworthy on two counts. First, it records Mayers's recommendation to Newman of three Calvinist authors: "My Dear Friend with this you will receive Beveridge's *Private Thoughts* of which I beg your acceptance as a small token of my affectionate regard. . . . Did you ever read Dodderidge's *Rise and Progress* or Law's *Serious Call?*" Second, two evangelical principles are stressed: private scripture interpretation as the norm of judgment, and anti-world dualism:

> On perusing it [Beveridge] you will see that the opinions that we have discussed [are] deduced from the only authentic source [scripture]. To that source let me direct your attention   be more disposed to form your sentiments on religion from that, than to adapt and interpret it to your opinions   [spacing is original author's] I have of course had somewhat more experience of what is called the world, but I can assure you there is no real or substantial happiness to be found in its vain and unprofitable pursuits.

---

15   Newman, *Letters and Diaries*, vol. I, 29–30. Dated December 31, 1816.

Newman's Response: Personal Scripture Interpretation and Conscience,
Regeneration, and Loving Friendship[16]

In January 1817, Newman replied to Mayers in a three-paragraph letter, each of which reveals a relevant element. First, Newman expressed his thanks to Mayers and underscored the evangelical principle of personal scripture interpretation:

> I am very much obliged to you for your kind present. . . . Indeed I find I have very great need of some monitor to direct me, and I sincerely trust that my conscience, enlightened by the Bible, through the influence of the Holy Spirit, may prove a faithful and vigilant guardian of the principles of religion.

Here we see how easily Newman moved from the Bible-reading influence of his parents to that of Mayers. But along with the move came Mayers's evangelicalism, as well as one of Newman's earliest references to the primacy of conscience. However, in the second paragraph Newman addressed the key issue, regeneration, indicative of a dissonance in respect to evangelical doctrine:

> There is one passage [of Beveridge] that I do not quite comprehend; it is on the Sacrament of Baptism [and] how it could be that baptized infants, dying in their infancy, could be saved, unless the Spirit of God was given them; which seems to contradict the opinion that baptism is not accompanied by the Holy Ghost.

Over the next decade, this would be one of the major difficulties which Newman attempted to resolve, pitting his intellectual and theological development against his practical experience. As of 1817, however, we note that Newman experienced an intellectual dissonance with evangelical orthodoxy, since it clashed with his innate sensibilities even before he encountered it in Beveridge, as he wrote Mayers: "I had, before I read it, debated (it) with myself."

In the third and closing paragraph, Newman notably recounted his affectionate regard for, and his indebtedness to, Mayers:

> I hope I shall continue firm in the principles, in which you, Sir, have instructed me. . . . May that Holy Spirit by whom you were made the instrument of good to me, and by whom my heart was softened to receive your instructions, may he steer me safe through the dangers, to which I may be exposed at College.

---

16   Ibid., 30–31. Dated January 1817.

Thus, in Newman's responding letter we find an allusion to conscience and personal scripture interpretation, confusion over the doctrine of regeneration, and the high regard in which he held Mayers, especially for the latter's principles and instruction. The emotional, heartfelt, and personal comments are characteristic traits running through Newman's correspondence not only in this but in all relationships, as we shall see, evidencing the primary influence of the affections of the heart and interpersonal relations on his thought.

Further, these three categories indicate the intuitive (conscience and personal interpretation), intellectual (doctrinal confusion), and the interpersonal and affective (Mayers) elements influencing yet perplexing the young student. Mayers, however, responds to Newman's doubts with his primary letter in the series, a major systematic exposition of evangelicalism.

THE MAJOR MAYERS LETTER: *April 14, 1817* *Mayers's Evangelical Synthesis and Their Loving Friendship*[17]

MAYERS REPLIED TO NEWMAN IN THIS, THE MOST EXTENSIVE letter exchanged between them. Mayers is firm in addressing Newman's "unorthodox" leanings and details an elaborate exposition of evangelical doctrine regarding the interrelationship of baptism, regeneration, and conversion. The letter, a compact "systematic theological epistle," had a major impact on the sixteen-year-old Newman, who absorbed his elder's critique and exposition, although he reinterpreted these elements in the ensuing years from a different perspective on the dynamic process involved: that is, he considered regeneration and conversion necessary, as Mayers contends, but his thoughts on how and where they occur would shift significantly as his perspective evolved.

However, for the purpose of our study, the most important statement of Mayers occurs in the very last sentence of this lengthy letter:

> May you and I know by happy experience the influence of that Spirit, whose fruit is love joy peace etc 5 Gal 22 and then we shall not be solicitous to ascertain whether it was produced in Baptism or by subsequent operation of the Holy Spirit.

In such a lengthy letter dedicated to systematic theological argumentation, we find Mayers subordinating these intellectual questions about regeneration to their personal loving friendship.

---

17   Ibid., 32–34. Dated April 14, 1817.

This short closing is perhaps more relevant than the rest of the letter's theological analysis, for years later, when Newman had long separated himself from Mayers's evangelical doctrines, he emphasized not the intellectual differences between them, but rather the bond of the heart which characterized their relationship. For Newman, affectivity superseded the intellectual element. This was the enduring theological lesson which Newman learned from Mayers, notwithstanding the evangelical excesses in which that lesson was encased.

We should also note that several prominent themes of the letter — emphasis on the negative "unregenerate" state of human nature, the necessity of holiness[18] for regeneration, and the hard line which separates the regenerate from the unregenerate — will become major themes in Newman's earliest "*Parochial and Plain Sermons*" between 1825 and 1826. This link will be discussed more fully below. At this point the important note is that these theological seeds were planted as early as 1816, but even more importantly their influence was made possible by loving friendship. The heart, then, was the soil which nourished the theological seed, the same principle which Newman experienced in the loving relationship within his family. Thus we see a methodological consistency despite the intellectual excesses of this period. This dissonance was soon expressed in Newman's writings of the period.

Two Newman Letters: Evidence of the Conflict of Heart and Head

This loving friendship opened Newman's mind to the intellectual arguments of his mentor. But by 1820 the tension between heart and head, or between affectivity and intellect, was beginning to take its toll. On September 12, 1820, as Newman's school examinations of late November approached, he wrote Mayers of four conflicts or tensions he felt, symptoms of his reaction to the dissonance caused by evangelical excess.[19]

He described a desire for social isolation, the sin of coveting success, the conflict of his words with the feelings of his heart, and the "logic" of his "hypocritical" prayer. As for his desire for social isolation, he wrote:

---

18   For an examination of holiness in Newman, see Fr. Juan Velez, *Holiness in a Secular Age: The Witness of John Henry Newman* (New York: Scepter Publishers, 2017), 15, 17: "This work is a monograph on some of Newman's most important contributions to spirituality and theology. . . . (T)his book (is an) invitation to holiness in a secular age in light of the witness of Cardinal Newman." See also Ian Ker, *Healing the Wound of Humanity: The Spirituality of John Henry Newman* (London: Dartan, Longman, and Todd, 1993).

19   Newman, *Letters and Diaries*, vol. I, 86–87.

> I am more happy here, than I suppose I ever was yet; for the com-
> parative freedom from temptation I enjoy in having hardly anyone
> near me (I hope I do not speak presumptuously) leaves me at greater
> liberty to look into my heart, and to keep my thoughts on God.

The conflict of his heart and head concerning his scrupulous self-examination about academic success emphasizes the tension:

> As it is, I make my daily prayer, though I do not feel it as I ought
> to do, that I may not get any honors in the schools, if they are
> to be the least cause of sin to me. Yet with all the earnestness
> I assume, how little does my heart go with my words, or feel
> their extent. A very distinct thing to say so, when the trial is at
> a distance, and when the temptation comes in full force. [So] I
> continue to pray, "Let me get no honours here, if they are to be
> the slightest cause of sin to my soul."

He immediately followed this with a self-castigating charge of hypocrisy:

> But, while saying this, I often find that I am acting the part of
> a very hypocrite; I am buoyed up with the secret idea, that by
> thus leaving the event in the hands of God, when I pray, He may
> be induced, as a reward for so proper a spirit, to grant me my
> desire. Thus my prayer is a mockery.

Less than three months later, Newman would suffer his first of two breakdowns in the schools. This letter to Mayers contains evidence that the conflict over the nature of success, rooted in his Mayers-based evangelicalism and combined with his introverted personality,[20] played a major role in that event.

Five weeks after this traumatic event, Newman wrote Mayers a short recounting of the breakdown, with a revelatory personal interpretation:[21]

> I was unwell, low-spirited [and] so great a depression came on me,
> that I could do nothing. I was nervous in the extreme, a thing
> I never before experienced, and did not expect — my memory
> was gone, my mind altogether confused.

Newman followed this account with a major insight of his early years: "There is a great difference between believing a thing to be good, and

---

20 Terrence Merrigan has explored the impact of Newman's introverted personality on both his conversions and his theology in "Newman's Progress Toward Rome: A Psychological Consideration of His Conversion to Catholicism," *The Downside Review* 104 (April 1986): 95–112.   21 Newman, *Letters and Diaries*, vol. I., 99.

feeling it." In this concise comment, he summarized the conflict of heart and head, and his breakdown is an example of the dysfunction which resulted from this failure of integration.

However, Newman was a long way from actually realizing the depth of his own insight, for, as mentioned earlier, he went on to endorse an evangelical interpretation of the event:

> I am not only enabled to believe failure best for me, but God has given me to see it and know it.... Honour and fame are not desirable.... I trust I may have always the same content and indifference to the world, which is at present the prevailing principle of my heart — yet I have great fears of backsliding.

Newman closed this letter, his last in the series, on this evangelical note, which was an affirmation of his mentor's theological stance. In an earlier letter dated June 16, 1817, Mayers had written to "My dear Friend," cautioning him about the pitfalls at Oxford: "You will find the ridicule of the world among the strongest weapons Satan can employ, and one very frequently assumed by the Logicians of O. [Oriel]."[22] Mayers must have been heartened by Newman's evangelical interpretation of his academic difficulties, and he wrote him just five months later in the last letter of this series extolling the nature of evangelicalism: "The beauty of personal religion this is exactly what I like."[23]

Though Newman would eventually abandon much of the intellectual Calvinist influence of this period derived from Mayers and his recommended books, he always retained the more fundamental and important elements of their relationship, one which mediated the love of God through love of another. As with his family, Newman found in Mayers another witness to the truth, leading to God by living a life of love. However, these evangelical influences began to emerge in Newman's earliest theological writings, composed during this period, as his developing intellect assimilated these effects.

THE EVANGELICAL IMPRINT:
From Personal Influence to Theological Exposition —
The Earliest Theological Writings: 1821–1823

THE PERIOD 1821–1823 WAS A HIGH POINT IN NEWMAN'S EVANgelical commitment, as he records in his journal that "he was more devoted to the evangelical creed and more strict in his religious duties than at

---

22   Ibid., 36.   23   Ibid., 110.

any previous time."[24] During this period Newman composed his first theological writings. Three documents from this time provide evidence that his conversion of 1816, especially its evangelical coloring, infused his theological thinking with evangelical doctrine.

The First Document: "Comment on Philippians 2: 12–13"[25] — Evidence of Evangelical Influence

This document is dated June 1821, just months after his breakdown in the schools. Newman explains the biblical text "Work out your salvation" by an analysis of three key terms, or events: justification, regeneration, and sanctification, themes which had preoccupied him since 1816.

In Newman's analysis, justification is by faith alone, clarifying the meaning of "salvation" in the passage "because they were saved from that (eternal damnation) immediately on their justification and justified immediately on their believing."

Regeneration, on the other hand, is gradual compared to the "instantaneous" nature of justification. Sanctification, synonymous with holiness, is then acquired by means of efficacious grace, the work of which is both imputed and irresistible: "This will (the) Spirit imparts [and] it cannot be resisted." Newman's explanation of the process of sanctification is noteworthy in that it emphasizes two evangelical tenets. This "first stage of sanctification [is] by the exhortations of Scripture or of his ministers." The second emphasizes self-works: prayer, fasting, and communicating. The primacy of Scripture and personal acts are the chief means of developing sanctification, and these are also key evangelical principles. This first document, then, provides evidence that the evangelical creed was a prime influence on Newman's early theology.

The Second Document: "A Collection of Scripture Passages"[26] — Evangelical Doctrine and the Nature of Conversion: The Implication of Intuition

Fully entitled "A Collection of Scripture Passages setting forth in due succession the doctrines of Christianity," this document was written in the same year as the previous one and employs at least seven major evangelical themes in its interpretation of Scripture, yet its exposition of conversion relies more on the "textbook evangelical" description than Newman's own

---

24   John Henry Newman, *Autobiographical Writings*, ed. Henry Tristram (New York: Sheed and Ward, 1956), 80.
25   Thomas L. Sheridan, *Newman on Justification* (Staten Island: Alba House, 1967), 44–50.
26   Ibid., 50–57. Dated June 1821.

experience, which was incompatible with the former, especially its zealous character. The document espouses these evangelical doctrines:

1. Negative conception of human nature:
   Man now still owes obedience, but he is *incapable* of it because of the *total* corruption of his nature.

2 – 5. Predestination, the gratuity of election, final perseverance, and the concept of a vindictive God:
   Hence he (man) is condemned to eternal misery. . . . This justice, however, is tempered by the mercy of God, whereby *certain individuals* are predestined by God to be saved "for reasons not revealed to us" — but not because of any good in the individuals themselves. The rest are *left* to the condemnation which they have deserved.

6. Rejection of baptismal regeneration:
   What appointed mean could change so earthly an heart?. . . Did the waters of baptism? Easy receipt, and of inestimable virtue! . . . (So) simple remedy for the radical disease of our nature! . . . Alas, experience teaches a different lesson, and we are constrained to admit that neither the hand of the baptizer, nor the voice of him that exhorteth, nor the example of pious friends, nor afflictions, nor mercies, nor any thing human is a sure and certain method powerful to force "the gift of God."

7. Justification by faith alone:
   From whence then cometh his help? truly from the Lord who made heaven and earth! — happy, happy soul! lo, he hath laid hold on the appointed mean of justification, he hath brought down from above the robe of righteousness — he believeth!

These seven evangelical tenets imbue Newman's theological synthesis, but we find an important difference in the method employed in the second part of the document, which treats of conversion, compared to the first part, which treats of doctrine.

Newman's exposition of the nature of conversion provides evidence of the breach which was gradually developing between his evangelical intellectualism and his own personal experience of conversion. From another source, we find his noting that his conception of conversion was "from books" rather than from his personal experience, as he reflected five years later on this very document and the nature of his own conversion in his memoir entry dated July 26, 1826:

I have greatly changed my views on many points. I transcribe the following from loose notes which I find among my papers. It is written in 1821 and appended to a *description* of the ordinary *process* of conversion, (i.e., the hopes, fears, despair, joy &c &c of the person under conversion) which I then thought almost necessary to a true Christian. 'I speak of conversion with great diffidence, being obliged to adopt the language of books. For my own feelings, as far as I remember, were so different from any account I have ever read, that I dare not go by what *may* be an individual case.' That is, I wrote *juxta praescriptum*. I am persuaded that very many of my most positive and dogmatical notions were taken *from books*. In the matter in question (conversion) my feelings were not *violent*, but a returning to, a renewing of, principles, under the power of the Holy Spirit, which I had already felt, and in a measure acted on, when young.[27]

This reflection indicates that Newman's exposition of conversion was "textbook evangelical" and differed from his own experience. Further, his conversion experience was a renewing of "principles" already "felt" when young. This differentiation which Newman noted is of major import in that it emphasized the relationship of the heart and the head in his conversion experience, which clashed with his evangelical, academic, "bookish" conception. It was also an implication of the presence of the important dimension of intuition in Newman's developing theology. But the major note is that this breach would continue to widen over the next several years under different influences.

The Third Document: "The Nature of Holiness" 1822–1823[28] — The Emergence of the Primacy of Faith

This document is a further development of Newman's thought on conversion. First, he notes the requirement of conversion as "the necessity of a mighty revolution, a radical change of heart and sentiments taking place in every one who would be saved." Second, he notes that conversion is gradual: the "revolution of sentiment" is a "progress." In addition to its necessity and developmental nature, Newman finds three other factors which argue against a connection between conversion and baptism: rational reflection, tests based on Scripture, and repentance and faith. Newman finds that all three are usually present in conversion, but

---

27   Newman, *Autobiographical Writings*, 172.
28   Sheridan, *Newman on Justification*, 58–66.

not so in baptism. Thus, baptism and conversion are not mutual accompaniments, and if the latter is necessary for salvation, then baptism must logically fall short of sufficing for salvation. Newman then develops a six-stage process of conversion: awareness of sin and of God's holiness, sorrow for sin, belief, justification, peace with God and faith working by love, including good works. His scriptural exegesis reveals that baptism only appears at stages four and five, and

> We conclude therefore that baptism, *as such*, in no case conveys to the convert change of heart, but certain privileges, viz. justification, adoption, the right of asking for God's Spirit and the hope of heaven

and

> whatever change infant baptism effects, there is no reason for supposing its effects greater than those of adult baptism

but

> baptism, as such does not convey to the adult's soul the indispensable change, but certain privileges etc. *conditional* upon a previous alteration of sentiment.

At this stage, Newman is clearly committed to the evangelical interpretation of regeneration, and that it most certainly does not occur in the act of baptism.[29] This third document returns to the two other major themes of the first document, justification and sanctification, along with regeneration, as Newman attempts to synthesize the three.

Justification is "salvation from eternal misery" and is instantaneous. Regeneration is "salvation from the bondage of sin" and is a gradual process, beginning in justification. The link between the two is faith: "Faith is the principle and root of holiness in our souls (and) that first evidence of a new nature." Holiness, however, "consists in a certain state of the heart and affections [and] arises from a practical conviction of

---

29 Newman's evangelical theory of justification stands in opposition to the Council of Trent's "Decree Concerning Justification," wherein baptism effects justification and regeneration: "[I]n that new birth there is bestowed upon them, through the merit of His passion, the grace by which they are made just. . . . This translation however cannot . . . be effected except through the laver of regeneration or its desire, as it is written: *Unless a man be born again of water and the Holy Ghost, he cannot enter into the kingdom of heaven.*" *Canons and Decrees of the Council of Trent*, ed. H. J. Schroeder (London: B. Herder Book Co., 1955), 31.

the importance of eternal things." Practical conviction, or faith, is the source of holiness, and the occasion of justification and the beginning of the process of regeneration. Faith has now become a primary factor in Newman's soteriological understanding.

The value of these three documents is that they evidence Newman's initial forays into a theological exposition of his evangelical commitment. Three major points can be drawn from them. First, Newman was committed to an evangelical interpretation of the process of justification, regeneration, and sanctification, along with conversion. Second, a problematic distinction continues to exist as to just *how* these experiences actually occur — their causes and effects; in short, *how* God and man actually interrelate. This leads to the third major and perhaps most relevant point for our study: the nature and function of faith in this process.

FAITH AND THE AFFECTIVE AND AESTHETIC ELEMENTS OF RELIGIOUS CONVERSION

RETURNING BRIEFLY TO THE LAST DOCUMENT'S ANALYSIS OF the conversion process, two stages, the first and the fifth, yield important clues to the underlying essence of conversion, which is relationship, and the critical function of interpersonal dynamics in the entire process.

Stage one is "the sense of God's holiness and of our own vileness."[30] This is the moment of *awareness* and *presence* of the Transcendent Other and realization of the difference between oneself and that Other. This awareness is essentially *interpersonal*: it is *of* oneself *and* the Other *and* the relationship between them. In 1864, Newman described this stage regarding his own conversion of 1816:

> When I was fifteen, (in the autumn of 1816), a great change of thought took place in me. I fell under the influences of a definite Creed, and received into my intellect impressions of dogma, which, through God's mercy, have never been effaced or obscured. . . . I . . . believed that the inward conversion of which I was conscious, and of which I still am more certain than that I have hands and feet,) would last into the next life, and that I was elected to eternal glory. . . . I retained it until the age of twenty-one, when it gradually faded away; but I believe that had some influence on my opinions, in the direction of those childish imaginations which I have already mentioned . . . and

---

30 Sheridan, *Newman on Justification*, 64, 61.

> making me rest in the thought of two and two only absolute
> and luminously self-evident beings, myself and my Creator.[31]

This "thought" introduces an essential element in conversion, the aesthetic dimension, or the vision of a relationship with God. This perception which Newman experienced in 1816 transformed his human affections, developed in familial relations and in friendship with Mayers, into affection for God. This interaction of affectivity and aesthetic produces religious conversion, as the affections are now directed to the God imagined in, but transcending, the new vision. However, two other aspects are also involved. Through the description of this experience as a "thought," it obviously involved an intellectual element, and as a new vision and image, it involved the imagination also.

Stage five is "peace with God and faith working by love."[32] Here we find the genesis of an insight which would grow into the breach between Newman's evangelical doctrine and his personal experience until it split the two. The key link is Newman's reference to the nature of faith: "working by love." Faith is not merely an intellectual assent but rather an interpersonal experience — love. In brief, if faith is integral to conversion, and love is integral to faith, and love is an interpersonal experience, then the basis of conversion is love in an interpersonal relationship. This explains why Newman could relate his conversion experience of 1816 to his "feelings [as] a returning to, a renewing of, principles under the power of the Holy Spirit, which I had already felt, and in a measure acted on, when

---

31   Newman, *Apologia*, 16. Keith Beaumont offers an interpretation of this passage: "He refers to this experience and to the circumstances surrounding it — in a manner however which hides as much as it reveals — in a passage of his autobiography which constitutes perhaps the most celebrated passage in all his numerous and multifarious writings. The concluding formula, 'myself and my Creator,' has given rise to endless commentaries, many of them wide of the mark and some frankly grotesque. It has been alleged that Newman is inviting us to make of our 'self' a sort of cocoon in which we can shut ourselves away with 'our' God. How should we interpret this formula? And why, in particular, does the author place 'myself' before 'my Creator'? The explanation is quite simply that the very structure of the sentence expresses an *awakening of consciousness*. The fifteen-year-old boy becomes conscious of himself first, as a thinking, sentient, and self-aware being. Then, in the intimate depths of this consciousness of self, he discovers the presence of Another, in whom he recognizes God. The young Newman's experience is analogous to that of St. Augustine, expressed by the latter in the celebrated formula, 'God is more intimate to me than I am to myself' (*Confessions*, Book III, 6)." Keith Beaumont, *Blessed John Henry Newman: Theologian and Spiritual Guide for Our Times* (San Francisco: Ignatius Press, 2010), 12. Authorized biography for Newman's Beatification.
32   Sheridan, *Newman on Justification*, 61.

young."[33] This is an allusion to the consistency of his pre-conversion affectivity with that of his conversion experience: relationship is the common denominator, and love is its ground. The interpersonal relationships of home life were analogous to, and the human mediators of, his interpersonal relationship with God, culminating in his conversion experience. However, these realizations were clashing with the austere, intellectual theology of evangelicalism. This dissonance continued to develop, eventually causing Newman to reject doctrinal evangelicalism, but this was years away.

At this same time, Newman wrote a most valuable letter to the *Christian Observer* wherein he discoursed on a related topic, religious epistemology, which will be one of the major "tracks" on which he develops his thought in years to come. It is noteworthy in that the letter dates from the same period as the previous theological documents but adds further evidence that his own thinking and analysis of epistemology would not long abide the intellectual, theological, and experiential limitations of evangelical doctrine. Let us examine this document for that evidence.

The Religious Epistemology Track: Document 1 — The First Letter to the Christian Observer: An Epistemological Essay[34]

Reason, Newman writes, is a method for understanding a reality which is both external to, and greater than, the reasoning mind. Reason perceives pieces of, but less than, the whole. Thus, the essay's themes are the limitations of reason and the implications of these limitations for man's knowledge, especially when applied to religious categories. As an example, Newman analyzes how the mind works on mathematical problems, leading to conclusions about reason's limits and value, resulting ultimately in an insight into the role of à priori speculations in our thinking:

> No science perhaps is more adapted to confirm our belief in the tenets of Christianity than that of mathematics, when cultivated with a proper disposition of mind [by] making us sensible of the contracted range of our imagination and judgment; by shewing us how little we know, how little we can comprehend, and how erroneous oftentimes are the conclusions to which à priori speculations would lead us.

The nature of mathematical study is objective since "passions and feelings and prejudices are excluded; there is nothing to excite hope, or

---

33 Newman, *Autobiographical Writings*, 80.
34 Newman, "To the editor of the *Christian Observer*," in *Letters and Diaries*, vol. I, 102–5; May 1821.

gratify desire; nothing to be gained or to be lost." However, such objective reflection leads to the insight that a dimension of reality is beyond rational comprehension: "And yet even here, when there is no temptation to be dissatisfied with truth, or to be afraid to avow it, (as, often unhappily, is the case in matters of religion,) many things occur; at which we cannot but wonder, and for which we can give no reason."

Reason, then, delivers our understanding to the door of wonder, enabling us to know some things, but leads us more importantly to understand that there are some things which we do not know. The major pitfall at this juncture is intellectual arrogance, the presumption that reality conforms to our ability to comprehend it, resulting in objections to any thinking that reality extends beyond rational comprehension:

> Who will not confess the rashness and arrogance of such objections, and of our attempting to give an opinion respecting the propriety of the plan approved by the Creator, while our judgment is in our present feeble state, and our knowledge of the system of the universe, and of the adaptation of its parts, is even more limited than that of the fly in the fable, who saw fit to find fault with the architectural proportions of one of the noblest buildings in the world?

At this point in the essay, Newman has drawn his comparison of the two major foci into sharp contrast: the rational dimension of the mind versus the nature of reality, the latter so obviously transcending the limits of the former. Using this framework, he transfers the argument to the topic of religion and revelation: "Apply the confession to religion — how little do we know of the ways of God, and how unequal are our faculties to judge of what we do know?" Again employing the rationalist-suprarationalist analogy, Newman characterizes the opposition:

> 'If the Gospel were written on the sun,' said Paine, 'it would be believed by all.' To these and similar suggestions of unbelief, how striking is the answer of the Apostle: 'Nay, but, O man, who art thou that repliest against God?'

Newman describes these matters as the *difficulties* of revelation, which he answers by means of his epistemological analogy. He continues, however, into the even more perplexing areas which he calls the *contradictions* and *impossibilities* of the divine mysteries: the Trinity, the Incarnation, the nature of evil, human freedom, and others. These second species of objections may be answered from the same analogy . . . when we are informed how many apparently contradictory propositions in science are reconciled: [then] If persons would but consider the analogy, if they would but apply something of the same temper and calm judgment to religion which they do not refuse to science, there would be but few objectors to the truths of the Bible.

Newman then goes on to analyze why the analogical method fails for many:

> But their passions are brought into play: they fear least the Gospel should be true; they hate the light, their heart is not inclined to spiritual duties and therefore they approach the examination of the Scriptures with prejudice; they decide superficially and turn away in disgust [and] this very thing is done daily with the Bible. Men begin at the wrong end of the scale of reasoning; and having refuted, as they conceive, a doctrine by arguments resting on the basis of pre-conceived ideas, they proceed up the ladder, and arrive at once, at the portentous determination, that all the proofs that have been advanced in support of that doctrine, and the book which contains an avowal of that doctrine, must be erroneous. It is in this spirit that they lay down the unphilosophical axiom, 'a true religion can have no mysteries;' and then infer either that Christianity is not a true religion, because it contains mysteries — or that it contains no mysteries, because it is a true religion. Nothing can be more illogical, more unworthy of a person of science than such conclusions; but where the passions of men are aroused, and their interests concerned, little regard is paid to consistency or impartiality.

Thus, passionate self-interest can render reason illogical. In this, perhaps Newman's earliest extended exposition of method, we find numerous points relevant to our study:

1. Method is a relationship of two entities: the mind's ability to comprehend and the reality within which that mind dwells.

2. Reality, then, has an objective, external, transcendent dimension which the mind can only partially perceive.

3. The nature of understanding, whether in science or in religion, is grounded in the same phenomenon — the mind's ability to comprehend, interacting with the larger reality of which the mind is a part.

4. Both science and religion have a content which is partially knowable yet partially unknown, the realm which is the object of wonder.

5. Thus, mysteries of revelation are no less real than the unexplainable wondrous phenomena of science.

6. The intellectual method of analogy is the key means to grasping this truth.

7. Prejudicial preconceptions are the key factors causing a rejection of this method, resulting in illogical method and erroneous conclusions.

In regard to Newman himself, several points are noteworthy regarding his intellectual development at this stage:

1. Though at the height of his evangelical period, of which personal, self-interested traits are the hallmark, Newman is extremely critical of precisely these elements, yielding evidence that the dissonance between evangelical extremism and his own developing epistemological philosophy was increasing. This "ultraism" will soon provoke discord within the Newman home.

2. The focus on method as a determinant of content is a major note of this essay.

3. The use of the principle of analogy is prominent, most relevant in that we find here the grounding of this principle in Newman's own original thinking, prior to his encountering it a few years later in Butler's *Analogy*. Thus, Butler's ideas confirmed a tendency of thought already present in the young Newman's mind.

4. Newman's reference to the passionate bias which he terms "that fatal distemper of the soul" is relevant on three counts: first, he himself would shortly be reprimanded by his father for the very trait he here criticizes (evidence of the dissonance) and second, this issue of "temper" would play a major role in the upcoming debates in which he engages with his brother Charles, crystallizing his first Oxford University Sermon of July 2, 1826: "The Philosophical Temper, First Enjoined by the Gospel." Third, it was another allusion to that area of mind, the intuition, which would assume a major position in Newman's theology. But Newman had miles to go before he could rest in such a synthesis, a journey marked by the dissonance between his evangelical intellectualism and its clash with his emerging epistemological philosophy. This is also early evidence of a philosophy of mind which would be incompatible with another influence that he would soon encounter, liberalism, to be discussed later in this chapter.

This essay is a most valuable record of young Newman's thought on the nature of the mind and method and the role of analogy in the process of understanding, as well as those factors which obstruct understanding. Five decades later in the *Grammar*, Newman would still be developing his thought on these issues, and it is noteworthy to see that they were primary elements in his thinking even at this young age.

But as a conclusion to this stage, let us step back and situate Newman's early theological writings in the context of his life, including the Mayers correspondence as a resource. This will yield additional insight as to how and why he formed his theological positions. Also, these "situations" of practical experience are more significant in this process than generally recognized, and are therefore most relevant.

By 1821, we find that Newman's developing intellect and his religious intuition were failing to harmonize. Newman had come to a major crossroad in his early life. In 1816 he experienced a religious conversion with primarily affective and aesthetic elements which also "spoke" to his threatened family situation resulting from the collapse of his father's bank. Enter Rev. Mayers, a man of great credibility as a spiritual witness to the truth. However, along with Mayers's religious integrity came the intellectual flaw of evangelical excess. In fairness to Mayers, the correspondence depicts him to be a mild rather than an extreme evangelical at least in practice if not in thought, and this may explain the attraction of the practical-minded Newman to him. In fact, as we have seen, Newman described his own conversion as a non-typical Evangelical type, probably more akin to Mayers's own state.

Why then was Newman so influenced by the intellectual nature of Mayers's recommended Calvinist books, especially if Mayers the person was perhaps more moderate? Let us re-examine the earlier quote from the *Apologia*: "Above and beyond the conversations and sermons of the excellent man, long dead, the Rev. Walter Mayers, of Pembroke College, Oxford, who was the human means of this beginning of divine faith in me, was the effect of the books which he put into my hands, all of the school of Calvin."[35] Beyond the personal influence of Mayers, these evangelical authors provided Newman with an intellectual defense in support of his childhood religious intuition and experience. The hard-line dualism of evangelicalism, with its pessimistic interpretation of material existence and its "other world" emphasis, was intellectual medicine for a spiritually weakened young Newman, whose pristine view of reality was beginning to disintegrate. The result was an inevitable clash between the lure of evangelicalism, which ironically served to insulate Newman from the demise of the religious milieu of his youth, and the remaining vestiges

---

35 Newman, *Apologia*, 25.

of that experience: home life itself. Home life and evangelicalism were now on a collision course.

In sum, the Mayers correspondence, as well as the three major theological documents Newman authored during this period, plus his first letter to the *Christian Observer*, provide evidence of the following important insights for our study:

1. The stability of Newman's home life and its loving milieu, built upon loving interpersonal family dynamics supported by Church tradition, was threatened.

2. Newman sought shelter from this threat in the dualistic doctrine of evangelicalism, primarily through the influence of his loving friendship with his spiritual mentor of the period, Rev. Mayers.

3. The intellectual tenets of evangelicalism, however, did not harmonize with his own emerging religious intellectualism. His reflections on faith, grounded in affectivity, did not mesh with evangelicalism's "ultraism."

Following this path, let us examine where the dissonance was heard most acutely — home. This will offer further valuable information on the influences bearing on Newman's ongoing conversion experience.

STAGE THREE:
The Clash of Home and Family with Evangelicalism

WE AGAIN LEARN A SIGNIFICANT FACT, NOT FROM THE APOLO-*gia* but from Newman's correspondence and journal, regarding his state of mind in the early 1820s. Between June and September of 1820, he was conscious of the onset of a mental and moral change, of becoming in solitude "graver and graver."[36] On September 2, 1820, he wrote his mother that he was "miserable" and "not at all so myself."[37] His correspondence over the next three months, particularly in regard to his impending degree examinations, indicates a mind in torment, even to the point of considering success a sin. The tension between evangelical intellectualism and Newman's feelings mounted and in late November, during his exams, he literally broke down. He wrote his father on December 1 that "my nerves quite forsook me and I failed."[38] His journal recorded that same day "he had overread" and "broke down, lost his head, [and] had to retire."[39] Again that same day he wrote to an unidentified source, "I was so nervous,

---

36 Newman, *Autobiographical Writings*, 45–46.
37 Newman, *Letters and Diaries*, vol. I, 86.
38 Ibid., 94. 39 Ibid., 94, n. I.

I could not answer a half dozen questions. The nervousness, I may add the illness, continued whenever I approached the schools, and, after a week's procrastinated efforts, I have this morning, retired from the contest."[40]

Vital information continues to emerge from related correspondence. He wrote his mother on December 3 that "my sole anxiety in very truth arose from the fear I entertained of disappointing you and the college."[41] Again, Newman's chief feeling was tied to family.

As noted previously, a most revealing document is the letter Newman wrote to Rev. Mayers on January 3, 1821, shortly after the breakdown.[42] Unwell, depressed, and extremely nervous, Newman noted the great difference between believing and feeling something to be good, a recognition of the dissonance between his feelings and evangelical intellectualism, a dissonance resulting in, or at least substantially contributing to, his breakdown.

This dissonance brought on by the introduction of evangelicalism began to strain home life. Newman's journal recorded a nasty confrontation at home on September 30, 1821, when he and his younger brother Frank were home from Oxford. Frank, who had also been indoctrinated into evangelicalism, refused to copy a letter for Mr. Newman on the grounds that it should not be done because it was Sunday.[43]

> Septr 30. Sunday
>
> After dinner I was suddenly called down stairs to give my opinion whether I thought it a sin to write a letter on a Sunday. I found dear Francis had refused to copy one. A scene ensued more painful than any I have experienced. [Note: Newman sided with his brother against Mr. Newman]. . . . I have been sadly deficient in meekness, long suffering, patience, and filial obedience. With God's assistance, I will redeem my character.
>
> Oct 1 Monday
>
> My Father was reconciled to us today. When I think of the utter persuasion he must entertain of the justice of his views, of our apparent disobedience, the seeming folly of our opinions, and the way in which he is harassed by worldly cares, I think his forgiveness of us an example of very striking candour, forbearance, and generosity.

Here we find Mr. Newman, the loving and forgiving earthly father, once again a witness to the heavenly Father, a personal testimony leaving

---

40 Newman, "Letter to an unknown correspondent" in *Letters and Diaries*, vol. I, 95.
41 Ibid., 95–96. 42 Ibid., 99. 43 Newman, *Autobiographical Writings*, 176.

its imprint on his son. But the dissonance continued. While home for the holidays three months later, Newman received a lengthy warning about what his father perceived as a dangerous intolerance in his son's perspective and accompanying behavior. It was a severe caution regarding Newman's increasing evangelical extremism, which his father called "ultra" tendencies. Newman recorded this very memorable admonition at length in his journal, evidence of the building dissonance: [44]

> Sunday. January 6. (1822)
>
>   After Church my Father began to speak to me as follows: 'I fear you are becoming &c. . . . Take care [because] you poured out [Scripture] texts in such quantities. Have a guard. You are encouraging a nervousness and morbid sensibility, and irritability, which may be very serious [and] it is a disease of the mind. Religion, when carried too far, induces a softness of mind [and] no one's principles can be established at twenty [and] in two or three years will certainly, certainly change. . . . You are on dangerous ground. The temper you are encouraging may lead to something alarming. . . . Do nothing ultra. . . . I know you write for the *Christian Observer*. My opinion of the *Christian Observer* is this, that it is a humbug. . . . That letter was more like the composition of an old man, than of a youth just entering life with energy and aspirations.'

Newman then recorded his reaction:

> O God, grant me to pray earnestly against any delusive heat, or fanatic fancy, or proud imagination of fancied superiority, or uncharitable zeal. Make me and keep me humble and teachable, modest and cautious.

At this point, Newman was in the seventh year, and the apex, of a religious conversion grounded in affective and aesthetic elements but with a significant intellectual element, primarily influenced by evangelicalism. These two events involving his father have significant importance in a study of his conversion. The first scene of confrontation leads Newman to conclude, if we read the implications of his journal entry, that their relationship, especially in light of his father's exemplary behavior, was more important than the principle on which the dispute began. In fact, that is never even mentioned again in the account by Newman. It is the relationship which is of much more concern.

---

44   Ibid., 179–80.

The second incident, his father's severe admonition regarding Newman's self-indulgent evangelical temper, elicits a similar response. He takes it to heart and is deeply moved. We find in his father's warning, moreover, a focus on Newman's temper, which is also the theme of his letter to the *Christian Observer* just months earlier. It is, in effect, a father's challenge, a warning that Newman's head and heart were discordant. The temper which Newman analyzed as an impediment to grasping the truth of religion is the very same factor which is causing a self-centered certainty that obstructs true understanding. These fatherly words of wisdom led Newman to pray against such distemper and for humility and teachableness. These themes — temper, humility, and teachableness — will become high points of two early Newman sermons: the latter two, of the *Parochial and Plain Sermon* of December 18, 1825, entitled "The Inward Witness to the Truth of the Gospel," and the former, as mentioned, of the first *Oxford University Sermon*, preached just six months later on July 2, 1826, entitled "The Philosophical Temper, First Enjoined by the Gospel." At this point, the primary focus is on the depth of the relationship of father and son. The latter was opened to the sagacious observations of the father through their affectionate relationship developed over more than twenty years. Once again, it was the nature of the interpersonal relationship which made possible the openness and acceptance, the trust and belief, which led to fuller intellectual understanding. Newman's theological reorientation, then, ultimately resulting in several of his major writings of this period, was in major part a result of the loving father-son relationship.

On January 11, 1822, just five days after his father's severe admonition, Newman records a characteristically very brief yet momentous note in his journal which underscores the powerful influence which this relationship had on him.[45]

> Jany 11 Friday
>   My Father said this morning I ought to make up my mind what I was to be. . . . So I chose; and determined on the Church. Thank God, this is what I have . . . prayed for.

Two notes are in order regarding this entry. First, it occurred so soon after the admonition, and Newman's response was so immediate, that it makes the elder Newman's influence on his son seem even more strikingly powerful. Secondly, given the great concern about his son's religious development and its apparent "ultra" tendency, it seems almost equally amazing

---

45   Ibid., 180.

that we find no record of the elder Newman's response to his son's choice of the Church as a vocation, and this may indicate that the son's faith in the wisdom of his father's counsel was equally balanced by the father's trust in his son's decision. Faith and trust, as the two necessary elements in relationships, are thus evidence that the loving relationship which existed between father and son was the ground from which each could be open and receptive to the other. Thus, loving interpersonal relationship was the basis on which Newman's theological discernment advanced. Further evidence of this effect is found in two documents written by Newman soon after his father's admonition, which we will now examine.

TWO POST-ADMONITION DOCUMENTS OF 1822:
Greater Awareness, Continued Dissonance — The English
Essay for the Oriel Fellowship: *"Know Thyself"* and
The Second Letter to the Christian Observer

IN AUGUST OF 1822, NEWMAN WROTE AN ENGLISH ESSAY FOR the Oriel Fellowship. Entitled "Know Thyself,"[46] it is an argument against arrogant self-sufficiency, advocating the development of self-awareness as the source of a necessary humility before the mysteries of nature and revelation, echoing the theme of his earlier letter to the *Christian Observer*. In this essay, Newman, evidently displaying the conscious effect of his father's admonition, constructs a balanced interpretation of how to attain true self-knowledge by means of an analysis of "two opposite faults which we find very often combined in the same individual," self-conceit and diffidence. He concludes his analysis thus:

> The desirable self-confidence which lies between the extremes of self-conceit and diffidence is for the most part the result of general good sense. The arrogant man thinks himself positively excellent; the person who forms a proper estimate of his own powers is aware his excellence, as indeed the word implies, is relative only [and] the difference which exists [therefore] between himself and his fellow-creatures dwindles into nothing. Thus there is little danger of his being deficient in humility — he humbles himself before the mysteries of the book of nature, and with still deeper abasement before those of a still holier revelation; from him we may expect at once caution and enterprise, being alike removed from the self-sufficiency of the arrogant and the despair of the diffident.

---

46 Newman, *Letters and Diaries*, vol. I, 147–49.

The key term in the previous analysis is arguably that of awareness. However, awareness, like conversion, is not an all-at-once experience, but develops in levels or degrees. This becomes evident when we compare Newman's apparently well-balanced analysis with the document he authored just one month later, another letter to the *Christian Observer*,[47] which stands in sharp contrast to the prize essay.

Herein Newman wrote, "It is to those who have not yet commenced their collegiate residence that I chiefly address myself [since] students are not sufficiently aware of the danger beforehand."

In advising new students from his own experience, it is noticeable that he has acquired some, but far from a high, degree of self-awareness in that he promulgates evangelical principles in his instruction to them. The world and the Christian, for example, are in opposition: "[The student's] chief temptations are the more dangerous, because the world tells him that the passions and motives which as a Christian he has to dread are in themselves honourable and useful."

The logical result of this tendency, as we have seen, is an exaltation of failure:

> Failure perhaps is the only thing that can prove the state of his heart, by manifesting his cheerfulness under disappointment, [and] he may feel disposed to pray even for failure [in order] to vindicate [the] real character of his religious principles.

Thus, the principles of evangelical dualism and the praise, and even the seeking, of failure and a cheerful response to it provide evidence that Newman's evangelical commitment was still deeply rooted. He then listed the effects of this dualism: mental conflict, great anxiety, depression, seclusion, solitude, melancholy, and nervousness, all of which form "a paradox worthy of Christianity."

In conclusion, we find Newman's thought very affected by the counsel of his father. The Oriel Fellowship Essay is a major indication of that influence, raising Newman's consciousness to a higher level of self-awareness. But Newman had not overcome the negative dualism he acquired from evangelicalism. The dichotomy was still very much present, although Newman was now aware of its presence, since the tension between his affectively grounded religious epistemology and his evangelically influenced conversion was mounting.

---

47 Newman, "To the editor of the *Christian Observer*," in *Letters and Diaries*, vol. I, 150–54: September 22, 1822.

Another influence had emerged during the early 1820s which saved Newman from going over the precipice of evangelical excess, but this influence would be both helpful and yet the source of another major challenge. We now turn to that intellectual frame of mind which provided the next major element in Newman's development: Liberalism.

STAGE FOUR:
Convolution of the Conflict

FROM EVANGELICALISM TO LIBERALISM

IN APRIL 1822, LESS THAN A YEAR AND A HALF AFTER HIS breakdown in the schools, Newman was elected a Fellow of Oriel, an event which he called "the turning-point of his life." With a rejuvenated spirit, he became a member of the "School of Speculative Philosophy in England."[48] Our examination of this period from 1822 through 1828 proceeds by the same method as the Mayers—evangelical phase. Once again Newman was introduced to new influences which were of both an interpersonal and an intellectual nature, with Newman's receptivity of the latter character-istically conditioned by the former. These influences, however, were of a much different nature. Whereas evangelical conversion stressed emotion and feeling as a symptomatic "truth-check" of the convert's religious state, the intellectuals of Newman's newfound Oriel Common Room interpreted these excesses as evidence of just the opposite—an anti-intellectual, anti-rational emotional state, far off course from the liberalizing, extremely rational method by which they assessed truth.

As Newman stated in his *Autobiographical Writings* of January 1823, he pre-ferred "virtue over religion," an axiom of the liberal mind, and he contended in correspondence against Rev. Mayers on theological issues. Although ironically Mayers had cautioned Newman at the beginning of his college days about the threat to his religious views from the logicians of the liberal school, and his father cautioned him regarding evangelicalism, Newman had to find truth for himself, "wherever it is." In this pursuit, from 1822 until 1828 Newman would drink heartily from the other side of the cup of excess, imbibing the heady wine of rationalism which flowed freely from the table of the Oriel Common Room. Two major figures, Richard Whately and Edward Hawkins, would each in their own ways contribute to Newman's personal, intellectual, and theological development during this period.

---

48   Newman, "Letter to Mrs. Newman," in *Letters and Diaries*, vol. I, 134–35; April 16, 1822. Newman, *Autobiographical Writings*, 63.

From the *Apologia*, the *Autobiographical Writings*, and the *Letters and Diaries*, we again find Newman's characteristic dual focus regarding these personal influences. First and most importantly, his concrete experiences with them affected his heart, his religious sensibilities. This, as with Mayers, was the dominant motif: the veracity of the personal relationship as an insight to truth. Once again we find it to be the foundation for the intellectual influences which followed. Only after Newman entered into intimate and loving friendships with these parties does the intellectual dimension begin to flower.

It was Whately and Hawkins who took the young Newman under their wings and helped him develop as a person, as did Mayers. Their loving kindnesses affected Newman even more so than their intellects, as many years later he would write of how he yet held them in high affection, despite the theological and political differences between them.

Here the *Apologia* is uncharacteristically more revealing of their interpersonal relationships as the primary factor conditioning intellectual influence. Regarding Hawkins, Newman wrote, "I can say with a full heart that I love him, and have never ceased to love him." But why did Newman feel this way? "He was the first who taught me to weigh my words, and to be cautious in my statements."[49]

The operative words in Newman's description are "taught me." Again we see the personal bond qualifying the influence of Hawkins. Also in this account, as with the account regarding Whately, Newman placed this description of the personal affect prior to his description of the intellectual influences Hawkins was to have on him, which were quite substantial. Through Hawkins (and his recommended book, Sumner's *Apostolic Preaching*), Newman "was led to give up my remaining Calvinism, and to receive the doctrine of Baptismal Regeneration."[50] Yet this was not all Hawkins imparted to Newman. "There is one other principle, which I gained from Dr. Hawkins, more directly bearing upon Catholicism, than any that I have mentioned; and that is the doctrine of Tradition." Along with this he advanced the proposition that "the sacred text [Scripture] was never intended to teach doctrine, but only to prove it, and that, if we must learn doctrine, we must have recourse to the formularies of the Church; for instance, to the Catechism and to the Creeds."[51]

The intellectual beginnings of an interest in Antiquity, the Fathers, and the seeds of the development of doctrine can be traced to Newman's relationship with Hawkins, whose critique of Newman's very first sermon dissuaded Newman from the evangelical hard-line he had adopted at

---

49 Newman, *Apologia*, 29. 50 Ibid. 51 Ibid., 30.

the outset of his parish ministry. This intellectual influence would soon complement Newman's actual experiences with his parishioners, eventually causing Newman to refocus his theological and moral positions. But once again, as with Mayers, the essential note is that Newman was opened to Hawkins's theological insights by a loving interpersonal relationship.

Of Whately, the *Apologia* is equally revealing. "I owe him a great deal. He was a man of generous and warm heart." But on a more personal note, "While I was still awkward and timid in 1822, he took me by the hand, and acted toward me the part of a gentle and encouraging instructor. He, emphatically, opened my mind, and taught me to think and to use my reason [and] I became very intimate with him in 1825."[52] The deep impression of Whately's fatherly guidance is quite obvious. But it reached even deeper levels in Newman's description of their relationship after they came to differ theologically.

> I have always felt a real affection for what I must call his memory; for, at least from the year 1834, he made himself dead to me.... Yet I loved him too much to bid him farewell without pain.... I believe that he has inserted sharp things in his late works about me. They have never come in my way, and I have not thought it necessary to seek out what would pain me so much in the reading.[53]

Again we find this intimate interpersonal relationship described at length, as with Hawkins, and likewise prior to the account of theological influence. By so doing, Newman continued to underscore the fact, even by means of literary structure, that for him the heart conditioned the head. Once Newman's heart was opened, Whately's theological influence entered. Whately

> was, first, to teach me the existence of the Church, as a substantive body or corporation; next to fix in me those anti-Erastian views of Church polity, which were one of the most prominent features of the Tractarian movement.[54]

However, the operative principle is that once again the interpersonal relationship, the meeting of hearts, emerged as the key factor conditioning Newman's intellectual development. With Newman, when the interpersonal experience resonated with truth through love, the intellectual effects easily followed. In respect to intellectual development, the important note regarding Newman's relationship with both men is that they were primary

---

52 Ibid., 31.   53 Ibid., 31–2.   54 Ibid., 32.

sources of liberal influence. Middleton records that "Whately's line of thought [was] definitely liberal in tendency,"[55] and Maisie Ward recounts:

> At the time the Liberalism of the Noetics was certainly less apparent to Newman than it later became, [which] was characterized by its spirit of moderation and comprehension, and of which the principal ornaments were Copleston, Davison, Whately, Hawkins, and Arnold.[56]

In a note in the *Apologia*, Newman clarified what he came to understand as Liberalism:

> Now by Liberalism I mean false liberty of thought, or the exercise of thought upon matters, in which, from the constitution of the human mind, thought cannot be brought to any successful issue, and therefore is out of place. Among such matters are first principles [and] the truths of Revelation. Liberalism then is the mistake of subjecting to human judgment those revealed doctrines which are in their nature beyond and independent of it, and of claiming to determine on intrinsic grounds the truth and value of propositions which rest for their reception simply on the external authority of the Divine Word.[57]

However, a note should be made that, as Ian Ker quotes from Newman's *My Campaign in Ireland*, Part I:

> There is another kind of Liberalism of which Newman is very much in favor, [and] he promptly makes the important modification, 'that there is much in the liberalistic theory which is good and true; for example, not to say more, the precepts of justice, truthfulness, sobriety, self-command, benevolence, which ... are among its avowed principles, and the natural laws of society.'[58]

Newman's *Apologia* description of liberalism, however, was written in 1864, and he was vulnerable to its appeal some forty years earlier when he "was beginning to prefer intellectual excellence to moral; I was drifting in the direction of the Liberalism of the day. I was rudely awakened from my dream at the end of 1827 by two great blows — illness and bereavement."[59]

---

55 Middleton, *Newman at Oxford*, 42.

56 Maisie Ward, *Young Mr. Newman* (New York: Sheed and Ward, 1948), 76.

57 Newman, *Apologia*, 29.

58 Ian Ker, *Newman and the Fullness of Christianity* (Edinburgh: T & T Clark, 1993), 32–33.   59 Newman, *Apologia*, 33.

Once again, we find a familiar pattern: Newman's interpersonal relationships laid the foundation for the intellectual effects which followed: from home and family to God and Church, from Mayers to evangelicalism, and from Whately and Hawkins to Liberalism.

The very end of the previous quotation contains yet another reference to the same pattern, although it is couched in the *Apologia*'s characteristic understatement. Newman noted that he was saved from the excess of Liberalism by "illness and bereavement." Bereavement is the sole word we find to indicate the devastating blow Newman would suffer upon the sudden death of his dear sister Mary. This will be analyzed more fully in chapter two, but the connection made by Newman at this juncture is evidence that his relationship with Mary, a matter of the heart, was the spiritual medicine which helped cure his intellectual liberalizing excess. This would mark another major example that relationships cued Newman's intellect: first, home life; second, Mayers; third, his father and his admonitions and counsel to choose a vocation; fourth, Whately and Hawkins. But two other cases of such examples can be added to the list, and both involved family: the loss of his father and his resultant responsibility for his brother Charles's religious disaffection. In late 1824 and through 1825, these personal experiences, primarily of the heart, would once again reshape Newman's insights, affecting his conversion journey.

STAGE FIVE:
Experience Beyond Words

MR. NEWMAN'S DEATH AND THE
SHATTERING OF THE EARLY PARADIGM

MAISIE WARD STATES THAT "1824 WAS THE LAST YEAR IN WHICH THE family was whole and complete."[60] Newman's diary states only the facts:[61]

Wednesday 29 September
    Aunt came to town. Dr Clutterbuck came for the last time —
at 1/4 to ten at night my dear Father ceased to breathe — Charles,
Francis and myself slept in the parlour in our clothes. my Father
died.

And two days later he wrote:

Friday 1 October
    Saw my dear Father for the last time — began sermon Eph v, 14

---

60   Ward, *Young Mr. Newman*, 105.   61   Newman, *Letters and Diaries*, vol. I, 93.

The *Autobiographical Writings* adds the emotions to this rather factual account:

> Sunday Octr 3
>
>   That dread event has happened. Is it possible! O my Father, where art thou?

and

> On Thursday he looked beautiful, such calmness, sweetness, composure, and majesty were in his countenance. Can a man be a materialist who sees a dead body? I had never seen one before. (His last words to me, or all but his last, were to bid me read to him the 33 chapter of Isaiah. "Who hath believed" etc.)[62]

As we move from the diary to the journal accounts, we can sense a heart full of grief. It required the aesthetic distance of more than twenty years before Newman's heart could speak through the hero of his novel *Loss and Gain* about the effects of his father's death. The impact on this eldest son is emphasized by its position in the literary structure, the very ending of Part I, providing a major transition for the hero. It is worth citing at length, in that it synthesizes much of what has gone before:

> When Charles got to his room he saw a letter from home lying on his table; and, to his alarm, it had a deep, black edge. He tore it open. Alas, it announced the sudden death of his dear father! . . . It was a grief not to be put into words. . . .
>
>   It was the first great grief poor Charles had ever had, and he felt it to be real. . . .
>
>   He then understood the difference between what was real and what was not. All the doubts, inquiries, surmises, views, which had of late haunted him on theological subjects, seemed like so many shams. . . .
>
>   He felt now where the heart and his life lay. His birth, his parentage, his education, his home, were great realities; to these his being was united; out of these he grew. . . .
>
>   What is called the pursuit of truth seemed an idle dream. He had great tangible duties to his father's memory, to his mother and sisters, to his position; he felt sick of all theories as if they had taken him in. . . .
>
>   He could not do better than imitate the life and death of his beloved father. . . .

---

62 Newman, *Autobiographical Writings*, 202–3.

> A leaf had been turned over in his life. Youngest sons in a
> family, like monks in a convent, may remain children till they
> have reached middle age; but the elder, should their dear father
> die prematurely, are suddenly ripened into manhood when they
> are almost boys. Charles had left Oxford a clever informed youth;
> he returned a man.[63]

Thus does Newman recall the state of his mind and heart in the autumn of 1824, recounted through the thin veil of artistic license. His emerging rigorous rational development, under the influence of Whately and Hawkins, his acquired evangelical zeal engendered by Mayers, and the impact of his experiences as the curate of St. Clement's parish, a new role he assumed just three months before his father's death, were all drawn into sharpest perspective by the loss of the source of his earliest religious impressions, his father, and with it began the dissolution of the core of his religious sensibilities — his stable family life. Once again by means of experience Newman changed, as did his theological insights.

The contrast between the factual diary entries and the effusive prose of Newman's novel highlights the reemergence of a major Newman theme, the limitation of words and the mind's attempt to comprehend and express those experiences whose meaning extends well beyond categorization. For Newman, such a reality intimates the truth of a fuller reality beyond that which the mind can grasp, the realm of the supernatural. Once again, we find this perception to be a confirmation of his early childhood religious instincts.

Loss, however, would generate gain.

STAGE SIX:
The Loss of Fatherly Love and the Gain of Brotherly Responsibility

A THEOLOGICAL CATALYST

SIMULTANEOUS WITH NEWMAN'S DEVELOPING LIBERAL INFLU-ences and the grief of the loss of his father was his ongoing correspondence with his younger brother Charles. From all accounts a lifelong tormented, and tormenting, soul, Charles constantly challenged his older brother's theological beliefs. A product of their relationship was a generally over-looked series of important letters tracing Newman's evolving thought on a number of major theological issues.

---

63   John Henry Newman, *Loss and Gain* (London: Longmans, Green, and Co, 1911), 157–59.

The correspondence began in April of 1822, with another letter in August 1823 and picks up again in March of 1825, continuing through September of that year. In all, there are ten letters pertinent to this phase of our study, and they treat of such topics as the reasonableness of faith, the nature of revelation, anthropology, epistemology and the nature of the mind, method, temper, conversion, and especially two categories of major import in Newman's later work: intuition and testimony. These last two are also most relevant to our study in that they allude to the primary role of interpersonal dynamics in intellectual processing, with important implications for the nature of faith.

The correspondence with Charles is very valuable for a number of reasons: (1) It yields significant information on Newman's theological development; (2) It is generally neglected by other sources; (3) It was a primary influence on the major theological work Newman composed during this period, *The Life of Apollonius of Tyanaeus : with a comparison between the Miracles of Scripture and those elsewhere related, as regards their respective Object, Nature, and Evidence*. However, two other and more important reasons account for the relevance of the correspondence; (4) Newman was greatly concerned about Charles's spiritual state, a chronic problem for the family; (5) Of *most* relevance for this study is the fact that the correspondence began in earnest six months after the death of their father. From the commencement of the correspondence after their father's death, Newman wrote Charles no less than seven letters, almost all of which are of major theological significance. But what is of special note is that Newman was reacting to his new role as the head of the family. During this period, correspondence from his mother tells of her great fears about Charles, and Newman assumed the mantle of his recently deceased father. In Newman's admonitions to Charles one can hear the echoes of Mr. Newman to John Henry himself. As Maisie Ward writes, after the senior Newman's death, "His children became John's responsibility."[64] And so he shouldered it, as a loving son and brother, which is revealed by this extraordinary correspondence. Once again, the significance is that the heart was the inspiration for the theology of the correspondence. Characteristically, the impact of his father's death and his relationship with Charles are omitted from the *Apologia*, but *Letters and Diaries* discloses these bonds of the heart. Let us now examine these documents for evidence of these interconnections.

The following inventory organizes the correspondence by date and themes, keyed to the subsequent documents. All are letters exchanged between John and Charles, except as indicated:

---

64 Ward, *Young Mr. Newman*, 168.

1. THE PRIMACY OF PERSONAL QUALITIES[65]

NEWMAN HERE WRITES TO HIS YOUNGEST BROTHER A BRIEF and joyous letter the day following his election as a fellow of Oriel. The primary value of this letter lies in the description of personal qualities Newman perceives in his new peers: "I think myself honoured inexpressibly by being among such kind, liberal, candid, moderate, learned and pious men, as every act shows the fellows of Oriel to be." As is characteristically the case with Newman, he is first and most impressed by personal traits.

2. THE JOURNAL RECORD:[66]
Beginnings of the Theme, "Philosophical Temper," and the Nature of Revelation and its Relation to Reason, Conversion, and Grace

"IN WALKING HOME THIS EVENING WITH CHARLES I TOOK OCCA-sion to speak with him on the subject of religion," [and Charles said], "Why not read the Bible, and employ reason at once?"

---

65 Newman, *Letters and Diaries*, vol. I, 130–31. Letter dated April 13, 1822.
66 Newman, *Autobiographical Writings*, 192–93. Journal entry dated August 9, 1823.

Charles questioned any need for Scripture interpretation beyond personal, rational analysis, and Newman replied that revelation is supernatural, thus requiring grace for its interpretation: "I repeated my strong conviction that no one could understand the Scriptures fruitfully, unless it were given him from above."

Also, a sincere desire to grasp the truth of revelation supersedes denominational loyalty, which also includes an implicit reference to the primacy of conscience: "I did not confine salvation to one sect — that in any communion whoever sought truth sincerely would not fail of heaven."

In closing the entry, Newman noted three things:

> incumbent on every one, before he could pretend to judge of the Scripture doctrines — to read the bible constantly and attentively, to pray for grace to understand it incessantly, and to strive to live up to the dictates of conscience and what the mind acknowledges to be right.

Newman is advocating here a multileveled state of conversion as a prerequisite for judging doctrine: religious, in the act of constant, attentive Bible reading and incessant prayer for the grace of understanding; moral, in striving to live up to the dictates of conscience; and intellectual, what the mind acknowledges to be right.

Thus, this walk home with Charles led Newman to briefly systematize his thought on the nature of revelation and man's response to it, the necessity of conversion on its several levels, and the function of grace in this process.

Newman, however, was so moved by the discussion that he felt it necessary to continue it in a letter four months later.

3. TEMPER, METHOD, AND ANTHROPOLOGY[67]

> I CANNOT CONCLUDE THIS LETTER WITHOUT ADVERTing to the subject which engaged our attention, when walking to Town from Strand the beginning of August last.
>
> We find one man of one opinion in religion, another of another; and may thus be led hastily to conclude that opinions diametrically opposite to each other may be held without danger to one side or the other in a future state; but contradictions can no more be true in religion, than in astronomy or chemistry. . . . We are playing with edged tools, if instead of endeavouring perseveringly to ascertain what the truth is, we consider the subject carelessly, captiously, or with indifference.

---

67 Newman, *Letters and Diaries*, vol. I, 169–70. Letter dated December 12, 1823.

Thus, the temper with which one approaches the issue of truth, and the method employed in that search, are critical to the process and in fact are conditions of its veracity. Both of these themes Newman will continue to develop as the correspondence unfolds. Newman closes the letter, however, with a noteworthy anthropological insight:

> In every one of us there is naturally a void, a restlessness, a hunger
> of the soul, a craving after some unknown and vague happiness,
> which we suppose seated in wealth, fame, knowledge, in fact any
> worldly good which we are not ourselves possessed of.

This important reference indicates the moral necessity to discern what does, and what does not, fill that void. This speaks to the argument for objective truth against intellectual equivocation, which begets moral equivocation. Thus, Newman's discussions with his brother served to develop his intellectual positions, all the while rooted in fraternal concern as the interpersonal dimension once again influenced the intellectual.

It would be fifteen months until the next major letter to Charles in March 1825, and several major events had affected Newman during that interval, especially the death of his beloved father in September of 1824, which we have reviewed above, and then his ministry at St. Clement's, which he began in July of 1824, just before his father's death.

However, Newman penned a significant letter to Simon Lloyd Pope in February 1824, just two months following the preceding letter to Charles, continuing some of the same themes. Therefore, we will briefly examine it since it offers evidence of the effect of the dialogue with Charles on Newman's thinking.

4. ANTHROPOLOGY, REVELATION, CONVERSION, AND THE INTRODUCTION OF THE INTERPERSONAL CATEGORY OF TESTIMONY[68]

HEREIN NEWMAN REPEATS THE STRUCTURE OF THE ARGUMENT made to Charles in his previous letter:

> And it is the study of Scripture, it is this painful and contin-
> ued searching which gives us that "inward witness" it so often
> describes. . . . As we read, we see more and more. . . . It affects
> the heart, subdues the will and convinces the understanding,
> [but] we can expect nothing of these blessed advantages without

---

68 Newman, *Letters and Diaries*, vol. I, 170–72. Letter dated February 18, 1824 to S. L. Pope.

constant and earnest prayer for divine grace that we may be able really to understand what we read.

Here we find the interrelationship of revelation, grace, and conversion in its affective ("the heart"), aesthetic (seeing "more and more"), moral ("the will"), and intellectual ("the understanding") elements. But this dynamic begins in "painful and continued searching," reminiscent of the anthropological "void" mentioned in the previous letter, which man attempts to fill, resulting in the "inward witness" to the truth of this experience.

This last note on "inward witness" will become the theme of Newman's third earliest *Parochial and Plain Sermon* of December 18, 1825, less than two years later, and indicates the effect of the Charles dialogue on Newman's early theological writing.

But a subtle, yet perhaps the most important, reference in the letter is one which will become increasingly more dominant in Newman's thought during this period, that of testimony: "But the Bible itself says, 'to the law and to the testimony!'" Here we find the core principle which will soon be developed by Newman in his major theological work up to that point, his essay on *The Miracles of Scripture*, which elucidates personal credibility as the requisite trait establishing the authority of witness.

A major note should be made here of the importance of this insight and its connection to Newman's future thought. The nature of witness and personal credibility are factors of interpersonal dynamics. Moreover, these elements are intimately related to his exposition of the theory of development. Further, all of these complement the strength of the argument from personality which he would later derive from Keble, which itself is an expansion of the argument from analogy which he was soon to find in Butler. So it is that in this letter we find Newman's joining the testimony of Scripture witnesses to the "internal witness" of the scripture-reader, an intricate analysis of interpersonal dynamics, evidence that such dynamics are at the center of his thought.

Now let us move on to his letters of the following year.

5. THE LETTERS OF 1825

AS NOTED, JUST THREE MONTHS AFTER NEWMAN BEGAN HIS parish duties at St. Clement's in July of 1824, his father died. Beginning about five months later, Newman began a series of letters to Charles during 1825, numbering seven in all, which are important documents cataloguing the development of Newman's theological thinking at the time. These invaluable records are generally overlooked and, in addition to his intellectual development, they continue the principle that his theological progress was grounded in an affectionate interpersonal relationship.

5A. On *Temper* and *Epistemology*[69]

Charles had written to John on February 23 that he had "come to a judgment which will no doubt surprise you; it is entirely against Christianity; which I expected to find synonymous with wisdom and knowledge, but which is far otherwise."[70]

John responded with a major letter regarding epistemology, particularly the nature of the mind and à priori dispositions. In doing so, he noted the distinction between the roles of logic and moral feeling in the act of judgment: "Your letter of the 23rd ult. did not so much surprise, as grieve and distress me. . . . You are not in a state of mind to listen to argument of any kind." He then gave a major analysis of his brother's current state, which had caused him to have a methodical predisposition against religion:

> You have had much to bear. . . . Now you are in an unquiet state
> of mind altogether at variance with that calm, equable, candid,
> philosophical temper which is necessary for balancing such nice
> matters and adjusting such difficult questions as many of these
> connected with religion. You are apt in *every thing*, not only in
> religious inquiries, to be self-willed to decide precipitately, to run
> away with a part for the whole, to form conclusions from very
> partial inductions. . . . You have very little judgment. . . . And
> you consider [caution] as timidity and meanness; . . . This very
> same caution is a quality indispensably necessary not only in
> political and metaphysical discussions, but also in chemistry and
> natural philosophy.

The first half of the letter is personal — Newman's analysis of Charles's mental state and how that state has predetermined his judgments. This serves as the motivation for the second half, as he moves into a formal analysis of the nature of judgment: "Yet how monstrous is it to attempt overturning a system by *a-priori* objections to its doctrines; while the great body of external evidence on which it is founded remains untouched." Newman then elaborates on the nature of evidence:

---

69 Ibid., 212–15. Dated March 3, 1825.   70 Ibid, 212.

> Remember too the external evidences are built upon the obvious and general canons by which we judge of the truth or falsehood of *every thing* we hear; not on rules peculiar to religion. . . . The internal evidence depends a great deal on *moral feeling*; so that if we did not agree, we might accuse each other of prejudice or pride: the external is founded on purely logical principles.

Here we find Newman's distinguishing between the method of logic, which judges all external evidence, and that of "moral feeling," which judges internal evidence. It appears at this stage that Newman clearly separates "objective, logical" method from "subjective," "feeling," or intuitive method. It should be noted that he was at this time under the increasing influence of the "Logicians of Oriel," as Mayers termed them, and had been since 1822. Thus these letters naturally express the effects of that influence. However, in addition to the analysis contained in the letter, we find sprinkled throughout numerous references and indications that it was Newman's heart which was at the root of his analysis: his concern and love for his brother.

> I am sometimes much affected to think of what you have borne; I think I see your state of mind too well, and love you too dearly to feel impatience at any opinions you advance; I write from a full heart. . . . I am your affectionate brother; I am a natural advisor and friend; Pray excuse me if I appear to have said any thing hastily or severe: I have not wished to do so.

Even as Newman was advancing his thinking on the relationship of mental method to judgment, he clearly indicated that the goal of this process was grounded in loving concern for his brother, once again evidence that the interpersonal relationship drove his intellectual development.

These epistemological issues and their relationship to religion continued to intrigue Newman during this period. In fact, the very next day after this letter, he wrote to his mother that he had "undertaken for the Encycl. Metrop. the memoir of Apollonius Tyanaeus and the Argument on Miracles, as connected with it. It is a very difficult subject, and I hesitated before I accepted it."[71] But the evidence supports the conclusion that to a great degree Newman's debates with Charles during this period provided an important, if not the primary, impetus. This becomes increasingly evident as Newman picked up the theme of the previous letter, the grounds of religious belief, in his next letter to Charles just three weeks later.

---

71   Ibid., 216.

5B. The Logic of Faith and the Illogic of Unbelief: The Heart, not the Intellect, as Center[72]

This letter indicates the extent to which Newman's mind had taken up the issue of miracles. Having just agreed to write a major article on the subject, he now posed a list of thirty-five questions to Charles, of which fifteen concern miracles, three conversion, six belief, and four mental processes. But his opening paragraph contains the most valuable information as he elucidated the relationship of the heart, and faith, to reason. Here we again find evidence of his preoccupation with questions of epistemology and method, the responses to which determine positions regarding faith and religion: "I consider the rejection of Christianity to arise from a fault of the *heart*, not of the *intellect*; that unbelief arises, not from mere error of reasoning, but either from pride or from sensuality."

Here Newman makes a key observation most relevant to our study: belief is a matter which transcends reason in that it is of the heart, a term clearly linking belief with the affections. The essence of belief, then, is relatedness, an experience beyond mere intellectual processing. Newman continues:

> A dislike of the contents of Scripture is at the bottom of unbe-
> lief. . . . Thus unbelievers (as I observed in my last letter) reverse
> the legitimate process of reasoning. . . . There is at bottom that
> secret antipathy for the doctrines of Christianity, which is quite
> out of reach of argument.

Newman contends that a rejection of religion which goes beyond reason is at the root of unbelief: "I do not then assert that the Christian evidences are *overpowering*, but that they are *unanswerable*; nor do I expect so much to show Christianity *true*, as to prove it *rational*; nor to prove infidelity *false*, so much as *irrational*."

Here we find evidence in Newman's early thought that, based upon an epistemological analysis, belief is the terminus of a rational process, whereas unbelief is an irrational violation of that methodical process.

In this letter we find Newman's continuing elaboration of the relationship between the heart and the head. With the *Miracles* article on the table and driven by the fraternal love in his heart and the intellectual stirrings of his mind, he combines them both in this valuable document from his early period. In concluding the letter, Newman added his characteristic note from the heart, again indicating the motivation behind his intellectual analysis is his deeply rooted affection for his brother:

72   Ibid., 219–21. Dated March 24, 1825.

I cannot conclude without some allusion to the great pain in having to write a letter of this description to one so dear to me. To be entering into a defense of Christianity against a brother, is, I will not merely say, a novel and astonishing, it is a most painful, a most heart-rending event. It is indeed almost useless to express my feelings on the subject: words are after all but declamation.

5C. On the Nature of Method and Revelation as Supra-Rational[73]

Just three weeks later, Newman wrote the longest letter in the series, devoted in the main to the nature of method.

In my first letter I gave my opinion that you had taken up the subject under discussion quite *at the wrong end*: that instead of beginning with the external evidence you had most illogically plunged into the consideration of the *contents* of the Bible. . . . It is unfair to form your judgment of a revelation from its moral system in the manner you are doing.

Here he continued to press the issue of the nature of method:

A person who judges of the contents of [the] revelation by his own preconceived notions would infallibly have pronounced the revelation spurious. Here he would act illogically; *not* because *prior* to the revelation (using all the light he had) he had come to the *probable* conclusion [against the revelation]; but that *now*, when a professed revelation was offered him, he *assumed* that his opinion [was] so demonstratively true, that instead of examining the claims of the revelation he might try it by its *contents*. A reasoner of this description would be rightly called prejudiced and opinionated.

The key distinction, then, is that of the *contents* of revelation from its *credentials*. Revelation must be judged, therefore, by the latter, not the former. To do otherwise is faulty method, which produces faulty results.

If the contents of a professed revelation on divine things are to be made the test of its genuineness, no revelation could be made for us: for scarcely two persons can be got together, who will agree in their antecedent or self-originated ideas of God and his purposes toward man.

Revelation, then, is supra-rational in nature, and that fact must be taken into account when attempting to grasp it: "A revelation [thus] would

---

73   Ibid., 224–28. Dated April 14, 1825.

contain many particulars beyond the reach of our present reason." The important fact is to recognize and observe this distinction in practice:

> The credentials then of a revelation are for the most part distinct from its contents — and by the former is it primarily to be tried; [and] so much then on the first point (viz.) the unfairness of deciding on the merits of Scripture by an examination of its contents instead of its evidences: a task to which we are quite inadequate.

Newman then applied his analysis directly to Charles in the second part of the letter, objecting to "your rejecting the *credentials* of Christianity because you dislike the *contents* [and] your assuming that unassisted reason is competent to discover moral and religious truth." This last state of mind Newman attributed to Charles's being "under the influence of pride." But where does this polemic lead? Newman closed the discussion by citing the two aspects of the fundamental doctrine of Christianity, "that the mind cannot arrive at religious truth 1st without a revelation, 2nd without God's dispersing its prejudices in order to its *receiving* that revelation." Thus, the mind cannot grasp religious truth because the mind is insufficient to that task. For the apprehension of this truth there are two requisites: a revelation and an assistance to overcome the limitations of prejudices — the pride of the self-sufficing power of reason. But revelation and assistance are essentially interpersonal dynamic acts: revelation is self-disclosure, and assistance is the aid of grace. So here we find Newman's epistemological argument on method grounded in interpersonal dynamics, specifically self-giving and charitable acts of disclosure and help. In this letter, Newman again integrates method and interpersonal relations, with the true essence of the former modeled on the latter.

5D. *Intuition and Religious Epistemology*[74]

This letter consists of a single long paragraph one page in length and repeats many of the arguments previously raised. However, Newman introduced a new element into the discussion, intuition, a major theme of his next two letters as he began to work out the interrelationship, systematically, between it and revelation and method, then its function in anthropology and its relation to grace, and lastly its relation to testimony. In this letter intuition is described as the locus of man's supra-rational sensitivity. Regarding revelation he asks

---

74   Ibid., 240–41. Dated July 7, 1825.

> What if it were *impracticable* to give us other kind of evidence than is given? *This* is the true state of the case. . . . The contents are not to be brought into evidence for or against revelation, *because* man is not in a state to judge of them; not, that is, from the *fault* of the *contents*, but from the weakness of man. And this is the case in other subjects. Des Cartes (for example) by attempting to prove to himself mathematically his own existence . . . attempted to apply demonstrative proof to a proposition which could only be proved by what metaphysicians call *intuition*.

Newman here posits this faculty as the supra-rational component of man's epistemological structure. He continued this theme in his next letter, albeit less directly.

5E. An *Interpersonal Synthesis*: Intuition, Anthropology, Grace, and Epistemology[75]

While repeating much of the same argument on epistemology, Newman now added a connection of intuition with natural feelings and the desire for grace to assist in understanding:

> Let me observe too you have not noticed my observations on the importance of prayer for divine guidance in these difficult and momentous inquiries — observations not grounded on the precepts of Christianity, but on the natural feelings of every one who acknowledges a Providence, and confirmed by the actual practice of almost every country and age.

Thus, Newman recognized the innate "natural feelings" or intuition of a need or desire for assistance from a higher power, the Transcendent Other, in grappling with ultimate questions, which is a description of intuition. Again we find that Newman pushes the limits of the argument beyond the bounds of "demonstrative proof" and into an area where deductive logic fails. This area is noticeably interpersonal, as man intuits a need for superhuman assistance from the Transcendent Other. Though Newman does not specifically utilize such personalist terminology here, his meaning is quite clear. The dynamics involved in the self-disclosing, self-donating acts of God's revelation to man are essentially the laws of interpersonal love which are felt and known in a manner which transcends logic and described as intuition. Man's attempts to rationally explain the reality of love may come up short, or as Newman might very well put it, words

---

75   Ibid., 246–48. Dated July 26, 1825.

cannot suffice, but man feels and knows its reality, its presence, its power, and its absence. Intuition, then, provides an epistemological complement to reason in that it aids in the discernment of religious truth which transcends thinking that is limited to its mere rational dimension. Intuition, then, opens the door to the reality of mystery, without contradicting it, but rather, sweeping up and transcending reason in its grasp of a fuller reality. It is, then, through intuition that man begins to perceive the reality of the mysterious dynamics of the Trinity as the interpersonal paradigm on which man's own nature is based, which then renders the mystery of the Incarnation intelligible, then inviting man's reciprocating response of love of God. Thus, in this letter we find Newman's working out his interpersonalist synthesis. But the overarching point should not be lost in this intellectual exposition: the ground and goal of Newman's argument is his love of his brother. His theological arguments are above all rooted in this very dynamic which he strives to understand and communicate to Charles — his love for him and his concern for his salvation. Thus, once again, love drives Newman's analysis.

5F. *Intuition and Reason in Method and Testimony*[76]

Continuing the themes of the previous arguments, Newman specifically addresses the question of method:

> To commence the examination of a revelation with its contents [was] a very suspicious circumstance. . . . Almost all unbelievers had adopted this method. . . . It follows that you are allowed to show if you can that Scripture contradicts itself — but observe another is not bound to see those inferences from doctrines.

This is a clear, major statement that method determines conclusions. Further, as cited in previous letters, method includes such personal dimensions as the disposition of the heart and the intuitive faculties.

On this issue of method and the intuitive and intellectual faculties, Newman points out the difference between *per*-ception and *con*-ception:

> For there is on *these principles* (natural feelings are to a *certain point* correct), no inconsistency in thinking mankind may be right in the feeling of dependence on a superior being, a subject on which there is a *general agreement*, and yet wrong in their conceptions of the *object* of that *dependence*, a point on which there is a *general disagreement*.

---

76   Ibid., 253–55. Dated August 25, 1825.

In sum, the conceptual, intellectual faculties attempt to order and structure what the perceptual, intuitive faculties feel and sense: the presence of the Transcendent Other. Newman then applied this perspective to his brother's charge that the Canon's credibility is suspect, based upon an objection to the inclusion of the book of Ezekiel and that therefore this compromises the credibility of Christianity itself.

Shifting the Canon discussion to the New Testament, Newman responded that "the New Testament is not *Christianity*, but the *record* of Christianity." This is a most important theme which holds prominence in his *Miracles* article which he was composing at this time, and we also found it in his letter to S. L. Pope. Scripture is a *record* of *testimony*, and it is the *testimony* to which the question of credibility must be directed. Testimony, however, is an interpersonal phenomenon involving, among other things, the degree of faith which one person can place in another. Scripture, then, is an invitation to trust the testimony of another, which involves judgment of the witness's credibility. We will examine this again in Newman's *Miracles* essay, but at this point it is noteworthy that he has added it to his development of themes in his correspondence with Charles.

5G. *Testimony, Method, and the Principle of Scriptural Development*[77]

This document is noteworthy as a record of Newman's early thinking on the theme of development and transmission, which would become a major preoccupation of his in years to come. It is related to the previous correspondence in its implicit discussion of method in respect to the question of the authenticity of Scripture. In his previous letter, Newman referred Charles to a paper he had written on the authenticity of the gospels (paper A),[78] prompting the present correspondence. He writes:

> You maintain that the gospels we now have are only in part the writing of the Apostles [and] thus that the present gospels are compilations, part being the original writing of the Apostles, etc, part not. That is, you *deny* their genuineness.... [For my] whole argument however I must refer you to my paper A — which I repeat, is equally directed against a partial as against an entire forgery.

Newman takes a strong position against Charles's assertions of development, holding for the principle of the gospels as "original memoirs":

---

77   Ibid., 258–60. Dated September 26, 1825.   78   Ibid., 255, n. 1.

> You say the Christian Elders, seeing heresy and foolish and per-
> verse opinions gaining ground on all sides perceived the necessity
> of separating the truth from the falsehood by means of authentic
> and standard histories of their Lord, and therefore compiled the
> Scripture gospels. Were not then the original memoirs of Matthew
> etc, which they then interpolated, already standard histories?

It appears by this last sentence that Newman means to say "*allegedly*
interpolated," which is then refuted by the sense of his next phrase, "already"
existing accounts; already existing histories require no interpolation. The
issue of development will, as stated, gain prominence in Newman's thought,
and it is helpful to recognize its emergence at this embryonic stage.

In closing this section, these eleven documents, especially the seven
written in 1825, provide an invaluable record of Newman's intellectual
development during this period, evidencing no less than sixteen major
categories, as outlined in the correspondence inventory at the outset
of this section. Reviewing that listing, we find interpersonal dynamics
underlying the categories he analyzed: "temper" or predisposition is
eventually perceived as a matter of the heart. This is a major factor in
the determination of one's method, which leads to an analysis of the
nature of the mind, with the question of method emerging as an ethical
matter: wrong method is a violation of the mind, usually grounded in
anti-personalist self-sufficiency and pride. This bears ultimately on the
act of faith and its opposite, unbelief. The reality of natural intuition,
however, offers evidence for Newman's positions on method and revelation, which he eventually synthesizes in the final interpersonalist category in the correspondence, testimony. Testimony is finally understood
as the ultimate interpersonalist element in the discussion of revelation
as found in Scripture.

Throughout this correspondence, Newman works toward logic as a
means of assessing truth, with intuition and "the heart" as keys to understanding that greater reality of which reason is a part. That greater reality,
of a God and man in relationship, of a God willing to self-disclose and
self-donate Himself for man, cannot be fathomed by mere reason but
points to the mystery of love and the truth of Christ, the archetypal
interpersonalist experience. Newman was attempting, successfully, to
transcend the limits of reason-based method (in the narrow, deductivist,
logical sense) as evidenced in the Charles correspondence. But in this very
act, Newman himself is a living witness to his own analysis. His loving
regard for Charles was the driving spirit behind his work.

CHAPTER ONE AND
OUR CONVERSION HYPOTHESIS

IN SUMMARIZING THIS PART OF OUR STUDY, LET US BRIEFLY recapitulate the influences which affected Newman's development up to this point. First, it was his home life which initially brought him into contact with the reality of love, especially his relationship with, and the example of, his father. This environment exposed him to the influence of religion, which complemented his intuition. Then it was the loving relationship with Rev. Mayers, which produced three major results. First, aided by grace, he perceived a new image of his relationship with God. This can be called an aesthetic conversion which involved the intellect as well as the imaginative and intuitive senses. Secondly, this insight produced an affective conversion by which Newman's affections were now directed to God. Both of these developments were grounded in the affectivity of family and friendship, as well as the religious images to which he had been exposed as a youth. Thirdly, he was so influenced by his affective relationship with Mayers that he accepted intellectually, and much too uncritically, the doctrines of evangelicalism, an acceptance which produced a moral dissonance in family relations, eventually causing a conflict with his father and ultimately within himself. During his Oxford period which followed, he was again greatly influenced by the affection shown to him by Whately and Hawkins, which opened him to the influence of their liberal thinking. In 1824, he suffered the trauma of his father's death. Responding to his family duty and especially to his mother's concerns, he then engaged his brother Charles in a long series of letters in an attempt to dissuade him from his negative religious predisposition. In each instance—family, father, Mayers, Whately, Hawkins, his mother and Charles—his intellectual development was motivated by the interpersonal dynamics of his relationships with those close to him. The intuition of Newman's heart often led him to act uncritically, evidenced by the fact that he would recant much of the intellectual influence he imbibed from those he loved. This tendency will play an even more prominent role in his dilemma over the nature of the one true Church in the years ahead. But the overriding note is that, though he would alter these intellectual positions, his heart remained unaffected, loving even those from whom he sometimes was estranged in great part. This can be attributed to the fact that *they*, not he, had altered their hearts towards him because *he* had altered his *head*. Thus, this period of Newman's conversion journey can be termed religious, as the product primarily of affective and aesthetic conversions. These two elements dominated his intellectual and moral sensibilities during this period. However, as a direct result of these influences, his intellectual development is significant in that he grappled with many themes which would become major issues in his theology. Among such themes are the principle of analogy which he was to discover in Butler, the question of religious epistemology, or the nature of faith, and the expression of that faith. This last theme entails the ecclesiological question of the one true Church and the development of doctrine, which will be the major foci of his theology when he approaches the traumatic issue of conversion to Rome. And most importantly, his early analysis of the nature of "temper" or self-willed predisposition as an affective aberration at the root of unbelief anticipates his own ultimate confrontation with self during his final conversion period in the mid-1840s. Finally, his thinking on intuition as a mode of knowledge is inseparably bound up with the imagination in the process of forming new and transformative aesthetic visions which promote conversion and without which it seems difficult to imagine the possibility of conversion. As our study progresses, we will see that these two poles of his thinking—on faith and religious epistemology on the one hand, and ecclesiastical doctrine on the other—actually form two parallel but independent "tracks" of his intellectual development until he effects a resolution through a synthesis which balances head and heart, the intellect and the affections, through the insights of the aesthetic dimension.

In closing Chapter One, we can conclude that Newman's first twenty-three years were driven by loving interpersonal experiences which produced an intellectual reflection on the nature of truth. He learned truth from experience, and experience served as the framework for the evaluation of intellectual reflection. This brought him to the realization of the importance of the act of faith as a product of love, an interpersonalist dynamic. Therefore, it seems appropriate to entitle this stage of our study "from human affectivity to religious faith." Chapter Two will pick up this theme, as the understanding of faith based in love becomes the ground for Newman's theological exposition over the next several years, culminating in the ascendance of the reality of the Church in his theology — transforming and expanding his perception and conception of the interpersonalist dynamic from a one-to-one with God to an incorporation of all others in that dynamic. In short, Mayers's "personal religion" will give way to a more communal understanding.

We will begin to see the effects of these factors on his theology in Chapter Two, which examines his movement "from religious faith to an interpersonalist theology."

These influences and their resultant changes provided a strong foundation for the experiences which followed in the next several years, which are the subjects of Chapter Two: the reality of parish work with his actual case histories bearing on actual versus textbook conversion; his earliest sermons; his intellectual encounter with the principle of analogy from Butler which, as we have seen, complemented his own thinking; his first major theological treatise on the miracles of Scripture; the emergence of the interpersonal shift in principle from self to Church-centered religion; and ultimately the deeply personal tragedy of his sister Mary's death. These six major factors continue the development of his interpersonalist-based theology, intellectual reflections which were heart-driven by interpersonal faith and love.

CHAPTER TWO

From Religious Faith to an Interpersonalist Theology: 1824–1827

INTRODUCTION

WE BOTH OPEN AND CLOSE THIS CHAPTER, WHICH TAKES US from 1824 through 1827, with stages of major personal experiences that had profound effects on Newman's theology, and between these poles we find six major stages of development, enumerated seven through twelve, following the pattern of Chapter One.

Stage seven examines the period of Newman's parish curacy at St. Clement's from mid-1824 through the spring of 1826, overlapping both his father's death and his correspondence with Charles. Newman's diary accounts are of great value regarding the conversion experiences of his parishioners, and these records are herein termed the "parish case records." These events are a major influence on his thought concerning conversion. As with the Charles correspondence in Chapter One, these records are generally overlooked in Newman studies and thus offer another original insight into his development at the time. Theory and practice, particularly Newman's concept of conversion and the reality of the conversion experience, clash in this environment, resulting in a significant intellectual change, altering his theology. Then we will examine the sermons of 1825, including two of Newman's earliest *Parochial and Plain Sermons*, as well as a series of other parish sermons which chronicle the evolution of Newman's thought on two major tracks — religious epistemology, which includes faith; and ecclesiology, a methodological mode which Newman will continue to employ throughout his conversion journey. This is Newman's first period of significant public theological exposition and thus identifies his positions on these issues at this time.

Stage eight reviews the effects of Joseph Butler's *Analogy* on Newman's intellect, striking a chord heard earlier by Newman himself. Newman came away from this reflection with insights which permanently shaped his later theological development. Thus this stage can arguably be termed the beginning of his intellectual synthesis.

Stage nine examines Newman's methodological transition from sermons to more lengthy, elaborate, and comprehensive intellectual exposition, through the writing of his essay on the Miracles of Scripture for the *Encyclopaedia Metropolitana*. This document is of primary value in its elaboration of personal witness as the fundamental element in the Scripture accounts, a theme he began developing in the previous sermons and which showed evidence of the effect of his own interpersonal relationships on his theological insights.

In stage ten we review two sermons written during the summer of 1826. The first, the initial *Oxford University Sermon*, formalized his thought on the issue of temper, over which he had jousted with Charles during the past two years. This sermon also witnesses the added import he gave to tradition and church, influenced by Whately and Hawkins. The second, another of his earliest *Parochial and Plain Sermons*, provides important evidence of his evolution beyond evangelical doctrine through a reflection on the nature of holiness and its implications, especially its necessary connection to morality.

Stage eleven reviews two documents, one from 1826 and the other from 1827, which emphasize his final turning from doctrinal evangelicalism toward a more communal understanding of church.

Stage twelve examines the personal experience which provided one of the major turning-points in his life, the sudden, tragic death of his beloved younger sister Mary. This soul-searing event, the pain of which bursts forth in his many letters and poems, is a catalyst which would reorder his thinking and unify many of the strands of thought resulting from the recent years of parish experience and theological writing. Intellect was once again reshaped by the heart, and the image of the unseen world, so impressed upon Newman through grief, informed his vision of reality. Thus, the affective, aesthetic, and intellectual elements interacted in the search for a resolution, and the vision of the Church as the meeting-place of God and man became more prominent.

Also during this stage Newman wrote a controversial sermon which elicited much criticism from his liberal Oriel colleagues. We will examine the effects of this controversy. Another experience of this stage, the effect of which will grow in prominence in years to come, was Newman's exposure to Keble's ground-breaking work *The Christian Year*.[1] Newman linked a

---

1   John Keble, *The Christian Year* (London: Frederick Warne & Co, 1827).

key element in Keble's work with the analogy principle of Butler as his theological development accelerated during this stage.

The six stages of Chapter Two complement the method begun in Chapter One: an analysis of Newman's theological exposition and the effects of "real" experience on his intellectual development. Through a review of his experiences and reflections, we find again that his heart and the mystery of the interpersonal dynamics of love grounded, shaped, and motivated his burgeoning intellect, as his imagination began to envision the Church, rather than the personal religion of evangelicalism, as the locus of the God-man encounter. We begin with an examination of Newman's curacy, which he assumed in 1824.

STAGE SEVEN:
Newman's Curacy at St. Clement's:
July 4, 1824–March 26, 1826

IN THE SPRING OF 1824, NEWMAN'S JOURNAL RECORDS A DECIsion which would profoundly affect the rest of his life:

> Sunday May 16
>   To day I have come to a most important determination. St Clement's Church is to be rebuilt. . . . It is proposed, Gutch the rector being incapacitated through age, to provide a Curate. . . . The curacy has been offered to me, and, after several days consideration, I have accepted it. . . . Mr Mayers advises me to take it; so does Tyler, Hawkins, Jelf, Pusey, Ottley.[2]

Of note is the reference to the role which the advice of his friends played in his decision. Two of the most influential people in his life to date, Mayers and Hawkins, were in favor of his accepting the curacy, and it is apparent that he sought this input prior to his decision. This parish service overlapped the death of his father and the Charles correspondence, while his liberal contacts, especially with Hawkins, were increasing.

Once again, due to the nature of the *Apologia*, we do not find any evidence of the effect of the parish assignment on Newman. However, the *Letters and Diaries* and the *Autobiographical Writings* recount no less than ten specific personal cases of major significance. They document Newman's reflections on his personal experiences with members of the congregation who were seriously ill or dying and generally in need of spiritual

---

2   Newman, *Autobiographical Writings*, 198–99.

counseling. These notes provide Newman's firsthand reflections on the reality of conversion, regeneration, faith, and grace. Such experiences of personal witness, so revealing as to the effect on Newman's intellectual and moral development, are a turning-point in his life as they lead him away from evangelicalism by calling into doubt its scriptural authenticity, a significant intellectual development grounded in interpersonal experience.

Following is a chronology of the ten major cases and their related themes.

NEWMAN'S PERSONAL CASE HISTORIES
St. Clement's Parish, July 4, 1824–March 26, 1826

NUMBER	DATE	NAME	THEME
	1824		
CASE 1	June–Aug.	Mr. Odcroft	Faith, conversion, and Newman's evangelical temper
CASE 2	June–Nov.	Mr. Swell	Suddenness of conversion
CASE 3	Aug.	Mr. Jones	The first evangelical admonition
CASE 4	Aug.	Mr. Bigg	The second evangelical admonition
	1824–1825		
CASE 5	Oct.–Feb.	Mrs. Flynn	The personal effect of conversion on Newman
CASE 6	Nov.–Jan.	Mr. Harris	The third evangelical admonition
CASE 7	Dec. (1824)	Mrs. Pattenson	Newman's "thrill" at effecting conversion and the evangelical interpretation of illness
	1825		
CASE 8	Jan. 1	Elizabeth Hale	The contrast of faith and theology
CASE 9	May 23	Miss Edgington	The impact of conversion on Newman
CASE 10	Aug 19	Mr. Claridge	Reflections on a sudden conversion

Less than two weeks after he began as curate at St. Clement's, Newman "began going through the parish, from house to house, to collect names, trades, etc."[3] He wrote his mother:

> about ten days ago I began my visitation of the whole parish, going from house to house, asking the names, numbers, trades, where they went to church etc etc . . . . It will be a great thing done — I shall know my parishioners, and be known by them.[4]

---

3   Newman, *Letters and Diaries*, vol. I, 179.   4   Ibid., 180.

In the course of his parish census, he had numerous experiences which promoted theological reflection. Let us examine, in chronological order, these ten major cases which so impacted Newman that he saw fit to make significant records of the experiences, which are relevant to our study of his conversion.

CASE 1. *Mr. Odcroft: Faith, Conversion, and Newman's Evangelical Temper*[5]

> [Appendix] 1824 June to Aug
> Odcroft — inflammation of liver (—) his illness lasted ten weeks (—) soon after his death, I heard he had been given to drinking — I fear I did not go to the bottom — but want experience — Though I told him openly the grand doctrines of Christianity, I did not say must be born again, but that he must have faith, abhorrence of sin, etc etc (—) He was one of the two first persons I attended — and I was too gentle — Lord, pardon me.

In this first major case recorded by Newman, we learn little about the parishioner, Mr. Odcroft, but significant facts emerge about Newman's perspective on his ministry. Newman criticized himself from his evangelically disposed perspective. He is not stern enough, "too gentle," and he failed to emphasize the need for conversion, stressing instead the need for faith, an indication that at this stage Newman separated the two. In addition to the fact that Newman had not yet worked out the relationship between faith and conversion, this document reveals his Calvinist predisposition. At about the same time, Newman recorded another case which caused him to reflect on the nature of conversion.

CASE 2. *Mr. Swell: The Suddenness of Conversion*[6]

> [Appendix] 1824 June to Nov
> Swell — an old man — afflicted with cancer in the throat, etc etc (a) very bad character — seemed to wish to RELY ON CHRIST, without change of heart. . . . Some time after, happening to call on him, I found him very different. . . . With great earnestness he begged me to pray for him. . . . After some days he was brought into great comfort and peace. . . . He grew weaker and weaker and at length departed (as I trust) in the Lord. Amen. His whole illness lasted about a year — and his agonies (according to the Physician who attended him) were indeed extraordinary. The

---

5   Ibid., 177. June–August, 1824.   6   Ibid., 177–78. June–November, 1824.

whole of this time God seemed to be drawing him and he at last owned it and felt it. There was something rather sudden in his (word illegible) *change* not in (two words illegible. In the transcription the last sentence reads:) There was something sudden certainly in the transition from obstinacy to terror and from terror to faith: but it might appear more sudden that (than) it really was — and all transitions must be more or less sudden.

Here we find Newman's reflection on the nature of conversion. Among its chief insights are: (1) Conversion may be more gradual than it appears; (2) All transitions are somewhat sudden; (3) The stages of the transition described by Newman, from obstinacy to terror and from terror to faith, describe the dynamics of interpersonal encounter. Obstinacy is self-absorbed isolationism. Terror implies a response to the encounter with a new and therefore potentially threatening Other. The awareness and realization of the presence of this Other, especially when perceived as more powerful, is at first threatening and even terrifying. But when love emanates from this Other toward its object, and when it is understood not as threat but as love, it can produce faith and trust in this Other. In his elucidation of these stages in Mr. Swell's conversion experience, Newman has noted the interpersonal dynamics which underlie the experience of conversion.

Another note regarding this record is the evangelical-inspired separation of reliance on Christ from change of heart. Given Mr. Swell's eventual conversion, it appears that his reliance on Christ was in fact indicative of a change of heart, even if not of the typical evangelical type. Newman's insight that the conversion was probably part of a process which began before the externally perceived event reveals the dichotomy in his own thinking between evangelical doctrine and his intuitive grasp of the interpersonal dynamics underlying religious conversion, a discrepancy which he would continue to confront in and through his parish experiences. But at this early stage of his ministry, Newman had a most influential exchange with Hawkins worthy of note.

THE HAWKINS INFLUENCE

DURING THIS PERIOD, NEWMAN SPENT A CONSIDERABLE amount of time with Hawkins. He states: "When I took orders in 1824 and had a curacy in Oxford, then, during the Long Vacation, I was especially thrown into his company,"[7] and they "had hall and Common Room to themselves [and] . . . he found in Mr. Hawkins a kind and able adviser."[8]

---

7 Newman, *Apologia*, 28.   8 Newman, *Autobiographical Writings*, 77.

Newman says of himself at this time that he "took for granted, if not intelligently held, the opinions called evangelical," which were reflected in his early sermons, "though mildly."[9] In fact, Hawkins criticized his first written sermon for its implied denial of baptismal regeneration and its high and rigid "line of demarcation" separating men into two classes, one virtually saints and the other virtually sinners. Newman cited Hawkins's admonition of his "either-or" perspective coupled with his recommendation of an academic text which would have a profound effect on Newman's evangelicalism:

> Men are not either saints or sinners; but they are not so good as they should be, and better than they might be — more or less converted to God, as it may happen. . . . St Paul . . . did not divide his brethren into two, the converted and the unconverted, but he addressed them all as "in Christ." Criticism such as this (had) a great though gradual effect [upon Newman], when carefully studied in the work from which it was derived, and which Hawkins gave him; this was Sumner's "Apostolic Preaching,". . . (which) was successful in the event beyond any thing else, in routing out evangelical doctrines from Mr Newman's Creed.[10]

We can now see the repetition of a familiar pattern. As with Mayers, Newman, so personally affected by Hawkins, was then open to his intellectual influence and recommended book. Hawkins had planted the first major seed of intellectual change in respect to Newman's interpretation of the conversion experiences of his parishioners, and that change was toward a more comprehensive understanding of the nature and effect of conversion. It is not a high, hard, either/or line separating people into two distinct categories, but a both/and phenomenon. People are both "not so good as they should be," and "better than they might be." This shift in the interpretation of conversion was reinforced intellectually by the *Apostolic Preaching*. According to these insights, many who would be considered unconverted by the standards of evangelicalism are in fact already converted. Conversion is therefore a matter of levels or degrees. Once again, Newman was confronted by dissonance, on this occasion caused by the failed integration of parish experience, reflection, and evangelicalism. The next two major cases continue to indicate the evangelical tendencies of Newman's early parish ministry.

---

9   Ibid.   10   Ibid.

CASE 3. Mr. Jones: The First Evangelical Admonition[11]

> [Appendix] 1824 Augt
>
> Jones very bad man — great drinker and swearer (and) he was certain 'he should be different if he recovered.' . . . I found that all the time he continued swearing etc as bad as ever — and spoke slightingly of me. . . . On finding out his duplicity, I expostulated with him very severely.

This case primarily witnesses Newman's evangelical response to the unsurprising backsliding of human nature. "I had somewhat suspected," he wrote of Jones's duplicity, and he reacted "very severely."

At about this time, Newman's correspondence reveals several other noteworthy themes. On August 30, 1824, he wrote to his mother: "It is quite idle to pretend to faith and holiness, unless they show forth their inward principles by a pure, disinterested, upright line of conduct."[12] For Newman, faith without works clearly does not suffice, which shows him at variance with evangelical doctrine. Morality and faith, for Newman, are intrinsically connected. On September 16, he wrote in his journal:

> Those who make comfort the great subject of their preaching seem to mistake the end of their ministry. Holiness is the great end. There must be a struggle and a trial here. Comfort is a cordial, but no one drinks cordials from morning to night.[13]

This doctrine reflects Newman's indebtedness to the evangelical Thomas Scott, "the writer who made a deeper impression on my mind than any other, and to whom (humanly speaking) I almost owe my soul. . . . For years I used almost as proverbs what I considered to be the scope and issue of his doctrine, *Holiness rather than peace*, and *Growth the only evidence of life*."[14] The next day, September 17, Newman wrote his friend Edward Pusey concerning his parish duties, making an important comment on his personal cases:

> The most pleasant part of my duties is visiting the sick — and I have seven or eight on my hands — and though there have been and are two or three most painful characters amongst them, yet on the other hand I have several most interesting cases. My visits quite hallow the day to me, as if every day were Sunday.[15]

---

11 Newman, *Letters and Diaries*, vol. I, 187–88. August 1824.   12 Ibid., 189.
13 Newman, *Autobiographical Writings*, 172.   14 Newman, *Apologia*, 26.
15 Newman, *Letters and Diaries*, vol. I, 191.

In these writings we find Newman's connection of faith and morality and at the same time a reiteration of early evangelical themes as found in Scott. This intellectualism was further impacted by his parish cases, which had now become the highlight of his duties, evidence that interpersonal dynamics had moved to the forefront of his ministry. However, the next major case recorded by Newman indicates the building intellectual dissonance as he reasserts traditional evangelical doctrines.

CASE 4. *Mr. Bigg: A Second Evangelical Admonition*[16]

> [Appendix] Sept
>   Bigg — middle aged or elderly man — I was called in when he was dying. . . . (He) had lived a pious and decent life. . . . The next day he was too ill to see me and died that evening. Alas! As I write this (next day) he may be exclaiming — 'that clergyman told me too truly about my perilous state!' O Lord God — [In transcribing Newman changed this to] he may be thinking how true in the main my words were!

Here we find a clear example of Newman's evangelical perspective. On the one hand everything recorded about this parishioner is positive: "quite sensible," "had great hopes of salvation — was no swearer — nor a miserable sinner relied on his works." Yet Newman's reminiscence is colored by the evangelical image of a vindictive God and a corrupt human nature.

Shortly after this case was recorded, Newman's father died. On October 18, 1824, he wrote to his mother about their great loss:

> The time may be comparatively distant, but still the days will come, when one after another we shall drop away like leaves from the tree; but, being as we trust in Christ, we shall meet one and all in heaven to part no more. . . . We shall meet, as our hope is, him, whom we have just lost.[17]

We have come to a major transition in Newman's early life, revealed by the six parish case histories which follow. Of the four cases already examined, the principal themes are faith, evangelical temper, and a few conversion reflections. But following his father's death, we find the beginning of a change in Newman, the significance of which we learned previously from *Loss and Gain* and which is evident in his reflection on the nature of reality, especially the existence of the unseen world, as he observed

---

16   Ibid., 192. September 1824.   17   Ibid., 195.

his dead father: "Can a man be a materialist who sees a dead body?"[18]

Subsequent to this event, the major cases recorded by Newman emphasize conversion: in four of the six it is the main theme, while another emphasizes the conflict of faith and reason, and the sixth is another evangelical admonition. If we examine these as two groupings split by Mr. Newman's death, we see a decided shift from the first group's concern with evangelicalism, as conversion is but a secondary issue. In the second group, however, conversion becomes the dominant theme as evangelical concerns are prominent in only one case. Let us now examine these six cases following Mr. Newman's death.

CASE 5. Mrs. Flynn: The Personal Effect of Conversion on Newman[19]

> Mrs. Flynn — young widow — in apparent decline from breaking blood vessel.... [S]he said she had always been very bad.... After attending her three weeks or a month, and reading the scriptures to her, [she said] I had enlightened her much. The day she died [she said] 'I trust entirely to Christ'.... I saw her three times this day.... [S]he had her senses and peace to the last. No case has affected me like this.

In the eight months of his parish ministry up to this point, this case most impressed Newman, and it centered on the conversion from a sinful life to an acceptance of the truth of scriptural revelation. But the key term in Newman's quotation of the parishioner's new state, which he records twice, is "trust," a term of interpersonal relationship and a key to the act of faith. The interrelationship of conversion experience and the dynamics of relationship move to the forefront of Newman's reflection by means of the case of widow Flynn. At about the same time, Newman records another major case, the last of his "evangelical admonitions."

CASE 6. Mr. Harris: A Third Evangelical Admonition[20]

> Harris — internal inflammation etc — given over — but recovered.... [He] exprest himself greatly benefitted and enlightened — trusted the sickness would be a warning to him — I cautioned him of the danger of backsliding and he seemed deeply sensible of it.... He has attended church very regularly since.

---

18   Newman, Autobiographical Writings, 203.
19   Newman, Letters and Diaries, vol. I, 196. Recorded between October 1824 and February 1825.
20   Ibid., 198. Recorded between November 1824 and January 1825.

The evangelical danger of backsliding is prominent in Newman's counsel in this case, and it is the last "evangelical admonition" found in the ten major cases he recorded, all of which occur in the early part of his ministry. The next major case, occurring at about the same time, begins Newman's shift to a significant focus on the conversion experiences of his parishioners.

CASE 7. *Mrs. Pattenson: The "Thrill" of Effecting Conversion and an Evangelical Interpretation of Illness*[21]

> Mrs. Pattenson — young married woman 22 in a decline — Happening to call by accident. . . . [I] asked if I should visit her — she said no — called again and again . . . [and] prevailed on her to let me read constantly with her. . . . I had no idea how ill she was. . . . (She was always sickly and she said) 'God has brought her to Himself by sickness. . . . He was all merciful and her soul was full of comfort.' . . . Her eyes looked at me with such a meaning, I felt a thrill I cannot describe — it was like the gate of heaven — I promised to call again in the evening — she was very thankful. — I did call in the evening — she had departed about an hour after I left her! — She told her friends she had had so pleasant conversation with me — so glad she was alone with me.

Here we have perhaps the most unique experience of Newman's involvement in the conversion of a parishioner. He is at first rebuffed, but he persisted, and began readings, presumably of Scripture, "constantly." His persistence yielded fruit as the young woman moved to a state of realization of God's mercy and thus comfort, a description of an interpersonal encounter and response. But the most noteworthy reference in the record is that of Newman's "thrill" at her converted gaze — "the gate of heaven." As the catalytic agent in her conversion, Newman was affected in a way rarely described with such emotion. This conversion-participation was increasingly more meaningful to Newman as his case histories continued. Newman does, however, make note of the woman's own evangelical-style interpretation of her suffering: "(She said that) God had brought her to Himself by sickness."

But in December of 1824, in the soul-searching shadow of his father's death and increasingly affected by the conversion experiences of his parishioners, Newman's understanding of conversion began to shift decisively.

---

21 Ibid., 199. Recorded December 1824.

Another major factor responsible for this change was the influence of his Oriel associates, as indicated by a diary entry on December 8, 1824:

> Pusey had told me Lloyd had been informed by a friend on good authority that my parishioners said they liked me very much but I 'damned them too much.' Being conscious of having said too little *on the whole* of future punishments (so Lloyd took it), I was at first perplexed — afterwards I thought it must mean I dwelt much on the corruption of the heart and that explained it — give grace![22]

Just eight days later, Newman noted a debate with Pusey on these subjects:

> Thursday Dec 16
> I am lodged in the same house with Pusey, and we have had many conversations on the subject of religion, I arguing for imputed righteousness, he against it, I inclining to regeneration from baptism, he doubting its separation &c.[23]

Here we find Newman's debating about evangelical beliefs, but the combined influences of parish experiences and his intellectual Oriel friends produced a major transition in his thinking which he recorded just a month after his debate with Pusey. But prior to that, on January 1, 1825, Newman recorded two other incidents worthy of note.

> Jan. 1 1825
> Mrs. Reeves tells me 'There are many proud ones hear me — and I gave them a hard blow the other day in my sermon' — Thank God, I know them not.[24]

From this parishioner's report, Newman hasn't lost his evangelical fervor, but his response indicates that the blow he struck was less than intentional, and therefore an indication that he no longer considered the evangelical mode of chastisement as necessarily the best for his ministry: "Thank God, I know them not." In this account we can hear the echo of his own insight just three weeks earlier: "I damned them too much . . . give grace!" As 1824 drew to a close, for Newman the scales of truth had tipped against evangelicalism.

On this same date, January 1, 1825, he recorded the eighth major case history, most notable for its methodological insight.

---

22 Ibid., 203.   23 Newman, *Autobiographical Writings*, 203.
24 Newman, *Letters and Diaries*, vol. I, 205.

CASE 8. Elizabeth Hale: The Contra$t of Faith and Theology[25]

> [Appendix] Hale Eliz: — young woman of 30, with cancer in throat, had been a very bad character — visited her and lent her books — but she is most unsatisfactory — I cannot make out whether she feels or not — fonder I fear, of reading tracts etc than the Bible.

Newman here alludes to his parishioner's preference for the logic of theological tracts to the faith-witness accounts of revelation, a preference he notes as his "fear," indicating his own position. Interestingly, he also describes the parishioner as possibly unfeeling, an implication of the connection of this lack of sensitivity to the coldness of logic. This was parallel to the argument he was simultaneously waging with his brother Charles over the nature of intellectual method. As a result of both parish experiences and intellectual influences, Newman was brought to the brink of a major change, as he wrote in his journal on January 13, 1825:

> I think, I am not certain, I must give up the doctrine of imputed righteousness and that of regeneration as apart from baptism. . . . It seems to me the great stand is to be made, not against those who connect a spiritual change with baptism, but those who deny a spiritual change altogether. (This refers to Dr. Lloyd. Decr 14, 1857) All who confess the natural corruption of the heart, and the necessity of a change (whether they connect regeneration with baptism or not) should unite against those who make it (regeneration) a mere opening of new prospects.[26]

We find in this entry, six months into his parish ministry, that Newman's evangelical hard-line conception of regeneration is breaking down. His parish experiences, added to the admonition of Hawkins months earlier, now reinforced by Lloyd and Pusey, all combined to cause a momentous shift in Newman's thinking.

Newman goes on to reflect upon four specific points regarding man's relationship to God. Three concern baptism: (1) Infant baptism makes sense only if it is the source of grace; (2) God can be bound by covenant (a term of relationship) to bestow grace through baptism; (3) Scripturally, this explains why Jesus bid children come to him. He then concluded that (4) "there should be no harsh line, but degrees of holiness infinitely small."[27] This was the culmination of a crisis in Newman's thinking that began at least five months earlier, as he recorded in his journal:

---

25 Ibid. Recorded January 1, 1825.   26 Newman, *Autobiographical Writings*, 203.
27 Ibid., 203–4.

Tuesday Aug 24 (1824)

Lately I have been thinking much on the subject of grace, regeneration, &c. and reading Sumner's *Apostolic Preaching*, which Hawkins has given me. Sumner's book threatens to drive me either into Calvinism, or baptismal regeneration, and I wish to steer clear of both, at least in preaching. . . . Last night I was so distressed about it. . . . The thought even struck me I must leave the Church. . . . I do not know what will be the end of it. I think I really desire the truth, and would embrace it wherever I find it.[28]

And just a week later he writes of an anxiety-producing visit with friends:

Friday Septr 3

Took tea with Mr Shepard. He and Mrs S. seem to wish me to be more calvinistic. What shall I do? I really desire the truth.[29]

These journal entries contain two important facts regarding Newman's intellectual state at the time. First, he was increasingly beset by doubts concerning the evangelical doctrines with which he had begun his parish ministry, and secondly, and most importantly, is the reference to truth. From it we can see the implication of an important insight indicative of Newman's method: truth is not to be assumed by the acceptance of denominational doctrine, but rather truth is the basis on which that doctrine must be constructed. In short, truth is the objective of the mind, and doctrines, as mental constructs, seek to express the perceived truth or, as Newman would later say, they are "approximations to truth."[30] The mysterious nature of truth, then, is the foundation of doctrine, and not the other way round. Wrestling with this dilemma produced the angst which Newman records in his diary entry of August 24, driving him into thoughts so extreme as to consider leaving the Church. We should note that just two months later he began his most important letters to his brother Charles, wherein he works out many of the questions which he raised above regarding the nature and truth of revelation and the proper intellectual method for ascertaining that truth.

But by the end of 1824, with the effects of assisting and witnessing his parishioners' conversions, and the influence of his Oriel friends, he began to construct a resolution, and it was in a direction against the assertions of evangelical doctrine.

Writing almost fifty years later in his *Autobiographical Memoir*, Newman himself summarized this personal transition with a specific note of this

---

28   Ibid., 202.   29   Ibid.   30   Newman, *Fifteen Sermons*, 340.

period as the beginning of the end of his evangelical commitment and the broadening of his philosophical perspective, as we have noted:

> Mr. Newman, then, before many months of his clerical life were over, had taken the first step towards giving up the evangelical form of Christianity. . . . Besides Sumner, Butler's celebrated work, which he studied about the year 1825, had, as was natural, an important indirect effect upon him in the same direction, as placing his doctrinal views on a broad philosophical basis, with which emotional religion could have little sympathy.[31]

From this evidence it is clear that Newman was in the midst of a great personal transition, and the causes of this evolution, when examined, are most relevant for our study. First, undoubtedly, his personal experiences in the parish were major catalysts, and second, his intellectual influences played a significant role. We have already seen the major influence of Hawkins, and that intellectual influence was grounded in their interpersonal relationship. But what of the two other intellectual influences bearing on Newman in December 1824 and January 1825, namely Lloyd and Pusey? Not surprisingly, we find the very same principle at work in these relationships. Newman was highly affected by the character of both men, especially their interpersonal qualities, and this led to their significant intellectual influence on him. As with Whately and Hawkins, the interpersonal relationship formed the foundation on which the intellectual influence could be built. Let us examine the evidence of Newman's relationships with Lloyd and Pusey.

THE INFLUENCE OF CHARLES LLOYD AND EDWARD PUSEY

FIRST WE WILL EXAMINE THE RECORD REGARDING THE PERsonal effect of Lloyd on Newman, and then the intellectual. Lloyd died suddenly after a brief illness on May 31, 1829, at the age of 45, and Newman wrote to his sister Harriett just a few days later that

> His death has shocked me much. . . . I had the greatest esteem, respect, and love for him, as a most warm hearted, frank, vigorous minded, and generous man. His kindness for me I cannot soon forget. He brought me forward, made me known, spoke well of me, and gave me confidence in myself. . . . I wish he had ever been aware how much I felt his kindness.[32]

---

31   Newman, *Autobiographical Writings*, 78.
32   Newman, *Letters and Diaries*, vol. II, 146.

More than a year earlier Newman had written:

> Lloyd is the new Bishop of Oxford. He is very kind, and takes
> great interest in my plan of reading the Fathers; but he says
> that our theological systems do not agree. They agree more than
> when I was in class with him, but I do not tell him so. I deeply
> feel his kindness.[33]

Here we find another reference to the interpersonal virtue of kindness
which deeply impressed Newman, and taken together with the previous
citation, we note the same affective ground of their relationship as we
have seen with Whately and Hawkins. Interestingly, Newman added an
additional note to the above letter to his sister Harriett which is of value:

> N. B. I have not mentioned him in my *Apologia* — for I was there
> concerned in tracing the course of my religious opinions, and
> the persons who contributed to form them. In this point of view
> I am not aware I owed any thing to Dr Lloyd. I left his lecture
> room in 1824, as I entered it in 1822, a calvinist.[34]

As we have established about the *Apologia*, personal influences are the
exception and not usually found since Newman designed it as a record
of the development of his religious opinions. Newman used the term
"religious" interchangeably with the term "doctrinal" in this regard, as
we have seen earlier,[35] and this fact becomes even more illuminating
for our study. It may have been that Lloyd had no direct effect on the
development of Newman's doctrinal positions, but the nature of their
relationship was conditioned by Lloyd's affective interpersonal qualities,
leading Newman to respond with "the greatest esteem, respect, and love
for him" and to declare "how much I felt his kindness." These are not the
statements of a detached, objective observer but of a person who *felt* the
effects of Lloyd's positive personality. Again, these affective experiences
opened the door to the intellectual effects of Lloyd which were of more
than passing worth. Perhaps Newman stated he could not trace any specific
doctrinal effects to Lloyd because Lloyd's intellectual influence went deeper
than the particularity of doctrines to the very nature of method, which
would make Lloyd's influence even greater. This, in fact, we learn from

---

33 Newman, *Autobiographical Writings*, 210.
34 Newman, *Letters and Diaries*, vol. II, 146. Note: Donald A. Wilthy corrects these
dates from 1824 and 1822 to 1826 and 1823, respectively. "John Henry Newman and
Dr. Charles Lloyd," *The Downside Review* (October 1993): 240.
35 Newman, *Letters and Diaries*, vol. I, 30, n. 1.

other sources. Lloyd, as Regius Professor of Divinity at Oxford, began a series of private lectures in 1823, and the subject is of significant import in relation to Newman's future work:

> He (Lloyd) employed his mind upon the grounds of Christian faith rather than on the faith itself; and, in his estimate of the grounds, he made light of the internal evidence for revealed religion, in comparison of its external proofs.[36]

Lloyd's theological teaching emphasized three factors, all of which appear to have left their intellectual influence on Newman: a thorough grounding in methodology which emphasized analysis and systematic argumentation, scripture, and a comprehensive philosophical, historical, and apologetic range.[37] Lastly, in Newman's journal entry of January 13, 1825, cited previously, at the height of his moment of transition away from evangelicalism, his reference to Lloyd clearly implicates the latter in Newman's altered position on baptismal regeneration. Also, note should be made that Lloyd approved of Newman's plan to read the Fathers, providing motivational support, if nothing more, to an instinct which would have profound theological repercussions.

Overall, the point of this review of Lloyd's influence on Newman is to note that it was fostered by the nature of their personal relationship. From that foundation, Newman, as was characteristic, would then open to the intellectual influence of the "other." The conceptual truth constructed by the intellect was borne out, and in fact occasioned, by the perceptual truth of the affective relationship. Newman's intuition opened him to Lloyd's intellectual influence.

Let us move on now to Pusey, who was elected a fellow of Oriel in April of 1823. Newman wrote of him, "He is a searching man, and seems to delight in talking on religious subjects."[38] On May 17, he continued his description of his new acquaintance:

> Pusey is Thine, O Lord, how can I doubt it? . . . (H)is devotional spirit, his love of the Scriptures, his firmness and zeal, all testify the operation of the Holy Ghost. . . . Yet I fear he is prejudiced against Thy children. . . . What am I that I should be so blest in my near associates?[39]

---

36 Newman, *Autobiographical Writings*, 71.
37 Wilthey, "John Henry Newman and Dr. Charles Lloyd," 237.
38 Newman, *Autobiographical Writings*, 190.   39 Ibid., 191.

Early in their relationship, Newman was characteristically impressed by the high, positive qualities of his new friend. In the previous record, however, is the telltale evangelical signature "prejudiced against *Thy children* (italics added)," evidencing the religious differences between them. By February 1 of 1824, Newman had grown even more admiring of Pusey, as his various journal entries indicate:

> Sunday Febr 1
>
> Have just walked with Pusey. He seems growing in the best things, in humility and love to God and man.[40]

> Monday March 15
>
> Took a walk with Pusey. . . . He is humility itself and gentleness and love, and zeal, and self devotion. Bless him with Thy fullest gifts, and grant me to imitate him.[41]

> Saturday April 17
>
> Pusey is so good and conscientious, he quite frightens me, and I wish him not to see what I do.[42]

We can easily see the high personal esteem in which Newman held Pusey. These noble, virtuous qualities so struck Newman that he found his friend worthy of imitation, and himself shamefully lacking. So it is that through the moral example of Pusey, he is opened to his intellectual influence, and combined with the influence of Lloyd, and these in conjunction with his parish experiences, we find a major shift recorded in the journal entry of January 13, 1825. It is of note that this entry is the very next one following Newman's discussions with Pusey in December in which Newman stated his views as diametrically opposite to those of Pusey on imputed righteousness, regeneration, and baptism — views which, as we have seen, Newman would virtually reverse the next month. Undoubtedly Pusey, by the force of his personal qualitative effect on Newman, was a major factor in this redirection. This once again underscores the theme that Newman was intellectually influenced as a result of the personal influence of their relationship.

To recapitulate, by January of 1825 Newman had shifted his thinking away from evangelical doctrines on a number of issues, and this change was brought about by the reality of conversion as he experienced it in his parish through his *interpersonal* relationships with his parishioners — the "thrill" — and the influence of his personal, affective relationships with

---

40 Ibid., 195–56. 41 Ibid., 197–98. 42 Ibid., 198.

his Oriel associates. *That* he changed and *why* he did so is now evident, but what that change consisted of, and the direction it was to take, we will now address. Newman's journal provides the evidence as he wrote just a month later:

> Monday Febr 21
> The necessity of composing sermons has obliged me to systematize and complete my ideas on a number of subjects. . . . Yet I hardly dare say confidently that my change of opinion has brought me nearer to the truth. At least, however, I may say that I have taken many doctrines almost on trust from Scott &c and on serious examination hardly find them confirmed by Scripture. I have come to no decision of the doctrines of election &c, but the predestination of individuals seems to me hardly a scriptural doctrine.[43]

This summary statement reveals a major fact. Newman describes the problem of method, first, in that the intellectual element of thought is increasingly his focus, brought about by the necessity of writing sermons for the parish, and secondly, that doctrine must be consistent with revelation. Since Newman had accepted certain doctrines from the evangelical Scott "almost on trust," he had obviously overlooked this rule of method: examination proved that certain evangelical doctrines were in fact unsupported by the revelation of Scripture. Ironically, this is the same methodological "predisposition" he debates in the correspondence with Charles and of which he himself has been guilty, only from a different perspective. An important note here is that this principle of accepting doctrinal positions of religious authorities on trust without validating them will be the same methodological flaw which will eventually "pulverize" his *Via Media* Church theory some fourteen years later. Now, however, his analysis has the unmistakable influence of Lloyd and his concern for method, as well as the liberal-rational influence of Whately and Hawkins. All these influences will soon combine to produce another stage in his development when he makes the intellectual transition from sermons to treatise since, as he wrote his sister Harriett at that time, "I am persuaded, as Whately suggested, that sermon writing *by itself* has a tendency to produce a loose rambling kind of composition, nay even of thought."[44] But before he would make that methodological transition, 1825 contained two other major experiences bearing on our study.

---

43 Ibid., 204.   44 Newman, *Letters and Diaries*, vol. I, 210.

First, Newman recorded the last two major parish case histories, and both centered on conversion. Then throughout 1825 he wrote four important groups of sermons relevant to our study: (1) Two of his first *Parochial and Plain Sermons*; (2) A series of six sermons on faith during the winter; (3) Followed in the spring by a series of three sermons on the nature of relationship, faith, and baptism; and lastly (4) Three sermons with a major ecclesiological theme in late 1825. These works were generally organized along the lines of the two tracks on which Newman was beginning to develop his theology — that of religious epistemology and that of ecclesiology.

We will complete the study of the parish case histories by reviewing these two conversions and their impact on Newman, and then proceed to examine the sermons, tracing the evolution of his theological exposition to his personal experience.

CASE 9. Miss Edgington: The Impact of Conversion on Newman[45]

> [Miss Edgington] got worse again and I renewed my visits from Febr 1825. Her case very interesting she had not thought very seriously of religion . . . while well — and did now. . . . [S]he gradually got weaker and weaker. . . . It is quite painful to look upon her. . . . [H]er sense of her own inward sinfulness seemed more strong. . . . [H]er soul, I trust, is holier than it was. . . . She took the sacrament (again), and about a week after departed, as I may trust, to the Lord who bought her — The case is very painful — it is like a sword going thro' my heart — Her mother has since told me she said that when I entered her room she thought of Jesus Christ in the picture. (Note.-) I could not learn that any thing was said about the 'new birth.'

Here we find a remarkable shift in Newman's account compared to previous cases. Despite the absence of an evangelical "new birth," he makes no admonitions and is seriously pained by the entire case, a "sword going thro' my heart." Miss Edgington's conversion is "soft" by evangelical standards, yet it is one of the most emotional and longest accounts recorded by Newman. It appears that both his evangelical temper and his intellectual positions were changing simultaneously. Conversion was now viewed as a painful but loving interpersonal transition rather than a merely authoritarian demand. Newman himself is within the experiential process of his parishioners as their loving spiritual facilitator, not on the outside as a cold tool of admonition. Newman's heart, affected by Lloyd and Pusey,

---

45   Ibid., 232. Recorded May 23, 1825.

had changed his head, which again in turn changed his heart, affecting his relationships with his parishioners as evidenced in this conversion case. Newman was now at the point of completing his personal transition which had kept him in turmoil since at least the previous August. Just six days after he wrote the previous conversion account, he was ordained and recorded in his journal a momentous change of position:[46]

> Sunday May 29
>
> My feelings [were] somewhat different from [last year]. Then, I thought there were many in the visible Church of Christ, who have never been visited by the Holy Ghost; now, I think there are none but probably, nay almost certainly, have been visited by Him. Who then will dare to say that any certain individual has completely emptied his soul of divine grace, and that not a drop remains at the bottom or on the sides of the vessel?

Newman had indeed come a long way from his early evangelical beliefs, but he was not yet completely convinced about baptism, as he went on to write in this account:

> Yet I do not even now actually maintain that the Spirit always or generally accompanies the very act of baptism, only that the sacrament brings them into the kingdom of grace, where the Spirit will constantly meet them with His influences.

On July 17 he concluded that the reason for "my change of sentiment as to regeneration" was that "in my parochial duties I have found many, who in most important points were inconsistent, but whom yet I could not say were altogether without grace."[47] Shortly after this journal entry, Newman recounted the last major conversion case in his diary.

CASE 10. *Mr. Claridge : Reflections on the Suddenness of Conversion*[48]

> [Appendix] Claridge - Aug: Man perhaps 35 — had been a coachman. . . . For some months past hearing he was in a declining way, I have called from time to time. . . . (T)he day before yesterday I was sent for — He seemed very near his end — and was very desirous of seeing me — he talked of God [as] most merciful in having spared him — and he ought to be most thankful. . . . Today I found that he had suddenly declared the weight of sin was suddenly taken off him and tears burst from

---

46   Newman, *Autobiographical Writings*, 206.   47   Ibid.
48   Newman, *Letters and Diaries*, vol. I, 252. Recorded August 19, 1825.

him and he said he was so rejoiced. . . . [I] was indeed much
perplexed — fearing to speak against the mysterious working of
God (if it was his working) yet equally fearing lest I should make
him satisfied with a partial repentance and with emotions. . . . I
am thinking of the cause of this. . . . [Is] it the work of the H. S.
(Holy Spirit) even in its suddenness?

Newman's diary noted that Claridge died ten days later, until which
time Newman visited him almost every day. This case indicates how "perplexed" was his thinking, to use Newman's own expression, on the nature
of conversion and the relationship between man and the Holy Spirit.

In closing this parochial stage of Newman's development, he himself
summarized it more than four decades later, reminiscing in his *Autobiographical Memoir*:

By personal experience . . . the religion which he had received from
John Newton and Thomas Scott would not work in a parish; . . . It
was unreal. . . . Mr Hawkins had told him beforehand; that Calvinism was not a key to the phenomena of human nature. . . . The
evangelical teaching, considered as a system and in what was
particular to itself, had from the first failed to find a response
in his own religious experience, as afterwards in his parochial.[49]

In concluding the opening section of this stage, we find that Newman entered parochial service with a strong evangelical predisposition,
but through the personal experiences of his parishioners' conversions,
combined with the intellectual effects of his interpersonal relationships
with Hawkins, Lloyd, and Pusey, he was moved to question major tenets
of evangelical doctrine, finally rejecting them. The death of his father
during this period, who was such a major influence in his life, added to
his theological reflection, as evidenced by the distinctly different interpretation and focus which Newman gave to the parish conversion experiences
before and after this event. Newman was deeply sensitized by his father's
death, and the effect is evident in his ministry. All these facts underscore
the conclusion that at the base of Newman's intellectual shift was the
affective nature of the interpersonal relationships he shared with those he
knew, and at the core of that base of interpersonalism is the experience of
faith. Faith, as we have seen, is an interpersonal dynamic and is integral
to, and perhaps definitive of, conversion. We have already seen in the
correspondence with Charles how Newman began to treat of faith, and

---

49   Newman, *Autobiographical Writings*, 79.

notably, this correspondence was written simultaneously with these parish conversion experiences. But Newman's development of his new theological insights — especially regarding human nature, revelation, conversion, faith, relationship, and ecclesiology — all clashed with his evangelical "baggage" and would be worked out in his sermons of 1825. We will now examine these documents to see what effect they had on Newman's theology of the period in light of the personal experiences just reviewed.

THE SERMONS OF 1825

NEWMAN BEGAN TO WORK OUT THESE PROBLEMS THROUGH his parish sermons, the major sources documenting his intellectual concerns and advances during this period. He realized the dilemma of the clash of his evangelical beliefs with his intuition and interpersonal experiences, but how did he make sense of, or harmonize, this discordance? The sermons of 1825 are the record of that attempt. We will review fourteen in all, forming two "tracks" along which Newman developed his thinking, that of religious epistemology and faith on the one hand and ecclesiology on the other, a method which he continued to employ, especially during his intellectual conversion phase. First, we will examine the series of six sermons he delivered from February to March on the subject of faith, evidence of the importance of this interpersonal experience in his intellectual development. Then in April and May he preached two sermons on the nature of relationship, and another in March of 1826, which is included in this group because of its thematic connection, as he wrestled to resolve intellectually the problems of justification, including infant baptism, sponsorship, and God's covenant with man. In a related *Parochial and Plain Sermon* in June, he examined the affective ground of religious knowledge, but still exhibiting the effects of evangelicalism. In another *Parochial and Plain Sermon* in December, he completed this track with insights regarding the heart as the ground of religious knowledge, obedience, and conversion, as well as connecting it to the importance of the testimony of personal witness as a key dimension of knowledge grounded in the heart. This theme bears on the major document he was composing at this time, his *Miracles* essay, which we will subsequently examine. Following these sermons on religious epistemology, we will then review Newman's second track of ecclesiology through three sermons delivered in November and early December, by which time his thinking has been considerably developed. These documents are indicative of a major change, the beginning of an intellectual synthesis, as he connected his previous themes to a new understanding of the Church, and they also indicate the influence of another major factor in his intellectual development, Butler's *Analogy*, especially its interpersonal significance.

THE RELIGIOUS EPISTEMOLOGY TRACK:
Documents 1–6 — *The Six Sermons on Faith:*
Toward an Interpersonalist Theology[50]

THE FIRST TWO OF THESE SERMONS ARE ENTITLED "THE NATURE and Object of Faith," and herein Newman crafts a definition and description of faith: it is "knowledge through a medium" and "more or less connected with the heart and affections."[51] It is, in other words, an awareness through an interpersonal dynamic encounter. But this faith "consists in being impressed with the reality of unseen things from confidence in the person who tells us of them." The catalyst of faith, then, is the credibility of the witness. The result is that it "produces very important effects upon the mind," and it also assists "fully to understand the peculiar article of a Christian's faith, that Jesus Christ came into the world to die for sinners."[52] Thus, the ground of faith is trust in personal witness, an affective act which also produces a new insight. Intellect, then, is grounded in affectivity.

But what is the context, or object, of this act of faith? The second sermon states that "the object of faith is the *holiness* and *mercy* of God. Faith is the *channel through* which this object operates upon the heart."[53] God's mercy is an interpersonal action from one Being to another. And what is the result of this encounter? It is nothing short of conversion:

> Real faith in the Son of God is so mighty a principle that it must work a change in the heart and reform and beautify the whole man. . . . The spiritual Christian is in a new world [with] a new sense given him. . . . [He] feels things unspeakable and incommunicable. . . . Faith gives a new meaning and import to the whole of life.[54]

And what is this new realization which the believer sees, the "new world," "new meaning and import"? It is the aesthetic vision of the loving interpersonal dynamic relationship which the believer now realizes to exist between himself and his God. He is in love, loving, and being

---

50 This series was preached between February 20 and March 27, 1825. We follow Sheridan's archival research: Sheridan, *Newman on Justification*, 91–97.

51 Ibid., 92. Published also in *John Henry Newman: Sermons 1824–1843*, vol. 5, ed. Francis. J. McGrath (Oxford: Clarendon Press, 2012).

52 Ibid., 92–93.   53 Ibid., 93.   54 Ibid.

loved. It is, then, "faith which worketh by love."[55] In short, the realm of the heart grounds the intellect and its vision.

The third sermon, "On Justification through Faith Only,"[56] offers another perspective on faith, influenced by Newman's evangelical background:

> The meaning of justification by faith alone . . . simply is that God will pardon and accept us in Christ without our deservings whenever we turn to Him and throw ourselves upon His mercy, and take Him for our only hope and salvation.[57]

But as the series continued, Newman developed this notion beyond the traditional evangelical sense. The fourth sermon, "Faith the evidence and principle of Newness of Heart," treats of the effects and validation of true faith:

> The only evidence that we did believe in Him, was the fruits of holiness and active obedience in our life and conduct. The great gift purchased for us by His death and now offered to our acceptance is sanctification.[58]

What we learn from this excerpt is that religious conversion through faith, if it is real, emerges in moral conversion. Obedience, our life and conduct become the yardstick by which we assess the truth of faith. Sanctification, or holiness, is the moral counterpart to religious faith. The next sermon develops further the interpersonalist nature of faith and sanctification by their connection to works.

The fifth sermon, "Necessary Connection of Faith and Works," stresses two important and reciprocal points: "Real faith cannot exist without good works. On the other hand, neither can good works exist without faith."[59] Sanctification, then, which is the evidence of true faith and conversion, is directed toward others as the realization, fruition, and witness of that truth.

The final sermon in this series, "Faith Connected with, and Confirmed by, the Inward Witness," is a commentary on the text of 1 John 5:10 — "He that believeth on the Son of God hath the witness in himself"— which Sheridan notes as "a very early example of an apologetic of immanence."[60]

---

55 Ibid.
56 Ibid., 94. Published also in *John Henry Newman: Sermons 1824–1843*, vol. 5. Dated March 6, 1825.
57 Ibid.   58 Ibid., 95.   59 Ibid., 96.
60 Ibid. Published also in *John Henry Newman: Sermons 1824–1843*, vol. 5. Dated March 27, 1825.

A key section from the sermon unites faith, revelation, and the discernment of truth:

> The man who believes on Christ, has another witness beyond the word of Scripture. He has an inward testimony, a consciousness within him, which confirms the statements of Holy Scripture in a most convincing manner, and puts the reality of religion beyond the reach of doubt and hesitation.[61]

Thus, faith produces an inward testament to the truth of scriptural revelation, and that faith is the interpersonal dynamic of belief in Christ. This faith, then, is the very ground for the acceptance of revelation, a very important fact which Newman addressed in the correspondence with Charles during this time. However, Newman added an important distinction. This inward witness

> springs from faith, but not at once and immediately from faith, but from faith through holiness; it follows the fruits of faith. Till faith has actually worked, there is no effect on the heart and life, which can constitute an actual witness and voucher to the truth of Scripture.[62]

This final clarification provides several points of note. First, faith *requires* works (holiness), since the internal witness to the truth of revelation follows the fruits of faith. Faith, then, is not mere intellectual assent, which would not move the heart. It is this movement of heart, this interpersonalist change, which constitutes truth's witness. Secondly, this connection of faith and works, when taken in light of the third sermon on justification by faith alone, substantiates Newman's doubts about evangelical presuppositions, doubts which were beginning to increase in early 1825.

In summarizing these six sermons on faith, we find that in Newman's thought, faith is an interpersonal dynamic leading to a new awareness of the loving relationship between God and man, with an affective ground and both implicit and explicit intellectual elements. The nature of this experience is beyond conceptualization and is thus primarily perceived intuitively through the aesthetic or imaginative vision of relationship. A product of this realization is the further insight of the dependence of man on God for His free gift of love which cannot be merited. However, good works are *evidence* of the conversion of the heart, as religious conversion produces moral conversion when faith becomes act, as man realizes that

---

61 Ibid.   62 Ibid.

sanctification is the necessary product of true faith. Faith, when carried out in good works, produces an "internal witness" or intuitive correspondence of the nature of that sanctification-action with the claims of revelation in Scripture. Faith, then, which is the cause of sanctification, is the internal ground of the believer's intuition to accept revelation. And since faith is an interpersonal dynamic of the mystery of self-donating love, the believer is moved to accept the biblical witness of Christ because it is precisely what his own experience has validated.

This series of sermons helped to develop Newman's early theology of faith. Then he preached three others, two in early 1825 and another in early 1826. The last one is included here due to its thematic relevance.[63] Though not as deliberately systematized as the previous group, they are unified by the theme of relationship and thus also bear on our theme of interpersonal relations and dynamics.

THE RELIGIOUS EPISTEMOLOGY TRACK:
Documents 7–9 — The Three Sermons on Relationship

ON APRIL 10, 1825, IN A SERMON ENTITLED "PERSONAL INTER-est in Christ,"[64] Newman's relationship themes of covenant led to important connections between sponsor, child, and baptism:

> A lively faith indeed is our only evidence of regeneration and justification. But both repentance and faith are presupposed to exist in every one who is brought to be baptized. And hence it is that we consider infants capable of the blessings of baptism, because [they] promise them both by their sureties.[65]

Following Sheridan, an analysis of this sermon statement provides Newman's critical new insight:

> The words 'they promise them both by their sureties' is a direct quotation from the Church Catechism, [which] Newman has been carefully studying recently. In it he has found one clue to the answer — for the moment at least — to the problem of how children can derive 'some spiritual benefit' from Baptism, a rite which he now clearly sees was intended by the Lord to be conferred upon them. The answer is the covenant: a self-dedication to God.

---

63   Regarding "On Infant Baptism," Sheridan dates its "projection" as "probably" 1825 from an archival study of Newman's preparation notes for the sermon (Sheridan, *Newman on Justification*, 100). Published also in *John Henry Newman: Sermons 1824-1843*, vol. 1. Both sources list the date of "On Infant Baptism" as March 12, 1826.

64   *John Henry Newman: Sermons 1824–1843*, vol. 5.   65   Ibid., 104.

> [But] how is self-dedication possible for a child? The *Church Catechism* provides the answer: his sponsors do for him what he cannot do for himself. This, then, is why the sincerity of the sponsors' intention is necessary for what we may call the 'validity' of the sacrament. They supply the all-important element: *faith*.[66]

While Newman goes on in this sermon to wrestle with the still unresolved issues of justification and regeneration, the important note is the recurrence of the theme of covenant. Newman takes this to new heights in his connection of the faith of the sponsor with the baptized infant, as the sponsor *gives* his own faith *for* the infant and in doing so *promises* to *foster* that faith. And faith, as we understand it, is loving relationship with God. The sponsor, then, becomes in a sense a surrogate Christ-figure, offering up to God that which the infant cannot, and through this love-act of faith-pledging, the sponsor creates a relationship, through himself, between God and infant. Relationship, then, is the key reality uniting Newman's thought on infant baptism and faith.

In a sermon delivered on May 8, 1825, "John's and Christ's Baptism compared,"[67] Newman continued the theme of covenant relationship and tied it to the early church tradition even while yet maintaining the evangelical position disassociating regeneration from the sacrament:

> It is thro' the sacrament of baptism that they have been admitted into the privilege of regeneration and adoption — though it is too true that numbers receive no ultimate advantage from that holy rite, but live and die unchanged and unrenewed in their hearts, yet as true is it that those who are living in the Spirit had through Baptism a right to that Spirit given and sealed to them. God's mercy may be extended further than it is revealed — but it is sure that it was by baptism that He commanded His apostles to make disciples and admit to the privileges of the kingdom.

Again, three important themes emerge. First, a covenant relationship is established in baptism. Secondly, this relationship creates a *right* to the Spirit, and thirdly, the revelation of Scripture (and hence the tradition of the early Church) affirms this. However, another most telling statement is Newman's claim that the power of the world of the Spirit "may be extended further than it is revealed." Newman would continue to struggle for some time with the implications of this realization.

---

66   Ibid., 104–5.
67   Ibid., 102. Also published in *John Henry Newman: Sermons 1824–1843*, vol. 5.

Newman breaks new ground and reinforces the theme of relationship when he analyzes the important role of the sponsor in baptism: "God acts by instruments; we cannot expect the blessing to descend on children when we fail to do our part." Sheridan gives a valuable interpretation of this passage: "So important is it (the right intention of the sponsor) that it is made a necessary condition for the sacrament to have its effect, viz., the admission of the child into a new covenant relationship with its creator."[68] This role of the sponsor is integral to the effect of the sacrament and mediates the relationship between child and God. This theme is continued and elaborated upon in the third and final sermon in this group.

Regarding the third sermon of this period on baptism, while in Newman's notes there is an outline for a sermon "On Infant Baptism" and, from the context of where it appears, it was probably "projected" about March 1825, its actual preaching was March 12, 1826.[69] The following excerpts from Newman's preparation notes are relevant to our study and indicate an influence on the preceding sermons:

> I. No age specified for Baptism — left them apparently to our discretion. Let us examine.
>
> 1. It is a benefit — the precise advantages — what is meant by being in covenant with God etc.
>
> 2. This is so great, that it is desirable we should possess it as early as possible.
>
> 3. Qu: whether infants can have the benefit? Qu — are conditions required? NO. Explain.
>
> 4. Confirmatory arguments — practice of the early Church, the Jews etc.

Three points are striking here. First, the controlling emphasis of the sermon is "being in covenant with God," or, in other words, relationship. Second, and printed emphatically in large type, is the "NO" answer to the question of required conditions: the covenant is gratuitous. Lastly, tradition serves as precedent, as witness. As Sheridan notes, "Furthermore, whereas, as we have seen, the sermons of the previous year in no way reflected his doubts on baptismal regeneration, this year's sermons now show a marked change in doctrine."[70]

But while the focus of these sermons may be Newman's attempt to resolve the doctrinal issue of baptism, this subject inherently involved the very nature of baptism itself — relationship. Thus, Newman's thought

---

68   Ibid., 103.   69   Ibid., 100.   70   Ibid., 99.

on this doctrine is driven by his vision of the nature of the God-man encounter. Sheridan also notes that "the same themes keep recurring here, both in diary and in his sermons. The covenant idea is the dominant one. . . . Even his attitude toward those with whom he comes in contact is no longer the same,"[71] and he refers to Newman's ordination day diary entry of May 29, which we have previously examined as an example. In other words, following his religious conversion Newman was moving toward a fundamental moral change promoted primarily by the inter-personal influences on his reflection. While his religious conversion was defined as his awareness *that* he was in relationship with an "Other," he was now seeking to rightly identify the primary locus of that encounter, which would result in his moral conversion expressed in its ecclesiastical dimension. However, his awareness at this time also contained a distinctively aesthetic element in his perception, his vision of the God-man covenantal relationship, a form of analogical reasoning from human to divine relationship. Thus we find affective, aesthetic, intellectual, and moral elements present.

The issues of covenant and relationship are the keys to a major advance in his thinking on faith and baptism and how the God-man relationship actually functions. In the sermon "On Infant Baptism,"[72] Newman formalized his thinking on the question:

> It may be said that the promise of the Spirit is made not to all who are baptized, only to those who have repentance and faith. . . . (C)hildren promise repentance and faith by their sponsors in baptism. . . . (T)heir sponsors promise they will do all in their power to lead them to God and will educate them in all the means of grace.[73]

Sheridan concludes that by early 1826, Newman "now connects the imparting of the regenerating Spirit directly and infallibly with Baptism, and decidedly not with the Evangelical act of 'conversion.' By this fact he can no longer be called an Evangelical."[74]

In summarizing these three sermons, we find the key focus is the creation of the covenant offered by God and accepted by man through his response of faith, which produces a moral in addition to a religious change. But through his appreciation for, and vision of, the power of the "unseen" spiritual world, Newman is also able to resolve the issue of the

---

71 Ibid., 101. 72 *John Henry Newman, Sermons 1824–1843*, vol. 1, 172–78.
73 Ibid., 176–77. 74 Sheridan, *Newman on Justification*, 121.

baptism of infants through the principle of instrumentality: the sponsor acts to form a covenant for the infant, freely promising to God the faith which the infant cannot. In so doing, the sponsor performs an act of love, the essence of relationship. Newman's insight clearly possessed not only an affective but also an aesthetic element in his vision of the relationship between God, infant, and sponsor, and the act of faith which unites them. The next sermon, delivered just after the two 1825 sermons on baptism, is Newman's second oldest *Parochial and Plain Sermon*, which contains an important epistemological theme related to our study.

THE RELIGIOUS EPISTEMOLOGY TRACK:
Document 10 — "Secret Faults":
A Sermon on the Affective Ground of Religious Knowledge[75]

THIS DOCUMENT, A COMMENTARY ON PSALM 19:12, WAS DELIV-ered at about the halfway point in Newman's parish ministry and is of primary significance, grounding the source of religious understanding and the subsequent intellectual grasp of doctrine in the heart. This fact, then, supports one of our main contentions, attributing to the heart and its methods the controlling role in grasping the truth of revelation.

> Self-knowledge is a necessary condition for knowing them [Christian doctrines, and] Men [think] that because they are familiar with words, they understand the ideas they stand for. . . . Self-knowledge is at the root of all real religious knowledge.[76]

Newman begins by making a connection between epistemology and truth, as well as addressing a familiar theme, the error of mistaking words for meanings. But how does he justify the assertion? "God speaks to us primarily in our hearts. Self-knowledge is the key to the precepts and doctrines of Scripture."[77] He then goes on to analyze the reasons for man's "secret" or hidden faults, the causes, both conscious and unconscious, of sin: we avoid self-analysis, we are untested, and even our strengths have weaknesses. In fact, the more we examine ourselves, the more weaknesses we find.[78]

A major note is Newman's assertion of the mode of communication of this self-knowledge, the heart. Revelation of Scripture, then, must speak to the heart if it is to produce that new awareness of self which leads to transformation and conversion. In order to discern the truth of Scripture,

---

75   John Henry Newman, *Parochial and Plain Sermons*, vol. 1 (London: Longmans, Green and Co, 1908), 41–56. Preached June 12, 1825. Hereafter PPS.

76   Ibid., 41–42.   77   Ibid., 43.   78   Ibid., 43–49.

and to follow Christ, we must feel the reality of His love and experience the transforming power of this encounter:

> For how can we feel our need of His help, or our dependence on Him, or our debt to Him, or the nature of His gift to us, unless we know ourselves?.... (I)f we cannot follow Him to the height above, or the depth beneath; if we do not in some measure discern the cause and meaning of His sorrows.... If you receive revealed truth merely through the eyes and ears, you believe words, not things; you deceive yourselves.... Without self-knowledge you have no root in yourselves personally.... Truth ... has never been ... more than a form.... They never have had experience of His power and love, because they have never known their own weakness and need.[79]

In this systematic exposition, the religious level expressed affectively ("feel") and the moral level ("follow") are sublated by the intellectual ("discern"), but a major note is that to "feel" presupposes knowledge of an intuitive, non-deductivist kind. This indicates that to "feel," which is an experience of the heart, is also a mode of understanding, and the ultimate ground of these processes is "the experience of His power and love."

This sermon, while treating of such an apparently negative topic as "faults," is actually a major systematic explication of the interpersonal nature of man and his necessary openness to the "Other," so readily revealed in Scripture. In order to find the true self, one must lose the isolated self by opening up to the love of this "Other." Again, the interpersonal dynamics of love and its transformative power are Newman's essential theological insights. Yet Newman retains his evangelical ability to "strike a blow" when he closes the sermon: "God give us all grace to choose the pain of present repentance before the wrath to come!"[80] But we must keep in mind two points: Newman was now in the ninth year of his evangelical phase, and conversion is gradual. The recent death of his father and the many personal experiences with his parishioners were slowly but surely working their effects upon him. He was definitely *changing*. This sermon at the midpoint of his Anglican ministry reflects a theological exposition of those changes, as he asserts that the primacy of interpersonal dynamics and the feeling of the love and power of Christ are the keys to knowing who we really are and what, or Who, we really need. Newman continued this theme of self-knowledge in his next *Parochial and Plain Sermon* of December 18.

---

79 Ibid., 54–55.   80 Ibid., 56.

THE RELIGIOUS EPISTEMOLOGY TRACK:
Document 11 — "*Inward Witness to the Truth of the Gospel*":
A Sermon on the Heart as the Ground of
Knowledge, Obedience, and Conversion[81]

NEWMAN MADE SIGNIFICANT ADVANCES IN THIS SERMON WITH the themes of religious epistemology, morality, and conversion, which are linked, in the final analysis, by the interpersonal experience of faith. Newman opens the sermon on a moral theme and then develops its intellectual implications. Speaking of a hypothetically well-trained religious student, but with undoubted autobiographical implications, he writes:

> They [religious teachers] set me on the way to gain a knowledge of religious truth. . . . They not only taught me, but trained me; they were careful that I should not only know my duty, but do it; they obliged me to obey. . . . This obedience to His commandments has brought me to a clearer knowledge of His truth, than any mere instruction could convey. . . . I have been taught by means of a purified heart, by a changed will.[82]

We find here that knowing follows doing, that doing provides a knowledge which promotes conversion. Thus, the importance of religious instruction lies in its inculcation of conduct. Doctrines are ultimately understood through experience, a theme consistent for Newman concerning the connection of "words" and "facts," of concepts and ideas, to reality.

But then Newman introduced a major new theme which goes to the heart of our study, the importance of the credibility of the teacher in the process of instruction. The pupil accepts the testimony of the teacher and believes it based upon the credibility of the instructor, asserting the primary function of interpersonal relationship in the decision to obey.

> We may sometimes hear men say, "How do you know that the Bible is true? You are told so in Church; your parents believed it; but might they not be mistaken? and if so, you are mistaken also." Now to this objection it may be answered, and very satisfactorily, "Is it then nothing toward convincing us of the truth of the Gospel, that those whom we love best and reverence most believe it? . . . Do we not receive what they tell us in other matters, though we cannot prove the truth of their information?"[83]

---

81 Newman, PPS, vol. viii, 110–23. Preached December 18, 1825.
82 Ibid., 110–11.　　　83 Ibid., 111.

Newman references the interpersonal relationship of love and reverence which is at the heart of belief as the source of accepting the testimony of another. In short, we believe those we love and who we know love us, and this dynamic is the foundation for the acceptance of the content of their instruction. But of special note is Newman's image of the example of teacher, that of the loving parent who teaches from the heart and who is not solely an "intellectual" instructor. Here again is evidence that a key Newman insight is rooted in his own early experience of a loving family. But then while he says that "this would be quite a sufficient answer," he states that he will give another, which also has major implications for our study. "I will show you that the most unlearned Christian may have a very real and substantial argument . . . of the truth of the Gospel, quite independent of the authority of his parents and teachers."[84] The answer, Newman states, is that the *knowing* is in the *doing*: "By obeying the commands of Scripture, we learn that these commands really come from God; by trying we make proof; by doing we come to know."[85] The key to this process lies in the subordination of the self to revelation, which then leads to a knowledge of God. Again, the knowledge is in the doing, or obedience:

> Consider the Bible tells us to be meek, humble, simple-hearted, and teachable. Now, it is plain that humility and teachableness are qualities of mind necessary for arriving at the truth in any subject, and in religious matters as well as others. By obeying Scripture, then, in practicing humility and teachableness, it is evident we are at least in the way to arrive at the knowledge of God.[86]

Submission leads to the discernment of truth, as this

> is the very beginning of wisdom, as Solomon tells us; it leads us to think over things modestly and honestly, to examine patiently, to bear doubt and uncertainty, to wait perseveringly for an increase of light, to be slow to speak, and to deliberate in deciding.[87]

Obeying Scripture, then, leads to religious truth because of the moral qualities it inculcates: teachableness and purity of heart.[88] Then Newman returns to a previous theme, self-knowledge: "Those who try to obey God evidently gain a knowledge of themselves . . . [and this is] the first and principal step towards knowing God."[89] Newman then succinctly and systematically structures the path from obedience to conscience to

---

84 Ibid., 112.   85 Ibid., 112–13.   86 Ibid., 113.   87 Ibid., 114.
88 Ibid., 115.   89 Ibid., 116.

morality to self-knowledge to knowledge of God, and ultimately to the realization of the necessity of conversion:

> For let us suppose a child, under God's blessing, profiting by his teacher's guidance, and trying to do his duty and please God. He will perceive that there is much in him which ought not to be in him.... Conscience ... will become a more powerful and enlightened guide than before.... He will understand and perceive more clearly the distance that exists between his own conduct and thoughts, and perfection.... (H)e will be humbled ... (and) feel, moreover, that even were he admitted into the Divine presence, yet, till his heart be (so to say) made over again, he cannot perfectly enjoy God. This, surely, is the state of self-knowledge.[90]

Newman then closes this section with a most relevant insight as to how this knowledge is realized. It is primarily felt, rather than consciously known, alluding again to the primacy of the heart, or an affective knowing or intuition, in this dynamic process: "I do not mean that all I have been saying will necessarily pass through his mind, and in the same order, or that he will be conscious of it, or be able to speak of it, but that on the whole thus he will feel."[91]

Again, we note the identity of *feeling* and *knowing*, as well as the fact that this describes an *interpersonal* dynamic at the root of the knowing. But Newman takes his analysis even deeper by alluding next to the situation of the "unlearned person" struggling for truth without benefit of religious instructors. What we find is a very relevant correspondence of the natural heart with the revelation of Scripture:

> When, then, even an unlearned person thus trained — from his own heart, from the action of the mind upon itself, (and) ... from an innate though supernatural perception of the great vision of Truth which is external to him (—) reads the declarations and promises of the Gospel, are we to be told that he believes in them merely because he has been bid believe in them? Do we not see he has besides this a something in his own breast which bears a confirming testimony to their truth?[92]

So it is that even the unlearned can perceive the correspondence of the truth of revelation with that of his own experience. This is, then, an intuitive isomorphism, a similarity in form and relations. But what

---

90 Ibid., 116–17.   91 Ibid., 117.   92 Ibid., 117–18.

Newman introduces next expands once again his theological analysis: the reality of mystery.

> He reads that the heart is "deceitful"... that he inherits an evil nature (and) here is a mystery... that it is a hard matter, nay, an impossibility, for us to appease His wrath. Here again is a mystery; but here, too, his conscience anticipates the mystery.[93]

The result, the mystery, is a paradox. On the one hand, there is the undeniable truth of the correspondence of internal feelings with scriptural revelation, yet there is an abyss between the corruptness of human nature and the perfection of God. But the paradox is resolved, the abyss bridged, by the ultimate personal act of the self-donation of Christ. This interpersonal act can convert mystery into belief:

> When he goes on to read that the Son of God has Himself come into the world (and)... died upon the Cross for us, does he not, amid the awful mysteriousness of the doctrine, find those words fulfilled in him which that gracious Saviour uttered, "And I, if I be lifted up from the earth, will draw all men to me?" He cannot choose but believe in Him.[94]

This mystery is the self-donation of love, and this revelation now becomes the primary teacher: "Here, then, I say, [so] he is in one way not taught of men, 'but by the revelation of Jesus Christ.'"[95] Then Newman reaches a methodological conclusion: "And the more he understands his own heart, the more are the Gospel doctrines recommended to his reason."[96] The mysterious revelation of Christ has spoken to, and the words ring true in, his heart. The heart, then, tells the mind this is true and it is "recommended to his reason" by the heart. The interpersonal dynamic felt in the heart is again the foundation for the recommendation of faith. This is, ultimately, a matter of first principles, since for others who do not believe, "You cannot convince them, because you differ in first principles."[97] Moreover, it is clear that these religious truths permeate, necessarily, all levels of our nature; religious, including the affective and the aesthetic, the moral, and the intellectual: "The truths of the Gospel...[are] realized in their own heart and conduct."[98] This leads to Newman's ultimate conclusion, which is of import regarding method: "Human knowledge, though of great power when joined to a pure and

---

93 Ibid., 118–19.   94 Ibid., 119.   95 Ibid.   96 Ibid.

97 Ibid., 122.   98 Ibid.

humble faith, is of no power when opposed to it, and, after all, for the comfort of the individual Christian, it is of little value."[99] Thus, reason without faith compromises, if not contradicts, theological reflection.

One final implication, which will become of great importance later in Newman's conversion experience, is that acceptance of authority is essentially a matter of faith and trust. This leads to an examination of the other track of ecclesiology on which Newman's thought was developing at this time.

THE ECCLESIOLOGICAL TRACK:
Documents 1, 2, and 3 — The Three Church Sermons[100]

SHERIDAN'S ARCHIVAL RESEARCH IS OUR SOURCE FOR THESE three sermons, and they indicate the influence of Butler and Whately on Newman's growing ecclesiastical perspective.[101] The first sermon in this series was preached on November 20, 1825 and contained the theme of covenant, which Newman expanded into an ecclesiological framework.

> The Holy Spirit is given generally to all the visible Church, i.e.,
> to all who are Christians and therefore the covenant . . . is upon
> all who are by baptism admitted into the Christian body. . . .
> To the whole body then of the church is the Spirit given.[102]

Then we see a decisive departure from the evangelical doctrine of the necessity of extraordinary conversion: "God's time is already come, it was the time of baptism. . . . All are invited to Christ through baptism as the means of His grace."[103] Now Newman emphasizes the key advance made in this sermon series: the primacy of the church as the locus of this experience: "How do we become entitled to the gift of Christ's Spirit? We answer, by belonging to the body of His church — and we belong to His church by being baptized into it."[104]

---

99 Ibid., 123.

100 Sheridan, *Newman on Justification*, 113–17. Preached November 20, November 27, and December 4, 1825. All three sermons are published in *John Henry Newman: Sermons 1824–1843*; the first, "Our admission into the church our title to the Holy Spirit" in vol. 5; the second, "On the communion of saints," in vol. 4, and the last, "On the use of the visible church," in vol. 4.

101 "In view of this 'discovery' of the sacramental principle from his reading of Butler, we can better appreciate the significance of three sermons preached toward the end of 1825, in other words, a short while after he had finished reading the *Analogy*. . . . (W)hile the Church's independence was Whately's main concern, his conversations with Newman also had the effect of underlining much of what Newman was reading in Butler on the subject of the Church." Sheridan, *Newman on Justification*, 112–13, 116.

102 Sheridan, *Newman on Justification*, 113.   103 Ibid.   104 Ibid.

Newman closes the sermon by forging a necessary connection between membership in the true church and morality: "Our state was changed at baptism, whether our hearts were changed, our present conduct must declare."[105] Then he asserts the fact that conversion is a gradual process, a critical issue which Hawkins had called to his attention previously, another departure from evangelical thinking:

> Undoubtedly every true Christian has the *principle* of holiness within him, he has the *nature* of godliness. One believer may be better than another, and have made greater advances toward the entire renovation of his heart. But he only differs in *degree* from the other, not in *kind*.[106]

Thus, Newman defined the special route to God: the Spirit is present in the community of the Church, and man enters the Church and encounters the Spirit through baptism. That is not the end, but rather the beginning, of the relationship, the "bottom rung of the ladder," so to speak. The way up the ladder, or deeper into relationship, is through holiness, or good works toward others wrought by loving faith. And by linking communal membership with baptism, Newman achieves not only systematic continuity with his previous sermons but also asserts the continued primacy of interpersonal relations, as evidenced in baptism.

Most notably, the introduction of ecclesiology, especially such a communal interpretation, is a significant departure from the self-oriented, personal religion of evangelicalism.

The second sermon in the series, "On the Communion of Saints," delivered one week later on November 27, provides a unification of several major themes:

> The office of the Holy Spirit is to be considered not only with reference to the growth in grace of individual Christians, but also as regards the edification of the general body of believers. . . . We profess to acknowledge a Holy Catholic Church, that is, a Holy universal church — for catholic means universal. This universal church is not the church of this country, or of that, but of all. It is the general and united company of all believers [for] it embraces all men so far as they are quickened by the Spirit of God, all that in every place call upon the name of Jesus Christ our Lord.[107]

Newman has clearly established his view of the Church as a divine reality transcending denominational or national lines, a theme we have

---

105   Ibid., 114.   106   Ibid.   107   Ibid., 114–15.

seen developing earlier and which will become of increasingly greater importance as his conversion process continued in his search for the true Church. But here he emphasizes the roles of the Spirit and of Christ in that mystical body, with believers as members through faith. Then he goes on to describe the tripartite, interpersonalist, moral essence of this community:

> Yet we must not consider the Holy Spirit as uniting us only to Him. The same Divine Agent also unites us to one another. Not only is our fellowship with the Father and with His Son Jesus Christ, but if we walk in the light as He is in the light we also have fellowship with one another. This is called the communion of saints.[108]

Sheridan aptly summarizes this as "the Communion of Saints effected by the Holy Spirit, produced by means of identity of will and object, and consists in mutual love."[109]

Newman's theology has reached a new plateau in his conception of this communal Church characterized by the ground of faith, mutual love. This comprehensive perspective brings to fruition a number of the elements from his previous sermons. But a final distinction remains — that of the visible and invisible Church, which is the subject of the last sermon in this series, "The Use of the Visible Church," delivered a week later on December 4.[110] The focus of this sermon is the visible church as the ordinary means of grasping revelation, perhaps serving primarily to indicate the presence of another major influence on Newman's thinking at this time. We can readily see that a major advance had occurred in Newman's thinking in these last three sermons. While they certainly relate to the themes of the earlier groups, such as faith and its grounding in love, and the nature of relationship which is at the center of faith, his pneumatology-based ecclesiology is almost a surprising harmonization of these elements. What, then, gave rise to this synthesis? We learn from his diary that on Saturday, June 25, he began reading Joseph Butler's *Analogy of Religion*,[111] and that as late as October 12 he writes that he read "part of Butler's *Analogy*,"[112] indicating that he had not yet finished the work, no doubt due to the constraints of parish duties. However, these last three sermons show the unmistakable effect of Butler's principle of sacramentality, a major intellectual influence on Newman's development. We will review this influence in the next stage of our study, but note it here as an important influence on Newman's changing theological perspective.

---

108 Ibid., 115. 109 Ibid., 114. 110 Ibid., 115.
111 Newman, *Letters and Diaries*, vol. I, 238. 112 Ibid., 262.

SUMMARY OF THE SERMONS OF 1825

IN SUMMARIZING AND CLOSING THIS STAGE OF NEWMAN'S development, we find the year 1825 to be a time when his significant interpersonal experiences were impressing upon him the "real" nature of things. The recent death of his father, the conversion experiences of his parishioners in which he was so intimately involved, his fraternal responsibility for his brother Charles, as well as his friends from Oriel all coalesced, resulting in a sharp clash between Newman's previously held evangelical doctrines and the meaning and import of all these influences, most of which were incompatible with evangelicalism. The fourteen sermons of 1825 which we have examined are a record of Newman's attempt to synthesize these highly charged interpersonal encounters in a comprehensive, intellectual, theological framework.

Commencing his reflections along the track of religious epistemology, the nature of faith was the theme of the series of six sermons in the winter of 1825. Here Newman made major advances in epistemology with significant implications for method. Faith is the awareness of an interpersonal relationship with God, intuitively perceived, a gift of unmerited love, and the evidence of its presence is conversion of the heart expressed in "good works," which are essentially interpersonal acts of love. This interpersonal dynamic of faith leads to an insight of divine truth mediated by revelation. Faith, then, is necessary to grasp the mediative nature of revelation, an insight indicative of the direct influence of analogical reasoning on Newman's theology.

The nature of faith as grounded in relationship leads to Newman's second series of sermons on that subject, overcoming the sharp dualism of evangelical thinking through an analysis of the sacramental nature of relationship as Newman focused on the function of the sponsor in infant baptism. The sponsor's faith, offered up for the infant, creates a tripartite relationship between God, sponsor, and infant, thereby breaching the abyss of dualism through the formation of this "covenant." Newman references early Church tradition as the authoritative witness for the credibility of these conclusions, and we begin to see the emergence of the Church as an element in his theological work.

Thus, Newman synthesized faith and its implications for relationship with the Church's traditional practice of infant baptism. His first *Parochial and Plain Sermon* which we examined develops a theme from the series of sermons on faith: the intuition of the heart is the key to self-knowledge, which in turn is the key to apprehending the truth of revelation. Here

Newman elaborates an important epistemological advance by asserting that intellectual knowledge is grounded in the heart's intuition: the heart informs the head of the truth of scriptural revelation. Man's nature, then, is grounded in the intuitive perception of the heart, essentially an interpersonal experience. We then examined another *Parochial and Plain Sermon*, preached at the close of 1825, which elaborated upon his epistemological framework by grounding religious knowledge in ethical conduct. By *doing* we come to *know*, especially through trusting obedience to loving witnesses of the truth. The primary means by which this is developed is through the mediation of truth by loving teachers, a connection of interpersonal dynamics with the ground of ethical insight. In such manner is religious knowledge attained. Again by analogical reasoning, this experience leads us to see the truth of revelation mediated through the truth of the interpersonal experience. This experience of analogical reasoning is also available to all men "naturally," without the assistance of loving teachers, because man's innate intuition alone can analogize from personal experience to the claims of revelation, in which case revelation itself becomes the teacher: the heart identifies itself in Scripture. Newman again stresses his methodological point in that the heart recommends truth to reason. The epistemological as well as the moral implications of this conclusion are that true knowledge, beyond mere "intellectual" assent, requires an act of faith, a deep, interpersonal, loving encounter which expands the context and field of knowledge, enabling the "experience-revelation analogy" to be made.

Having worked through his thoughts on the interpersonal nature of faith and the grounding of religious truth in the intuitive perception of the heart, Newman made another major advance in the late fall when he preached his series of sermons on ecclesiology, commencing the second track of his reflections. The Church is envisioned as a communal, interpersonal locus of the encounter of the Spirit with man, a community characterized by faith and realized by sharing the love given by God to man with other men, a tripartite, trinitarian-patterned reality. We also see here the direct effects, recently confirmed in Butler, of Newman's analogical reasoning, which assists him in overcoming the evangelical division between the visible and invisible Church: the visible is the instrument for grasping the invisible.

In these fourteen sermons, Newman's primary focus is the nature of faith, conceived as an interpersonal dynamic grounded more deeply in man than the intellect can conceive, but yet validated as true because in a mysterious, supra-logical way, we know it, or feel it, to be so. God, man, Church, the mysteries of revelation, and the moral implications are synthesized, and the evangelical dualism is transcended by the method of analogical reasoning. Superseding the method of mere syllogistic logic, it has its ground in the heart's perception of truth, which is then correlated with experience and revelation. And what is the ultimate basis of this heart-driven method? It is precisely what Newman had written a few years earlier in 1820–1821 in his private notes, which he discovered in 1874 when he was editing his papers: "The reality of conversion — as cutting at the root of doubt, providing a chain between God and the soul (i.e. with every link complete) I know I am right. How do you know it? I know I know. How? I know I know I know &c &c."[113]

This statement summarizes quite succinctly the elements of intuition and knowledge, relationship and faith, and conversion which Newman worked out at length in the sermons of 1825. These were theological fruits of his intellectual reflections on the intuition of his own personal experiences enlightened further by the disclosures of revelation. Let us now note briefly the major influence upon these last sermons of 1825, Butler's *Analogy*, which also had a great impact on all of Newman's future thinking.

STAGE EIGHT:
The Influence of Joseph Butler's Analogy

THE INTELLECTUAL SYNTHESIS BEGINS

A STATEMENT FROM THE INTRODUCTION OF JOSEPH BUTLER'S *Analogy* succinctly summarizes the analogical method of reasoning which Newman adopted in late 1825 and which would have a profound and permanent effect on his theology:

> If there be an analogy, or likeness, between that system of things and dispensation of Providence which revelation informs us of, and that system of things and dispensation of things which experience, together with reason, informs us of, i.e., the known course of nature; this is a presumption that they have both the same author and cause; at least so far as to answer objections against the former being from God, drawn from any thing which is analogical or similar to what is in the latter, which is acknowledged to be from him; for an Author of nature is here supposed.[114]

---

113   Newman, *Autobiographical Writings*, 150.
114   Joseph Butler, *The Analogy of Religion Natural and Revealed, to the Constitution and Course of Nature*, ed. 15 (New York: Mark H. Newman, 1843), 108.

We will continue to see these effects even more than four decades later, as this natural-supernatural framework is a major theme of the *Grammar*. But here in his conclusion Butler interrelates several major elements which have been preoccupations for Newman, the development of which Butler presumably influenced:

> And it is intuitively manifest, that creatures ought to live under a dutiful sense of their Maker; and that justice and charity must be his laws, to creatures whom he has made social, and placed in society. . . . Inattention, among us, to revealed religion, will be found to imply the same dissolute moral temper of mind, as inattention to natural religion.[115]

Here knowledge is linked to intuition, morality is an innate sensibility, and man's nature is essentially interpersonal, as are such "laws" of God as justice and charity. The rejection of this divinely created natural schema, a fact which implies that nature itself is a supernatural manifestation, is due to an "immoral temper of mind" — the very element of predisposition which we have seen Newman criticize, especially in his correspondence with Charles, and then ultimately condemn as irrational and a violation of the mind's own laws of operation.

Newman makes prominent reference to Butler's work in the *Apologia*, referencing it as one of his earliest and major influences, especially for "two points, which are the underlying principles of a great portion of my teaching."[116]

> First, the very idea of an analogy between the separate works of God leads to the conclusion that the system which is of less importance is economically or sacramentally connected with the more momentous system, and of this conclusion the theory, to which I was inclined as a boy, viz. the unreality of material phenomena, is an ultimate resolution.[117]

The sacramental principle, discovered intellectually in Butler, was intuitively perceived in the religious imagination — the *intuition* — of the young Newman in and through the loving security of home life, as we have noted. But when Newman actually discovered Butler is of note. The *Apologia* states that "it was about this date [1823], I suppose, that I read

---

115 Ibid. It is noteworthy that the last chapter of the *Grammar of Assent* is divided into sections entitled "Natural Religion" and "Revealed Religion." Newman devotes several pages to a discussion of Butler and the principle of analogy at the end of the work.
116 Newman, *Apologia*, 30.   117 Ibid.

Bishop Butler's *Analogy*."[118] However, as we have seen, his diary notes an entry of June 25, 1825, "Began Butler's *Analogy*,"[119] and again on October 12 of the same year, "Read part of Butler's *Analogy*."[120] Thus, it appears that "about 1823" is actually the summer and fall of 1825 — *after* the death of his father, while he was heavily engaged in theological correspondence with his new responsibility, Charles, and during the midst of his parish ministry. These personal experiences seem to have been militating for an intelligible context within which they could be rendered intelligible. They were all *parts* but cried out for a synthesis which would both do them all justice while rendering their meaning intellectually comprehensible. Analogical reasoning was the methodological principle which facilitated this synthesis.

In addition to analogy, Newman took another principle from Butler: "Secondly, Butler's doctrine that probability is the guide of life, led me, at least under the teaching to which a few years later I was introduced, to the logical cogency of faith, on which I have written so much."[121]

This principle, when developed further by Keble, will deepen its impression on Newman in years to come. So through Butler we find the beginning of an intellectual synthesis which, when completed, will provide evidence to support a contention of our study: that, for Newman, his religious intuition was grounded in interpersonal love, and that in turn drove his conversion experience, which in turn drove his theological reflection and in the process shaped his method, its presuppositions and sources. We will see this principle again in stage eleven in regard to Newman's developing ecclesiastical theology. Butler's lifelong influence on Newman, as we noted in its appearance in the *Grammar*, will be referenced throughout our study as Newman's conversion experience evolves.

We have already seen how perplexed Newman was by the conversion experiences of his parishioners. The sharp contrast between "unreal" evangelical doctrines and parish reality produced an intellectual dissonance. Newman needed not only an intellectual advance, but a methodological transition as well in order to work out and harmonize these disparate elements. He discovered the first in Butler and created the second by use of the extended article or treatise rather than the sermon. We have already noted that he felt this need to expand and systematize. The parish supplied the context while Butler supplied the method. The result was the *Scripture Miracles* article he authored for the *Encyclopaedia Metropolitana*, Newman's most elaborate theological document to date, which contains keys to his early, and

---

118   Ibid.
120   Ibid., 262.

119   Newman, *Letters and Diaries*, vol. I, 238.
121   Newman, *Letters and Diaries*, vol. I, 30–31.

subsequent, theological development. We now turn to the *Miracles* Essay to examine the effects of Butler on this major stage in Newman's development.

STAGE NINE:
A Methodological Transition — From Sermon to Treatise[122]

THE STRUCTURING OF AFFECTIVITY
THROUGH THE NATURE OF WITNESS

ON MONDAY, JUNE 6, 1825, NEWMAN RECORDED IN HIS DIARY the first note of his work on the miracles of Scripture,[123] and on Saturday, April 29, 1826, he noted: "Sent off parcel containing Essay on Miracles to Smedley."[124] In the nearly eleven months which it took him to complete the essay, five major influences were simultaneously at work: his correspondence with Charles, his parish duties, especially the conversion experiences of parishioners, his extensive theological development through his sermon compositions, the effects of his liberal Oriel associates, and the intellectual impact of Joseph Butler's *Analogy*. These combined influences resulted in a methodological shift in Newman's exposition as he utilized this form for a more elaborate treatment of his theological interests. This treatise was not only a methodological advance for Newman, allowing another context in which to apply his analogical method, but it was also a high point in his theological development, advancing two major premises in support of Scripture miracles: the interpersonal category of witness testimony as the essential factor in evaluating miracle claims, and the innate capacity of the human mind, especially evident in the peasant motif, to grasp these truths of revelation. Another major advance is Newman's application of Butler's second major principle, "probability as the guide of life,"[125] as a philosophical retort to the rationalists' principle of antecedent improbability. We can readily see the continuity of these themes with Newman's previous work, and we now examine the *Miracles* essay for evidence of their further elaboration. Newman devoted fifty-five pages to his two-part essay.

Newman asserts that the core of the credibility of miracles is the nature of the witness on whom the argument for miracles rests. He clearly indicates that this is the major focus of the essay as he begins the final section "On the Direct Evidence for the Christian Miracles" with this reference to belief in personal testimony:

---

122 John Henry Newman, *The Miracles of Scripture Compared with Those Related Elsewhere, As regards their respective Object, Nature, and Evidence* (Glasgow: Bell, and Bain, 1826), 341–97.   123 Newman, *Letters and Diaries*, vol. I, 236.
124 Ibid., 283.   125 Newman, *Apologia*, 30.

> Important as are the inquiries which we have hitherto prosecuted, it is obvious they do not lead to any positive conclusions, whether certain Miraculous accounts are true or not. . . . The quality of the testimony on which the accounts rest can alone determine our *belief* in them.[126]

Newman then specifies two requisites for the credibility of a witness: character and competency.

> The credibility of Testimony arises from the belief we entertain of the character and competency of the witnesses [and] when information is *unexpected*, or *extraordinary*, or improbable, our only means of determining its truth is by considering the credit due to the witnesses.[127]

Moreover, this is a basic epistemological principle: "This is true, not only in the case of Miracles, but when facts of any kind are examined into."[128] This reasserts the earlier theme of our study that belief is an interpersonal dynamic. The credibility of a witness's testimony is judged by the honesty and competency of the witness.[129]

Honesty consists essentially in high moral standards, and Newman specifies six qualities "prejudicial to their character for *honesty*," all of which are moral shortcomings. Competency, on the other hand, consists in having "ascertained the facts which they [the witnesses] attest, or who report *after examination*. . . [for] Miracles require the testimony of eye-witnesses."[130]

In terms of competency, personal experience of a miracle is required due to the nature of the event. But, as with honesty, the personal character of the witness is a crucial element, and Newman lists numerous impediments to good character which compromise or invalidate testimony. But here he introduces a relevant theme bearing on epistemology. Competency is *not* a matter of education. That is, it is not an acquired trait as much as it is innate, in the sense that the human mind is intrinsically capable of perceiving revelation, and thus miracles. The educated person can, in fact, miss the forest for the trees:

> Yet while we reasonably object to gross ignorance or besotted credulity in witnesses for a miraculous story, we must guard against the opposite extreme of requiring the testimony of men of science and general knowledge. Men of philosophical minds are often fond. . . [of] arranging, theorizing, and refining. . . [rather

---

126 Newman, *Miracles*, 386.   127 Ibid., 387.   128 Ibid.
129 Ibid., 389.   130 Ibid., 390.

than] giving a plain statement of facts ... [and] they are insensibly led to *correct* the evidence of their senses with a view to account for the phenomenon (as) they think it *should be*, not as *it is*.[131]

Thus the extremes at both ends are to be avoided. Just as gross ignorance would invalidate testimony, so can a narrow perspective, which may be more subtly present in the method of the "educated" mind, though it is just as compromising. Here Newman unites several major themes, asserting the credibility of witnesses, even uneducated peasants, the innate nature of the human mind, and the analogical perspective of a multi-leveled reality:

> As Miracles differ from other events only when considered *relatively* to a general system, it is obvious that the same persons are competent to attest Miraculous facts who are suitable witnesses of corresponding natural ones. If a peasant's Testimony be admitted to the phenomenon of meteoric stones, he may evidence the fact of an unusual and unaccountable darkness.... To say, that unlearned persons are not judges of the fact of a Miraculous event, is only so far true as all Testimony is fallible and liable to be distorted by prejudice [for even unlearned persons can distinguish] rightly *on the whole* between the effects of nature and those of a power exterior to it.... Practical intelligence is insensibly diffused from class to class.... Here Science has little advantage over common sense; a peasant is quite as certain that a resurrection from the dead is Miraculous as the most able physiologist.[132]

In short, the natural mind, which can apprehend nature, can thus apprehend that which is not of nature and thus has the capacity to grasp the miraculous. Newman then applies this to the ultimate function of the miracle, conversion. If we recall that awareness or apprehension is part of the initial religious stage of conversion, and then follow Newman's analogical argument for the apprehension of an external order and the relationship of the physical and the moral orders and its Governor, we can readily see how the divine message contained in the miracle of revelation, grounded in the interpersonal dynamic of the credibility of witness, ultimately causes the conversion of those who believe the miracle's witness. The links between religious conversion, with its affective and aesthetic elements, and moral conversion, and analogical versus strictly logical perception are forged by means of interpersonal dynamics. And again, Newman references the early Church members, specifically the

---

131 Ibid., 392.   132 Ibid., 392–93.

Apostles and their converts, as the chief examples of this dynamic of miracle witness-conversion:

> The original witnesses of our Saviour's Miracles were very far from a dull or ignorant race.... The conviction wrought in the minds of these men was no bare and indolent assent to facts which they might have thought antecedently probable or not improbable, but a conversion in principles and mode of life [and] ... the practical nature of the belief produced proving that it was founded on examination of the Miracles.[133]

Conversion is, as we have seen, rooted in the heart, and here Newman makes the fundamental connection of witness, a form of interpersonal dynamic, with conversion. Both are in fact grounded in an act of faith, which was previously determined to be basically interpersonal. Thus, we find further evidence here that Newman's theology is essentially interpersonalist. Then in closing the essay Newman alludes to an ecclesiological theme also linked to conversion:

> Here the evidence for the Scripture Miracles is unique. In other cases the previous system has supported the Miracles, but here the Miracles introduced and upheld the system. The Christian Miracles in particular were received on their own merits; and the admission of them became the turning point in the creed and life of the witnesses.... The Apostles went out of their way to debar any one from the Christian Church who did not believe them as well as themselves... (by) excluding from their fellowship of suffering any who did not formally assent as a necessary condition of admittance and first article of faith, to one of the most stupendous of all the Miracles, their Master's resurrection from the dead.... It may even be said, that if the single fact of the Resurrection be established, quite enough will have been proved for delivering all the Miracles of Scripture.[134]

Thus, Newman closes this article, his most significant single theological document to date, by uniting conversion, witness, church, miracles, and faith, all of which are interpersonal experiences. This, then, is the ground of his theology, intellectually influenced by the effects of Butler's analogical method and probability principle but also driven by his personal experiences as son, curate, brother, friend, and pupil. These last two factors note the effect of his Oriel influences, which had a marked effect on the "logic" of the

---

133   Ibid., 393.   134   Ibid., 394–96.

treatise, one of its fundamental characteristics and the source of an increasing extremism, due to these "liberalizing" tendencies, which Newman himself will soon realize and which we will examine at the close of this chapter.

However, in regard to this article, many years later Newman noted that the general positions taken in the essay attained further development in the areas of intellectual certitude and ecclesiological implications:

> The main difference between my Essay on Miracles in 1826 and my essay in 1842 (on Ecclesiastical Miracles) is this: that in 1826 I considered that Miracles were sharply divided into two classes, those which were to be received, and those which were to be rejected; whereas in 1842 I saw that they were to be regarded according to their greater or less probability, which was in some cases sufficient to create certitude about them, in other cases only belief or opinion.
>
> Moreover, the argument from Analogy, on which the view of the question was founded, suggested something to me besides, in recommendation of the Ecclesiastical Miracles. It fastened itself upon the theory of Church History, which I had learned as a boy from Joseph Milner. It is Milner's doctrine, that upon the visible Church come down from above, at certain intervals, large and temporary Effusions of divine grace.[135]

These comments indicate that Newman's "intellectual synthesis" had only just begun. In that light, we now move on to the next major stage in Newman's development during this period, evidenced by two major sermons delivered shortly after the completion of the *Miracles* essay, which are termed "theological sermons" because they address substantially theological rather than strictly or primarily pastoral issues.

STAGE TEN:
The Continuing Synthesis —
Two "Theological Sermons" of the Period

"THE PHILOSOPHICAL TEMPER, FIRST ENJOINED BY THE GOSPELS"[136]

WE FIND IN THIS DOCUMENT, PREACHED JUST A LITTLE MORE than two months after the completion of the *Miracles* essay, Newman's attempt to synthesize numerous major themes.

---

135   Newman, *Apologia*, 40.
136   Newman, *Fifteen Sermons*, 1–15. Preached July 2, 1826.

He argues, first, for the complementarity of reason and revelation, since both are grounded in the same larger system, and then for the moral basis of the scientific, reasoning mind, both of which he addressed in the *Miracles* study. Thirdly, he takes up the question of method in the pursuit of truth: the outcome of investigation is a product of the method employed, which raises the issue of method to the moral level. We have seen this debated in his correspondence with Charles. But what is proper method, and how is it learned? Discipline teaches method and, correlated with Scriptural revelation, it imparts the requisite qualities of humility and teachableness, themes of his *Parochial and Plain Sermons*. At the close Newman returns to his present interest, analogy, attributing the error of scientific method to the rejection of revelation and the subsequent unnatural separation of the two orders, the physical and the moral. The solution lies in early religious training for the inculcation of a proper understanding of the relationship of the two orders, again a previous theme. But for our purposes, the key theme emerges in Newman's assertion that Christianity is the first religion to teach the necessity of revelation for philosophy and that Christianity, by means of its moral requisites, promotes universal good and brotherhood — interpersonal elements.

The primary point of this sermon is that Christianity is interpersonal in nature. If knowledge and morality are best advanced by Christianity, then its nature must be observed, and its nature is interpersonal dynamics: "It was Christianity which first brought into play on the field of the world the principles of charity, generosity, disregard of self and country, in the prospect of the universal good."[137] All of these qualities are moral and are terms which imply a receiver of the act, performed for the good of the other, even if not for the benefit of the doer. This is the interpersonal essence of Christianity, establishing the norm for the religion. What is the great danger to Christianity? It is the spirit of separatism, of religion from reason: "There is much danger lest the philosophical school should be found to separate from the Christian Church. And this evil has in a measure befallen us."[138] And what is the safeguard? "That it does not increase, we must look to that early religious training, to which [all] persons [should] be submitted."[139] Returning again to a major theme of the *Parochial and Plain Sermon*, Newman asserts the interpersonal nature of religious experience through the office of teacher, which, as we have seen in his case, is the loving, believing parent.

This sermon is not only a major synthesis of numerous previous themes, but it primarily highlights the interpersonal nature of Christianity which correlates with the intellectual apprehension of truth. It is a

---

137 Ibid., 10.   138 Ibid., 14.   139 Ibid., 14–15.

direction-marker in Newman's development as the realities of tradition and the Church are now moving into view as primary factors, indicating the influence of Whately and Hawkins. But perhaps it is better said that these realities are moving *back* into view, recollecting that the period of evangelicalism caused a temporary absorption with self and private religion, which was always at odds with Newman's intuition and his prior and most seminal influence, the warmth of love radiating from the religious-inspired hearts of home. Let us turn now to the second of our "theological sermons" which involves a treatment of method and morality.

"HOLINESS NECESSARY FOR FUTURE BLESSEDNESS" [140]— THE MORAL AND SALVIFIC IMPLICATIONS OF ANALOGICAL REASONING

THIS SERMON, A COMMENTARY ON HEBREWS 12:14 — "HOLINESS, without which no man shall see the Lord"—was preached the month after the previous *Oxford University Sermon* and integrates several major themes by means of analogical reasoning, displaying again the effects of Butler's work. This major document from the period incorporates numerous themes: the relationship of the physical and heavenly worlds, morality and the nature and necessity of holiness, conversion, the Church, and interpersonal dynamics at the center of the process:

> This text (is) . . . a chief truth of religion in a few words (for) it is declared in one form or other in every part of Scripture. . . . The whole history of redemption, the covenant of mercy in all its parts and provisions, attests the necessity of holiness in order to salvation. . . . [It is] some awful irreversible law in the nature of things and the inscrutable determination of the Divine Will.[141]

Here the moral order, holiness, is linked by the structure of reality to the physical order, but only by the interpersonal category of grace, even though the ultimate nature of this relationship remains shrouded in mystery to the human mind:

> A way has been opened through God's grace for his salvation, without being informed why that way, and not another way, was chosen by Divine Wisdom. Eternal life is "the gift of God". . . . He may prescribe . . . (its) terms. . . . He had determined holiness to be the way of life.[142]

---

140 Newman, PPS, vol. i, 5–13. Preached August 1826.   141 Ibid., 5.
142 Ibid., 5–6.

That holiness is the way to eternal life is a content of revelation. *Why* it is so is the mysterious content of the will of God. But for our purposes we find in the opening pages of the sermon, first, the insight of the analogical method which perceives the interrelationship of the physical and moral orders, and then the interpersonal dynamic at the core of the process by which man achieves salvation: the "gift" of eternal life is essentially an interpersonal act, and its reception is qualified by the requirement of, in essence, the same behavior: holiness being essentially an interpersonal, moral act or state. Thus, the key insight here is the analogical reasoning, not only by which Newman integrates the two orders of existence, but also by which he interrelates the beings on each level: the graciousness of God requires the graciousness of men to others.

Newman then turns from the function of holiness to a description of what it is, and this is best rendered in his description of the *unholy* person, who is isolated, self-centered, and in essence *unrelated*: "A mind contented with itself [and] an isolated being [who] could not *bear* the face of the Living God [for he would say] 'Let us alone! What have we to do with thee?'"[143]

We once again see the personalist root of Newman's thought regarding the very nature of our being and its dynamism. But is there an earthly manifestation of this post-earthly level of existence? For Newman, it is the Church. "Heaven then is not like this world; I will say what it is much more like — a *church* [for] here we hear solely and entirely of *God*."[144] Church, then, is the mysterious nexus of God and man promoting reciprocal selfless relationship, which is the essence of holiness. Its antithesis, which drives man from God, Church, and others "is a moral malady which disorders the inward sight and taste; and no man labouring under it is in a condition to enjoy what Scripture calls 'the fulness of joy in God's presence.'"[145]

Newman adds a traditional evangelical perspective to the definition of holiness as "inward separation from the world,"[146] and follows with a succinct contrast of moral states and levels of existence: "Heaven would be hell to an irreligious man."[147] In summation of the first part of the sermon, Newman concludes that "holiness is . . . the condition for our admission into heaven [and] necessary from the very nature of things."[148] In this statement he has synthesized much of what has preceded in this study.

Following this conclusion, though, he offers much evidence in support of our personalist theme as the heart of his theology:

---

143 Ibid., 8.   144 Ibid., 7.   145 Ibid., 8–9.   146 Ibid., 8.
147 Ibid., 9.   148 Ibid., 8.

> Now then I will mention two important truths which seem
> to follow from what has been said: 1. If a certain character
> of mind, a certain state of the heart and affections, be neces-
> sary for entering heaven, our *actions* will avail for our salva-
> tion. . . . Good works . . . [are] required . . . [because] they are the
> means [of] . . . strengthening and showing forth that holy prin-
> ciple which God implants in the heart.[149]

Newman's second truth concerns our major theme, conversion, and
its relation to holiness: "No one is able to prepare himself for heaven,
that is, make himself holy, in a short time; [for] is not holiness the result
of many patient, repeated efforts after obedience, gradually working on
us, and first modifying and then changing our hearts?"[150] Returning to
themes developed in previous sermons, Newman recalls that obedience
and effort, over time, change the heart, or convert it. But true obedience is
not legalistic in that it includes the affective, interpersonalistic dimension,
which becomes apparent when as he describes those who separate the two,
"that their obedience, so to call it, has been a matter of course, in which
the heart has had no part."[151]

In closing, Newman adds a final note supporting our interpersonalist
theme by relating change, or conversion, to the Spirit's gift of Itself within
us, a theme of immanence which we have seen before and will see again,
especially in his *Lectures on Justification* treating of the Indwelling of God:

> While we thus labour to mold our hearts after the pattern of the
> holiness of our Heavenly Father . . . [We] are not left to ourselves,
> but that the Holy Ghost is graciously present within us, and
> enables us to triumph over, and to change our own minds.[152]

This document advances but reshapes evangelical doctrine, tracing the
necessity of morality from the design of human nature, an insight obfus-
cated by the myopic vision of self-absorption, and in the process providing
evidence to support the contention that interpersonalist dynamics are at
the core of his theology.

We have already noted the effect of Whately and Hawkins on Newman's
thought in regard to the Church and tradition, respectively, and we now
turn to several documents from 1826 and 1827 which show the ascendancy
of these elements in Newman's developing theology. He was now on the
brink of a major transition highlighted by his emerging ecclesiological
perspective driven by his personalist intuition and intellectual insights. His
new vision of the Church is evidence of the aesthetic element in his theology.

---

149 Ibid., 9–10   150 Ibid., 10–11.   151 Ibid., 12.   152 Ibid., 13.

STAGE ELEVEN:
From Evangelicalism to Church

FROM PERSONAL TO COMMUNAL RELIGION

IN 1826 AND 1827, NEWMAN PRODUCED TWO OTHER DOCUMENTS which indicate his continuing separation from evangelicalism through the issue of baptismal regeneration and his new image of the Church as community. While turning away from evangelical self-absorption, Newman was turning toward the reality of the Church reconceptualized as the requisite milieu for personal salvation. This amounted to a growing realization of the primacy of the interpersonal, communal, social nature of salvation.

On November 19, Newman delivered a sermon "On the One, Catholic, and Apostolic Church,"[153] espousing his "branch theory" highlighting the social nature of the Church and his vision of the unity of its visible and invisible dimensions. This is further evidence of Newman's developing realization of the relational nature of the plan of salvation, and it clearly indicates, in the imagery of the Church, an aesthetic element. The unmistakable influence of Butler's sacramental principle and analogical reasoning is evident.

Then in February of 1827, Newman composed his "Paper on Infant Baptism."[154] By synthesizing the arguments from tradition (practicing and thus advocating the rite), Scripture (which has no evidence opposing it), and theology (baptism is regeneration!), he underscored the social aspect of God's covenant with man. He is now in opposition to the evangelical requirement of moral conduct as a necessity for regeneration, which is now replaced by the eye of faith, which "sees" baptism for the supernatural reality that it truly is — a sacrament, a mystery of divine-human interrelationship which is beyond the merit of man, and dependent upon the grace of God.

In Sheridan's words, "In his rejection of the Evangelicals' subjective criterion of membership in favor of the objective criterion of baptism, we see Newman's definitive break with Evangelicalism."[155]

In one sense this is *where* we see Newman's break, but *how* and *why* are the foci of this study. It was a return, in realization, to the religious intuition of his early life which had conditioned his religious conversion of 1816, wherein he experienced his first major consciousness of the presence of God, a reality embedded deep in his religious intuition and fostered through his home-life relationships. From 1816 until 1827, he sought to

---

153 Sheridan, *Newman on Justification*, 125–27. Also published in John Henry Newman, *Sermons 1824–1843*, vol. iv.   154 Ibid., 127–32.   155 Ibid., 134.

sustain the truth of that conversion experience by means of decisions which best approximated that intuition. For years he believed this was through the doctrines of evangelicalism. However, his advancing intellect, with liberalizing influences, and personal experiences gradually led him to see the flaws in the evangelical system as he wrestled to bring both into a perspective consistent with his conversion experience. The record shows that his theological development was inseparable from, and dependent upon, his conversion-state, which was struggling to align itself with his religious intuition. The issue of infant baptism provided a theological corrective, while the increasing emphasis on, and image of, the nature of the Church as the mediator and facilitator of man's personal relationship with God was moving into primary view.

These two documents, the first dealing with ecclesiology and the second with the nature of baptism as relationship, correspond to the more explicit "two-track" method of Newman's thinking, especially during his intellectual conversion stage regarding religious epistemology and faith on the one hand and ecclesiology on the other — the two tracks of Newman's developing theological method. However, one last but important element, again bringing his mind and heart into unavoidable conflict, was yet to come during this phase, and for this we turn to the final stage of this period.

STAGE TWELVE:
The Growing Breach with Liberalism and the Catalyst of Suffering

IN 1827 NEWMAN'S INTELLECTUAL PENDULUM REBOUNDED from the excesses of evangelicalism to the mentality of his liberal Oriel influences. However, three major experiences caused him to change direction once again.

First, on April 15, 1827, Newman delivered a sermon, "On the Mediatorial Kingdom of Christ,"[156] with which Whately, Hawkins, and Blanco White all found fault. The *Letters and Diaries* record Newman's memo, written the next month on May 13, reacting to their criticisms. The value of this document lies in its revelation of Newman's concern for the *method* underlying his presentation and the critiques, indicative of a difference which would eventually become a breach between his more encompassing "aesthetic" method and the more narrow "partial view" of his colleagues. Nonetheless, he had eased into their intellectual camp more than he

---

156   Published in *John Henry Newman: Sermons 1824–1843*, vol. i.

realized, as he wrote that "Arianism (in the main) is true — so is Sabellianism — so (in its first outline) Unitarianism — but none the *whole* truth — yet for *particular purposes*, according to particular occasions, it may be useful to represent the Catholic doctrine in this or that form."[157] Newman was beginning to prefer the "strength" of reason to the wonder of the mysteries. The slide from Evangelicalism into Liberalism, however, is an almost natural progression which Newman would later critique, as Ian Ker has pointed out: "He blamed the rise of Evangelicalism on the 'lowminded' Latitudinarians or liberal Anglicans of the 18th century 'who had robbed the Church of all her more beautiful characteristics.'"[158]

During this year, several other events transpired which reinforced the primacy which interpersonal relations continued to play in Newman's life. In September he read Keble's *Christian Year*, a work which he referenced in the *Apologia* as "an original note (and) a new music," and "religious teaching so deep, so pure, so beautiful."[159] Keble, he noted, reaffirmed the two major principles he had learned from Butler, those of sacrament and probability as the guide of life. However, these were "recast in the creative mind of my new master."[160] Keble was to provide Newman's intellect with the key to the assent of faith, which identified with Newman's childhood religious intuition: the argument from personality. However, the following personal encounters are further evidence that affectivity clearly dominated Newman's focus during this period. In late 1827, Newman was forced to choose between Keble and his mentor from his early days at Oriel, Hawkins, as they were both in competition for the vacated Provost's post. Newman's *Letters and Diaries* recounts a dramatically revealing letter which Newman wrote to Keble regarding his decision to support Hawkins. Despite the intellectual influence on Newman of Keble's *Christian Year* and the awe in which Newman had held Keble from his earliest days at Oxford, *Newman based his support for Hawkins on the depth and quality of their interpersonal relationship.* Keble was perceived by Newman in his early Oriel days as aloof and disapproving because of Newman's evangelical tendencies, and this feeling of personal rejection, a matter of affectivity, was Newman's primary decision-making factor: "I have lived more with Hawkins and therefore understand him more (whereas) I have had few opportunities of your society,"[161] he wrote. Almost forty years later Newman recollected,

---

157   Newman, *Letters and Diaries*, vol. II, 15–16.
158   Ker, *Newman and the Fullness of Christianity*, 37.
159   Newman, *Apologia*, 36.   160   Ibid., 37.
161   Newman, *Letters and Diaries*, vol. II, 44–45. Letter dated December 19, 1827.

"I knew Hawkins, and he had taken me up while Keble had fought shy of me."[162] To his friend Pusey he wrote more than fifty years later, "I voted for Hawkins from my great affection and admiration. I have never ceased to love him to this day."[163] And so it was that the heart of Newman was to inform his decision between Keble and Hawkins, a decision once again grounded in the heart, the locus of religious intuition.

The primacy of Newman's heart, however, was being seriously jeopardized by the encroaching liberal effects of Oriel. Just as evangelicalism's excesses had exacerbated his feelings, liberalism did the same for his intellect. But less than three weeks after Newman wrote Keble, he suffered a blow which traumatized both mind and heart.

On January 4, 1828, while at dinner and sitting next to her oldest brother, Newman's youngest sister Mary became ill and retired abruptly. By the next evening she was dead.[164]

Characteristically, Newman's diary sparsely notes the tragedy: "Wednesday 5 January 1828 We lost my sister Mary suddenly."[165] A year later to the day, Newman could only write: "Monday 5 January a well known day."[166]

Much like the brief entry recording the death of his father in 1824, Newman's writing indicates a constant theme: words fail to express the reality. Mary was an extraordinarily special person to Newman. Her innocence and joyful spirit gave her an other-worldly, almost sacramental quality which once caused him to comment in his journal: "It must have been in October, 1826 that, as I looked at her, beautiful as she was, I seemed to say to myself, not so much 'Will you live?' as 'How strange that you are still alive!'"[167] He wrote Robert Wilberforce just a week after her death:

> She was gifted with that singular sweetness and affectionateness of temper that she lived in an ideal world of happiness, the very sight of which made others happy. All that happened to her she could change into something bright and smiling like herself — all events, all persons (almost) she loved and delighted in — and thus, having lived in this world as if it were heaven, before she discovered (as she must in time) that it was not so, she has been translated into the real and substantial heaven of God.[168]

---

162   Ibid., 44, n. 1. Letter dated April 9, 1866.
163   Ibid., 45, n. 1. Letter dated June 29, 1882.
164   Ward, *Young Mr. Newman*, 149–51.
165   Newman, *Letters and Diaries*, vol. II, 47.
166   Ibid., 113.
167   Newman, *Autobiographical Writings*, 213.
168   Newman, *Letters and Diaries*, vol. II, 148–50.

During the ensuing year we find some twenty letters exchanged between Newman, his mother, and his sisters sharing the grief of Mary's loss. But once again it is in his artistic work that we find him able to reveal his deepest feelings. In his *Verses on Various Occasions* he wrote two poems: *Consolations in Bereavement*, written in April, just three months after her death, and another, *A Picture*, written in August of that year. Both are records of extreme personal grief:

> Death came and went: that so thy image might
> Our yearning hearts possess,
> Associate with all pleasant thoughts and bright,
> With youth and loveliness;
> Sorrow can claim,
> Mary, nor lot nor part in thy soft soothing name.

> Joy of sad hearts, and light of downcast eyes!
> Dearest thou art enshrined
> In all thy fragrance in our memories;
> For we must ever find
> Bare thought of thee
> Freshen this weary life, while weary life shall be.
> Oxford.   *April, 1828.*[169]

> Such was she then; and such she is,
> Shrined in each mourner's breast;
> Such shall she be, and more than this,
> In promised glory blest;
>
> When in due lines her Saviour dear
> His scattered saints shall range,
> And knit in love souls parted here,
> Where cloud is none, nor change.
> Oxford.   *August, 1828.*[170]

Six months later he again wrote Robert Wilberforce about the extreme pain he was suffering over Mary's loss. He "cannot reconcile my imagination to the fact," he cries, as the grief "almost overpowers me during the day."[171] The experience jolted and redirected Newman, who "was beginning to prefer intellectual excellence to moral; I was drifting in the

---

169 John Henry Newman, *Verses on Various Occasions* (London: Longmans, Green, and Co, 1910), 28.

170 Ibid., 32.   171 Newman, *Letters and Diaries*, vol. II, 82.

direction of the Liberalism of the day. I was rudely awakened from my dream at the end of 1827 by two great blows — illness and bereavement."[172]

In terms of the perspective of this study, Meriol Trevor provides an excellent interpretation of the influence of Mary's death on Newman:

> But how could Mary's death or a nervous collapse [which he suffered the previous November] affect this intellectual drift? The loss of Mary revived all Newman's sense of the overpowering reality of the unseen world [and] . . . a sense of the reality of the supernatural world so vivid as to make the world of nature seem veil; such a spirit and imagination could never fit itself into the world of common-sense morality and intellectual abstraction inhabited by Whately and his friends of the liberal school. Mary's going out of his world strengthened Newman's sense of exile in it, which success had been undermining, [and her death] did for him what falling in love does for some people — opened his heart to a more sensitive sympathy with others. . . . [Thus] the pain can be fruitful.[173]

In closing this chapter, we note that Mary's death brought Newman home, in a real sense, to the source of his religious intuition — interpersonal love. Though by this time far beyond the little boy described at the outset of the *Apologia*, the grief which the mature Newman recounts in his poems and correspondence of 1828 was grounded in the reality of that early religious intuition, watered and fed by the loving relations of family life which first taught him the reality of the unseen world and the love of God through Christ through Church through Scripture, all through love of, and in, family. This was the source of Newman's first and religious conversion, a coming to fruition of his affective and aesthetic conversions of heart and imagination, which his subsequent moral and intellectual development sometimes approximated, sometimes distorted. This religious conversion was the foundation which would provide the ground for his theological development. His theological writing of this period yields evidence to the effect that his theology and method were shaped by, and served to understand and express, his conversion experience and its relationship to his innate religious intuition. The tension of this relationship would produce the potential for deeper and more enlightening conversions.

---

172   Newman, *Apologia*, 33.

173   Meriol Trevor, *Newman: The Pillar of the Cloud* (New York, Macmillan, 1962), 75.

CONCLUSION: PART I

NEWMAN'S RELIGIOUS CONVERSION
AND OUR CONVERSION HYPOTHESIS

THE LITERATURE FROM THIS PERIOD PROVIDES AN INSIGHT into how Newman's theology evolved, which is not readily revealed by an examination of the theological documents—sermons, Encyclopaedia articles, essays, the *Apologia*. It is only by studying those sources in the light of the personal correspondence, private journals and diaries, and artistic works that we come to a fuller, more accurate understanding of the forces which drove Newman's theology. In so doing we are faithful to a principle of Newman himself, that all "theorizing" must be rooted in concrete experience. By means of this method we learn that Newman's theology was inspired by the concrete religious experiences of early family life, including his baptism into the Church as a community and a loving family. This was not merely an "institutional ceremony," as he would later rail against those who would interpret it as such. The developments and strengths of Newman's religious intuition, quickened by these experiences, led to his first major conversion in 1816, in which the religious dimension of conversion dominated—the acute awareness of the presence of a loving God, occasioning his *Apologia* statement of that event: "The thought of two and two only absolute and luminously self-evident beings, myself and my Creator . . . [as] I only thought of the mercy to myself."[174]

Two relevant notes are in order regarding this statement. First, Newman also stated that it was rooted in his previously developed religious intuition, which included his sense of the "unseen" world even prior to this realization. The conversion was "in the direction of those childish imaginations which I have already mentioned, viz. in isolating me from the objects which surround me, in confirming me in the mistrust of the reality of material phenomena."[175] From his own words, then, we can trace Newman's religious conversion of 1816 back to his religious intuition, which included affective and aesthetic elements.

But another important fact is disclosed in the same paragraph, previously stated above. Along with his religious conversion through the acute awareness of God, he *intellectually* accepted the

> doctrine of final perseverance. I received it at once, and believed
> that the inward conversion of which I was conscious (and of
> which I still am more certain than that I have hands and feet,)

---

174 Newman, *Apologia*, 25–26.   175 Ibid., 25.

would last into the next life, and that I was elected into eternal glory [and] I retained it till the age of twenty-one, when it gradually faded away.[176]

Along with this religious conversion, which was sustained throughout his life, Newman also accepted the *intellectual* doctrines of evangelicalism. Here the multifaceted nature of conversion is revealed. The intellectual dimension, with its moral effects, would approximate but eventually distort Newman's interpretation of his religious intuition. Thus, by 1820, as he has stated, he was "miserable" and growing "graver and graver," breaking down in November of that year. But by 1821, the intellectual dimension was shifting, and for the remainder of this phase of his development he struggled to harmonize his intellectual grasp of his religious conversion. This emerged in 1827–28 with his rejection of the "unreal" basis of evangelicalism, when the vision of the Church, with all of its relational and familial overtones, began to assume a more prominent role in his theology. Thus it was that his moral sense was jolted as he realized a dichotomy between it and his religious intuition. We see at this stage the emergence of his notion of conscience, inseparably wed to innate religious intuition. Having grappled for years with the reality *that* a loving God was present in his life, he confronted the moral dilemma of *what* earthly form revealed this presence. He was on his way to resolving the initial problem that, though it may begin in the realization of the innate personal relationship with God through religious intuition, it must extend beyond the isolated enclosures of self-absorbed evangelicalism to the more social and communal relationship, the Church. He began to discern the pattern or analogy that a fuller understanding of the revelation of Christ and its promise of salvation lies in the self-donating, communal reality of which the Church is the *right* witness. Thus, with the emergence of his Church as a primary factor in his development toward the close of this period, he was on the verge of moving from the predominance of religious conversion to moral conversion in his assumption that his Church of England was indeed the locus in, through, and by which religious conversion thrives and continues to reveal the truths which alone satisfy the human thirst for God. This he believed, and thus began the second phase, dominated by his quest for a moral solution.

A study of the documents of this period reveals that his method, the sources he chose to employ — and exclude — in his work, and what presuppositions and beliefs governed those choices were a result of, and were

---

176　Ibid.

dependent upon, his conversion-state, an interrelationship of religious intuition and awareness, intellectual discernment, and moral commitment, all grounded in an essentially interpersonalist dynamic relationship with God and others through the Church.

However, the intellectual dimension at this period of his religious conversion, though subordinate to the affective and aesthetic elements, was itself dominated by its evangelical beginning which emphasized the one-to-one relationship of the self to God, epitomized by Edward Copleston's[177] comment to the young Newman whom he encountered alone in solitary reflection in 1823: "Numquàm minus solus, quàm cùm solus."[178] Rendered as "Never less alone than when alone," Cicero's axiom expressed the two dominant elements of this phase of Newman's conversion journey. The aesthetic image of a very personal relationship with God is a trait of his "first conversion," which is accompanied by the redirection and expansion of his affections, so well developed in his family milieu, from the visible world to that newfound Source of affection, God. But the axiom also contains the implication of a self-centeredness in that turn toward God, which is a trademark of the evangelical as well as the liberal intellectualism he acquired during this period, and the accompanying morality. However, his first *Oxford University Sermon*, on the other hand, clearly identified the essential moral element at the heart of Christianity's interpersonalist essence. But in this tension we find the dissonance between head and heart, affections and intellect.

The identification of the presence of these elements is consistent with our conversion hypothesis, as are the various parts of the conversion process: the developmental aspects of complementarity, simultaneity, reciprocity, and especially primacy of the element which dominated this period, the affective. Also present in the aesthetic element are its religious, Christian, and imaginative dimensions, as that element operates to promote "movement toward harmonization." The functions of conversion are present in varying degrees: the vision of the Transcendent Other, change of heart, knowledge of being loved, faith, and reciprocal forgiveness. The effects of conversion as well are identifiable: the ongoing experience of the Transcendent Other, sacramental insight and experience, and obedience. Lastly, the sources of conversion as graced, personal, and relational are also present.

---

177 Edward Copleston (1776–1849) was Provost of Oriel from 1814–1827, when he became bishop of Llandaff. Ker, *Apologia*, 525, n. 56.

178 Newman, *Apologia*, 34; Cicero, *Officiis*, III. I, 1; *De Re Publica* I, xvii, 27.

However, our hypothesis also indicates that conversion is ongoing and as such is open to change. Newman was on the verge of a second conversion, from the primacy of affectivity and aesthetic elements to the primacy of moral ones in his search for the right locus of the God-man encounter. As that element of conversion changes, it has a reciprocal effect on all other dimensions. We will now seek evidence of that occurrence in the second major phase of Newman's conversion journey.

PART II

Exoriare, Aliquis![1]

("Arise, avenger!")

NEWMAN'S MORAL CONVERSION
1828–1833

---

1 Newman, *Apologia*, 49: "Virgil, *Aeneid*, iv. 625. From Dido's great soliloquy on hearing that Aeneas had deserted her."

CHAPTER THREE

Newman's Moral Conversion:
1828–1833

INTRODUCTION

IN THIS CHAPTER, I ASSERT THAT FROM 1828 THROUGH MID-
1833, Newman experienced a prolonged search for the right ecclesiastical
expression of his religious conversion, which culminated in the vision
of a reformed Church of England. En route to that decision two forces
were at work, both rooted in his affectivity. First, there was his drive to
willfulness, expressed in the Oriel tuition controversy, and his coming to
terms with that drive while seriously ill in Sicily in 1833, the immediate
catalyst, in large part, of his moral conversion. For these events we study
his personal papers—letters, diaries, journals, poems—which, as noted in
Part I, reveal Newman the person. Then there is Newman the theologian,
expressed in his formal writings of the period, which disclose an incisive,
analytical, and synthesizing intellect which, ironically, could conceive of
the fullness of the Christian heart, yet he himself, at this stage, could not
attain it. This internal conflict was due to a willful temperament which
caused an affective, aesthetic, and intellectual dissonance that provides
evidence to support several major tenets of our thesis: the nature, structure, and dynamics of conversion, affectivity as the root of all subsequent
conversions and the ground of both intellectual and moral conversion;
the developmental principles which indicate that each element of conversion—affective, aesthetic, intellectual, and moral—mutually influences
the others; that Christian temper, a disposition of affectivity characterized
by self-denial and concern for the other, is essential for affective conversion; that the aesthetic element functions to synthesize the other elements;
and lastly, that loving personal relationships of home and friends are the
human instruments by which Newman first learned of, and then through
which he submitted to, that Transcendent Other. In the end, for Newman
the Church was modeled on home and friendship.

Structurally, first we examine Newman's dispute with Edward Hawkins
over the function of the Oriel tutor, revealing Newman's willful and anti-
authoritarian nature. Then we examine several examples of his theology

of the time: (1) his series of sermons on the liturgy relevant to the nature and dynamics of conversion and the importance of submission of the will; (2) two sermons which thematically introduce (3) *The Arians of the Fourth Century*, characterized by its analysis of the temper, or affective disposition, as the ground of heresy and conversion; and (4) a key sermon on affectivity, grounding Christian love in interpersonal relationships of home and friendship, from which is formed the Church-home analogy. We close with an analysis of the rejection of Rome and the crisis in Sicily, when he came to a point of spiritual catharsis resulting in the realization of his own willful temper. This insight produced a moral conversion to a vision of a reformed Church of England as the true *locus* where, as the heir to the apostolic Church, he believed he experienced, albeit temporarily, the true earthly encounter with that Transcendent Other.

STAGE ONE: The Oriel Tuition Controversy

THE FOLLOWING SECTION EXAMINES AN EVENT IMPORTANT FOR our understanding of Newman: the controversy of the Oriel tuition. Having commenced in late 1828 under veiled circumstances, the issue flared into the open in the spring of 1830 as Newman and two tutor colleagues, dissatisfied with the traditional system of instruction and having implemented their own reforms, refused to submit to the authority of the provost, Edward Hawkins, who ordered them to return to the old system. Given the substantial influence which Hawkins had had on Newman, this controversy, and particularly Newman's behavior toward Hawkins, provide insight into the dynamics of Newman's affective, moral, and intellectual state, leading to the conclusion that his self-interested willfulness shaped his moral and intellectual development, causing an internal dissonance reflected externally in his relations with Hawkins. More than forty significant documents provide a thorough record of the history of the controversy, with Newman and Hawkins exchanging eighteen letters. The controversy highlights the particular dimension of Newman which is the focus of the chapter—his willfulness and his problem with submission to authority, and the influence this affective drive had on his intellectual and moral development.

> Friday 20 January arranging accounts etc. Principal returned — arranged (i.e. in Provost's absence) that I should be Tutor at Oriel beginning Easter Term.[2]
> Saturday 8 April Term commenced — settled the lectures.[3]

---

2   Newman, *Letters and Diaries*, vol. I, 272.   3   Ibid., 282.

These 1826 diary entries indicate the beginning of Newman's tenure as tutor, which lasted until the spring of 1831. Newman appeared to have carried out his duties in the usual manner, as he described the official method of instruction and the function of the tutor:

> It had been usual to draw it up [the academic schedule and assignments] without any regard to the existing relations between each Tutor and his own pupils, all the Tutors becoming lecturers for the occasion to all the Undergraduates, whether their pupils or not, and taking this or that class by rotation, indiscriminately, whomsoever it was composed of.[4]

Newman functioned as a tutor in this manner for about three years, even though he had expressed personal dissatisfaction with it.[5] By 1829, two new tutors had been appointed, Robert I. Wilberforce and Hurrell Froude, who were equally dissatisfied with the prevailing system. Together they formulated a plan for a new method of instruction, but perhaps most important was their judgment that they could take it upon themselves to implement the changes without consultation with, or approval from, Edward Hawkins. The senior tutor, Joseph Dornford, confirmed this in a letter to Newman dated December 26, 1828: "And now for your new plan of Lecturing. . . . I perfectly agree with you here that we are not at all bound to consult anyone but ourselves on the adoption of it."[6] The need for the change centered in the concept of the tutor. Newman described his pastoral vision of the office as superior to the impersonal concept of the traditional system:

> The principle now introduced was that each Tutor should in the first place be responsible and consult for his own pupils, should determine what subjects they ought to have lectures in, and should have the first choice as to taking those lectures themselves, and should in the second place consult for the pupils of others. Otherwise they considered the office of Tutor became that of a mere lecturer, and that teaching was not an act of personal intercourse, but an ungenial and donnish form.[7]

---

4 Newman, *Autobiographical Writings*, 99. 5 Ibid., 89.
6 Newman, *Letters and Diaries*, vol. II, 206–7.
7 Newman, *Autobiographical Writings*, 99. The essential point of the controversy rested in Newman's concept of the tutor as primarily responsible for the individual students assigned to him by the provost, especially in regard to their spiritual formation. Thus, he considered the function chiefly pastoral. This resulted in the tutorial system reforms, which allowed the tutors to separate their pupils from the rest of the student body for selected instruction. Hawkins, on the other hand, believed that this pastoral function

Underscoring the clandestine nature of their strategy was a letter Newman wrote to his friend Samuel Rickards on February 6, 1829: "The most
important and far-reaching improvement has been commenced this term:
a radical alteration (not *apparent* on the published list) of the lecture system . . . but we do not wish these to be talked about."[8]

Almost fifty years after these events Newman summarized the communication between Hawkins and the tutors on the issue, an account which
does not appear to support his claim that Hawkins was aware of their plan:

> Accordingly in the beginning of 1829 they resolved on acting
> on their own view of the matter. They did not formally com-
> municate to the Provost what they were doing, though he was
> from the first made aware of it. . . . Their Lecture Table . . . was
> a matter for their own discretion.[9]

From these sources it is clear that the tutors were not completely forthright with Hawkins regarding their changes. When Hawkins became aware
that the changes had been implemented, and without his consent, the
dispute over the tutor's function escalated into one of authority: whose
right was it to define the role of the tutor? Before we examine the ensuing
confrontation, we should note another significant event that occurred
prior to that conflict, which caused the beginning of the rift between
Newman and Hawkins and which may very well have turned Newman
against Hawkins prior to the tutor controversy.

In the winter of 1829, just as the tutors were implementing their
reforms, Newman entered into "the first public event I have been concerned in,"[10] his involvement in the Peel affair. Sir Robert Peel represented
the university in Parliament. For many years he opposed Catholic emanci-
pation in Ireland, but in 1829, as a leader of the Tory government which
feared that a civil war was brewing in Ireland, he reversed his position. As
a result, two issues arose. First, there was his political inconsistency, and
then there was the issue of Church-state relations. Peel's opponents, who
included the rebellious tutors, thought the University seat in Parliament

---

could be accomplished within the traditional academic framework which assigned
students indiscriminately to tutors for instruction. This seemed to subordinate the
pastoral function to the academic. Newman believed such discrimination aided in
the fulfillment of the tutor's primary function, the pastoral, while Hawkins held that
it worked to the detriment of the student body as a whole.

8 Newman, *Letters and Diaries*, vol. II, 118.

9 Newman, *Autobiographical Writings*, 99–100.

10 Newman, *Letters and Diaries*, vol. II, 125.

should represent the school's underlying Church sentiments without appearing to be merely an extension of government policy. Peel resigned his seat over the controversy but decided to seek re-election in February of 1829, persuaded to do so by a group of supporters, one of whom was Hawkins. In letters to his sisters Newman berated the actions of the "meddling Provost," an indication of the beginning of the rift between them:

> Peel resigned. . . . This was a great thing, and among others I exerted myself to gain it. Unluckily our meddling Provost just then returned from London, where . . . he suddenly formed a committee . . . for Peel.[11]
>
> Well then — take the case — Mr Peel changes his mind on the Catholic question, resigns his seat — and . . . meddling individuals put him up again.[12]

Peel was defeated, and Newman wrote his mother that "we have achieved a glorious victory."[13]

The tuition revisions and the Peel affair set the stage for confrontation, which began in the fall of 1829. The tutors, however, were able to operate for almost a year before Hawkins got wind of their changes. The first report of confrontation over the revisions occurred through an entry in Newman's diary on November 2, 1829: "Monday 2 November important College meeting with the Provost (*doubtless about Lecture List*)."[14]

The very same day Newman wrote to the senior tutor, Dornford, with his summary of the situation. This letter contains several major facts which run through the entire controversy: Hawkins's clear objection to the tutors' reforms and the value he saw in the traditional system, the high esteem in which he held the tutors, and the very personal, affective nature of his communications. These facts are valuable in that the correspondence exchanged during the controversy indicates that it was Hawkins who consistently separated the questions of policy, authority, and personal relationship, while Newman did not. As the following correspondence reveals, it is Hawkins who appeared temperate and open, whereas Newman was intemperate, rude, and eventually insubordinate. Ultimately it was this tendency to willfulness which led Newman to challenge Hawkins boldly and even to extend his reforms beyond their initial state, deliberately provoking Hawkins. Newman bluntly refused to submit to Hawkins's authority, which became the major issue of the controversy. As evidence of the above, we begin with Hawkins's letter to Dornford, who, upon

---

11 Ibid., 122. 12 Ibid., 127. 13 Ibid., 125. 14 Ibid., 172.

learning of the tutors' reforms, apparently did not disclose to Hawkins his prior knowledge and assent to the reforms:

> I thought it absolutely requisite before matters got worse to strike a blow at the mischievous system which you described of three tutors conferring together upon alternatives to our System without consulting the Dean or the Provost. . . . I venture to say [the old system] has worked well in practice as well as appeared good in conversation or theory. . . . [As for] the value of such men as your three colleagues . . . I have a very high value for them all three . . . [a] high estimate of every one.[15]

Hawkins both valued his tutor staff and opposed their reforms. However, a restrained Hawkins took no other action for almost six months, at which time he requested from Newman details of the reforms. Newman replied in a brief note: "It is founded on these principles — that the tutors have full authority to arrange their lectures together without consulting the Provost."[16] Newman then gave Hawkins a breakdown of the new lecture structure. The very same day, Hawkins replied in a lengthy letter again praising the tutors and quite conciliatory in nature, although he reiterated his support for the old system and especially noted his duty and authority to maintain it: "I was extremely sorry to find . . . that there had been so much irritation and misunderstanding." So that his personal feelings might be understood, Hawkins then quoted from his letter to Dornford which praised the tutors, but ultimately upheld the old system:

> Whatever I have expressed on the system of Tuition in Oriel, I have considered myself discharging a very *imperative* but *most painful* duty. I considered myself officially bound to maintain the *principles of a system*, which I knew I had received, and which I was persuaded was in the main correct. That such a system had been delivered into my hands was a *fact* on which I could scarcely be mistaken.

Not only was his position clear, but his temper was moderate and open-minded while asserting the authority of his office. He closed by implying to Newman that the tutors ought to consider submitting to his authority:

> [I] only feared lest conscientious scruples should drive men whom I valued and esteemed to resignation of their offices — a thing evidently possible — though I conceived it absolutely

---

15 Ibid., 201.   16 Ibid., 208. Dated April 28, 1830.

unnecessary, because there was another course equally natural and horourable for them to pursue.[17]

Newman replied the following day in a brief letter notable on several counts. It offered Newman's evidence as to why the old system did not work adequately, but even more importantly it began by referencing a problem which is a key to the significance of the entire tuition dispute for Newman: "Why cannot a Provost speak to his Fellows except through an organ?"[18] Newman was vexed at what he perceived as Hawkins's impersonal manner of communicating. Recalling that his personal intercourse with Hawkins was the very factor which caused Newman to support Hawkins over Keble for the Provostship, this note of personal affront was more significant than it might at first have appeared, as subsequent correspondence reveals. This document is the first evidence that it was the personal dimension of the issue, or rather the impersonal dimension, as Newman saw it, that played a major role in Newman's reaction to Hawkins. In addition to the intellectual question of which system was better, Newman was affected by his perception of the manner in which Hawkins dealt with him.

This document is also noteworthy on another count. Nowhere in Newman's reply does he respond to the question of Hawkins's authority. Thus, when taken as a whole, we find a personally offended Newman who ignored the authority of his superior, while contesting his judgment. A last observation is that Newman's tone is blunt and confrontational in sharp contrast to the conciliatory nature of Hawkins.

Hawkins's response, written the same day, supports this analysis. Hawkins takes up the sole issue of Newman's personal affront, even leaving aside the question of the system itself:

> I abstain of course from making any remarks at present upon the notes on the Lecture-system which you have sent me.... But really you are not doing me justice in your question 'Why cannot a Provost speak to his Fellows except thro' an organ?'[19]

Hawkins goes on to object to Newman's perception of personal affront. The entire purpose of his note was his concern for Newman's feelings. But just a few days later, Newman, in another letter to a friend, implied that he had no intention of changing his position.[20]

The controversy took another turn at this time, revealed in two letters which Edward Copleston, the former provost, sent to Hawkins, both dated

---

17 Ibid., 209–10.   18 Ibid., 211.   19 Ibid., 212.   20 Ibid., 213.

May 3, 1830.[21] Copleston was critical of Newman's temper and attitude toward authority, while noting Hawkins's "equanimity":

> The Head may reasonably require to have a control in the system of education. Nothing indeed can be plainer than that this is the spirit of the Oriel Statutes. . . . I must here add by way of parenthesis, that the style and tone of Newman's letter to you is by no means in accordance with that spirit. . . . From what you say of Newman's religious views, I fear he is impracticable. . . . Newman ought to acknowledge that he has been wrong in practicing this reserve towards you. It is utterly inconsistent with every liberal view of the relation in which he stands to the Head of his college. . . . You have suggested, I think, the best method. . . . The tutors must recognize a very different sort of relation between them and the Provost. . . . Adieu. . . . You are better able than I am to contend with annoyances, and I have often admired and envied your equanimity under them.

Not only does Copleston support Hawkins's authority in opposition to Newman's position, but he also alludes to a most important aspect for our study: Newman's temperament. It is this intemperance on Newman's part which led him to confront Hawkins's authority and then to go to even greater lengths to provoke Hawkins. But Copleston's letters provide one other element, the strategic insight which Hawkins will use against the tutors:

> The Provost might retaliate by refusing admission to pupils under them. . . . I might be led, if the opposition was obstinate, to support my own views, by assigning pupils, as they enter, to those tutors who agreed with me. This I should signify beforehand. . . . Still my main hope of success in correcting these aberrations would rest on the manifest intention of the Statutes they have sworn to obey.

Hawkins soon implemented this advice. But again we note Copleston's reference to authority and the obligation of the tutors to so comply. Newman, however, would have none of this, nor would Froude and Wilberforce. However, Dornford wrote to Newman, on the same day that Copleston wrote to Hawkins, on this very issue of authority: "I never meant to say that we were justified in continuing a course which the Provost had distinctly condemned."[22] For Dornford, the principle of authority superseded the merits of the respective systems.

---

21   Ibid., 213–15.   22   Ibid., 215.

Two days later Newman wrote an insubordinate letter to Hawkins interpreting Hawkins's position to imply that the tutors were merely assistants to the senior tutor. Newman stated that he will "comply with your call to retire . . . on the understanding that . . . to all but to the Senior Tutor the name, not of *Tutor*, but of *Assistant Tutor*, shall be assigned. . . . Without such an engagement, I do not feel obliged to resign."[23] Hawkins replied to Newman's provocation the same day:

> I would rather, indeed, consider the letter *unread*, for it is written under much, I might also say entire, misconception of my views. . . . Let me once more beg you to do every thing in your power to stifle and utterly remove all feelings of this kind. I am confident they ought not to exist at all. And I fully expect that when you cease to think yourself slighted or harshly treated in the matter (and assuredly I never intended to do either,) you will view the whole subject in a very different light.[24]

Again we note contrasting tempers in this exchange. Newman extended the parameters of the controversy and did so in a confrontational manner, whereas Hawkins continued to refrain from the immediate issue to attend to Newman's misconceptions and feelings, which he did in a most conciliatory manner.

Following this, Hawkins drafted to Newman the longest and most comprehensive letter in all of the controversy's correspondence.[25] Again, this document can be examined for both its temper and its argument. As for temper, Hawkins held to his concern for their relationship and Newman's feelings, a concern which Hawkins felt was not reciprocated:

> I wish to *write* to you on this subject . . . lest not only my meaning but my *sentiments* should be misconceived. . . . It was with very great pain that . . . I learned from you that I had wounded your feelings and offended you. . . . You told me so very distinctly. . . . Had you not . . . I must have inferred it from the tone of the notes which you have subsequently sent me, which did not become a Fellow writing to the Provost, much less one friend addressing another.

Again, Hawkins was most concerned with their relationship and Newman's feelings, after which he then made his argument. In summary, he claimed he was not informed that the new system was actually in operation, that Newman's objectives could be attained within the old system, and that

---

23   Ibid., 216. Dated May 5, 1830.   24   Ibid.   25   Ibid., 228–33.

the new system was in fact dangerous: "You have carried a good principle (I mean that of Private Tuition) too far...[and] in the end occasion very serious mischief." But then Hawkins identified a principle of Newman's behavior most relevant to our study:

> I regret to find that you have also grounded your own system upon a Theory of your independence with respect to your colleagues and the Provost alike inconsistent . . . both with the practice of the College and with the spirit of the Statutes even of the university and much more with the spirit of our own Statutes.

Newman's independent streak was rightly noted by Hawkins, and it was this tendency which precluded Newman from responding to Hawkins's conciliatory overtures. In refusing to do so, Newman was also challenging tradition, as Hawkins thus bolstered his case:

> I may indeed be not unreasonably prejudiced in favor of a system to which I have been accustomed for many years, and which has been cordially approved of by men of no mean judgment in such matters and of considerable experience. . . . I ask nothing more than that you will not at once, but *gradually*, return to the old system.

Despite Hawkins's lengthy letter of some 3700 words and his advisement that Newman take his time to respond, Newman fired off a relatively short letter the very next day, with a characteristic display of temper: "I have been surprised and pained on finding you expressing your persuasion more than once that I am acting under the influence of personal mortification or other absurd uneasiness." Newman then counter-argued: "My chief private objection to the system you propose, is, that . . . the mere lecturing required of me would be incompatible . . . to that more useful private instruction," then adding the key point for our analysis, his refusal to submit to Hawkins's authority: "This to me is an *insuperable objection*. . . . I cannot act on the *principles* of your system . . . and . . . shall feel myself bound in honor to retire at the end of this term."[26]

Newman then escalated his confrontation with Hawkins in a letter just a few days later. Hawkins had rejected Newman's distinction of tutor and assistant tutors in his major letter. But in a display of provocative one-upmanship, Newman used Hawkins's non-distinction of function as support for his own argument for personal independent authority:[27]

---

26 Ibid., 233–34.   27 Ibid., 237–38. Dated June 13, 1830.

> I gather from the circumstance of your declining to make any dis-
> tinction in the Calendar between the Senior and other Tutors that
> I am (as I always thought) a Tutor in an University sense . . . and
> that my pupils are really committed to me . . . because they are
> committed to no one else.

Newman seemed insistent on flying in the face of Hawkins's authority, as he constructed a position inviting, or demanding, that Hawkins
terminate him as tutor by insisting on functioning as tutor as he saw
fit until Hawkins removed him: "Retire of my own accord, I think I
never can. . . . I cannot justify myself in withdrawing . . . without such
an exprest [sic] wish to that effect on your part." In his closing remarks
Newman revealed a willfulness and commitment to self-interest, indicative
of his temper during this period:

> Whereas I cannot change my system of tuition, I must with-
> draw. . . [not] voluntarily. . . . [but] at your desire . . . by making
> your will a condition of my retaining it. . . . I have no reason to
> be dissatisfied with my own conduct, and see the whole matter in
> too clear a light to expect any change in my opinion. . . . Strong
> views necessarily lead to strong resolves which no words can
> soften down . . . which at first sight may have appeared to you
> harsh or uncalled for.

On the same day that Newman wrote this letter he received another
quite lengthy one from Hawkins,[28] who was, while conciliatory in tone,
adamant in his position, and he introduced several new elements into the
controversy. First, he attributed Newman's state of mind to overwork, an
interpretation which irked Newman. But then, after yet another detailed
review of the controversy, he cited the core factor in Newman's behavior
most relevant to our study: Newman's refusal to submit to authority. "But
it appears to me, my dear Newman, that, under a deep sense of your own
responsibility, you have a little forgotten that of the Provost." Hawkins
then implemented the alternative suggested earlier by Copleston: "If
you cannot comply with my earnest desire, I shall not feel justified in
committing any other pupil to your care."

In sharp contrast to Newman, Hawkins's tone throughout was conciliatory even when issuing his ultimatum, and his sincerity was reinforced
by his lengthy and well-reasoned analysis of all the issues. This considerate
temper softened his use of authority:

---

28   Ibid., 239–41.

> I endeavoured to place myself in your situation, and therefore
> asked nothing of you which you might not honourably and, as I
> should hope, conscientiously concede. . . . My earnest wish and
> desire was to retain you in office . . . and I was most reluctant
> to allude to any other course which might have anything of the
> air of a threat.

Two days later Newman responded with characteristic intransigence as
well as a rejection of Hawkins's rationale for his state of mind: "I cannot
alter my views . . . tho' to refer to my over work and depression of spirits
is . . . quite foreign to the purpose."[29]

The controversy which flared into the open in April was now, by mid-
June, a crisis of authority versus personal judgment, and it was clear
that Newman would not submit, but rather would continue his "rebel-
lion." Shortly thereafter, on July 9, Newman composed a memorandum
summarizing the controversy,[30] a document most noteworthy on three
major points: (1) Newman's belief in the subordination of public to
private relations with students; (2) the necessarily related question of
Hawkins's authority; and lastly and perhaps most importantly, (3) the
very interpersonal issues which really disturbed Newman, causing what
we may call an affective aversion to Hawkins.

> That the *private relation was subordinate to the public* (the particular
> to the general, if it must be worded) *this* was the principle which
> I never heard of as belonging to Oriel, and to which I have con-
> sistently been opposed.
>   On a second meeting he took an opportunity of telling
> us . . . that we must *obey him* and it was not open to *consult* him.

Newman's affective aversion to Hawkins was interwoven in the argument "in principle," but this predisposition on Newman's part appeared
to underlie and thus affect his intellectual analysis. This was most clear
when Newman himself linked his deliberate failure to expressly inform
Hawkins of the changes in the tuition system to Hawkins's perceived
temper and his conduct in the Peel affair:

> And I will own, I did not force myself to effect an interview with
> him for the purpose of communicating to him beforehand my
> intentions, because I knew it was the habit of his mind to raise
> difficulties in every subject proposed to him — because I had

---

29 Ibid., 241–42.   30 Ibid., 246–50.

long considered him an eminently impractical man. . . . It was but a month or two after our first adapting our modified plan, that he put an end to all frank and easy intercourse between himself and us by his conduct on the occasion of Mr. Peel's resignation of the representation; of which I shall say nothing.

The second count of Newman's disaffection with Hawkins arose from Newman's affront with what he perceived as the provost's impersonal mode of communicating, referenced earlier but reiterated in this memo, underscoring its importance to Newman:

Yet I could not help feeling there *was a fault somewhere* in his arrangements, that he should need express his feelings to us *through an organ,* an expedient only resorted to when necessary and often (as in this case) failing its purpose. I thought and think that a Provost ought to be on those easy terms of intercourse with his Fellows as to supersede the necessity of such second-best contrivances; and, in thanking him by note for his kind expressions of regard I attempted in a few words to hint this feeling of mine to him.

Could this be the same Hawkins whom Newman had, only some 30 months earlier, supported for provost over the esteemed Keble? Newman's own explanation to Keble at that time contrasts sharply with his perception of, and feelings toward, Hawkins now:

His general views so agree with my own, his practical notions, religious opinions, and habits of thinking, that I feel vividly and powerfully the advantages the College would gain when governed by one who pursuing ends to which I cordially approve would bring to the work powers of mind to which I have long looked up with great admiration.[31]

Just a month after this letter Newman wrote the provost-to-be Hawkins a letter on the tuition system, which is likewise ironic due to his current feelings: "As to your remarks about Tutorial arrangements, I confess I have a very strong opinion, but still not one which I will venture to oppose to your judgment."[32]

Returning to the current memorandum, we find that Newman closed it by an admission that Hawkins was perhaps not as closed-minded as previously indicated: "At the Provost's request, (who by this time showed

---

31   Ibid., 44.   32   Ibid., 51.

himself more reasonable than he had hitherto done < been>) I had sent him the particulars of our lecture-system for his inspection."[33]

What conclusions can be drawn from this memo, especially in light of Newman's previous feelings for Hawkins? By Newman's own linking of events, Hawkins's politics offended him and caused him to be less than frank about the tuition reforms. Newman seemed to force his rationalization for this when he says he "long considered him an eminently impractical man," in light of his letter to Keble wherein he specifically called Hawkins "practical." Not only did Newman personalize their political differences, he then was personally offended by Hawkins's mode of communicating, "through an organ," an affront which Newman referenced on several occasions during the controversy. When taken in light of Newman's admission that Hawkins was "more reasonable" than he thought previously, it can be concluded that Newman's personal desires, both politically and academically, led him to vilify Hawkins, an act which seems unjustified by the correspondence record. This vilification, motivated by Newman's willful temperament, led him to his ultimate decision to defy Hawkins's authority.

During the controversy Newman wrote a letter to S. L. Pope on another subject, his resignation from the Bible Society, of interest in that it referenced Newman's analysis of the principle of action. This he believed was based in affectivity, which is also the ground of intellect, and which can be applied most appropriately to our analysis of Newman's own actions:

> Practical matters cannot be defended by argument, or explained on paper — (i.e. except accidentally) — they are determined by the ἦθος (ethos) of the agent — who (whether he be correct or not) still adopts his measures, not on a process of reasoning which words will do justice to, but on feeling, on the dictates of an internal unproduceable sense.[34]

This epistemological/psychological analysis, not directly connected to the controversy at hand, reads like an ironic description of Newman's own conduct. Here he found grounds for an affective base to action, the realm of an unproduceable sense manifest in feeling, a description of intuition, underlying the level of the reasonable, practical mind. The academic principles of the tuition dispute may have been practical indeed, but we can detect an affective base beneath Newman's reasoning which

---

33   Ibid., 249.   34   Ibid., 264.

produced an equally affectively grounded result: a defiance of Hawkins's authority. Shortly we will see how this same principle emerged as the major factor in Newman's analysis of the temper of heresy and its anti-authoritarian spirit; but having gathered this insight from Newman, let us return to the tuition controversy.

The dispute simmered until the fall of that year when Newman and Hawkins again exchanged correspondence. On October 12, Newman reasserted his independence and refusal to submit to Hawkins's authority in a characteristically curt and rude note:

> I have rights which I dare not voluntarily relinquish.
>
> In sending you this note, I have no thought of giving either you or myself the trouble of a renewal of our correspondence — I merely wish to recall to your mind the view which I had occasion to lay before you in my letters of last term.[35]

Hawkins replied the same day with his characteristic open-minded restraint:

> My dear Newman,
>
> Perhaps we had better not mix up discussions on the tuition with the business of this week.... Afterwards, I shall be most happy to talk with you or write to you, as far at least as we may agree in thinking it likely that discussion can lead to any beneficial results.[36]

Newman responded immediately, spurning Hawkins's openness:

> My dear Provost,
>
> I am sorry you should think I want discussions, or (if not so) imply the possibility of their being of service. I beg you will entirely believe they are quite unavailing: Next week I shall be out of Oxford.[37]

Less than two weeks later, Newman wrote to the senior tutor, Dornford, that he clearly had no intention of complying with Hawkins's directive, but would continue on with his own system:

> My dear Dean,
>
> I am concerned to find that you should think that I still continue connected with the College system of tuition. Of course I have arranged my Pupil's lectures for myself.[38]

---

35   Ibid., 294.   36   Ibid.   37   Ibid., 295.   38   Ibid., 296.

Hawkins, having been informed of Newman's actions by Dornford, immediately responded, upset that Newman was making further changes in the tuition system in open defiance of his authority. Even though Hawkins noted that this letter was never sent, it provides further specific evidence that Newman was now the antagonist in the conflict:

> The system of absolute separation of the Pupils which I presume you mean to adopt by the terms of this note . . . excludes even that degree of communication of the pupils which your plan of 'Public Lectures' admitted. Could I expect then that . . . you intended to go still further, and shut out all communication with the other Tutors, or with the Dean?[39]

Newman's next letter is again sharp:

> I think it best . . . to transcribe part of my letter of June 14. . . . 'If you leave me Tutor in the way you propose, it is not under the idea of my probably changing my mind . . . or . . . of my engaging any Tutor's pupils but my own.'[40]

Hawkins responded a few days later noting Newman's previous one sentence as a weak justification for his actions: "I had certainly forgotten the sentence you quote. . . . I did entertain hopes of your changing your mind. . . . And I regret exceedingly to find those hopes fading away more and more."[41]

A few days later Newman wrote one of his sharpest letters:

> By withdrawing my supply of Pupils you are gradually destroying my interest in the College. . . . I do not feel bound to make those concessions in . . . Public Lectures, which I was ever willing to make when I was recognized by you as one of the College Tutors. . . . Under the circumstances I feel no call on me to undertake even for a time a disagreeable service. . . . It is a great satisfaction to me to feel that I have from the beginning done all in my power to convince you I was as much in earnest as yourself.[42]

After this, Hawkins made no further attempts to convince Newman to remain as tutor, nor did he take any other action against Newman. The situation continued on into the spring of 1831, with no record of correspondence. Finally, in April 1831, Newman wrote to Hawkins, officially resigning as tutor: "I have resolved at the end of this term . . . to

---

39 Ibid., 297.   40 Ibid., 336.   41 Ibid., 298.   42 Ibid., 300–1.

surrender into your hands the few pupils you then will have left to me."[43] Hawkins responded in a most kind-hearted note, even allowing Newman to continue his private instruction of his remaining pupils if he so chose:

> I shall never cease to regret you have thought it necessary to abandon a situation in which you were so eminently useful.... I certainly can have no wish that you should give them up, if you should be able and willing to give them the benefit of your instruction.[44]

A diary entry for June 11, 1831 reads: "Second day of Collections (examinations) — finished *my* men — and so ends my Tutors work!"[45] As for the two other rebellious tutors, Froude and Wilberforce, the former resigned his position about four months before Newman's resignation, while the latter did so three months after Newman. The tutor controversy was now closed.[46]

THE POST-CONTROVERSY EVIDENCE

THREE LETTERS WHICH NEWMAN WROTE SHORTLY AFTER THESE events provide further evidence as to his temper during this period. To his sister Harriett he wrote these words of self-description: "If times are troublous, Oxford will want hot-headed men, and such I mean to be."[47]

Shortly thereafter, he wrote to his friend Rickards on a number of subjects, including the tuition dispute, and his interpretation of Hawkins is noteworthy:

> As to the business of the Tuition, there was no help for it. The Provost wished to take from me all discretionary power. It was impossible I could walk, look, talk, and eat by rule, and a bad rule, as I thought. It was not a question of degree, but from the first he would hear of no compromise; so there was an end of it.[48]

Then, in the final relevant letter of the controversy, Newman wrote another Oriel Fellow, William James. This final interpretation of the events

---

43 Ibid., 326.   44 Ibid.   45 Ibid., 324.

46 Two major effects of the tutorial controversy, ironically, were the Oxford Movement and Newman's study of the Fathers: "Humanly speaking," Newman later reflected, the Tractarian Movement "never would have been, had he not been deprived of his Tutorship, or had Keble, not Hawkins, been Provost." Ker, *John Henry Newman: A Biography*, 41. Also, "The incident was important because it . . . enabled him to get on with his reading of the Fathers," which would have extremely significant effects. Sheridan Gilley, *Newman and His Age* (Westminster: Christian Classics, 1990), 74.

47 Newman, *Letters and Diaries*, vol. II, 367.   48 Ibid., 370–72.

implied that Hawkins had been less than forthright and refused to discuss the question, engaged in false flattery, and was rash. Regarding his pupils, Newman held that

> I thought that I, to whom they were confided, was to be the ultimate judge in what lectures they were placed. . . . Some discretionary power . . . was essential to my having any moral influence or control over my Pupils. . . . The Provost . . . refused to discuss the question. . . . I have proof that he was not careful to master my view. . . . He did not believe me, and attempted to flatter me, as if I were a child and could not see through him with half a glance. . . . Having a great notion of the necessity of firmness, forgetting that boldness without knowledge is rashness, and without strength, is pertinacity, he persisted. . . . He thought me angry and put out . . . You will smile perhaps at my vehemence.[49]

CONCLUSION

WHAT CAN WE CONCLUDE FROM THIS REVIEW OF THE TUITION controversy? Perhaps Newman's own reflection some twenty years later is the guide to its interpretation: "It is impossible to deny that it would have been better to have mentioned the new plan of Lecturing to the Provost in the first instance."[50]

This statement gives added insight into the original facts and assertions of the case. Here we find Newman admitting that the new plan was in some major way withheld from Hawkins. Yet at the time Newman had made quite a point of Hawkins's alleged knowledge of the plan. Taken in light of the detailed, extensive, and sensitive responses of Hawkins on this issue throughout the controversy, this admission by Newman provides a ground from which to analyze his conduct during the affair. Aside from the obvious disagreement in principle over the nature of the tutor, which could be described as both intellectual and moral in nature, the correspondence reveals the affectivity — the will, desire, and ultimate concern — of the principals in the dispute. Newman stressed self-determination over external authority, personal discretion over submission to the judgment of a superior, exclusivity with respect to his pupils over inclusivity of other pupils, and an offensive relations-damaging communication style over an interpersonally sensitive one. Perhaps Evangelicalism and the Church of England influenced his path in that both

---

49 Ibid., 375–76.   50 Ibid., 250.

of these communities stressed and opposed the same factors. For all of these reasons we can conclude that Newman, despite the intellectual and moral assertions of his position that the tutor was essentially a pastoral role in contrast with what he perceived as Hawkins's impersonal, traditional interpretation, exhibited what may be called an affective dissonance expressed in his temperament, ironically the very same principle which he had discerned in his brother Charles's behavior. This produced two major effects. The first was internal and had two aspects. First, as his affectivity centered on self, it influenced intellectually and morally the position he maintained during the dispute. How his intellect perceived the facts of the controversy and the ethical interpretation he made of them were shaped by his affective disposition. But a second aspect is that his affectivity itself was divided in that his will was actually split in conflict between his drive for self-interest and his drive for God. This affective bifurcation was generally unconscious until his realization of it during his Sicilian crisis a few years later. This first effect then produced the second, external effect, which was his interpretation of Hawkins's position — and person. In conclusion, this apparently academic controversy yields evidence that Newman judged and reacted to Hawkins and the issues from a self-interested ground of affectivity which produced a dissonance, which becomes clearer not only through his behavior toward Hawkins but especially in light of the evidence which follows regarding his intellectual and theological insights at the time of the tuition dispute. This review analyzes Newman the person and his experiences as revealed through his personal correspondence. We will return to this dimension of his willfulness in the final section of this chapter when we examine his experiences during his Mediterranean trip, wherein Hawkins and the tuition dispute, as well as his obstinate affectivity, return as the major foci. But what is important for our study is that we have established through this review three insights: (1) affectivity as the ground of the intellect and the moral sense; (2) affectivity admits of two essential aspects, the drive for self and the drive toward God; and (3) these dimensions of the human person interact with reciprocal influence.

Having established this from an analysis of a major event in Newman's life, let us now move on to examine the work of Newman the theologian. Here we see another dimension, that of his incisive theological insight capable of producing an imposing intellectual synthesis. At the same time, however, it underscores our thesis that what the theologian could conceive he could not yet put into action — and thus the existence of his inner struggle. From these two dimensions, his life and his theology, we seek a basis for a better understanding of the nature of conversion and its implications for theology, especially as he developed it along the tracks of religious epistemology and ecclesiology.

STAGE TWO:
Newman's Theology of the Period

A. AN EARLY SYNTHESIS OF THE
TRACKS OF FAITH AND CHURCH:
The Liturgy Sermon Series, January 31–April 4, 1830[51]

INTRODUCTION

WHILE THE TUITION DISPUTE WAS IN ITS EARLY STAGES, NEW-man composed a series of ten sermons on the liturgy motivated by a book on Church reform proposing changes in the liturgy, which Newman saw as dangerous primarily because of its potential impact on the affections. In a letter dated January 21, 1830 to another Fellow of Oriel, E. M. Rudd, Newman described the liturgy as the means by which the Church promotes affectivity, inculcating religious affection in people since childhood (again the recurrent motif), and her prayers and Creed as the ground of objective truth in an age indisposed to it:

> The advantages . . . are not balanced by the hazard. . . . Associa-tions . . . with the liturgy and affection for it is the great hold of the Church in the minds of the multitude. . . . They feel little her abstract claims on their reverence. . . . The influence she exerts in the hearts of her people is chiefly by . . . attachment to those prayers . . . heard from childhood. . . . Should we not dread dis-turbing this feeling? . . . And (to) question the Athanasian Creed [is] an extreme danger of countenancing the false liberality of the age which would fain have it believed that differences of *opinion* are of slight consequence. . . . The very talk about alteration will move irreverence towards the Service in an age particularly inclined to self-confidence and irreverent presupposition.[52]

Here Newman again noted the primacy of affectivity as the ground of intellect, and thus the Church's great function is in its promotion. The

---

51 Newman: *Sermons 1824–1843*, 55–113. See also Robert C. Christie, "Conversion Through Newman's Liturgy Sermon Series of 1830," in *Newman Studies Journal*, vol. 3, no. 2 (Fall 2006): 49–59.   52 Ibid., 191.

liturgy sermon series substantiates these two themes of our thesis: affectivity as the ultimate ground of intellect and morality, and thus conversion, as well as the reciprocal dynamic relationship these elements share. Newman composed a succinct systematic theology in these ten documents which informs us of his thinking on the broadest scale to date. Notably, his concern for the promotion of religious affectivity through liturgical practice will be at the heart of his dispute with Anglican authorities in the early 1840s.

But this series is noteworthy also because it was the continuation of a key theme. Here Newman specifically developed his concept of temper, the personal dimension that expresses affectivity, initially addressed in the Charles correspondence and arguably the major theme of his first book, *The Arians of the Fourth Century*, which he began to write just about a year after these sermons.

Lastly, this series is valuable in that it reveals Newman's incisive theological insights, offering a contrast to his motives and conduct in the tutor dispute, and thus supporting our perception of his personal dissonance.

THE FIRST TWO SERMONS:
An Overview of the Series

THE FIRST SERMON OF THE SERIES PROVIDES NEWMAN'S OVERview of the entire subject: the nature of liturgy, how it functions, and, of especial interest for our purposes, its objective: conversion.

> Liturgy ... is a service for the people. . . . [I]n the New Testament it means helping *Christians* in any public way. . . . But . . . as applied to the forms of Common Prayer . . . the word *liturgy*, as found in the Prayer book, means *the form in which the Christian priest conducts and presents to God the joint worship of the congregation.*[53]

Having established the ecclesiastical nature of liturgy and introduced the function of the priest, Newman expanded upon the priestly office by referencing tradition, while also linking this sermon thematically with his earlier referenced sermon of 1826, "Holiness Necessary for Future Blessedness:"[54]

> God had ... given him [St. Paul] the office of preaching to the Gentiles ... and so preparing them through sanctification for

---

53 Newman, *Sermons: 1824–1843*, ed. Placid Murray, vol. i (Oxford: Clarendon Press, 1991), 60–61.   54 Newman, PPS, vol. i, 1–14.

heaven[55]. . . . What St. Paul was by office to the Gentiles . . . are all Christian ministers . . . to the Christian community.[56]

Having rooted the priest's function in tradition, Newman developed its one objective, conversion: "The Christian minister's one object [is] to bring men near to God . . . and as a means . . . to convey . . . sanctifying influences of divine grace. This, I say, is his only object."[57] How is this accomplished? By promoting affective, moral, and intellectual conversion, that is, "whenever he is enabled to do good . . . whenever he raises one good thought or desire in another's heart, or urges him to one good action."[58] Then uniting tradition, liturgy, and conversion, Newman references Romans 15:27: "'That I should do this liturgy, this public service for Jesus Christ to the Gentiles' i.e. that of converting them to Christianity."[59]

But Newman perceived a distinction between Anglican liturgical practices and those of both the Jewish and Roman Church traditions, the latter two similar, he believed, in their separation of priest and congregation in worship, a practice which contrasted with the former. We find here a typically anti-Roman temper on Newman's part, focusing on the nature of the priest as facilitator of conversion:

> Do not confuse the liturgy or service of the Christian priest with that of the Jewish (which) did not offer up the prayers of the people. . . . He did not pray with them, he prayed apart from them — and they prayed by themselves. . . . We see this error among the Roman Catholics — the indolence of the human heart has led them literally to change the office of the Christian priest into that of the Jewish. . . . The people have no active share [and are] passive. . . . The priest works out their salvation for them. . . . This is a doctrine easy to the corrupt heart . . . which almost dispenses with the necessity of selfdiscipline — whereas . . . faith . . . sets the mind . . . to . . . that long difficult selfdenying process of sanctification.[60]

While Newman may have been incorrect about Roman liturgical practice, a fact borne out by his contact with the Sicilian churches just three years later, his insight on the nature of conversion is most relevant to our study. Most of all, conversion is rooted in the heart, the seat of affectivity, and it was his objection to passivity and non-participation of the heart which is most prominent here. If conversion is a matter of the heart, and the goal of the liturgy is conversion, then liturgy must move the heart.

55 Newman, *Sermons*, 1824–1843, 58.   56 Ibid., 59.
57 Ibid.   58 Ibid.   59 Ibid., 60.   60 Ibid., 63–65.

Newman closed this opening sermon with four criteria for liturgy: communal, common form, and confession of obligation. Notably, all of these are interpersonal in nature, involving an Other as the object of the liturgy and also an other as the co-participant. The Other-to and the other-with are inseparable entities in Newman's liturgical schema.

The second sermon defined the three "peculiar" uses of the liturgy: it teaches doctrine, it teaches and forms character, and lastly it promotes charity as the fulfillment of the "whole law." Newman began by noting the requisite public nature of liturgy: "To united prayer the blessings peculiarly Christian are attached." Then he added the ecclesial specifics: "The *Keys of His Kingdom* . . . [are] the *sacraments* and they [priests] hold them. . . . The Christian priest implies a congregation. . . . When many pray together, one must lead. . . . He enables Christians to pray *at once* — he makes a Church."[61]

But the three peculiar uses of the liturgy, because of their communal nature and purpose, require a common form. Here we note that Newman's analysis identified the affective base of both liturgical form and objective: that of the promotion of relationship, a theme he previously developed in his sermons of 1825. It is already clear that Newman's breakdown of the three peculiar uses of the liturgy correlates with those personal elements of conversion which are the subject of our study: doctrine with the intellect, character formation with the moral, and charity with the affective, through the liturgy's appeal to the aesthetic element of imagination. But essential to his analysis was that each use is grounded in relationship, or the promotion of an Other to other affectivity. To understand this further, let us next examine his three sermons on doctrine.

THE THREE SERMONS ON LITURGY AS TEACHING DOCTRINE

"THE FIRST USE OF OUR PRAYER BOOK THEN OR LITURGY . . . is . . . a record of the *doctrines* of the gospel . . . God's will and our relations to Him."[62] Sermons three, four, and five treat of specific doctrines, and notably all are affectively rooted. Sermon three holds that "the Liturgy, *first*, teaches doctrine—viz concerning God[63] . . . . The Book of Common Prayer teaches the doctrine of the Trinity."[64] Here Newman united form, content, and method: "The *Creeds* (of course) contain the most *direct* information concerning this great and fundamental doctrine . . . and the Athanasian Creed draws out the true doctrine of Scripture into a still more exact

---

61 Ibid., 69.   62 Ibid., 71.   63 Ibid, 75.   64 Ibid.

form."[65] Then he added an affective note on method, soon to be prominent in his *Arians* analysis of the Alexandrian Church's method in its concern for the convert: "It is not my purpose to *prove their doctrines* . . . but to *teach* the truth—and . . . in the most gentle and persuasive way."[66] Notably, this distinction between proving and teaching was one which he learned a few years earlier from Hawkins.

Newman closed this sermon on the doctrine of God with a synthesis of Creedal form and a previously discerned theme, personal witness, both of which he then transposed the personal relationships with his sister Mary, his father, and Walter Mayers, who died suddenly on February 22, 1828,[67] into liturgical context:

> Our public prayers — Many of them are the very words of the Apostles and Prophets . . . whose lives we rightly look up to as patterns for our virtue — and they are the words used by those whom we loved personally and who are gone before us to their reward.[68]

By means of his interpersonalist analysis Newman vivified the concept of doctrine. We not only share creedal affirmations with the very eyewitnesses of Truth, but also with those whom we hold in our own hearts. Past, present, and future interpersonal relationships are at the center of Newman's analysis of the doctrinal function of liturgy.

The fourth sermon is based on the text of Matthew 19:17: "If thou wilt enter into life, keep the commandments." Newman develops the relationship between doctrine and moral precept by connecting salvation to liturgy through the experience of faith, concluding that liturgy-engendered faith is but one side of the same coin, with obedience the other, having momentous ramifications for salvation: "The Liturgy teaches doctrine — concerning the duty of man . . . our acceptance depends on *faith*. . . . Redemption . . . can be secured only by *continual* asking — i.e. a habit."[69] The important insight for us is the interrelationship of the intellectual and moral spheres. Doctrine is essentially of the former, and notions of duty and habit of the latter. This formed his synthesis that faith and obedience are, in a sense, two modes of the same reality, a theme related to his 1825 sermons.

---

65 Ibid.   66 Ibid., 76.   67 Newman, *Letters and Diaries*, vol. II, 57.
68 Newman, *Sermons, 1824–1843*, 79.
69 Ibid., 80–81. This sermon was eventually published in Newman, PPS, vol. iii, 6, as "Faith and Obedience."

The two states of mind are altogether one and the same. It is quite indifferent whether we say a man seeks God in faith, or . . . by obedience[70]. . . . Not a single act of faith can be named but what has in it the nature of obedience.[71]

Newman then extends his analysis further into the nature of obedience, which is relevant to our study on two counts: he probes its nature to its affective root and by so doing offers an ironic contrast between Newman the theologian and Newman the tutor: "To believe is of the heart, and to obey is of the heart. . . . Obedience . . . belonged to the same temper of mind as faith."[72] Then Newman pressed his analysis of affectivity further into its interpersonalist depth in the act of surrender, the very quality required, according to our hypothesis, of final, unconditional conversion:

From the beginning to the end of Scripture, the one voice of inspiration consistently maintains . . . this one doctrine, that the only way of salvation . . . is the surrender of ourselves to our Maker . . . and this state of mind is ascribed in Scripture sometimes to the believing, sometimes to the obedient.[73]

And what disposition, or temper, runs counter to this spirit?

Man is proud, or . . . self-righteous, not when obedient, but in proportion to his disobedience. To be proud is to rest on one's self . . . but a really obedient mind is necessarily dissatisfied with itself, and looks out of itself for help. . . . As a man obeys, is he drawn to faith.[74]

Here let us compare Newman the theologian, on the one hand, and Newman the tutor, on the other. Both the correspondence to Hawkins and these sermons were written at about the same time, yet what is most striking is that his analysis of doctrine to its affective root reveals the very temper which Newman lacked in his Hawkins dealings. We can see from this that Newman's theological insight outpaced his own affective development. What his intellect could conceive, his heart could not implement, causing an internal dissonance externally exhibited in his willful refusal to submit to authority, underscored by the manner or tone in which Newman communicated. Thus, Newman's own theological analysis becomes the very yardstick by which we can measure the harmony of his development, and at this point in time the heart of the tutor did

---

70 Newman, PPS, vol. vi , 80, 85.
71 Ibid., 85.   72 Ibid., 81.   73 Ibid., 82–83.   74 Ibid., 82.

not harmonize with the mind of the theologian, a contrast traceable to Newman's willful affective disposition.

Newman's fifth sermon, closing out his reflections on doctrine, continues his analysis of faith, grounding it in grace: "There is not any one doctrine insisted upon by the Church more immediately practical than this — the necessity of the continual aid of divine grace in order to our pleasing God."[75] The important implication is that, if grace is the source of our pleasing God, then it is also the source of faith. But the response to grace must be active and not passive, as Newman referenced through Luke 13:

> Strive — mere seeking is not enough — many seek with half hearts, but Christian seeking is a striving. . . . Turn to Him with all our hearts [and] serve by obedience. . . . Hate ourselves [and our] low selfishness . . . indolence [and] unbelief. . . . [D]eny ourselves . . . lest we seek merely, not strive.[76]

We can summarize these first five sermons as an understanding of liturgy in its various aspects. It promotes conversion through the office of the priest who unites the aspirations of the community. He does so by teaching who God is and how we attain relationship with Him through the truth of the Creed, by the affective response of faith to the teaching of His doctrine, and the moral imperative of obedience consistent with that faith. All of these require His help, attainable only through a full-hearted, affective seeking which inspires and grounds that faith and obedience.

Now let us examine the last five sermons in the series, which extend and deepen Newman's analysis of liturgy and conversion. These treat primarily of the moral sense and its ultimate ground in Christian love, the expression of religious affectivity.

THE FIVE SERMONS ON LITURGY AS
TEACHING AND FORMING CHARACTER:
Sermons Six and Seven on the Character of Faith and Hope

"THE LITURGY, SECOND, FORMS THE CHARACTER — VIZ TO faith[77]. . . to hope[78]. . . to self denial."[79] So Newman introduced each of these three sermons on a particular character trait which the liturgy promotes. The first sermon linked the liturgy with faith and included an important epistemological analysis:

---

75 Newman, *Sermons, 1824–1843*, vol. ii, sermon 12; no. 5 in the liturgy series, p. 84.
76 Ibid., 85–86.   77 Ibid., 87.   78 Ibid., 90.
79 Ibid., 96. This sermon actually follows no. 8 in the series and will be treated in that order.

Baptism is the only essential test . . . the only essential bond of fellowship . . . the symbol of that one party which Christ has sanctioned — and those who . . . look for other tests . . . walk by sight not by faith.[80]

Newman would develop one of these themes two years later in his *University Sermon*, "Contest Between Faith and Sight,"[81] which indicates his further separation from evangelicalism over the issues of baptism and conversion. But here his analysis was specifically concerned with the unity of tradition, community, and faith through liturgy. The sermon concluded with an insight into the relationship of liturgy-engendered faith to love:

All through the Liturgy . . . the Church speaks in the temper of faith. . . . Observe how faith leads to love. We do not love each other because we do not believe we are what Christ and the Apostles say we are . . . joint members of Christ — This is the true union which exists between us, for all worldly relations tend to a speedy termination.[82]

This is a valuable insight for our study in that Newman traces an affective defect, the failure to love, to a failure to believe, a disposition which the Church through her liturgy reverses. Love is generated by the liturgy's promotion of faith. Newman also perceived an intellectual dimension of faith in that "we do not believe we are what Christ and the Apostles say we are," the contrast of knowledge by sight versus that by faith. This reciprocal influence of faith and love, of intellect and affection, is consistent with our thesis. "This temper of faith" includes, by use of the term temper, both cause and effect aspects, and Newman used "temper" to express a multidimensional state, sometimes highlighting the intellect, sometimes the moral, sometimes the affective dimension. But whatever is highlighted, the principle is that they are inseparable, which emphasizes their reciprocally influential natures.

Temper is an even more prominent notion in the following and seventh sermon of the series: "The Liturgy . . . forms the character — viz to hope."[83] First, Newman defined hope: "the patient subdued tranquil cheerful thoughtful waiting for Christ."[84] But how is this accomplished? "In order to have attained to Christian hope the mind must have gone through previous discipline which has already wrought it into a calm

---

80   Ibid., 88.   81   Newman, *Fifteen Sermons*, 120–35.
82   Newman, *Sermons, 1824–1843*, vol. i, 88–89.   83   Ibid., 90.
84   Ibid.

and quiet temper. . . . Hope is a *subdued* temper. . . . It is not a passionate longing, an intemperate rash emotion."[85]

If we reflect upon Newman's dispute with Hawkins, we find again in Newman's own theological analysis of the temper of hope additional evidence of his own personal dissonance, since he did not attain the very state which he described as Christian hope. We find a familiar note when Newman's analysis continues, tracing hope to its affective root:

> Christian hope is cheerful . . . a merry heart is a continual feast < Prov 15 >. . . . The secret deep in the heart unconsciously spreads . . . over . . . thoughts and feelings . . . from a source of which the Christian himself is not aware.[86]

Here Newman added to the intellectual aspect of hope its affective ground by reference to the characteristic locus of affectivity, the heart. But he also provided a key insight into the dynamics of hope. Its source lies in this deep, preconceptual level of affectivity, affirming another significant point of our thesis: affectivity is the ground of the dynamic of conversion. This is related to the movement stated earlier in the sermon on grace, which is an affective dynamic, as the ground of faith.

Then Newman connected affectively based hope with the liturgy and its inherent focus on the community and others rather than absorption with the self, two aspects which are also affective in nature:

> Above all our hope is perfected by its peculiar Christian object . . . a personal but not a solitary consolation. . . . We are not allowed to regard ourselves as individuals but as members of one body. . . . It should be our endeavour to train our hope upon this habitual love of the general Church. . . . It is one great benefit resulting to us from public worship, that we are taught thus to neglect our slight griefs, to think of those of others.[87]

One final note should be made of a brief but significant image which Newman employed near the sermon's end regarding the actualization or objective of the heart's impulse: "Who does not feel his heart stir within him at the thought of attaining to that beloved home, where our Lord is gone before us?"[88] For Newman, home and heart are synonymous. We explored this aspect earlier in our study, and it is of note that Newman chose this image of the place wherein he first experienced the quickening of his own affections to express the ultimate end of those

---

85 Ibid.   86 Ibid., 91.   87 Ibid., 92.   88 Ibid., 93.

instincts — togetherness with Christ. Newman also referred to this home as "glimpses of heaven," a metaphor expressing that the state to come is like the state where he first loved and was loved — home.

Though Newman's theological synthesis here is profound, it again indicates that the "temper" which the Christian ought to attain through the liturgy has not been successfully reached by the theologian himself, as the history of the tuition dispute revealed, offering further evidence of the dissonance within.

This completes our review of Newman's sermons on the formation of character and the liturgy. In the remaining three sermons Newman treats of three other habits of character or temper which are both the culmination, and the means by which to attain the culmination, of the ultimate relationship with God sought by the heart. The first treats of reverence for tradition and its affective base, followed by two on the objective of conversion, the promotion of Christian charity preceded by self-denial as the requisite habit by which it is attained. These contain further evidence supporting our thesis.

SERMON EIGHT ON REVERENCE FOR THE OLD PATHS

THE EIGHTH SERMON, "STEADFASTNESS IN THE OLD PATHS,"[89] was a commentary on Jeremiah 6:16 wherein Newman offered a valuable epistemological comparison of scientific and religious knowledge, and then indicated the relationship of knowledge to morality, and ultimately to its affective base. Reverence for, and adherence to, tradition is the path to self-fulfillment, and this is a function of the liturgy. But again we note an ironic contrast between Newman's theology and his conduct toward Hawkins and the "old system." The sermon opens with a thematic statement: "Reverence for the old paths is a chief Christian duty . . . as continually expressed in the Prayer Book—not to slight what has gone before."[90] Then Newman contrasted epistemological modes:

> God has given us no authority in questions of science. . . . The world is more learned in these things than of old. . . . There is no limit to the progress of the human mind here. . . . But let us turn to that knowledge which God has given, and which therefore does not admit of improvement by lapse of time; this is religious knowledge . . . given . . . by revelation.[91]

Then in rapid order Newman relates intellectual to moral knowledge and traces them to their affective base:

---

89 Newman, PPS, vol. vii, 18, 243–57.   90 Ibid., 243.   91 Ibid., 245–46.

> Do we think we become better men by knowing more? Little
> knowledge is required for religious obedience. We have all of us
> the means of doing our duty; we have not the *will*, and this no
> knowledge can give. We have need to subdue our minds, and
> this no other person *can* do for us.[92]

The submission of the will, an affective dynamic, is the ground of the
performance of our duty. But whence comes the content of that duty?
"Practical religious knowledge . . . is a personal gift . . . from God."[93] This
theme recalls the earlier sermon on grace and implies that the essence of this
knowledge is affective. Grace, as a gift, is an interpersonal dynamic exchange.

Near the close, Newman examines the Scripture citation on which the
sermon is based, and it is noteworthy to review it briefly in connection
with our thesis because it implies a relationship of affectivity and morality.
Newman calls the statement "sweet music": "Thus saith the Lord, Stand
ye in the ways, and see, and ask for the old paths, where is the good way,
and walk therein, and ye shall find rest for your souls."[94] The exhortations
"to stand," "to see," and "to ask" are all implicitly acts of submission of
personal will, while the old paths, the good way are acts of intellectual
and moral discernment, but which are unattainable without the will's
submission. Lastly, to find rest for the soul is a description of the interpersonal dimension of affectivity, the self-actualization or fulfillment of the
soul. The dynamic which begins in submission, or intrapersonal affective
development, reaches its terminus in rest, or interpersonal affective union.
Thus, the internal ordering of affectivity, morality, and intellectuality
moves the self beyond itself and into relationship with the Transcendent
Other. Newman's theological synthesis provides evidence to support our
thesis regarding both the presence and the reciprocal interaction of the
elements of conversion, as well as the ground of conversion itself.

However, we now return to the recurrent dichotomy which this sermon series presents. After such an insightful "theoretical" examination
of these issues, Newman authored another synthesis of affective, moral,
and intellectual conduct which is again striking because in the Hawkins
dispute he hardly practiced what he preached:

> We shall think less of circumstances, and more of our duties
> under them, what ever they are. In proportion as we cease to
> be theorists, we shall become practical men; we shall have less
> of self-confidence and arrogance, more of inward humility and

---

92   Ibid., 247–48.   93   Ibid., 249.   94   Ibid., 252.

diffidence; we shall be less likely to despise others, and shall think of our own intellectual powers with less complacency.[95]

This character description offers further evidence that Newman's theology and his actions were certainly at odds. The temper described by the theologian and the actions of the tutor were distinctly different, reflecting his internal dissonance.

SERMON NINE ON SELF-DENIAL

THE NINTH SERMON DEALS WITH THE LENTEN LITURGY AND self-denial as the requisite for Christian love, with again a characteristically affective ground: "The Atonement, our bond of union, is brought home to our affections especially in this season."[96] Here the term "temper" is the dominant motif, and it is expressed in all three areas of relationship: "The peculiar Christian temper ... to *Almighty God* ... is *hope* ... to his neighbor it is *love* ... to himself it is *selfdenial*."[97] Then Newman defined the theme of the sermon, self-denial, referencing Luke 9:

> Here He shows us from His own *example* what Christian selfdenial
> is — viz not a mere refraining from sin ... but a giving up what
> we *might lawfully* enjoy. ... The Christian feels the need of this
> habitual selfcontrol ... schooling his will daily, that it may be
> submissive. ... He denies himself ... because it is good ... [and
> he] triumphs over himself.[98]

Self-denial, then, is key to forming the will so that it develops the capacity for submission, and this positive interpretation of self-denial makes it possible to see it as a good. But in addition, it is the degree of self-denial expressed here which is relevant for us: even that which might be lawfully, and rightly, enjoyed. We need to say little more here about the clear dichotomy between Newman's theological insight and his steadfast commitment to his own views in the tutor dispute, except to note that the evidence mounts. Submission was not a word which the tutor was prepared to utter, or perhaps even capable of uttering, at this time.

One final note on this sermon should be made since it bears on Newman's temperament, which influenced his ecclesiology at the time. For the independent-minded Newman, matters of self-denial were strictly personal, beyond the right of the Church to impose without violation of personal freedom: "They are in individuals the free sacrifice of the heart,

---

95 Ibid., 251.   96 Newman, *Sermons, 1824–1843*, vol. i, 96.
97 Ibid., 99.   98 Ibid., 99, 103–4.

of the Spirit of Liberty. . . . Our Church could not in her services press them forcibly upon us without erring." But Newman does not stop here, immediately attacking the Roman Church for what he perceived to be this violation of individual freedom:

> It is the very sin of the Roman Church that she has usurped power over mens' [sic] consciences in these matters and, unlike a kind mother, *compelled* her children to be sad or mirthful in order and by measure. . . . This tyranny is her especial offense against the Spirit of Christian liberty. . . . We on the contrary are are [sic] bid none of these things. . . . Therefore, our Church leaves the modes and particular acts of selfdenial to the conscience of each of us.[99]

This note of independent-mindedness, facilitated by the Church of England, was characteristic of Newman's temper toward Hawkins. This sermon, with its theme of self-denial, sets the stage for the culmination of the series in Newman's analysis of Christian charity.

SERMON TEN ON CHRISTIAN CHARITY

IN THIS SERMON, NEWMAN TREATS OF THE VERY CORE OF RELI-gious, affective conversion: Christian love: "The Liturgy forming the character—viz to Charity—the Litany."[100] Newman referenced Galatians 5:22–23 as his theme:

> The fruit of the Spirit is love, joy, peace, long-suffering, gen-tleness, goodness, faith, meekness, temperance. . . . I will now describe the nature of *Christian love*, in which (St Paul tells us) is the fulfilling of the whole <social> law <Rom 13> and show how our hearts are trained to the exercise of it by the services of the Prayer Book.[101]

Then referencing St John — "Little children love one another . . . because it is all in all"— Newman proceeded to offer his personal insights on this exhortation of revelation. Here we note its obvious interpersonal nature, but one which is dependent upon a prior intrapersonal synthesis of affec-tivity, morality, and intellect. Once again, we cannot help but contrast these theological insights with Newman's own conduct toward Hawkins:

> Now this spiritual or Christian temper of mind . . . contains . . . humility . . . selfdenial . . . brotherly affection . . . attention to small ordinary duties influencing the conduct in all the daily

---

99   Ibid., 104–5.   100   Ibid., 106.   101   Ibid., 106, 109.

business and family relations of life . . . making him amiable, kind, cheerful, considerate and affectionate as a friend companion and associate . . . a *habit* within us.[102]

This affective temper also is a moral obligation, based on revelation:

> This affectionate attention to others in ordinary affairs and the minute parts of our conduct is a part of the Christian duty of love . . . the pattern which our Savior has set us. . . . All revelation has proceeded from the same condescending love — though God is high, yet hath He respect unto the lowly.[103]

This final sermon, while offering excellent theological insight into the nature, ground, and dynamics of Christian love, again contributes to the evidence that Newman the theologian and Newman the tutor were two dimensions of this great personality which had yet to be successfully integrated. We need only reflect upon one aspect of his description of Christian love in light of Hawkins's wounded response to Newman precisely on this point. Newman wrote above that such love makes one "amiable, kind, cheerful, considerate and affectionate as a friend companion and associate . . . a *habit* within us."[104] Just two months later, as previously noted, Hawkins would reply to Newman that "the tone of the notes which you have subsequently sent me did not become a Fellow writing to the provost, much less one friend to another."

The last five sermons in this series are especially notable since they treat of several themes which relate to the core of our thesis. Through the liturgy's formation of moral character, a connection is forged with the intellectual or doctrinal nature of the first five sermons. Also the concept of temper is introduced and gains greater emphasis as the series unfolds, and it is temper as an affective force which Newman will discover as the key to understanding the root of heresy in *Arians*. But the series culminates in the final sermon with an examination of the terminus of Christian character formation, love, which is inseparably connected to the formation of affective temper.

This examination of these sermons on the liturgy indicates, on the one hand, a rich, almost systematic theology based on liturgy, but also provides evidence that Newman's intellect and the self-willed independent thrust of his affectivity were dissonant. Clearly, his theology was influenced by his intellectual understanding of affectivity, and his imagery of home with its obvious implications of his positive affective experiences added its own influence. But an unresolved conflict existed between his intellect

---

102 Ibid., 110.   103 Ibid., 110–11.   104 Ibid., 110.

and his affectivity and also within his affectivity itself, most noticeably in his willfulness, a battle which would emerge again during his visit to the Mediterranean two years after these sermons and less than a year after he resigned as tutor. Lastly, noting the summary of the ninth sermon, Newman's independent streak seems to have been influenced by the Church of England, which likewise led to his disparagement of the Roman Church. This would also be a prominent factor during his Mediterranean journey.

Another note of interest is that of the absence, any time the sacraments were mentioned, of any reference to penance, the sacrament of submission. In fact, he even cut short one Book of Common Prayer specific reference to the biblical exhortation on forgiving sins, indicating that perhaps his independent drive found this exhortation a matter for strictly private reflection.[105] This is consistent with the problem of the integration of his intellect and affectivity.

This sermon series, so rich in its theology, is an example of Newman's dissonance when viewed in the context of his conduct. Later on in 1834, when reviewing his Sicilian crisis over willfulness, he himself noted the irony of his preaching, but not possessing, the Truth, confirming our conclusion.

Next we consider two major sermons which both introduce the themes of Newman's major work of the period, *The Arians of the Fourth Century*, and serve as a second example of this dissonance in Newman's conversion journey.

B. THE TWO PREAMBLE SERMONS TO ARIANS

I. THE SECOND UNIVERSITY SERMON:
"The Influence of Natural and Revealed Religion Respectively"[106]

PREACHED ON APRIL 13, 1830, JUST NINE DAYS AFTER THE LAST sermon in the liturgy series, this sermon is a compact version of *The Arians of The Fourth Century*, thus serving as a major preamble to that work. Newman marshaled previous influences from Butler (and Keble, though unstated) and applied them to the question of truth as given by nature and revelation. In doing so he resolved the intellectual dilemma by connecting the issue to its personalist, affective base, the Incarnation. Through this historical fact, doctrine is born. Schism was then seen as an intellectual error which denied the reality of a personal God encountered in the revelation of Christ. Thus, as Newman said, the Church stands or falls on the doctrine of the Incarnation; if no Incarnation, then no

---

105   Newman, *Sermons, 1824–1843*, vol. I, 79.
106   Newman, *Fifteen Sermons*, 31.

personal God, no Church, and no moral order beyond the conflicting codes of natural humanist thinking.

As for Butler's influence, "The relation of Revealed to Natural Religion . . . the two systems coincide in declaring the same substantial doctrines . . . an argument contained by implication, though not formally drawn out, in Bishop Butler's Analogy."[107]

And then the intellectual dilemma of revelation in the Incarnation:

> Scripture completes the deficiency of nature . . . to discern in it one solitary doctrine, which . . . has no parallel in this world, an Incarnation of the Divine Essence . . . the doctrines of the Divinity of our Lord, and of the Personality of the Holy Spirit. . . . The denial of these . . . is the great guilt of anti-Trinitarians . . . and throw(s) back the science of morals and of human happiness into that state of vagueness and inefficiency from which Christianity has extricated it.[108]

This personalism, we have seen, was implicit in Butler but explicit in Keble's *Christian Year*, so influential on Newman as he recounted in the *Apologia*:

> The second intellectual principle which I gained from Mr. Keble . . . [was] ascribing the firmness of assent which we give to religious doctrine . . . to the living power of faith and love which accepts it. . . . Faith and love are directed towards an Object; in the vision of that Object they live. . . . Thus, the argument from Probability . . . became an argument from Personality . . . one form of the argument from Authority.[109]

Newman then traced the failure of a moral system based solely on nature to its denial of the personalism of God inherent in creation through Christ, who is the nexus of the moral, natural, and supernatural orders: "A mere moral strain of teaching duty and enforcing obedience fails . . . because it does not urge and illustrate virtue in the Name and by the example of our blessed Lord . . . (and mercy pre-eminently)."[110] We note here, in Christ's person and the pre-eminence of His mercy, the affective nature of His personal revelation, which is discarded when the intellect rejects the doctrine, and with this rejection comes the downfall of the moral system so grounded: "Every spirit that confesseth not that

---

107 Ibid. This is the subject of the final chapter of Newman's *Grammar of Assent*, indicative of Butler's lifelong influence.   108 Ibid., 31–32.
109 Newman, *Apologia*, 37–38.   110 Newman, *Fifteen Sermons*, 34.

Jesus Christ is come *in the flesh*, is not of God. . . . It reverses . . . all that the revealed character of Christ has done for our faith and virtue."[111] The Incarnation, then, reveals to us Christ's personal character, and so the truth of revelation lies in His historical fact, which is the basis for, and from which springs, doctrine:

> And hence the Apostles' speeches in the book of Acts and the primitive Creeds insist almost exclusively upon the history, not the doctrines, of Christianity. . . . By means of our Lord's Economy, the great doctrines of theology [are] taught, the facts of that Economy giving its peculiarity and force to the Revelation.[112]

To reject this is the "peculiar perverseness of schism, which . . . consulting the opinions of mankind as to the means of obtaining happiness . . . undertakes . . . an examination of man's nature, as if the only remaining means of satisfying the inquiry."[113]

We find here a composite of Newman's thinking from the influences of the mid-and-late 1820s. These factors were applied to the intellectual problem of the synthesis of natural religion and revelation (or reason and faith), the lines of which argument Newman sketched out in this sermon. The issue centers on the dominant fact of revelation, the mystery of the Incarnation, which is an aspect of the mystery of the Trinity. The rejection of this mystery is ultimately a rejection of the affective nature of that revelation. These themes will be taken up shortly in *Arians* and thus this sermon is a preamble to that analysis of doctrine and heresy. But of importance for us here is Newman's explication of the affective root of that mystery, which relates to an implication of our thesis: the source of conversion as itself the affective giving of the grace of faith which makes conversion possible. We now move on to examine the second preamble sermon to *Arians*.

2. THE SYNTHESIS CONTINUES:
The Sermon on the Affective Nature of Doctrine:
"The Mystery of the Holy Trinity"[114]

THE SPRING OF 1831 WAS AN ACTIVE PERIOD FOR NEWMAN, AND a few points of interest are noteworthy to situate the second sermon in its context. On March 9, Hugh James Rose wrote to Newman suggesting that the latter write, in addition to a work on the Thirty-Nine Articles which Newman had earlier proposed, "as a preliminary to a work on these Articles in which all the great doctrines of Christianity are treated, a *History of the*

---

111 Ibid., 35.   112 Ibid.   113 Ibid., 32–33.
114 Newman, PPS, vol. vi, 24.

Councils, in which so many of them (one may say all) were discussed."[115] On March 28, Newman replied to Rose indicating his qualified agreement to write both articles.[116] Responding quickly, Rose replied on March 30 to Newman's concern about the scope of the project: "I should say that my object in proposing to you a History of the Councils was precisely that it might serve as an *introduction to* your work on the Articles. The Councils chiefly to be dwelt on are those in which the great points of faith were discussed or great heresies censured."[117] In Newman's qualifying letter he proposed treating of numerous topics in his Articles work which, we will see, were eventually subsumed into the Councils' article, which became *The Arians of the Fourth Century.* Just two weeks later, on April 13, Newman wrote to Hawkins resigning as tutor at the end of the term.[118] On May 29, he preached the sermon on the Trinity which we now review. On June 22, he entered in his diary the notation of his commencement of work on *Arians:* "Wednesday 22 June 1831 began my studies *up at Rose Hill—I suppose those for the Nicene Council.*"[119]

Newman grounded his discussion of the Trinity in the biblical revelation of Matthew 28:19: "Go . . . teach all nations; baptizing them in the Name of the Father, and of the Son, and of the Holy Ghost." This exhortation is both intellectual and affective ("teach") and interpersonal: "This . . . ordinance of discipleship was to be administered in the Name — of whom? . . . of Him whose disciples the converts forthwith became . . . of that God whom . . . they confessed . . . obey[ed] . . . and trusted."[120] Christ's directive, then, was addressed to both the mind and the heart. The convert not only learns a teaching but enters into a relationship. But the important question immediately arises: who is that Other, the Object in the relationship?

> Yet when Christ would name the Name of God, He does but say, 'in the Name of the Father, and of the Son, and of the Holy Ghost.' I consider, then . . . there is a difficulty, *till* the doctrine of the Holy Trinity is made known to us. What can be meant by saying, in the Name, not of God, but of Three?[121]

Newman answered that the names are "*correlatives*, one implies the other . . . the Three Sacred Names . . . have a meaning relatively to each

---

115 Newman, *Letters and Diaries,* vol. II, 321.   116 Ibid., 320–21.
117 Ibid., 323.   118 Ibid., 326.
119 Newman, *Letters and Diaries,* vol. II, 338. Note: Italicized material was interpolated into the *Letters and Diaries* from a Newman notebook.
120 Newman, PPS, vol. vi, 343–44.   121 Ibid., 344.

other, and not to any temporal dispensation."[122] Newman then performed an epistemological analysis: "There can be no greater obscurity than a mystery; and . . . the Sacred truth . . . is a perplexity to the convert."[123] But here is the very ground of the intellectual error of the heretic:

> For the point . . . is the improbability that Our Lord should introduce an obscurity of mere words, with none existing in fact, which is the case in the heretical interpretation. . . . If there be an eternal mystery in the Godhead . . . there could not be but a difficulty in the words in which he revealed it . . . the plainest and most exact form of speech which human language admits of.[124]

Newman considered the problem to be that of comprehending the implicit Trinitarian relationship:

> The difficulty is not in any one (Name) singly; but in their combination. There is no difficulty, except as is in the nature of things, in the Adorable Mystery spoken of, which no wording can remove or explain. . . . If there is confusion of language . . . this arises from our incapacity in comprehension and expression. . . . That simple accuracy of statement which would harmonize all of them is beyond us, because the problem of contemplating the Eternal, as he is, is beyond us.[125]

We note here an implicit intellectual drive, in the impulse for harmonization, to achieve what can best be termed an aesthetic synthesis, aesthetic in the generic sense of the whole, the entire view. Newman then proposed a concise statement on God's nature, drawn from Scripture:

> I propose to state the doctrine . . . disclosed to us in . . . Scripture. . . . Now, it may be asked, in what sense 'one'? . . . I answer, that God is one in the simplest and strictest sense . . . as being individual. . . . In him there are no parts or passions . . . nothing of quality . . . whole, perfect, and simple, and . . . one in Himself, or, as the Creed speaks, one in substance or essence.[126]

But in the comprehension of the mystery, intellect fails: "We men are incapable of conceiving of Him as He is; we . . . attain . . . glimpses . . . partial views . . . we call by different names, as if He had attributes."[127] Again Newman identified the problem as intellectual, an incapacity of conception, and he implied another dimension of insight, previously noted, in the

---

122 Ibid., 344–45.　　123 Ibid., 346.　　124 Ibid.
125 Ibid., 347, 350–351.　　126 Ibid., 347–49.　　127 Ibid., 349.

terms "glimpses" and "partial views." These are symptoms of an inherent aesthetic desire for wholeness, completeness. The result is what may be termed an "intellectual aesthetic affectivity" with the inherent limitation imposed by utilizing concepts to represent images of a whole.

Further, the employment of "as if" in the cognitive process is a clue to another device utilized by the intellect: analogy. Both analogy and the notion of aesthetic in relation to the intellectual comprehension of the divine mystery are developed at length in *Arians*. Newman then offered a valuable distinction: "I am not attempting to explain *how* the mystery is, but to bring out distinctly *what* we mean by it."[128] *How* is an intellectual grasp, whereas *what* is the perception that the reality is so, without asserting its conceptual understanding. This provided the point of transition to the disposition which promotes an understanding of the mystery, the requisite quality of unconditional conversion, submission: "If we find it tries us . . . whether for our reason, or our imagination, or our feelings, let us . . . submit to it each of our faculties."[129] Again, Newman ultimately traced the ground of the intellect's grasp to affectivity. Then he united the principles of analogy and aesthetic in relation to human nature and its partial perception of the divine:

> We are endowed by nature and through grace with a por-
> tion of certain excellences which belong in perfection to the
> Most High. . . . Earthly things are but partial reflexions of
> Him. . . . But there are certain other disclosures . . . concerning
> the Divine Nature . . . of which we have no image or parallel in
> ourselves . . . and call unintelligible . . . and mysterious because
> we cannot account for them.[130]

The subtle implication brought out by the use of the analogy of the human to the divine is precisely the intellectual fact to which the heretical mind is blind: that the divine ultimately transcends the human in a way which renders the analogy, beyond that point, useless. Mystery or unintelligibility are expressions of this fact, an implicit reference to the Transcendent Other for which there is no human analogy. Using the term analogically, one sense of the divine is on the order of personhood. Scripture identifies God as personal:

> This mention of Word . . . Wisdom . . . Presence . . . Glory . . .
> Spirit . . . Breath . . . Countenance . . . Arm . . . and Hand of
> the Almighty is too frequent, and with too much of personal

---

128 Ibid., 352.   129 Ibid., 353.   130 Ibid., 354, 356, 354.

characteristic, to be dutifully passed over by the careful reader of Scripture.[131]

By emphasizing that there is something like a person inherent in what we mean by God, Newman analyzed God-talk and God-man relations down to their personalist bases. It follows then that affectivity is the basis of such thinking, since these intellectual concepts stem from that base. Our concepts, then, must take into account not only what can be known about interpersonal dynamics, but even more importantly, to prevent error, what we can't or don't know. Here Newman synthesized principles of analogy and aesthetic to emphasize the ultimate ground of interpersonal relations, the affectively based act of faith:

> We understand things unknown, by the pattern of things seen and experienced. . . . Earthly things are partial reflexions of Him . . . and if Scripture reveal to us aught concerning Him, we must be content to take it on faith, without comprehending how it is, or having any clear understanding of our own words.[132]

This theme of the affective base of the intellectual dilemma of comprehending the Trinity is explored at length in *Arians*, but Newman sketched out the lines of that argument here. He closed the sermon with a synthesis interrelating the mystery as understood through revelation which is, on the one hand, like personhood, yet on the other completely beyond its limitations. Doctrinal creeds expressing this mystery are the objects of believers, but the unbelieving heretical mind rejects these creedal conceptualizations, because they accommodate non-conceptualization. In the end, the ultimate warning is ironically against willful affectivity:

> This mystery is in the New [Testament] clearly declared. . . . Thus, the words of the Creed hold good . . . and . . . other views . . . whether Sabellian, or Arian, or Tritheistic, without denying in words the Holy Three, do deny Him in fact, and in the event, and involve their willful maintainers in the anathema.[133]

Notably, the heretic is characterized as willful, a trait of affective defect, which, as we have seen, goes to the core of the dissonance between intellect and heart. How is this overcome? By conversion, which includes (1) change of heart, (2) submission, (3) sanctification, and then, emphasizing the reciprocal nature of this dynamic, (4) an intellectual grasp with an aesthetic dimension of the image of the God-man relationship: "May we

---

131   Ibid., 356.   132   Ibid.   133   Ibid., 357, 359–60.

never inquire without a careful endeavour, with God's aid, to sanctify our knowledge, and to impress it on our hearts, as well as to store it in our understandings."[134] Notably, this multi-dimensional description of conversion contains the four elements of our hypothesis.

The sanctification of knowledge. This phrase grounds the rest of the process which Newman described and, as seen earlier in our study, sanctification or holiness is the development of a submissive disposition of the self to the Transcendent Other, which is an affective temper or conversion. This change then illuminates our previously limited knowledge, taking our understanding to a new level of insight. But simultaneous with this experience is the fundamental change of heart which occurs at the moment, and in the act, of submission. This is precisely the dilemma for the unsubmissive heart of the heretic, who then rejects the intellectual concept which only the affectively grounded heart can accommodate. We will now move on to see how Newman explored these subjects in *Arians*. But the major point is that Newman the theologian, who was capable of such penetrating intellectual insight, was himself troubled by an affective dissonance. We will see this dissonance expressed in *Arians* in his attacks upon the Roman Church, and it reoccurs during his Roman visit in 1833. From these facts we can conclude that his affective dissonance influenced his intellect in the creation of an ecclesiastical image representative of his affectivity. Thus, his theology was the intellectual expression of, and inseparably linked to, his affectivity. The result was his vision of, and moral conversion to, a reformed Church of England as the true and good actualization of that affective drive, a vision he would later see as faulty.

C. THE ARIANS OF THE FOURTH CENTURY:
A Study of Temper: Affectivity as the Ground of Intellect and Conversion[135]

NEWMAN'S WORK ON *ARIANS*, HIS MAJOR WORK OF THIS PERIOD and perhaps his most seminal document, extended from June of 1831 until July of 1832, filling almost 400 pages, and its major themes examine the core of fundamental theology. From an understanding of revelation drawn from Scripture, Newman unearthed a line of continuity from the early church to the Alexandrian, distinguished most importantly by a personalist method which disclosed the truth of revelation by means of a disposition,

---

134   Ibid., 361.
135   Newman's historical work had a relevant application: "In his study of the Arian heresy, Newman has contemporary religious liberals very much in mind." Ker, *Newman and the Fullness of Christianity*, 34.

or temper, which facilitated that process. Briefly summarized, the method was analogical, economical, and aesthetic, and the accompanying temper was that which promoted the virtue of concord, a synonym for harmony. The aesthetic element assists the intellect in questions of method, while the affective element engages the desires of the heart in its search for fulfillment. These dimensions are reciprocally influential. The heart motivates and drives the mind, but the mind, in its methods of ascertaining what it believes to be the truth, through the moral determinations which the intellect affirms, affects the heart. Thus, moral judgments and intellectual affirmations exist in a necessary reciprocal relationship with affectivity. They can promote, or retard and damage, each other, but are inseparable. Such is the fruit of Newman's analysis. Its irony is that it offers further evidence that though he was able to bring great powers of intellectual analysis to bear upon these subjects, the very temperament which he understood so well intellectually eluded him personally. Again, Newman provides the diagnostic tools for his own evaluation.

One last note from Newman's personal life will help situate his concern with temper in *Arians*. In early 1829 his correspondence with his brother Charles resumed, and his diary records no less than eight exchanges of letters till the end of the year, picking up again in the spring of 1830.[136] Charles was insistent on reopening the previous discussion which culminated in Newman's analysis of an affective predisposition against religion as the faulty methodological ground of Charles's position. At first Newman refused to reopen the discussion,[137] but he was once again moved by his mother's anxiety over Charles.[138] Shortly thereafter he wrote to Charles one of the lengthiest letters of his life, some 24 pages in all.[139] Newman revisited the old theme and described it very much as we find it in *Arians*; judgments against doctrine are caused by intellectual, methodological error grounded in affective distemper.[140] Newman concluded the letter with a tenet which is an apt introduction to the *Arians* study: "It is a *fundamental* doctrine of Scriptures that the mind cannot arrive at religious truth without a revelation — *I think it never can.*"[141]

---

136 Newman, *Letters and Diaries*, vol. II, 131, 142, 165–68, 171, 173, 206.

137 Ibid., 244.   138 Ibid., 228.

139 Ibid., 266–81. The reprint of the letter reduced the size length of the original.

140 Ibid., 270–78.

141 Ibid., 281. *Arians* is not only as an historical analysis of the grounds of heresy in the fourth century but also an allegory of the contemporary liberal crisis in the English Church. As Ian Ker states: "*The Arians of the Fourth Century* may be primarily a historical work, but its author's own theological prescriptions are never far from the

In his opening analysis of the birth of heresy from the spirit of Judaism, Newman referenced the Anglican divine Hooker, who grasped a
fundamental relationship: "The mind . . . feeling present joy, is always
marvelously unwilling to admit any other cogitation, and in that case,
casteth off those disputes whereunto the intellectual part at other times
easily draweth."[142]

Further, Judaism, as an influence in the Antiochene Church which was
the seedbed of the Arian heresy, is termed a "self-indulgent religion. . . . It
necessarily indisposed the mind for the severe and exciting mysteries . . .
which fell as cold and uninviting on the depraved imagination . . . and
heard but 'a hard saying' in what was sent from heaven as 'tidings of great
joy.'"[143] These are the beginnings of that basic disposition or temper
which constitute a major focus of *Arians*.

Prior to an examination of the important conflict of tempers in the
early Churches, we should note with irony the cause of this conflict, as
Newman perceived it: the failure of ecclesiastical authority. Once the
apostolic age ended, and with it the testimony of the original witnesses,

> no sufficient ecclesiastical symbol existed, as a guide to the mem-
> ory and judgment. . . . The absence of an adequate symbol of
> doctrine . . . had not yet been superceded by the authority of an
> ecclesiastical decision. . . . The Church was . . . not yet willing to
> impos[e] an authoritative creed. . . . The leaders of the Church
> were dilatory in applying a remedy. . . . They were loth (sic) to
> confess, that the Church had grown too old to enjoy the free,
> conspicuous teaching with which her childhood was blcst.[144]

---

surface. Like contemporary religious liberalism, Arianism, unlike earlier heresies, was
originally a 'sceptical rather than a dogmatic teaching', aiming 'to inquire into and
reform the received creed, rather than to hazard one of its own', and as such enjoying
all the advantages of the 'assailant' over 'the assailed party' in 'finding' rather than
'solving objections'. In disputing the orthodox creed, the Arians, too, were guilty of
misapplying human reason to the mysteries of revelation." Ker, *John Henry Newman:
A Biography*, 48. Notably, the tuition dispute intertwined the liberal-Church conflict.
Newman referenced this interrelationship regarding the Peel affair, Hawkins, and
the tutors: "Mr. Peel . . . had offered himself for re-election . . . [and it] was far more
than a question of politics and political expediency; it was a moral, an academical,
an ecclesiastical, nay a religious question. . . . Their [the tutors'] opponents were
liberals, and the liberal side . . . was the anti-Church, anti-Christian side." Newman,
Autobiographical Writings, 97.

142   John Henry Newman, *The Arians of the Fourth Century* (London: Basil, Montague,
Pickering, 1876), 19.   143   Ibid., 18–19.   144   Ibid., 35–37.

The seeds of ecclesiastical discord were planted by the failure of Church leaders to fill the void occasioned by the reality of passing time. Original witnesses passed on and their testimony of truth had to be transmitted, but how? Such was the dilemma for the early Church, and its response was "dilatory." The absence of Church authority gave rise to a spirit of self-determination. Ironically, this is the very principle, the assertion of authority, which will cause Newman to shortly reject Rome. A second irony is that he will also soon criticize the Anglican leadership for *its* lack of assertion of authority.

Aligned with this failure of authority was the influence of the Sophist intellectual school whose method emphasized a "sceptical rather than a dogmatic teaching . . . proposing to inquire into and reform the received creed, rather than to hazard one of its own. This was the artifice to which Arianism owed its first successes."[145] Beginning in the Antiochene Church with Paulus of Samosata, it was continued by Arius, who:

> went on to argue that 'if the Father begat the Son, certain con-
> clusions would follow'. . . . His heresy . . . [was] founded in a syl-
> logism. . . . Arianism had in fact a close connexion with the
> existing Aristotelic school . . . as that philosopher's logical system
> confessedly is to baffle an adversary, or at most to detect error,
> rather than to establish truth.[146]

Continuing his analysis of the intellectual or methodological nature of the Arian claims, Newman wrote:

> The minds of speculative men were impatient of ignorance, and
> loth to confess that the laws of truth and falsehood which the
> experience of this world furnished, could not . . . be applied to
> another. . . . Hence, canons grounded on physics were made
> the basis of discussions about possibilities and impossibilities in
> a spiritual substance . . . as those which in modern times have
> been derived from the same false analogies against the exis-
> tence of moral self-action or free-will. . . . Accordingly . . . those
> who would not believe the incomprehensibility of the Divine
> Essence . . . conceive[d] of it by the analogy of sense, and use[d]
> the figurative terms of theology in their literal sense.[147]

Newman provided a statement from Epiphanius as a succinct summary of this intellectual-methodological aspect of the heretical mind: "'Aiming,'

---

he says, 'to exhibit the Divine Nature by means of Aristotelic syllogisms and geometrical data, they are thence led on to declare that Christ cannot be derived from God.'"[148]

However, it was at this point that Newman perceived dependence of the heretical intellect on the temper which grounds that intellect. Temper, as an expression of affectivity and will, is arguably the single most pervasive theme of *Arians*, and it is equally important in our thesis. As we have seen, temper occupied much of Newman's theological thought at the time, and his own intellectual work was substantially grounded in his own temper.

In the second statement above on the formation of the heretical mind, Newman linked the intellect with temper by means of the descriptions "impatient of ignorance" and "loth [sic] to confess." Here we note his development of the principle that will and affectivity, or temper, shape the intellect. Earlier Newman had identified the historical genesis of this disposition as the "unchristian temper" which pervaded the region prior to the Arian controversy, characterized by "love of singularity, the spirit of insubordination and separatism, and the gloomy spiritual pride which . . . history evidences."[149] Newman accumulated evidence of a predisposition of negative affectivity which is essentially self-centered and destructive of interpersonal relations. Echoing the long-standing debate with his brother Charles, the opening chapter of *Arians* asserts a fundamental principle: temper determines method, or put another way, the predisposition of affectivity shapes the intellectual canons of the individual. Paulus of Samosata, of the Antiochene Church, embodied that temperament "with a rapacity, an arrogance . . . extraordinary profaneness, and a profligacy . . . a supercilious spirit" with a resultant heretical theology "concerning the Person of Christ . . . certainly derogatory of the doctrine of His absolute divinity and eternal existence."[150] But Newman identified the moral sense as another important influence upon the intellect, which also bore on Paulus's theological development: "His heresy was a kind of Judaism in doctrine, adopted to please his Jewish princess [Zenobia][151] . . . who possessed influence enough over the Christian body to seduce the Metropolitan himself from the orthodox faith."[152] This led to an assault on the heart of revelation itself, the mystery of the Incarnation: "A tendency to derogate from the honour due to Christ . . . was . . . created by an observance of the Jewish rites . . . by that carnal, self-indulgent religion."[153] Newman then linked the slackening

---

148 Ibid., 35.   149 Ibid., 16.   150 Ibid., 4–5.   151 Ibid., 5.
152 Ibid., 12.   153 Ibid., 18.

moral state of the Church at Antioch with both the breakdown of faith (an affectively based act) and doctrine (an intellectual representation of faith):

> Men like Paulus were but symptoms of a corrupted state of the Church. The history of the times gives us sufficient evidence of the luxuriousness of Antioch; and it need scarcely be said, that coldness in faith is the sure consequence of relaxation of morals.... When the spirit and morals of a people are materially debased, varieties of doctrinal error spring up, as if self-sown, and are rapidly propagated . . . evidencing the latent connexion between a judaizing discipline and heresy in doctrine.[154]

In this analysis Newman forged the connection between temper, morality, and intellect. Temper is the driving force which shapes the intellect, but morality, a product of the intellect by means of the temper, likewise influences the intellect. In other words, Newman described the reciprocal dynamic relationship between these entities. Thus far Newman was sketching out the negative or heretical temper and its influences. Let us now examine his analysis of positive affective temper and its effects on morals and intellect. This discussion was grounded in the cornerstone of Christian temper which the heretics rejected, personal witness. The heretics "rested their cause on their dialectical skill, and not the testimony of the early Church,"[155] a statement which recalls the theme of the *Miracles* essay. With this reference to testimony Newman affirmed the key reality of interpersonal dynamics, which beckons forth faith in spite of the limitations of reason. An important insight drawn from Newman's analysis is the erroneous understanding of man's relationship to God, which can be derived from erroneous liturgical symbols, which in turn produce erroneous intellectual conceptualizations which, through the principle of reciprocal influence, damage the affections. Newman, reminiscent of his liturgy sermons, describes the interaction:

> The mere performance of the rites of the Law, of which Christ came as anti-type and repealer, has . . . a tendency to withdraw the mind from the contemplation of the more glorious and real images of the Gospel; so that the Christians of Antioch would diminish their reverence towards the true Savior of man, in proportion as they trusted the media of worship provided for a time by the Mosaic ritual.[156]

---

154 Ibid., 9, 18, 21.   155 Ibid., 30.   156 Ibid., 19.

Newman's introduction of the act of trust into the liturgical process, which he developed in the liturgy sermons, indicates its interpersonal nature, which is a further development of the understanding of Christian temper. Testimony, witness, and trust are terms of relationship to an Other, wherein we see the opposite in the heretical temper. It is this contrast of reverence for the "old paths" of the tradition, its witnesses and teachers, and thus implicitly their authority, which separates the Christian from the heretical temper. Newman quoted Alexander on this point: "It is one of the first accusations brought by Alexander against Arius and his party, that 'they put themselves above the ancients, and the teachers of our youth, and the prelates of the day; considering themselves alone to be wise, and to have discovered truths, which had never been revealed to man before them.'"[157] Recalling Newman's earlier sermon on reverence for religious teachers and how that was provided through relationship, we can see in this statement the self-centered temper which declares itself as its own authority and deduces truth from that ground. This temper severs relationship and, if truth be a product of relationship, as the Christian temper senses, then truth is obscured and error issues forth. However, this analysis is nonsensical to the heretical mind because, through its temper, its method for evaluating truth-claims has been reduced to subjectivist principles. The Christian temper, on the other hand, is distinctly Other-centered, or objectivist and intersubjectivist, in its methodology. We find evidence of this temper in the Antiochene Church's contrast with the Alexandrian Church, the latter characterized not by a self-centered judgment of the truth-claims of revelation but rather by a submission to the voice of revelation in order to grasp its truths, with a notable humility born of subordination. This produces faith:

> It is scarcely the attribute of a generous faith, to be anxiously inquiring into the consequences of this or that system, with a view to decide its admissibility, instead of turning at once to the revealed word, and inquiring into the rule there exhibited to us.[158]

Newman then cites important examples of Christian temper in the early Church at Alexandria. This begins his argument for consistency of tradition between it, the original witnesses, and the Church of England, and thus the Anglican claim of apostolic succession. Two major examples of the affective Alexandrian temper are the character of the Church's

---

157   Ibid., 36.   158   Ibid., 46.

writings and that of its religious education system. The former are imbued with interpersonalistic qualities, with their object always concern for the other, the convert:

> The writings of its theologians would partake largely of an exoteric character. I mean, that such men would write . . . with the tenderness or the reserve with which we are accustomed to address those who do not sympathize with us, or whom we fear to mislead or to prejudice against the truth, by precipitate disclosures of its details.[159]

Thus a gradual disclosure of truths, or economic method of writing, was employed solely out of concern for the convert. Tenderness, reserve, and humility were all qualities of concern for the other and characteristic of the Alexandrian temper. Its catechetical school emphasized obedience, which implicitly included submission to the authority of religious teachers: "A previous season of preparation, from two to three years, was enjoined, in order to try their obedience, and instruct them in the principles of revealed truth . . . before reception into full discipleship . . . of believers."[160]

All of these qualities of Christian temper which the Alexandrian Church possessed can be called those of religious affectivity. Newman drew a second and parallel description of the Christian temper from Scripture, at the same time making an argument for the legitimacy of the Alexandrian Church. Newman stated that conversion is wrought by an affective process: "As to Scripture . . . no one sanction can be adduced . . . in behalf of the practice of stimulating the affections . . . in order to the conversion of the hearers."[161] However, faith is brought about by that moral habit, obedience, which is affective in nature:

> On the contrary, it is its uniform method to connect the Gospel with Natural Religion, and to mark out obedience to the moral law as the ordinary means of attaining to a Christian faith. . . . Converts . . . were . . . distinguished by a strictly conscientious deportment.[162]

Obedience, as we have already seen, is an interpersonal dynamic, and therefore affective, which implies both relationship and submission to an other. Clement of Alexandria was referenced as a prime illustration of that Church's method which, of especial note, was consistent with Scripture, and both contrasted sharply with that of Antioch: "It had the distinct

---

159 Ibid., 42.   160 Ibid., 44.   161 Ibid., 46.   162 Ibid., 46–47.

object of interesting the learned heathen ... [and the] desire to rouse the moral powers to internal voluntary action, and their dread of loading and formalizing the mind."[163] We note here the relationship of the affective, moral, and intellectual dimensions in one process, but also of importance is how they interrelate. Foremost is the generating force of the process, the affective drive, which emanates from the teacher as a desire to rouse the hearer to desire the object of such movement. This is described as engaging the moral powers to act, or in short, to promote the desire to do good, all the while exhibiting care not to over-intellectualize the process. This of course does not mean that the intellect is not engaged in the process of moral discernment, but quite the opposite. Such discernment always includes intellectual engagement, even if just implicitly, but it is easily possible that an overly stimulated intellect may result in a moral confusion due to the ultimately mysterious nature of divine truth. It is this dilemma which the Alexandrian teachers sought to avoid.

One last quality is stated by Clement which should not be overlooked in that it recalls the theme of the early Newman sermon on holiness and it is also affective in nature: "Our ears must be sanctified as well as our tongues, if we aim at being recipients of the truth."[164] Sanctification, or holiness, is a condition for grasping truth. Thus, the intellect's understanding is dependent upon affective and moral development. Newman concluded that Alexandria is methodologically, and thus temperamentally, consistent with Scripture, and thus the legitimate heir to Apostolic succession: "The Fathers considered that they had the pattern as well as the recommendation of this method of teaching in Scripture itself."[165] In fact, the two sources of divine truth, Scripture and tradition, are two sides of the same coin in that they are both based upon the same fundamental fact: personal witness. It is the experience of witness which the tradition expresses in its doctrine and creed. On this point Newman cited Irenaeus:

> We know the doctrine of our salvation through none but those who have transmitted to us the gospel, first proclaiming ... then delivering it in the Scriptures ... the traditionary and the written doctrine together ... substantially one and the same.[166]

Not only does the interpersonalist fact of witness ground doctrine and its transmission, but such witness is also affective in character, by the example of St. Paul, whom Newman referenced through Augustine: "He was made all to all men ... from the affection of a sympathizer ... with

---

163   Ibid., 48–49.   164   Ibid., 49.   165   Ibid., 54–55.   166   Ibid., 54.

compassion . . . to the little ones dispensing the lesser doctrines . . . but the higher mysteries to the perfect, all . . . true, harmonious, and divine."[167] Not only did Paul teach with an affective disposition, but his teaching was of mysteries which are harmonious, a reference to their aesthetic quality, one which is then reflected in the function of the early Church, "the chief office of the early traditions, viz. that of interpreting and harmonizing the statements of Scripture."[168]

Newman identified yet another principle of method shared by both Scripture and tradition, allegory, which is described as "the representation of truths, under a foreign, though analogous exterior . . . of adumbrating greater truths under the image of lesser."[169] But the crucial insight was the purpose of allegorical method, which is nothing short of, first, affective conversion, through the aesthetic or imaginative aspect of allegory, which then makes moral and intellectual conversion possible:

> Scripture assigns the same uses to this allegorical style, which were contemplated by the Fathers . . . viz. of trying the earnestness and patience of inquirers, discriminating between the proud and the humble, and conveying instruction to believers.[170]

Another dimension of method, previously noted in Paul, is that of economy, or the gradual unfolding and thus partial withholding of the truth. Economical and allegorical methods are two means of achieving the same end, conversion: "To contrast the two with each other, the one may be considered as withholding the truth, and the other as setting it out to advantage."[171] But we are brought back to the primacy of affective conversion as the ground of intellectual conversion by this statement from Basil on the use of the economical method by Gregory of Neocaesarea: "He did not think it necessary to be very exact in his doctrinal terms, when employed in converting a heathen; but in some things, even to concede to his feelings, that he might gain him over to the cardinal points."[172]

The failure to grasp this methodological fact is at the root of heretical intellectual error, which is an aesthetic flaw, grounded in an affective defect: "This distinction our heretical opponents could not enter into, much as they pride themselves on the subtlety of their intellect."[173]

Economy is crucial not only for our understanding of the nature and consistency of Scripture and early Church teaching but also because it is the mode of divine communication, both in creation and in all of revelation:

---

167 Ibid., 53.   168 Ibid., 56.   169 Ibid.   170 Ibid., 59.
171 Ibid., 65.   172 Ibid., 70.   173 Ibid.

> The doctrine of the Economy...[is] exemplified in the dealings
> of Providence towards man.... It might with equal fitness be
> used ... for the work of creation itself.... All those so-called
> Economies ... which display His character in action, are but
> condescensions to the infirmity and peculiarity of our minds,
> shadowy representations of realities which are incomprehen-
> sible to creatures such as ourselves, who estimate everything
> by... parts and whole.[174]

The method of revelation grounding Scripture and tradition is both
interpersonalist, "the influence of being on being,"[175] and implicitly
aesthetic. But this brings us to the central insight, which is the affective
ground of "God's method":

> The popular argument from final causes...[is] an Econo-
> mia ... teaching ... the active presence of Him, who ... dwells
> intelligibly, prior to argument, in ... heart and conscience.... This
> general principle seems to have cut all the ties and to be floated
> off...[in] interminable scepticism; yet a true sense of [our] own
> weakness brings it back, the instinctive persuasion that it must
> be intended to rely on something, and therefore the information
> given, though philosophically inaccurate, must be practically
> certain; a sure confidence in the love of Him who cannot deceive,
> and who has impressed the image and thought of Himself and
> His will upon our original nature.[176]

We find in this pastoral-systematic statement at one and the same
time the influences of the arguments from authority and personality in
a sacramental context, derived from Butler and Keble, and the seeds of
the arguments for certainty and the illative sense which Newman will
explicate in the *Grammar of Assent*. There is no mistaking that the function
of the teaching is to arouse a realization of the existing interpersonal and
dependent relationship between God and the self, one which is so intimate
that it can be described as an indwelling or interpenetration. This is the
living presence of the Transcendent Other, an affective relationship by its
very nature, which through the imaginative aspect of the aesthetic element,
and then through reflection, becomes intellectual. Clearly, however, this
mutual indwelling affectivity is the essence of true reality and relationship,
and thus the ground of all method and, by extension, the temper which
necessarily grounds method. When the intellect rejected this concept of

---

174   Ibid., 75.   175   Ibid.   176   Ibid., 76.

the "whole" of reality, based upon a presumption of the power of its own intellectual operation, it produced the aesthetic flaw in heresy:

> The greatest risk will result from attempting to be wiser than God has made us, and to outstep . . . the limit of our range. . . . Intellectual ability should do no more than enlighten us in the difficulties of our situation, not in the solution of them.[177]

An appropriate recognition of our intellectual limitations leads to the opposite, affective response: "This is but the duty of implicit faith in Him."[178] However, the value of Newman's analysis of the intellectual error in heretical method was in his attribution of that mistake to its affective base, its temper, "the cold disputatious spirit, and the unprincipled domineering ambition, which are the historical badges of the heretical party."[179] These were defects of the heart, essentially interpersonalist, and they sowed the seeds which grew into the intellectual methods of heresy. In speaking of the Arian school specifically, Newman noted those negative traits clearly identifiable as damaging to the affections:

> Its disputatious temper . . . melancholy temperament . . . an abstraction from sense, and an indifference to ordinary duties . . . walking by an internal vision of the truth, not by . . . a tedious and progressive reason,[180] and bold, irreverent inquiries and the idle subtleties . . . are the tokens of the genuine Arian temper.[181]

It is this predisposition of temper which caused the Arian mind to reject the truths of Scripture because it misunderstood the methods by which they were communicated:

> The Arian . . . ask[ed] . . . why he should believe our Lord's divinity. . . . Allegorisms did not silence him, while it suggested the means of evading those more argumentative proofs of the Catholic doctrine . . . built upon the explicit and literal testimonies of Scripture . . . by a forced figurative exposition . . . and extended the application of the allegorical rule.[182]

Newman pinpointed the intellectual contradiction in Arian method, on the one hand implicitly rejecting the allegorical description of the relationship between Father and Son, yet implicitly utilizing the same principle to deny the Son's divinity. Newman offered yet another description of the heretic as "timid and narrow-minded . . . unwilling to receive the truth

---

177 Ibid. 178 Ibid. 179 Ibid., 97.
180 Ibid., 109–10. 181 Ibid., 113–14. 182 Ibid., 114.

in that depth and fullness in which Scripture reveals it."[183] Intellectually narrow and anti-aesthetic, the heretic was driven by a willful temper.

The preceding material from Newman's 130-page opening chapter revealed a theology of conversion dynamics wherein temper, the moral sense, the imagination, and the intellect function in reciprocity. Temper, associated with affectivity, was the ground of the process. In successive chapters Newman applied this schema to the doctrinal controversy of the fourth century, continuing to flesh out these dynamics. In his analysis of creedal formation and imposition, Newman combined an ecclesiastical critique with his conversion hypothesis to explain the cause of the conflict.

With increasing distance from the age of the original witnesses of divine truth, and a crisis developing in the absence of that authority, Church leaders responded by reformulating the principle of authority from that of the original witnesses to that of teachers as transmitters and "the especial guardians of divine truth."[184] Newman underscored the primacy of this interpersonal, affective relationship which we have seen throughout our study:

> Truth . . . its due resting-place . . . is the Christian's heart. . . . Here, again, is strikingly instanced the unfitness of books, compared with private communication, for the purposes of religious instruction; levelling, as they do, the distinctions of mind and temper by the formality of the written character, and conveying each kind of knowledge the less perfectly, in proportion as it is of a moral nature, and requires to be treated with delicacy and discrimination.[185]

Truth is communicated through the person of the teacher, and so it is in affective relationship that acceptance of the teaching, or conversion, is accomplished, a dynamic from heart to heart, resulting in an affectively driven faith:

> Before the mind has been roused to reflection . . . it acquiesces, if religiously trained, in . . . implicit acknowledgment of the divinity of Son and Spirit. . . . This is the faith of uneducated men, which is not the less philosophically correct . . . because it . . . [is] not conceived in those precise statements which presuppose the action of the mind on its own sentiments and notions.[186]

In one of his passages of greatest synthesis, Newman immediately moved from the facts of this experience to the cause, which identified the

---

183 Ibid., 126.　　184 Ibid., 135.　　185 Ibid., 138.　　186 Ibid., 143.

affective temper, influenced by its "vision" or aesthetic perception, as the foundation of both the moral and intellectual senses, and we also note the familiar familial analogy utilized:

> Moral feelings do not directly contemplate and realize to them-
> selves the objects which excite them.... A child feels not the
> less affectionate reverence towards his parents, because he can-
> not discriminate in words, nay, or in idea, between them and
> others. As, however, his reason opens ... the ground of his own
> emotions and conduct towards them ... are the correlations
> of their peculiar tenderness towards him [and] authority over
> him.... He might trace these ... to the essential relation itself
> [and] his ... debt to them for the gift of life and reason.... His
> intellect contemplates the object of those affections, which acted
> truly from the first, and are not purer or stronger merely for
> this accession of knowledge.... The mind ... cannot refrain
> from the attempt to analyze the vision which influences the heart,
> and the Object in which that vision centres; nor does it stop till
> [it expresses] in words ... what has ... been a principle both of
> its affections and its obedience. But here the parallel ceases....
> Reason can but represent it in the medium of those ideas which
> the experience of life affords.

However, the principle of reciprocity can cause an errant intellect to damage the affections: "Unless these ideas ... be correctly applied to it, they re-act upon the affections, and deprave the religious princi-ple.... [T]he intellectual representation should ever be subordinate to the cultivation of the religious affections."[187]

It is the nature of the intellect to express the experience of relationship. It is through this process that creeds are born: "The intellect demands a formal statement concerning the Object of our worship ... and a system of doctrine becomes unavoidable.... Creeds tranquilize the mind; the text of Scripture being addressed principally to the affections, and of a religious, not a philosophical character."[188] Thus, doctrine is the product of intellectual expression of relationship, and creeds fulfill the aesthetic function by synthesizing the feelings of the affections and the concepts of the intellect. Further, a similarity exists in the ground of doctrine and the object of Scripture, which is the affections, or the religious character: "The Sacred text ... forms ... the religious temper."[189] But if creeds are deduced from Scripture it is essential to understand the Sacred text, and

---

187   Ibid., 143–45.   188   Ibid., 146.   189   Ibid.

to do so requires an aesthetic sense: "Scripture . . . and the faith which it propounds . . . [is] scattered throughout its documents, and understood only when they are viewed as a whole," which is the same sensibility described above as the "vision which influences the heart." The terminus of this aesthetic, affective dynamic is faith: "Faith [is] rather . . . a character of mind than [a] notion."[190]

Then Newman's anthropological insight was reflected in a statement regarding human nature, which implied that its essence lies in the affections rather than the intellect: "Nature . . . unites mankind by the sympathy of moral character, not by those forced resemblances which the imagination singles out."[191]

We can now summarize the interrelated dynamics of Newman's analysis. The essence of human nature lies in the formation of the human heart, which is accomplished through Scripture and the doctrines contained therein, through the teaching authority of the heirs to the witness tradition, and expressed in their creedal statements. These statements tranquilize the intellect in accord with the impulses of the affections, and perform an aesthetic, synthesizing and ultimately satisfying function, culminating in the interpersonal act of the will — faith.

In contrast to the Christian heart, or temper, is that of the heretic which, through its self-interestedness, misapprehends the analogical mode of Scripture doctrine, forcing a literal, human-centered logical interpretation:

> The meaning of Scripture . . . we may not deduce by [an] argu-
> mentative . . . process. . . . The case is analogous to that in which
> the evidence for Natural Religion is presented to us [and] our
> notion of the incommunicable nature of God . . . by a figure of
> speech. . . . The mysterious view of the doctrine evidently lies in
> our inability to conceive a sense of the word person . . . leading
> us to consider *personality* as equivalent . . . to the unity and inde-
> pendence of the immaterial substance of which it is predicated.[192]

The mystery which is rejected by the heretical mind is essentially beyond reason: "On these two truths the whole doctrine turns, viz. that our Lord is one with, yet personally separate from, God."[193] The key error in Arian method was the application of rational technique to personal relations, but the latter not being reducible to the former: "The love for two intimate friends, or for a brother and sister, or for . . . parents . . . arises from the incommensurableness . . . of the respective feelings. But false doctrine

---

190 Ibid., 147.   191 Ibid.   192 Ibid., 151–53.   193 Ibid., 156.

forces us to analyze our own notions, in order to exclude it."[194] Thus, doctrinal error was the end product of methodological error, itself the product of temper. A major contrast of Catholic and Arian tempers, which determines their respective doctrines, holds:

> There are no signs of an intellectual curiosity in the tenor of these Catholic expositions, prying into things not seen as yet; nor of an ambition to account for the representations of the truth given us in the sacred writings. But such a temper is the very characteristic of the Arian disputants. They insisted in taking the terms of Scripture and of the Church for more than they signified.[195]

This temper also produced an anti-aesthetic dimension in Arian method: "They took only just so much of [Scripture] as would afford them a basis for erecting their system of heresy by an abstract logical process . . . reasoning from . . . one or two Scripture terms . . . into . . . the principle."[196] The very opposite of this heretical temper, which is the culmination of the temper's development, is that which Newman noted in his liturgy sermons, concord, which is both affective and aesthetic in nature:

> Concord is . . . the perfection of the Christian temper, conduct, and discipline . . . almost . . . the sole precept of the Gospel. It required a far more refined moral perception, to detect and to approve the principle on which the internal peace is grounded in Scripture; to submit to the dictation of truth . . . as a primary authority in matters of conduct; to understand how belief in a certain creed was a condition of Divine favour, how the social union was intended to result from an unity of opinions.[197]

Thus, again we see that submission to the truth, or obedience to authority, is essential to developing the temper of concord, which itself is essential to grasping the principle of concord in Scripture. Further, there is an implicit aesthetic sense in the relationship between belief, doctrine, and God-man and man-man relationships. In the final analysis, affectivity is the very source of desire: "We desire to revere what we already love. . . . The truth [is] revealed to us in Scripture . . . to humble and to win over . . . those who really love it."[198] It is the essence of these dynamics that they both begin and terminate in affectivity. Toward the close of his work, Newman synthesized faith, intellect, affection, morality, and

---

194 Ibid., 164.   195 Ibid., 223.   196 Ibid., 220–21.
197 Ibid., 244. For the liturgy's development of concord see Newman, *Sermons, 1824–1843,* 74.   198 Ibid., 273.

relationship: "The right faith . . . is the only true aliment of the human mind . . . which influences the heart to suffer and to labor for its sake."[199] The figure who most exemplified the temper of Christian concord was the leader of the Alexandrian Church during the period of the Arian heresy, Athanasius, who provided the line of consistency from the early witnesses to the Church of the fourth century. Such unity was reflected in affective and aesthetic identification: "Athanasius . . . evinces an admirable tenderness and forbearance . . . with a temper and candour, which . . . evidences . . . Christian charity. It is this union of opposite excellences, firmness with discrimination and discretion, which is the characteristic praise of Athanasius."[200] Newman sought such a line of continuity for his Church of England at the close of *Arians*, a continuity with apostolic witness and the Alexandrian Church, in the form of a latter-day Athanasius. In the closing sentence, he issued a clarion call ironically self-prophetic of the role he would shortly assume as one of his Church's leading reformers: "Our Athanasius and Basil will be given us in their destined season, to break the bonds of the Oppressor, and let the captives go free."[201]

SUMMARY OF THE *ARIANS* REVIEW

IN SUMMARY, *ARIANS* HIGHLIGHTS THE PENETRATING THEO-logical analysis which Newman brought to bear upon the nature of heresy, as Ian Ker so succinctly stated:

> The historical originality of Newman's first book lay in ascribing the origins of the Arian heresy to Antioch rather than Alexandria and to Aristotelian rather than Platonic influence; its theological topicality lay in the parallel it openly drew between Arianism and contemporary religious liberalism. [202]

However, Ker also cites a fact which contains a clue about Newman's ongoing conversion journey when he notes one reason the book was rejected by its originally intended publisher: "Newman's theological views, particularly on tradition, seemed more Roman Catholic than Protestant." And so it is of substantial note for us that in the process of his historical analysis he also provided a loosely constructed systematic of the nature of conversion and faith, the affective, aesthetic, moral, and intellectual elements of those entities, and their reciprocal dynamic interrelationships, consistently affirming Christian temper, or affectivity, with concord as its

---

199   Ibid., 355.   200   Ibid., 356.   201   Ibid., 394.
202   Newman, *Apologia*, 527.

fullest realization, as the ground of the processes. Our analysis of Newman's theology yields results supporting several of the major assertions
of our thesis: the nature of conversion, its affective ground and various
other elements, and the reciprocal dynamics of these parts, as well as
interpersonal relations, especially engendered in family life and friendships,
as the key to understanding the influence of affectivity on Newman's theology. At this point in his life, his affectivity was exhibited in a significant
dissonance. On the one hand, he displayed a brilliant theological grasp
of affectivity's nature and dynamics, first experienced in family life and
thus its primary model, which resulted in his religious conversion of 1816,
begetting the realization *that* he lived in graced relationship to a Transcendent Other. On the other hand, however, he was driven by a willful
temper in a continual search for the earthly *locus* of that Other, seeking
its intellectual representation. Beginning in his moral commitment to
Evangelicalism, it increasingly gave way to the Church of England as the
realization of that vision. In 1833, the search reached a climax, temporarily,
in his commitment to a reformed Anglican Church, while he rejected the
authoritarian Rome. This can be termed his moral conversion, which was
only a halfway house in his conversion journey. But as further evidence
of the primacy of affectivity in Newman's thinking and its connection to
relationships of family and friends, we now examine a key sermon which
he preached during his composition of *Arians*, dedicated to the theme of
affectivity. Given the time of its composition, we can presume it both
influenced, and was influenced by, his thinking in *Arians*.

D. NEWMAN'S AFFECTIVITY SERMON:
"The Love of Relations and Friends"[203]

ALMOST MIDWAY THROUGH THE WRITING OF ARIANS, NEWMAN
preached this sermon which expounds the nature of Christian love, the
temper at the heart of his *Arians* analysis. Here Newman traced the ground
of Christian love to the affections, a theme of his liturgy sermons, and
then grounded the affections in the selfless relationships of home life.
These two aspects substantiate dual themes of our thesis, first, that for
Newman affectivity is the ground of conversion, promoting intellectual
and moral development, and second, the ground of religious affectivity
which leads us to feel and know our relationship to God is perceived
through the vision of human relationships of home and friends, which
were the primary personal influences in Newman's life.

---

203   Newman, PPS, vol. ii, sermon 5, 259–64. Preached December 27, 1831.

Newman defined love as an affective, other-directed interpersonal state which includes three dimensions: submission, tolerance, and kindness, and it is necessarily moral, that is, not mere abstraction but active movement of the self toward, and for, the other,

> and therefore, must begin by exercising itself on our friends around us . . . by trying to love our relations and friends, by submitting to their wishes, though contrary to our own, by bearing with their infirmities, by overcoming their occasional waywardness by kindness.[204]

This is the method by which "we form in our hearts that root of charity."[205] Newman expressly criticized "universal" or abstract love when it is conceived apart from, and at the expense of, family and friends:

> The love of our fellow Christians and of the world at large . . . is the love of kindred and friends in a fresh shape. . . . A man, who would fain begin by a general love of all men . . . does harm . . . sacrificing individual to general good. . . . Abstract notions . . . often forget to take any thought of those who are associated with themselves.[206]

The model of Newman's theology of love is drawn from the example of Christ, related by St. John, on whose feast day this sermon was delivered. Newman reflected upon the human, affectionate Jesus in contrast to the concept of a less-than-humanly divine, dispassionate "universally loving" Christ:

> It might be supposed that the Son of God Most High could not have loved one man more than another. . . . Yet we find that our Saviour had a private friend; and this shows us, first, how entirely he was a man, as much as any of us, in His wants and feelings; and next, that there is nothing contrary to the spirit of the Gospel . . . in having our affections directed in an especial way towards certain objects, towards those whom the circumstances of our past life, or some peculiarities of character, have endeared to us.[207]

The pattern of true love is contained in the revelation of Jesus's personal relationships, grounding all further manifestations: "With our Saviour's pattern before me . . . the best preparation for loving the world at large . . . is to cultivate an intimate friendship and affection towards those who

---

204 Ibid., 261.   205 Ibid.   206 Ibid., 260, 262.   207 Ibid., 259.

are immediately about us."[208] The revealed pattern for us was in the interpersonal relationship of Jesus and St. John who "had the unspeakable privilege of being the friend of Christ. Thus he was taught to love others; first his affection was concentrated, then it was expanded."[209] Thus, for Newman affectivity grounds both the intellect and morality, supporting a major assertion of our thesis:

> It has been the plan of Divine Providence to ground what is good and true in religion and morals, on the basis of our good natural feelings. . . . Consider how many other virtues are grafted upon natural feelings.[210]

In the final major theme of the sermon, and again supporting one of our major assertions, Newman held that this affectivity is first experienced and learned in the home, through parents:

> What we are towards our earthly friends in the instincts and wishes of our infancy, such are we to become towards God and man in the extended field of our duties as accountable beings. To honour our parents is the first step towards honouring God.[211]

Here Newman returned to the theme which Part I of our thesis developed at length, that Newman's personal home life experiences of interpersonal love were the affective grounds of all the theology which followed, assuming the always-present influence of grace doing its work in the dynamic process. Immediately following this statement Newman made what is for us a most notable analogy between Church and home, one which is recurrent throughout his work: "Hence our Lord says, we must become as little children, if we would be saved; we must become in his Church, as men, what we were once in the small circle of our youthful homes."[212] In the affections associated with home life Newman finds the ground for a wider, social love:

> I have hitherto considered the cultivation of domestic affections as the source of more extended Christian love. . . . I cannot fancy any state of life more favourable for the exercise of high Christian principle, and the matured and refined Christian spirit . . . than that of persons who differ being obliged to live together, and mutually to accommodate to each other. . . . This is one among the many providential benefits . . . of the Holy

---

208 Ibid., 260.   209 Ibid., 262.   210 Ibid., 260.
211 Ibid.   212 Ibid.

Estate of Matrimony; which not only calls out the tenderest and gentlest feelings of our nature, but . . . must be in various ways more or less a state of self-denial.[213]

The affective relationships of home also engender moral conduct so infused with self-sacrifice that it transcends merely good behavior, relating not only man to man but man to God as well. By analogy, these human relations promote participation in, and knowledge of, the divine:

But what is it that can bind two friends together in intimate converse for a couple of years, but the participation in something that is Unchangeable and Essentially Good, and what is this but religion? Religious tastes alone are unalterable.[214]

Then echoing themes of the liturgy sermons and *Arians*, Newman addressed the affective Christian temper's opposite, which is selfishness and independence:

Nothing is more likely to engender selfish habits (which is the direct opposite and negation of charity), than *independence*. . . . Men who have no tie on them . . . no calls on their daily sympathy and tenderness . . . no one's comfort to consult, who can move about as they please, and indulge the love of variety . . . are very unfavourably situated for obtaining that heavenly gift, which is described in our Liturgy, as being 'the very bond of peace and virtues'. . . . We are not our own.[215]

Newman described that state which is destructive of, or at the least an impediment to, the development of Christian affectivity: independence of self from real affectionate involvement with others, characterized by the absence of self-denial. Ironically, it was precisely this state of independence and self-will which characterized Newman's dealings with Hawkins at this time, which supports our thesis that, while Newman understood from experience the nature and feelings of Christian affectivity, and could render them so eloquently in theological reflection, he displayed the very opposite tendency in his own conduct. On this point, we now turn our attention to an examination of his Mediterranean experiences, which provides evidence that he became startlingly aware of this dissonance, which will move us toward our conclusion that he achieved a moral conversion wrought by a changed affectivity, promoted by an aesthetic element, the vision of a reformed Church of England as the intellectual correlative of

---

213 Ibid., 263.   214 Ibid., 264.   215 Ibid., 263–64.

that experience. This sermon, however, in conjunction with the sermons on the liturgy, the *Arians* preamble sermons, and *Arians* itself, forms the theological aspect of this period, evidencing a heightened intellectual grasp of domestically engendered affectivity which was not yet fully incorporated into his temperament, thus causing his affective dissonance. Shortly after completing *Arians*, Newman set sail for the Mediterranean and a confrontation with, and partial resolution of, this internal dissonance.

STAGE THREE:
Confrontation with Willfulness and Moral Conversion

INTRODUCTION

THIS CLOSING SECTION WILL BRING THE CHAPTER BACK TO whence it began as Newman confronted the realization of his willfulness, especially in his dealings with Hawkins, eventually recalling the irony that the sermon he preached the day before he left England for the Mediterranean was on this very subject, willfulness. This experience, along with the tutor dispute, furnished the experiential pole of this period, in contrast to the insights of the theology he developed at the time, and thus supports our assertion of the presence of an affective dissonance. However, the tension of this dissonance will eventually produce conversion.

About five months after completing *Arians*, Newman accepted an offer to accompany Hurrell Froude and his father on a Mediterranean trip, undertaken primarily for the health of the younger Froude, who was chronically ill. They departed England on December 8, 1832. During the first part of the journey Newman visited Rome where he and Froude met twice with Dr. Wiseman, a Roman clergyman, to explore the common grounds between the two churches with an eye toward some kind of reconciliation. The contacts with Wiseman and other encounters with the Roman Church during this trip had both positive and negative effects on Newman, revealed through his personal correspondence, diaries, journals, and poetry. These sources support our thesis that his aversion to Rome was due to an affective dissonance, rooted in Rome's requirement of submission, again raising the issues of authority and personal judgment. Here again our methodology utilizes these personal documents to obtain a different perspective from that offered by his theological work. But in order to understand what happened to Newman in the spring of 1833 we begin by reviewing events in reverse order, first examining the root of that affective dissonance which burst forth during the second part of the trip when, on April 9, Newman parted company with the homeward-bound Froudes and returned to Sicily alone, where he confronted his internal dissonance, resulting in a life-changing moral conversion. Then we will return to review the ecclesiastical effects which had been wrought by that dissonance in the form of his rejection of Rome, which remained an unresolved dimension of his conversion.

THE SICILIAN EXPERIENCE[216]

FOR ACCOUNTS OF THESE EVENTS WE HAVE THREE RECORDS. First, he wrote to Frederick Rogers one month after this experience, and in July and August he wrote two letters to Henry Wilberforce in response to the latter's letter of concern and joy at Newman's safe return home. These letters form the most immediate documentation of the crisis, and they are supplemented by a later account of the events by Newman written at intervals in 1834, 1835, and 1840, and reviewed and edited by him again in 1876. These documents furnish us with, first, the facts of the episode, and second, Newman's interpretation of those facts.

Having parted company with the Froudes on April 9, Newman arrived in Messina on April 21 and, hiring a guide who accompanied him throughout his ordeal, he made his way inland. About nine days into the trip, Newman felt a fever coming on, which grew progressively worse:

> I having noticed feverish symptoms in me the foregoing day, (e.g. I could not eat at Catania on April 30) & that night being almost choked with a feeling[217] . . . I had the fever. . . . Numbers were dying of it. . . . My attendants thought I could not get over it. . . . I was so reduced that I could not lift my hand to my mouth to feed myself . . . but in ten days I was able to travel. . . . The only remaining signs of my illness now are my hair falling off and a slight cough.[218]

These details of his illness come from all three of the letters written within 90 days of the crisis. But it was in the last of the three, written to Wilberforce on August 4, that we find an account of Newman's reflection upon the episode which underscores our thesis. Through illness Newman realized the destructive nature of his willfulness:[219]

---

216 Louis Bouyer considers Newman's Sicilian experience "his greatest inward struggle" and a "plunge into the depths of his being" (*Newman*, 146, 150).
217 Newman, *Autobiographical Writings*, 122.   218 Ibid., 117–18.
219 Bouyer interprets the experience as "mainly a matter of self-will." Bouyer, *Newman*, 147.

> It was a lonely situation. . . . Yet I had once . . . quite a revela-
> tion come to me . . . of God's love to His elect, and felt as if I
> were one . . . Not that I can describe the feeling in words. Then
> I was much relieved the next day, by being able to discover, as I
> thought, sins in my conduct. . . . I came to think that there was
> something of willfulness in my coming to Sicily.[220]

Not only was there a willfulness in his specific intent to return to Sicily,
a decision which the Froudes opposed,[221] but Newman also reflected
that this willfulness was of a deeper, character-defining nature, with a
connection to his conduct toward Hawkins:

> And then I felt more than I had done the willfulness of my char-
> acter generally, and I reflected that I was lying there the very day
> on which three years before I had sent in my resignation of the
> tutorship (or something like it).[222]

Though Newman acknowledged his willfulness, at the same time he
indicated that he had not yet overcome it, since he was "unrepentant" of
what he did, even if critical of how: "And, though I could not (and do not)
at all repent doing so, yet I began to understand that the manner was hasty
and impatient."[223] The following year Newman reflected again upon his
Sicilian crisis, interpreting the events as punishment for his willful temper:

> It was a judgment for profaning the Lord's Supper, in having
> cherished some resentment against the Provost for putting me out
> of the Tutorship . . . [and] for my willfulness in going to Sicily
> by myself. . . . As I lay in my bed the first day . . . I . . . felt God
> was fighting agst me — & at last I knew why — it was for self-
> will. . . . I bitterly blamed myself, as disrespectful and insulting
> to the Provost, my superior.[224]

Newman's reflections caused him to connect his realization of willfulness with another insight "that the very day before I left Oxford, I
had preached a [University] Sermon against willfulness, so that I seemed
to be predicting my own condemnation . . . and whether in me was not
fulfilled the text 1 Cor xi : 29 – 32 (as I still think it has been)."[225] The
Pauline reference concludes with an interpretation of his illness as an act of
God's judgment for his own good: "When, however, we do fall under the

---

220 Newman, *Autobiographical Writings*, 118.   221 Ibid., 125.

222 Ibid., 118.   223 Ibid.   224 Ibid., 121, 124, 126.

225 Ibid., 118.

Lord's judgment, he is disciplining us, to save us from being condemned with the rest of the world."[226] And this illness and judgment were for the willfulness in his general character just as it had been in Saul's, the subject of his *University Sermon*. The irony of the connection provoked a change in Newman, first by an affective sense or feeling that something was not right, that God had been against him. This brought about the intellectual reflection with Saul as partners in willfulness, an apparent function of the analogical imagination. Through the reciprocal effect of that intellectual realization, produced by the dynamics of his internal affective dissonance, Newman underwent both an affective and moral change. But before noting the changes, we should examine Newman's analysis of the nature of Saul's willfulness, which will shed light on the nature of that affectivity which so affected him at this time.

THE SERMON ON "WILFULNESS: THE SIN OF SAUL"[227]

DELIVERED JUST FIVE MONTHS PRIOR TO HIS CRISIS, THIS SER-
mon offers additional evidence that Newman possessed an internal affective dissonance which provoked the heightened realizations during his illness. The sermon was an incisive analysis "of the nature of religious faith . . . by which I mean an implicit reliance . . . a surrender . . . to Him"[228]. . . . "The trial . . . is one of Faith in opposition to self-will,"[229] underscoring the fact that faith is essentially affective. In the person of Saul, Newman found the disposition of temper with which he would soon identify:

> Saul seems to have had . . . a certain perverseness of mind,
> founded on some obscure feelings of self-importance . . . called
> pride . . . a reluctance absolutely to relinquish its own inde-
> pendence of action . . . connected with . . . that one fatal defect
> of mind . . . corrupting the integrity of his faith . . . wilfulness,
> the unaccountable desire of acting short of simple obedience
> to God's will, a repugnance of unreserved self-surrender and
> submission to Him.[230]

This drive is nothing less than the anti-authority principle in human nature: "Wilfulness [is] a characteristic of human nature . . . an unaccount-able and instinctive feeling to resist authority as such."[231]

Lastly, Newman deduced the reciprocal nature of affectivity, the intel-lect, and moral conduct, which affirmed affectivity as the ground of the

---

226   Ibid.   227   Newman, *Fifteen Sermons*, 156–57. Preached December 2, 1832.
228   Ibid., 156–57.   229   Ibid., 173.   230   Ibid., 158, 161.
231   Ibid., 170, 169.

dynamic, reciprocal process. The will, an expression of affectivity, directs the intellect: "A perverse will easily collects together a system of notions to justify itself in its obliquity."[232] This was the principle at work in Saul:

> By wilful resistance to God's will, he opened the door to those evil passions which . . . ended in an overthrow of the mind . . . by the removal of true religious principle. . . . Derangement was the consequence of disobedience. . . . Wilfulness [is] a natural principle of disorder. . . . His moods and changes . . . were . . . the convulsions of the spirit, when the governing power was lost.[233]

Thus, willfulness produced unbelief: "He fell from his election, because of unbelief — because he would take another part, and not the very part which was actually assigned him."[234] However, it is an affective conversion of the heart which disposes the mind to what can be called Newman's expression of an aesthetic vision of truth: "But those minds, which naturally most resemble the aboriginal chaos, contain within them the elements of a marvellous creation of light and beauty, if they but open their hearts to the effectual power of the Holy Spirit."[235] And how is this accomplished? Through submission to the truth of revelation, we overcome self-will, we trust in faith, and we shape our moral character: "Revelation puts us on a trial . . . of obeying for obedience-sake, or on Faith. . . . Revelation provides us with an important instrument for chastening and moulding our moral character, over and above the matter of its disclosures."[236]

This sermon provides an insight into the grounds for Newman's self-condemnation, and it also supports our thesis of the affective ground,

---

232 Ibid., 164.   233 Ibid., 164–65.   234 Ibid., 166.
235 Ibid. This reference to the "light and beauty" which inheres in the human mind through an "open heart" to the Spirit is indicative of the intuitive recognition of divine presence which Newman was soon to experience among the Catholic peasants of Sicily. Newman confirms this influence: "Then, when I was abroad, the sight of so many great places, venerable shrines, and noble churches, much impressed my imagination. And my heart was touched also. Making an expedition on foot across some wild country in Sicily, at six in the morning, I came upon a small church; I heard voices, and I looked in. It was crowded, and the congregation was singing. Of course it was the mass, though I did not know it at the time. And, in my weary days at Palermo, I was not ungrateful for the comfort which I had received in frequenting the churches; nor did I ever forget it. . . . Thus I learned to have tender feelings towards her [the Roman Church]; but still my reason was not affected at all. My judgment was against her, when viewed as an institution, as truly as it ever had been. This conflict between reason and affection I expressed in one of the early Tracts, published July, 1834." Newman, *Apologia*, 65.   236 Ibid., 172.

with an accompanying aesthetic image, and its reciprocal relationship with the intellect and the moral sense.

Examining Newman's self-reflections, we find, first, his realization of the dissonance existing between his affective state of willfulness and his intellectual understanding of its moral consequences, especially in regard to the Hawkins affair, and then an important revelation of a dissonance within his affective state itself.[237] This produced a partial affective conversion, causing a moral conversion. Accompanying his realizations of willfulness and remorse over his behavior, he also had "quite a revelation . . . of God's love to His elect, and felt as if I were one . . . an instance of God's mercy to me; not that I can describe the feeling in words." From his description, we can conclude that what Newman felt was an affective experience, deeper than intellect, beyond words. In the midst of his realization of his sinful willfulness, he still felt the personal presence, love, and grace of God directed toward him. This affective experience appeared to have provoked what we interpret as a key statement differentiating his errant temperament and behavior from the true aspiration of his soul. "But after all I was comforted by the thought that...'I have not sinned against the light,' and repeated this often."[238] This was Newman's plea that, although he had erred in his conduct due to his willfulness, he had not understood until this moment that his self-centered acts against his fellow man were actually against God Himself. Immediately following this is his conversion-confession:

> And then I thought I would try to obey God's will as far as I
> could . . . walking in the way of God's commandments and put-
> ting myself in the way of His mercy[239]. . . . I had a strange feeling
> on my mind that God meets those who go on in His way . . . that
> I must put myself in His path, His way, that I must do my part.[240]

We can arguably hold that according to his accounts of this day, May 5, Newman began an affective conversion of his willfulness which, in less than two months, culminated in both a moral and an intellectual conversion to a vision of a reformed Church of England as the true and good embodiment of that religious sentiment.[241]

---

237 Meriol Trevor interprets Newman's Sicilian trip as a reflection of the inner turmoil which we have been asserting: "The whole adventure perfectly realized in action the psychological and spiritual crisis within. . . . Perhaps that obscure intuition of his drove him back to the beautiful terrible island he called men's tomb." Trevor, *The Pillar of the Cloud*, 121.   238 Newman, *Autobiographical Writings*, 118. 239 Ibid., 119.   240 Ibid., 127.
241 Jean Smith's comprehensive analysis of Newman's Sicilian expeditions synthesizes the influence of suffering, the affection of strangers, and the possible ecclesiastical

In a final extract from his reflections a year after the crisis, which proved that this conversion was only partial, Newman offered a searing self-analysis which differentiated his substantial intellectual ability from his state of heart, a dissonance which resulted in a "hollowness" of his preaching the Truth without possessing it:

> The self-reproaching feelings increased. I seemed to see more and more my utter hollowness.... My professed principles ... felt...[as] mere intellectual deductions from one or two admitted truths.... I have a vivid perception ... of certain admitted principles ... a considerable intellectual capacity of drawing them out ... & a rhetorical ... power to express them.... Loving the Truth, but not possessing it.... I believe myself at heart to be nearly hollow — i.e., with little love, little self-denial. I believe I have some faith, that is all.... This statement will account for how I can preach the Truth without thinking much of myself.[242]

By his own account, his gifted perception, intellectual capacity, and rhetorical power pale next to his affective failure of possessing the Truth. In revealing terminology, he is "at heart" nearly hollow, with "little love, little self-denial." But the saving grace was a desire for That which eluded him: "Loving the Truth ... I have some faith." His faith underscored the dichotomy within his affectivity, an admission both of a failure due to willfulness and of an implicit desire for a better relationship with God, very similar to the tension revealed by his statement during the crisis that he had "not sinned against the light."

The spiritual crisis in Sicily raised to consciousness the long-existing internal conflict of which his father had cautioned him years earlier, and which damaged his relationship with Hawkins. He realized it was a question of heart. The tension between doing his own will and doing God's will forced him into an unnatural affective bifurcation. The result was a

---

effects of the experiences: "Now, after a double crisis, spiritual and physical, of near-death and rebirth ... we cannot tell what deeper resonances the spirit of the place set up within him below the level of consciousness; perhaps it surfaces in that keener awareness of the Church (for years to come, of course, the Church of England) as 'Mother', which recurs in his verses and sermons from now onwards. Here and now, what he had experienced ... was hospitality, the mercy of Catholics, the kindness of a good house, whence he was sent on with commendations to friends, to Palermo, and the final stage of his journey home." "Newman and Sicily," ed. Rosemary Smith, *The Downside Review* (July 1989): 176.

242 Newman, *Autobiographical Writings*, 125.

spiritual metamorphosis and a change of heart, a desire to conform his will to God's. But what would be the intellectual and moral expression of that conversion? He resolved the question by formulating the image of a reformed Church of England. He was finally conscious of his affective dissonance, but he attained only a temporary resolution, a partial solution: the realization *that* the Transcendent Other was manifested and encountered in His most revealed form *in* a reformed English Church, resolving, for now, *where* this encounter occurred. *Arians* provided the intellectual justification to recognize the Church of England as the contemporary heir to the Alexandrian and hence the apostolic tradition. However, that Church required a "second reformation" to avoid the pitfalls of liberalism, just as the Church of the fourth century required the assertion of Church authority to combat Arianism. But the Church of England would be only a temporary solution until the next manifestation of the dissonance.

Now we examine the road not taken in 1833 when Newman was attracted to, but ultimately rejected, the alternative of the Roman Church during the earlier part of his Mediterranean journey with disparagement characteristic of his temper. His Roman antipathies, as they existed in 1833, were not without their ambivalences, which were the seeds of his intellectual conversion which lay ahead.

THE ENCOUNTER WITH ROME AND ITS REJECTION

"A UNION WITH ROME, WHILE IT IS WHAT IT IS, IS IMPOSSI-ble,"[243] was the comment Newman wrote to John F. Christie on the very same day that he and Froude met with Dr. Wiseman in Rome just three days before the end of their five-week visit. The significance of Newman's conclusion was that it was rooted in that same willfulness which Newman confronted just one month later in Sicily. But why did Newman meet with Wiseman to discuss "union" with Rome, and why did he balk? It was nothing short of the issue of submission of his independent self-will to a greater authority. But this occurred at the end of the Roman visit, and to understand fully Newman's feelings toward Rome we must examine the experiences which led him to seek out Wiseman. In the process we will also discover a heightened motivation for his reform of the Anglican Church, and the ambivalence of both his great impressions of, yet disgust for, the Roman Church. We begin in late 1832 just four days after sailing from Oxford, with Newman's dire perception of the state of the English Church reflected in his poetry:

---

243   Newman, *Letters and Diaries*, vol. III, 277.

> O Englishmen, truth-scorners brave!
>   How will ye weep the day
> When Christ reclaims the gift he gave
>   And calls the Bride away. [244]

The early part of the trip gave Newman much time for writing, and he communicated his attitude toward the "southern Churches" in this verse sent to Isaac Williams from Malta on January 16:

> O Lord and Christ, Thy Churches of the South
>   So shudder when they see
> The two-edged sword sharp issuing from Thy mouth,
>   As to fall back from Thee.
> And seek the charms of men, or Saints above,
>   To aid them against Thee, Thou font of grace and love. [245]

This vision of a troubled English Church, and of an even more dire situation existing in the "Churches of the South," framed the boundaries of the ecclesiastical dilemma Newman faced during his Roman visit. His impressions of the "southern Churches" were confirmed in late January by a visit to St. John's Cathedral during a stopover in Malta: "Most magnificent it is . . . but it is fearful to have before one's eyes the perversion of all the best, the holiest, the most exalted feelings of human nature . . . admirable if it did not go quite so far. . . . A sad presentiment, as if the gift of truth, when once lost, was lost forever."[246]

Newman identified the materialism of the southern Churches as a cause of their corruption, a theme he will reiterate in Rome. He then made another comparison with the English Church: "We have lasted longer than the South — but *we* are going (it appears) also."[247]

In addition to materialism, the liturgical excesses of the Churches were even more ominous: "The *fact* of the Greek Church invoking Saints, overhonouring the Virgin, and substituting ceremonies for a reasonable service . . . are the *prophetic* marks of Antichrist."[248]

Newman's arrival in Rome on March 2 gave rise to immediate paradoxical pagan and religious reflections of inherent evil contrasted with religious pleasure: "The first notion one has of Rome is as the great Enemy of God, the fourth monarchy — and the sight of the city in this view is awful — we need no tower of Babel."[249] His religious view of Rome contrasted, but not without significant flaw:

---

244 Ibid., 150.   245 Ibid., 198.   246 Ibid., 204.
247 Ibid., 204–5.   248 Ibid., 205.   249 Ibid., 231.

> As to the . . . view of Rome, the religious, here pain and plea-
> sure are mixed. . . . The Roman Clergy are said to be a decorous
> orderly body . . . and the appearance of the priests is superior. But
> there is (seemingly) timidity, indolence, and that secular spirit
> which creeps on established religion every where.[250]

In the same letter to his sister Harriett, he summed up his ambivalence
in verse:

> How shall I call Thee, Light of the wide West,
>   Or heinous error-seat?[251]

A few days later he again criticized the southern liturgies of the Greek
fasts and the Latin Masses as "a substitute apparently for moral obedience,
and an opiate to the conscience."[252] His earlier sense of the materialism
of the southern Churches was validated by his perceptions in Rome: "But
I believe all over Italy, and here pre-eminently, the Churches and the fine
buildings are the lure which makes the ecclesiastical body so timid and
poor-spirited. . . . They cannot bear to lose as a body such beautiful and
rich structures."[253]

The materialism and liturgical excesses led Newman to conclude that
they had resulted in "an over-abundance of formality, i.e. of outward
actions without *reverential* feeling." This, he felt, was England's warning:
"Yet it is useful to dwell upon this, because it is so likely to be the case with
ourselves at home."[254] But on March 18, after more than two weeks in
Rome, Newman wrote a summary impression which could be considered
an intellectual predisposition unsupported by fact:

> I cannot quite divest myself of the notion that Rome Christian is
> somehow under an especial shade as Rome pagan certainly was —
> though I have seen nothing here to confirm it. Not that one
> can tolerate for an instant the wretched perversion of the truth
> which is sanctioned here, but I do not see my way enough to
> say that there is anything peculiar in the condition of Rome.[255]

The need was for purgation, and not only for Rome: "By no means
short of some terrible conversion and thro' much suffering can the Roman
Church, surely, be reformed — nothing short of great suffering, as by fire,
can melt us together in England, one with another."[256]

But on March 25, Newman attended a Roman liturgy, and from the
account which he provided in a letter to his mother, which was extraordinary

---

250 Ibid., 232.   251 Ibid.   252 Ibid., 239.   253 Ibid., 246.
254 Ibid., 246–47.   255 Ibid., 258.   256 Ibid., 259.

in detail, it had a major impact on him. It appeared to have been the celebra-
tion of a Solemn High Mass at which the pope presided.[257] While on the one
hand he wrote that "not to speak of *doctrinal errors*, there is much unedifying
dumbshow," he was on the other hand so impressed by the overall ceremony
that he concluded, "And yet, as I looked on . . . I could only say in very perplexity my own words, 'How shall I name thee, Light of the wide west, or
heinous error-seat?'. . . . Who can separate the light from the darkness but
the Creator Word who prophesied their union? And so I am forced to leave
the matter, not at all seeing my way out of it. — How shall I name thee?"[258]

At this juncture in his Roman experience Newman had reached a crossroad. Despite its material, liturgical, and doctrinal excesses and errors, the
Roman Church seemed to possess some mystical dimension which Newman
perceived through this liturgical experience that threw him back upon his
earlier poetic reflection of Rome, questioning not only its nature but, in the
process, his own conclusions. Ironically, just the day before the liturgy,
Newman "went to hear Dr Wiseman,"[259] rector of the English College in
Rome, and shortly afterwards he and Froude met with him twice, on April 3
and April 6, to explore

> whether they would take us in on any terms to which we could
> twist our consciences. . . . Not one step could be gained without
> swallowing the Council of Trent as a whole. . . . We found to
> our horror that the doctrine of the infallibility of the Church
> made the acts of each successive Council obligatory for ever.[260]

This account, given by Hurrell Froude, marked a turning-point for
Newman. The Roman Church required that which Newman was not yet
prepared to give, submission of his will to the authority of Rome, although
he had ironically written to his sister of "the admirable system of the
Papacy as *an instrument of power*,"[261] the absence of which principle he
had discovered in *Arians* as the early Church's unintended catalyst for
heresy. On the very day after his last meeting with Wiseman he wrote to
another Oriel Fellow, Henry Jenkyns:

---

257   "On 25 March, Newman went to High Mass. . . . The Pope and his 'court' were
present." Ker, *John Henry Newman: A Biography*, 68.
258   Newman, *Letters and Diaries*, vol. III, 268. Letter to Mrs. Newman, Rome.
March 25, 1833. Newman's attendance at this liturgy appears to conflict with the
account of his Roman visit in Newman, *Apologia*, 48. Also, Ian Ker confirms this
liturgy as a Solemn High Mass (see previous note).
259   Ibid., 266; Newman, *Apologia*, 48.
260   Newman, *Letters and Diaries*, vol. III, 76.   261   Ibid., 190.

> The lamentable mixture of truth with error which Romanism
> exhibits — the corruption of the highest and noblest views and
> principles, far higher than we Protestants have, are malignant
> poisons. . . . A union with her on our part is impossible and
> ever will be.[262]

Two days later Newman parted company with the Froudes, they to
England and he to his great personal confrontation in Sicily with the very
condition over which he balked at Rome — submission. Writing to his sister en route to Sicily he commented, "A union with her is impossible. She
is the cruel Church — asking of us impossibilities, excommunicating us
for disobedience, and now watching and exulting over our overthrow."[263]

Just days before arriving in Sicily he wrote his last major letter on his
Roman experience to S. L. Rickards summarizing its paradoxes:

> We were 5 weeks at Rome. . . . [There was] the mixture of good
> and evil in it. . . . The Christian system there is deplorably cor-
> rupt — yet the dust of the Apostles lies there. . . . The spirit of
> the old Rome has possessed the Christian Church there. . . . They
> said 'nothing could harm Rome'. . . not unlike the temper which
> may have existed in Babylon. . . . Its policy is still crafty, relent-
> less, inflexible, and undeviating through a succession of rul-
> ers. . . . How a distinction is to be drawn between two powers,
> spiritual and devilish, which are so strongly united, is . . . much
> beyond our imagination. . . . But that it is incomprehensible is
> no objection to the notion of God's doing it. . . . Indeed . . . I
> have thought that [parable of the wheat and tares] . . . fulfilled
> in the Papacy.[264]

This summary of his Roman sojourn contains several of the perceptions
which will continue to work on Newman for years to come: the paradoxical, mystical nature of the Roman Church and its undeviating authority,
both symbolized in the Papacy, but likewise a confusion of the temper of
paganism with that of faith, caused by the nature of Roman faith: and submission to God's will and reliance on His guidance, which brings assurance.
Having rejected Rome's requirement of submission, and with his Sicilian
crisis just three weeks ahead, Newman pursued the only true and good
vision he could perceive: a reformed Church of England. These Roman
impressions will continue to affect Newman until his next major change
of heart, but for the moment his gaze and energy were focused on his dual

---

262   Ibid., 280.   263   Ibid., 284.   264   Ibid., 287–89.

objectives: the Church of England and home. On June 9, just days out from England, he wrote of the need to purge the Liberals from the Church:

> Ye cannot halve the Gospel of God's grace —
> — Men of presumptuous heart! I know you well.
> . . . .
>
> And so ye halve the Truth; for ye in heart
> At best are doubters whether it be true.[265]

And then he sounded the clarion call for Church reform:

> List, Christian warrior! thou, whose soul is fain
> To rid thy mother of her present chain —
> Christ will unloose His Church; yea, even now
> Begins the work; — and thou
> Shall spend in it thy strength, but, ere He save,
> Thy lot shall be the grave,[266]

Just four days later, Newman authored another poem again indicating the clash between reason and affection regarding the Church issue, a precursor of the personal battle he will wage just a few years hence:

> Oh that thy creed were sound!
> For thou dost soothe the heart, thou Church of Rome,
> By thy unwearied watch and varied round
> Of Service, in thy Saviour's holy home.[267]

It was on his voyage home that Newman composed "The Pillar of the Cloud,"[268] wherein the light against which he felt he had not sinned is now personified as the power which draws him forward. Again the imagery of home was employed to describe the end of the soul's journey:

> Lead, Kindly Light, amid the encircling gloom
> Lead Thou me on!
> The night is dark, and I am far from home —
> Lead thou me on!

And Newman acknowledged that this new relationship was previously frustrated by self-will:

---

265 Newman, *Letters and Diaries* vol. III, 319, and Newman, "Liberalism," in *Verses on Various Occasions* (London: Longmans, Green, and Co., 1910), 144–45.

266 Newman, *Letters and Diaries* vol. III, 319, and Newman, "Day-Labourers," in *Verses on Various Occasions*, 319.   267 Ibid., "The Good Samaritan," 153.

268 Ibid., "The Pillar of the Cloud," 156–57.

I loved to choose and see my path
. . . .
Pride ruled my will

The journey's end was a mystical vision uniting home and heaven as night gives way to morning, and the reunion with lost loved ones:

The night is gone;
And with the morn those angel faces smile
Which I have loved long since, and lost awhile.

At Sea. June 16, 1833

Newman synthesized his feelings in the combined realizations of family, home, Church, and England in the *Apologia's* succinct and dramatic description of his zealous return:

I . . . did not stop . . . night or day . . . till I reached England, and my mother's house. My brother had arrived from Persia only a few hours before. This was on Tuesday. The following Sunday, July 14th, Mr. Keble preached the Assize Sermon in the University Pulpit [entitled] "National Apostasy." I have ever considered and kept the day, as the start of the religious movement of 1833.[269]

With Rome rejected and the vision of "a work to do in England,"[270] Newman returned home with "the words, which had ever been dear to me from my school days, 'Exoriare, aliquis!' . . . I began to think I had a mission."[271]

CONCLUSION PART II:
Newman's Moral Conversion and Our Conversion Hypothesis

IN ANALYZING NEWMAN'S LIFE AND WORK DURING THIS period, we find a dissonance wrought by a tension within his own affectivity between self-will and submission to God's will, exemplified by the tuition dispute and the Sicilian crisis. We also found additional evidence that this affective element is the level of indwelling where God's grace touches man, and the response to that touch, or lack of response, shapes the intellectual and moral expression of that relationship. Once again, Newman's personal correspondence, diaries, journals, and poetry are the primary sources in understanding his actual conversion process.

---

269 Newman, *Apologia*, 50.   270 Ibid.   271 Ibid., 49.

However, in his theological work of the period, we discover an intellectual depth and conceptual understanding which far exceeded what Newman attained in his feelings and conduct at this stage in his life. From the liturgy sermons, *Arians*, and its preamble sermons we find a theology of the nature and dynamics of conversion so explicit that we can employ it to evaluate Newman's own ongoing conversion. From both Newman's life and theology we learn that all religious experience begins in the pre-conceptual depths of affectivity where man feels the presence of the Transcendent Other, and then that feeling moves out in the desire for an intellectual and moral expression of that encounter. And what is that expression? For this answer we turn to Newman's sermon on affectivity, wherein he synthesized religious affectivity, intellectual discernment, and moral commitment through and in the development of affective human relationships, especially family and friends, as analogies of our relationship to the Transcendent Other. Thus, Church, as the communal meeting-place of all parties, becomes a form of home, and in the process, Newman exhibits an imaginative, aesthetic element.

But in addition to this structure of conversion we also find the very important developmental principle. Each element — affective, aesthetic, intellectual, and moral — influences all others, which explains the importance of "right" symbols and creeds as expressions of affectivity. Just as the true symbol nourishes or "tranquilizes" the mind, so too can a false symbol damage the affections. And thus a moral commitment is required to that image which we believe to be true and thus good, as the representation of our affectivity. But this entire process of conversion depends on development of the proper Christian temper, concord, which facilitates this dynamic, and that temper requires submission of self-will, or the fundamentally affective act of faith.

Lastly, in the preamble sermons to *Arians*, and then further developed in that work, was the growing sense of an aesthetic dimension to the conversion experience, a vision of a total, complete relationship, the whole Truth, which for Newman was taking an ecclesiastical form. This dimension will take on added prominence when we examine the next phase of Newman's conversion journey.

But we can conclude that Newman reached a point in 1833 which can rightly be termed a moral conversion in his assertion of the image of a reformed Church of England as the specific realization of what his intellect discerned to be the fruits of his affective conversion in Sicily. That reformed Church, in Newman's vision, was heir to the original faith tradition of apostolic times and was thus validated, even to one with an unsubmissive temperament, as the true *locus* of the Transcendent Other.

Regarding Newman's moral conversions, Allen Brent offers an insightful analysis implicitly supportive of our thesis. He notes that Newman's conversion to Rome in 1845 was not only intellectual but moral and involved the issue of submission. However, Brent's perspective indicates that moral conversion is a transformation of the object of desire, implying also affective and aesthetic elements. Since Brent's analysis points to all four elements operating simultaneously and reciprocally, what he applies to Newman's Roman conversion applies to his conversion to the vision of a reformed Church of England as well:

> His subsequent biography may accordingly be argued to be the transformation of a '*vision* of power' into a suitable object of Christian reverence.... But ... to understand the change of Newman's *affective* stance towards Rome wholly in such terms would be to ignore a concomitant *moral* conversion.... [T]he transformation of Newman's *vision* was not only one of *intellectually* justifying the possession of that power but a *moral* transformation about in what that power itself really consisted.... [I]t was a *moral* conversion which the Roman Church of the nineteenth century was to find as problematic as his *intellectual* one.[272]

Taking Newman's own account of his thoughts toward the end of his Mediterranean trip, Virgil's cry, "Exoriare, aliquis!" ("Arise, avenger!")[273] expressed the nature of his moral conversion, and he wrote following this axiom, "I began to think I had a mission." That mission was his moral conversion to a vision of a reformed and supposedly apostolic Church of England, with the accompanying commitment to action.

Now we move on to examine the next phase of Newman's conversions, during which he continued to wrestle with willfulness and the image of a true Church model to correlate with his affectivity.

---

272   Allen Brent, "Newman's Moral Conversion," *The Downside Review* 104 (April 1986): 79, 87–88. Italics added to identify our four elements of conversion.
273   Newman, *Apologia*, 49: "Virgil, *Aeneid*, iv. 625. From Dido's great soliloquy on hearing that Aeneas had deserted her."

PART III

Securus Judicat Orbis Terrarum[1]

("The universal Church is in its judgments secure of truth")

FROM ENGLAND TO ROME:
Newman's Intellectual and
Unconditional Conversions
1833–1845

---

1 Augustine, Contra Epistolam Parmeniani, iii.3, as translated by Newman (Ess. 2.
101): "The universal Church is in its judgments secure of truth."

CHAPTER FOUR

Newman's Intellectual Conversion: 1833–1843

INTRODUCTION

IN THIS CHAPTER, I ANALYZE NEWMAN'S DEVELOPMENT FROM the dawn of the Tractarian movement in 1833 until his resignation as vicar of St. Mary's in September 1843,[2] during which period three stages are evident. First, from 1833 until mid-1839, Newman sought to construct a theory for the Anglican *Via Media*. Newman had not previously taken such deep interest in the Church of England, as Bouyer notes: "As for the Church of England as a whole, it may be said that he did not arrive at any thorough knowledge of it until the Tractarian Movement began."[3] That movement, the situation in the Church of England which gave rise to it, and Newman's theological writings of the period bearing on the *Via Media* will be examined. However, Newman was simultaneously working on a track other than ecclesiological. The nature of faith, and thus religious knowledge, once again became major interests especially at the end of this period, and so they provide evidence of the dual dynamic in Newman's thinking. The nature of the *Via Media* and the nature of religious faith ultimately clash. We will examine this conflict in the second stage of this period, from 1839 to 1841. Newman's unquestioned certainty that the *Via Media* was the true image of the Apostolic Church was challenged both by his own research and a contradictory image, Augustine's *securus judicat orbis terrarum*, and his position on the ecclesiastical issue began to change. At the very close of this period, two major events pushed Newman to a third stage: he became acquainted with the Irish Catholic priest Dr. Charles Russell, who "had more to do with my conversion than anyone else,"[4] and a series of "three blows which broke me" between July and November, 1841:[5] (1) the recurring image of the Church of England in

---

2   Newman, *Apologia*, 194.   3   Bouyer, *Newman*, 157.
4   Newman, *Apologia*, 178.   5   Ibid., 133.

schism; (2) the English bishops' condemnation of his Tract 90, Newman's "catholicized" interpretation of the Articles of the Church of England; and (3) that Church's accommodation of Protestantism by agreeing to participate in the creation of an interdenominational Jerusalem bishopric. These events plunged Newman into the depths of a great dilemma. If the Church of England were in schism, but Rome obviously corrupted by its additions to the primitive creed, where then might he find the true Church?

Stage three examines how Newman resolved this problem. His relationship with Dr. Russell deepened during this period. Perhaps most important of all in relation to Newman's intellectual conversion was the affective nature of their relationship. This was the ground from which Newman was exposed to Roman Catholic doctrine and devotional practices. It was the effect of this relationship which began Newman's turn toward Rome. Affectivity fostered his intellectual movement: "Not to take into account the effect of Dr. Russell's personal influence upon him would be a fatal omission. . . . Dr. Russell, for ever afterwards his 'dear friend,' and he alone, won, and retained until the end, not only his esteem, but his affection."[6] As with Mayers, Whately, and Hawkins during the early years of Newman's religious conversion, and with Keble and Froude during his moral conversion period, an affectionate personal relationship was once again the means by which Newman's intellectual development progressed. Newman's final two *University Sermons*, on Wisdom and on the Theory of Developments in Religious Doctrine, carry the influence of his relationship with Russell. It is of note that Newman dedicated his 1874 edition of his novel of conversion, *Loss and Gain*, to none other than Russell, and "it is a temptation to think that in *Loss and Gain* he was the prototype of the priest whom Charles Reding met in the train on his way to London after his last farewell to Oxford."[7]

Even though the effects of Newman's relationship with Russell eventually led to his intellectual conversion, as expressed in his fifteenth *University Sermon* on the Development of Religious Doctrine in early 1843, Newman had not yet attained the faith necessary to convert his intellectual conclusions into convictions. This prolonged crisis of faith lasted two years, until his action on October 9, 1845, when he finally submitted to the Church of Rome. This final stage is the focus of our fifth and last chapter. Here we will examine more fully the evidence for Newman's intellectual conversion to Rome as the locus of the true Church, which was the realization

---

6   Henry Tristram, "Dr. Russell and Newman's Conversion," *The Irish Ecclesiastical Record*, lxvi (September 1945): 189–200.   7   Ibid.

of the Augustinian imagery *securus judicat orbis terrarum*, and the moral force of the argument in its favor. Thus we will examine the evidence that affective, aesthetic, moral, and intellectual elements were interacting in a simultaneous, reciprocal, and complementary manner, and that during this period the intellectual element was the most dominant, thereby making it possible to identify it by that name, the period of Newman's intellectual conversion. Thus we will now examine Newman's intellectual conversion as it evolved in these three stages.

STAGE ONE: The Via Media

NEWMAN'S CHURCH IMAGE GROUNDED IN AN UNCRITICAL AND HUMAN-CENTERED FAITH

THE FOCUS OF THIS STAGE IS ON NEWMAN'S DEVELOPMENT OF an intellectual argument to support the Church of England's contention that it was the legitimate successor to the Apostolic Church, positioned between the "false" Protestant Churches and the "corrupt" Roman Church. We will examine why this became an important issue in 1833, the effects of that cause, and a brief history of the *Via Media*. Then we will review Newman's major theological writings of the period, which continue his two tracks on the nature of the church and the nature of faith, or religious epistemology. These tracks draw ever closer during this conversion phase, culminating, as noted, in the fifteenth *University Sermon* on the Theory of Developments in Religious Doctrine, which is the intellectual introduction to Newman's final unconditional conversion of submission.

THE CHURCH SITUATION IN 1833 ENGLAND

AS WE HAVE SEEN, NEWMAN RETURNED TO ENGLAND FROM his Mediterranean trip on July 9, 1833, and "the following Sunday, July 14, Mr. Keble preached the Assize Sermon in the University Pulpit. It was published under the title of 'National Apostasy.' I have ever considered and kept the day, as the start of the religious movement of 1833."[8]

What was that movement, its cause and objective? While Newman had been away, the government passed the Irish Church Reform Bill, abolishing ten sees of the established Church and instituting a tax on higher clerical incomes to support the Churches, replacing the "extremely unpopular Church rates, which were levied on the largely Catholic population."[9] This action conflicted with Newman's anti-Erastian view of the

---

8 Newman, *Apologia*, 50.   9 Ker, *John Henry Newman: A Biography*, 64.

Church, which he had imbibed years earlier from Whately, and thus he was at one with Keble's sermon which was given "against the background of the bill to reform the Church of Ireland, and (which) insisted that the Church was of divine origin rather than a department of the state."[10] Three months prior to this sermon Newman wrote to H. A. Woodgate from the Mediterranean in opposition to the Irish Bill and what it implied about the established Church, which was the "first serious hint"[11] of an actual movement:

> But to be serious on the subject of the Church, do you not think, now that the crown is but the creature of an Infidel Parliament, that the Bishops should not be appointed by it? . . . I think we ought to clamour . . . for a full and efficient reform . . . a return to the primitive state of the Church, when it was not a mere instrument of civil government, which it approaches to be now. I almost think the time is come to form clubs and societies under the title of Apostolical — that we may have some approximation toward a system of discipline.[12]

Shortly after Keble's sermon, a meeting was held of interested parties who decided to organize around one principle: Apostolical succession.[13] However, Newman himself had begun to emphasize another principle — popularity as an element of Church power, a principle which will come to fruition in Augustine's maxim just six years later. Between 1833 and 1841, this group published ninety articles or tracts, twenty-four of which Newman authored[14] (some sources count as many as twenty-nine[15]), including the controversial number 90 on the Thirty-Nine Articles of the Anglican Church, which brought an abrupt halt to the publications. We will examine five of those tracts which most directly relate to the development of his *Via Media*.

---

10 Newman, *Apologia*, 532, n. 141.

11 Ker, *John Henry Newman: A Biography*, 74.

12 John Henry Newman, *Letters and Diaries*, vol. III, ed. Ian Ker and Thomas Gornall (Oxford: Clarendon Press, 1979), 300.

13 Ker, *John Henry Newman: A Biography*, 81.

14 John Henry Newman, *List of Works Written and Edited by His Eminence Cardinal Newman, in the Library of Sir William H. Cope, Bast., at Bramshill* (Np: Publisher Unknown, 1885), 7–8.

15 John Henry Newman, *Tracts for the Times* (Np: Benedictine Classics, 2010). See also *Tracts for the Times* (*Works of Cardinal Newman: Birmingham Oratory Millennium Edition*), ed. James Tolhurst (Notre Dame: University of Notre Dame Press, 2013): "Newman, who edited the series, either wrote or compiled a third of the tracts."

A second major force that particularly piqued Newman and his allies, in addition to the Irish Church Reform Bill, was the Bill proposed in 1834, instigated by Dr. Renn Dickson Hampden of Oxford, to admit dissenters to Cambridge and Oxford without the required subscription to the Church's Thirty-Nine Articles, necessary for matriculation at Oxford and graduation at Cambridge. Hampden, who ironically had been appointed to replace Newman as a tutor, asserted in his formal pamphlet on the subject that "religion is distinct from Theological Opinion," "that a dogma was a theological opinion," "that speculation always left an opening for improvement," "that the Church of England was not dogmatic in its spirit."[16] Newman wrote bluntly to Hampden that these assertions "make a shipwreck of Christian faith," concluding that "such was the commencement of the assault of Liberalism upon the old orthodoxy of Oxford and England."[17]

At this point we should note that in this conflict over dogma, Hampden hit upon not only the primary Tractarian but also the lifelong theme for Newman: "First was the principle of dogma: my battle was with liberalism. . . . Such was the fundamental principle of the Movement of 1833."[18] In 1864 Newman summarized this overarching concern:

> The main principle of the movement is as dear to me now, as it ever was. I have changed in many things: in this I have not. From the age of fifteen, dogma has been the fundamental principle of my religion: I know no other religion. . . . well can there be filial love without the fact of a father, as devotion without the fact of a Supreme Being. What I held in 1816, I held in 1833, and I hold in 1864.[19]

This important synopsis, that dogma was always of ultimate concern from the moment of his first conversion, indicates further why we find it at the heart of Newman's intellectual conversion in his *University Sermons* on the subject, precipitating his *Essay on Development* in 1845. But the statement also indicates the fact that dogma is a lifelong reality, not merely some form of intellectualism to be mastered, but a living, ongoing mystery whose purpose it is to forever engage man's spirit. This fact underscores the ongoing essence of conversion, of which one form of expression is the lifelong encounter with revealed truth.

From the principle of dogma Newman was led to a second principle: "A visible Church, with sacraments and rites which are the channels

---

16   Newman, *Apologia*, 68.   17   Ibid.
18   Ibid., 61.   19   Ibid.

of invisible grace."[20] This thread also runs through Newman's lifelong religious experience:

> While I am now as clear in my acceptance of the principle of dogma, as I was in 1833 and 1816, so again am I now as firm in my belief of a visible Church, of the authority of the Bishops, of the grace of the sacraments, of the religious worth of works of penance, as I was in 1833. I have added Articles to my Creed; but the old ones, which I then held with a divine faith, remain.[21]

Thus, the dogmatic and ecclesiastical principles were lifelong concerns of Newman's spiritual journey, and, while they reached a certain extreme intensity and coalesced in the early and mid 1840s, they were ever present throughout his lifetime, underscoring the ongoing nature of that pilgrimage. Another important point is that Newman's concern for the dogmatic principle eventually led him to explore the nature of religious epistemology during this intellectual conversion period, expressed in his *University Sermons* and his *Lectures on Justification*. His concern for the Church principle, on the other hand, inspired many of his tracts as well as his *Lectures on the Prophetical Office*. He eventually synthesized these two tracks through the principle of the development of doctrine, at which point his own quest for certainty in the domain of religious knowledge and for the identity of the true Church was realized.

However, besides the dogmatic and Church principles, a third one drove Newman during the Movement, "and which I have utterly renounced and trampled upon since — my then view of the Church of Rome. . . . When I was young . . . I thought the Pope to be Antichrist," although the subsequent influences of Keble and Froude softened him on the subject. But at the outset of the Movement, "in 1832–3 I thought the Church of Rome was bound up with the cause of Antichrist by the Council of Trent."[22] Thus, from Newman's perspective the Movement was grounded in dogma, Church, and anti-Roman principles. We will now examine the relevant documents of the period as they relate to Newman's intellectual conversion.

NEWMAN'S CALL FOR CHURCH REFORM:
The Five Letters to The Record regarding Church Discipline

IN A SERIES OF FIVE LETTERS TO THE RECORD IN 1833, NEWMAN put forth his concept of the visible Church and the need for a reform of Church discipline. In his first letter of October 21, 1833, he stated:

---

20   Ibid., 62.   21   Ibid., 63–64.   22   Ibid., 64.

Now my notion of . . . the visible Church is this; that, besides
its being the bosom of the Church invisible (*i.e.* as having the
dispensation of the sacraments), it was intended as a *type* of it, and
a means toward forming it — a means, by preaching and teaching; and a type or figure, as holding up conspicuously before
the ungodly world, the rules of governance, the gospel system,
and the final separation of sinners from the elect. . . . I state my
belief that our present troubles are a judgment on us . . . for
our neglect of what our Church itself avows . . . the duty of a
strict discipline.[23]

In his second letter ten days later he advanced his attack on the laxity
of the Church in dealing with the liberal insurgents, providing much
scriptural evidence in support of his argument:

I ask the Church of England, *whether she warns her children against
the sin* of friendship with those who 'refuse to hear her'? . . . St
Paul says to Titus (iii, 10), 'A man that is an heretic, after the first
and second admonition, reject.'. . . Truly, the omission of the
practice has brought its cause with it in the present latitudinal
spirit which it has introduced into the Church.[24]

A week later he wrote, "The *duty* of discipline seems clearly marked
in Scripture; our *neglect* of discipline is undeniable."[25] His last letter of
November 14, 1833 alludes to another reason for the need of Church
discipline: the rise of the Papists. "I say then that the alarming increase
of the Papists is a strong reason for our stirring ourselves in the matter
of Church discipline. . . . (T)here is a prevalent feeling among the Papists
that England will in no long time be theirs." But here Newman refers to
the strength of Rome, a key to his next move:

Now their great advantage lies in this; that they all speak the
same thing. There is perfect organization in their clergy, perfect
accordance of profession in the people. . . . Protestants have had
nothing definite to appeal to, or point at, either in creed or in
polity . . . while the Papists *have* a Church, though it be a pillar
and ground of error . . . I say then, let us make the Church of
England, a bulwark against Popery, by advocating the restoration
of her discipline.[26]

---

23   John Henry Newman, *Letters and Diaries*, vol. IV, ed. Ian Ker and Thomas Gornall
(Oxford: Clarendon Press, 1980), 63–64.

24   Ibid., 76–77.   25   Ibid., 88   26   Ibid., 101–2.

In this series of letters at the outset of the movement we find Newman's call for Church reform centered on the dogmatic principle and stridently anti-Roman. Newman had also perceived the nature of the problem: external threats to the Church from both the state and the Papists, and internal threats from the liberals. The Tracts, however, which sought to remedy the problem, suffered from several inherent defects. They were written by a diverse number of authors, on diverse topics. In short, they lacked the very principle which grounded the strength of Rome: systematization rooted in a sound theology. The problem with the Anglican system, which consisted of the work of the Caroline divines, was that "most of their writings and ideas were of the nature of improvisations. . . . What had to be done was to bring out clearly the body of religious ideas needed to furnish a theological basis to the Anglican theory."[27] This led Newman to a study of the nature of the Anglican ecclesiastical system, expressed by the image of the Via Media.

THE HISTORY OF THE VIA MEDIA

THIS UNSYSTEMATIC ANGLICAN CHURCH NOTION WAS BORN during the reign of Queen Elizabeth when "some sort of via media had then to be discovered, not only if the religious but the political unity of the nation was to be secured . . . . The only workable solution was to make the Church very comprehensive and inclusive, in order that those who remained outside should have as little reasonable excuse as possible for dissatisfaction."[28] Described as a "vision" of the primacy of moderation in religion by the Whig Joseph Addison in 1711, this "Aristotelian mean between ecclesiastical extremes" subsequently "gained added strength from its consonance with classical and Enlightenment ideals of balance, proportion, and harmony . . . . The triumph of 'moderation' was assisted by a growing sense of security. It was easier for eighteenth-century Churchmen to maintain a stance of relaxed toleration once the Church of England no longer felt itself under much pressure from its rivals."[29] By 1833 these developments bordered on "officially sanctioned pluralism . . . a state system effectively governed by principles of indifferentism and secularism."[30] It was in light of this history and festering milieu that Newman

---

27   Bouyer, Newman, 162.

28   F. J. Foakes Jackson, Anglican Church Principles (New York: The Macmillan Company, 1924), 81.

29   John Walsh, Colin Hayden, and Stephen Taylor, eds., The Church of England, c. 1689–1833 (Cambridge: Cambridge University Press, 1993), 56–57.

30   Ibid., 62.

sought to restore Church discipline with an emphasis on dogma. Newman began with two *Tracts for the Times*, numbers 38 and 40 (some sources read "41"),[31] entitled *Via Media I* and *II*. However, we should note that Newman stated the dissonance between his mind and heart toward Rome as an affective attraction to it especially as a result of his Mediterranean experiences, while yet an intellectual aversion inculcated by his tradition:

> As a matter, then, of simple conscience, though it went against my feelings, I felt it to be a duty to protest against the Church of Rome . . . a duty, because the prescription of such a protest was a living principle of my own Church, as expressed . . . by a *consensus* of her divines. . . . I felt such confidence in the substantial justice of the charges which I advanced against her, that I considered them to be a safeguard and an assurance that no harm could ever arise from the freest exposition of what I used to call Anglican principles.[32]

Revealed in this passage is the critical fact that Newman grounded his belief in the Anglican system on a trust in the Anglican divines, an act of faith which would prove to be unsupported in fact and thus without intellectual basis and fatal to his vision of the *Via Media*. Günther Biemer, in his study of tradition in the history of Anglican theology, the ground from which Newman approached issues of tradition, offers a relevant summary analysis.[33] We now examine Newman's theological writings of the period on Church and tradition.

---

31 Newman, *List of Works Written and Edited by His Eminence Cardinal Newman, in the Library of Sir William H. Cope, Bast., at Bramshill*, 7–8.

32 Newman, *Apologia*, 66.

33 "Our enquiries into the theology of Anglicans in the first three centuries after the Reformation . . . gives us some indication of the dominant views at the time of the Oxford movement. We may now try to summarize the doctrine of tradition in Anglican theology. It seems that the Anglican Church always accepted tradition as a help to interpreting scripture, though there was always a rigorous Protestant line which took its stand on the unadulterated principle of *sola scriptura*. As source of faith, however, tradition was always rejected, with various degrees of sharpness, and there are only a few theologians who form an exception to this rule. The Tractarians occupy a special place within the framework of Anglican theology, in so far as Catholicizing tendencies were pushed as far as possible among them. The collapse of their efforts is linked with the reaction of strong Protestant and liberal forces in the Church of England. This is the historical and theological background against which the figure of John Henry Newman stands out. A child of his times, sensitive to all its problems, he takes up the principles, tests them and chooses among them, and follows them consistently to their logical end." *Newman on Tradition* (New York: Herder and Herder, 1967), 30–31.

NEWMAN'S VIA MEDIA

THE ECCLESIOLOGICAL TRACK:
Documents 1 and 2—
Tracts 38 and 40: Via Media I and II[34]

PUBLISHED ON JULY 25 AND AUGUST 24, 1834, RESPECTIVELY, these Tracts were written in the form of a dialogue between a traditional and a Tractarian member of the Church of England. Five prominent themes emerge: development of doctrine, thus already recognized at this early date, the Ancient Church as both the criterion and limits of the Articles, the function and effect of the Liturgy, and the need for anti-Liberal reform.

Development of doctrine:

> It is not unnatural that the Reformers of the sixteenth century should have fallen short of a full Reformation in matters of doctrine and discipline. Light breaks but gradually on the mind: one age begins a work, another finishes.[35]

> Fresh articles of faith are necessary . . . according to the rise of successive heresies and errors. These articles were all hidden, as it were, in the Church's bosom from the first, and brought out into form according to the occasion. Such was the Nicene explanation against Arius; the English Articles against Popery; and such are those now called for in the age of Schism.[36]

Newman added the following footnote to the 1883 edition confirming that he recognized, yet not to its fullest ramifications at the time, the principle of doctrinal development: "Here, as above, the principle of doctrinal development is accepted as true and necessary for the Christian Church."[37]

The Apostolic Church criterion:

> I cannot consent . . . to deprive myself of the Church's dowry, the doctrines which the Apostles spoke in Scripture and impressed upon the early Church. I receive the Church as a messenger from Christ, rich in treasures old and new, rich with the accumulated wealth of ages. . . . Our articles are one portion of that accumulation.[38]

---

34 John Henry Newman, *The Via Media of the Anglican Church*, vol. ii (London: Longmans, Green and Co, 1908), 21–48.
35 Ibid., 29–30.   36 Ibid., 40.   37 Ibid.   38 Ibid., 31.

The nature and limits of the Articles:

> Our Articles are . . . only protests against certain errors of a
> certain period of the Church. . . . I am bound to the Articles
> by subscription; but I am bound, even more solemnly than by
> subscription, by my baptism and by my ordination, to believe
> and maintain the *whole* gospel of Christ.[39]

Function and effect of the Liturgy:

> The Liturgy, as coming down from the Apostles, is the depository
> of their complete teaching; while the Articles are polemical, and
> except as they embody the creeds, are mainly protests against
> certain definite errors. . . . (T)he Liturgy, all along, speaks of
> the Gospel dispensation . . . a moral law . . . and that external
> observances and definite acts of duty are made the means and
> the tests of faith. . . . (I)t runs quite counter to the innovating
> spirit of this day.[40]

The need for anti-liberal reform: the subjectivity versus the objectivity of faith:

> We are now more Protestant than our Reformers[41]. . . . Now-
> adays, the prominent notion conveyed by it (faith) regards its
> properties, whether spiritual or not, warm, heart-felt, vital. But
> in the Catechism, the prominent notion is that of its object, the
> believing 'all the articles of the Christian faith,' according to the
> Apostle's declaration, that it is, 'the substance of things hoped
> for, the evidence of things not seen'[42]. . . . (A)nd besides, not a
> word said of looking to Christ, resting on Him, and renovation
> of heart. . . . I am speaking of that arrogant Protestant spirit (so
> called) of the day. . . . I cry out . . . that corruptions are pouring
> in, which, sooner or later, will need a second reformation.[43]

The nature of a reformation:

> I would do what our reformers of the sixteenth century did: they
> did not touch the existing documents of doctrine[44]. . . . (T)hey
> kept the creeds as they were; but they added protests against the
> corruptions of faith, worship, and discipline. . . . I would have

---

39 Ibid., 32. 40 Ibid., 46. 41 Ibid., 41.
42 Ibid., 43. 43 Ibid., 48.
44 Ibid., 38. Newman added a footnote to the 1883 edition that this point was "too
broadly contended for in No. 90," the final and controversial Tract on the Articles.

the Church do the same thing now. . . . (S)he should not change the Articles, she should add to them: add protests against the erastianism and latitudinarianism which have encrusted them.[45]

These early Tracts indicate several major principles which remain primary themes throughout Newman's conversion process: (1) On the one hand, the principle of development is acknowledged, but on the other Newman asserts a certain unchanging aspect of doctrine. Later in this period, Newman's work in his *University Sermons* on religious epistemology would sharpen these distinctions; (2) the Articles are recognized as but partial comments, and negative in content, of the "whole" gospel message; (3) this incompleteness of the Articles is underscored further by the assertion that the Liturgy contains the complete Apostolic teaching; (4) further, the contemporary spirit of the day, especially the liberal Protestant turn to the self, rather than to the Object of faith, had undermined the requisite moral dimension of faith; (5) thus, a reformation was needed to remedy the problem of theological content caused by the incompleteness of the Articles and the fact that all doctrine is contained in the Liturgy. However, two problems were outstanding: the Anglican schema lacked systematization, and action was needed to confront the Church's moral drift. Here we find the seeds of Newman's *Prophetical Office* as well as his *Lectures on Justification*, both written just a few years later, on the nature of the Church and the nature of faith. But in early 1836 Newman wrote two other Tracts, one asserting the Church of England over Rome and the other against the Rationalists, both of which are relevant to a study of Newman's search for the true Church.

THE ECCLESIOLOGICAL TRACK:
Document 3 —
Tract 71: On the Mode of Conducting the Controversy with Rome[46]

ON JANUARY 1, 1836, NEWMAN PUBLISHED TRACT 71 "ON THE Mode of Conducting the Controversy with Rome." This document asserts the legitimacy of the Church of England over that of Rome and as such presents one of Newman's most explicit statements on his vision of the true Church at that time. Newman based his positive case for the Church of England on two factors, possession of the sacraments and freedom from heresy:

> While we are able to maintain the claim of our clergy to the
> ministration of the Sacraments, and our freedom from any deadly

---

45   Ibid.   46   Ibid., 95–141.

heresy, we have nothing to fear from any of the historical disclosures which the envy of our adversaries might contrive against
our Church.[47]

Further, "our Articles, so far as distinct from the ancient creeds . . . neither are nor profess to be a system of doctrine."[48] On the other hand,
Rome asserts the primacy of an unscriptural tradition: "(C)ertain notable
tenets of Romanism depend solely on . . . Tradition, not on Scripture."[49]
Newman then lists seven "practical grievances" against Roman practice
dealing with sacraments, devotions, and, most notably, authority: "Consider the number of points of faith which the Church of Rome has set up.
You must believe every one of them."[50] A key point here is Newman's
rejection of the principle of infallibility, an extension of the authority
principle: "The primitive Church was never called upon . . . to pronounce
upon other points of faith[51]. . . . This is the question of a philosophical
mind, and the Church of Rome meets it with a theory . . . of infallibility. . . . But the English Church does not assume infallibility."[52] Ironically,
while Newman had noted the failure of authority in the fourth century
as the major factor in the spread of heresy, and while he was currently
calling for a restoration of Church discipline, he had not yet connected
the authority principle to the crucial issue of doctrine, as he would later
do. But he does maintain the essential objective, truth, which constantly
directed his mission: "Nor is it becoming . . . to dispute for victory not for
truth, and to be careless of the manner in which we urge conclusions."[53]

Newman then makes a major distinction indicative of his mind at
the time, that development was itself very much an undeveloped notion:
"There is . . . a want of correspondence between the appearance presented
by the Roman theology in theory and its appearance in practice. The
separate doctrines of Romanism are very different . . . in the abstract, and
when developed, applied, and practiced."[54]

Intellectually, at this stage Newman did not perceive identity in development. In closing his tract, Newman admits the flaw in the Anglican system
but contrasts it with the more serious Roman defect. The Anglican defects

> are but omissions. Rome maintains positive errors, and that under
> the sanction of anathema; but nothing can be pointed out in the
> English Church which is not true. . . . On the other hand, the

---

47 Ibid., 130.   48 Ibid., 136.   49 Ibid., 104.   50 Ibid., 108.
51 Here Newman is referring to points of faith other than the creed.
52 Ibid., 133.   53 Ibid., 102.   54 Ibid., 117–18.

omissions, such as they are, or rather obscurities of the Anglican doctrine, may be supplied for the most part by each of us for himself, and thus do not interfere with the perfect development of the Christian temper in the hearts of individuals, which is the charge fairly adducible against Romanism.[55]

Intellectually, Newman had not yet connected personal development and doctrinal development as grounded in a common principle, which he will do in his fifteenth University Sermon. According to Newman, the Anglican omissions were not errors, and the Roman enforcement of perceived errors impedes moral development, which Anglican restraint does not. Thus, the English Church has "mere omissions, not positive errors . . . and are . . . dissimilar from those . . . of Rome . . . (which are) clear and direct perversions and corruptions of divine truth."[56]

But beyond these facts of what Newman believed, why he believed them is revealed at the close of the Tract, a crucial revelation that the ground of Newman's intellectual position was his faith in the Anglican divines:

> The objections . . . against the English Church . . . are . . . dissimilar from those which lie against the Church of Rome, and which relate to clear and distinct perversions and corruptions of divine truth. Should it, however, be asked, whence our knowledge of the truth should be derived . . . it may be replied, first, that the writings of the Fathers contain abundant directions how to ascertain it; next, that their directions are distinctly propounded and supported by our Divines of the seventeenth century, though little comparatively at present is known concerning those great authors. Nor could a more acceptable or important service be done to our Church at this present moment, than the publication of some systematic introduction to theology, embodying and illustrating the great and concordant principles set forth by Hammond, Taylor, and their brethren before and after them.[57]

Here we find once again that Newman grounded his faith in the Anglican system on an assumed continuity between the Fathers and the Anglican divines, even though he admits to little actual knowledge of the works of the divines. This uncritical faith is the foundation of his Via Media theory, and, when that theory proved to be baseless, Newman himself would attribute his momentous mistake to this act of uncritical faith.

---

55 Ibid., 136–37.   56 Ibid., 140.   57 Ibid.

The second major fact is Newman's call for a systematic presentation of Anglican theology, a call which he himself will answer the following year in his *Prophetical Office*.

One final note adds to the importance of this Tract in the history of Newman's conversion. Twice Newman refers to the principle of a united Church, ironically a vision which will "pulverize" his own theory of the *Via Media* in just three short years:

> *How is it* that the particular Christian body to which I belong *happens* to be the right one?... Now the primitive Church answered this question, by appealing to the single fact, that all the Apostolic Churches all over the world did agree together[58].... Unity in the whole body of the Church ... is the divinely blessed symbol and pledge of the true faith.[59]

In conclusion of our review of this Tract, it contains six factors which influenced Newman's conversion process: (1) development of doctrine, (2) belief in Roman corruptions and (3) Anglican Apostolicity, (4) both grounded in an uncritical faith that the Anglican divines were consistent with the Fathers, (5) the need for a systematization of Anglican theology to prove this, and (6) an assertion of the principle of Church unity as a symbol of the true faith. We shall see the evolution of these six important factors in Newman's intellectual conversion as our study continues. Newman's sister Tract 73, written the following month, makes the case against Rationalism, and it is the first document of his parallel track of religious epistemology.

THE RELIGIOUS EPISTEMOLOGY TRACK:
Document 1 —
Tract 73: On the Introduction of
Rational Principles into Revealed Religion[60]

PUBLISHED ON FEBRUARY 2, 1836, THIS TRACT DEVOTES THE first third to an exposition of "The Rationalistic and the Catholic Tempers contrasted," while the two subsequent sections, in illustration, analyze the work of two Rationalist writers of the period. Newman recognizes three criteria of Rationalism which render it

---

58 Ibid., 132.
59 Ibid., 134.
60 John Henry Newman, *Essays Critical and Historical*, vol. 1 (London: Longmans, Green, and Co., 1895), 30–101.

a certain abuse of Reason; that is, a use of it for purposes for which it never was intended, and is unfitted: to rationalize in matters of Revelation is to make our reason the standard and measure of the doctrines revealed.... And thus a rationalistic spirit is the antagonist of Faith; for Faith is, in its very nature, the acceptance of what our reason cannot reach, simply and absolutely upon testimony.[61]

Rationalism is the antithesis of faith, whose consistent ground is testimony, as we have seen in Newman since his early work on miracles. Newman defines Rationalism's three cardinal tenets: (1) "Rationalism would account for everything."[62] "(T)his great assumption, that the object of Christian Revelation is ascertainable by us," Newman rebuffs. "Christianity," says Bishop Butler, "is a scheme quite beyond our comprehension.... Christianity is a particular scheme ... of various parts and a mysterious economy."[63] (2) Rationalism "finds fault with that disjointed and isolated character of the doctrines in the old Catholic creed, that want of system, which to the more philosophical mind of Bishop Butler would seem an especial recommendation from the analogy to the course of nature."[64] (3) Rationalism leads to the belief that the truth of doctrines can be gauged by their intelligibility. "Here, at length, Rationalism stands confused; doctrines, it seems, are not true, if they are not explicable."[65] The assumption of rationalism, then, is that divine truths are subject to the laws of logic and reason. This is "the spirit of the age ... arrogant and self-trusting[66] ... selfishness ... (with) everything subordinate to the individual."[67] Newman concludes the Tract with a description of that same temper which characterized his brother Charles's anti-religious attitude as well as the temperament he discovered at the root of the heretics of the fourth century: "There is a school of doctrine ... directing its attention to the heart itself, not to anything external to us ... (T)his doctrine is based upon error ... a specious form of trusting man rather than God."[68] This conflicts with the essence of revelation, which is grounded in mystery. Newman expresses the two aspects of revelation, the intelligible and the mysterious, in a key distinction: "A Revelation is religious doctrine viewed on its illuminated

---

61   Ibid., 31.   62   Ibid., 66.

63   Joseph Butler, *The Analogy of Religion Natural and Revealed, to the Constitution and Course of Nature*, ii, 4.

64   Newman, *Essays*, vol. i, 59.   65   Ibid., 60.   66   Ibid., 91.

67   Ibid., 54.   68   Ibid., 95.

side; a Mystery is the selfsame doctrine viewed on the side unilluminated."[69] Newman's insight is that Rationalism in matters of revelation is an intellectual error, and, most importantly, that error is due to a willful, self-centered temperament.

These four Tracts form the foundation for Newman's theory of the *Via Media* expressed in his *Prophetical Office*, published in 1837, a continuation of Newman's thinking on the track of Church and doctrine. The following year, 1838, his *Lectures on Justification* developed his thought on the track of faith and religious epistemology. Newman developed these two tracks relatedly but independently, a parallel process which continued through his *Tract 90* on ecclesiology and his *University Sermons* on religious epistemology, until he ultimately synthesized the two tracks in his fifteenth *University Sermon* and the *Essay on Development*. We will see the relationship between this parallel development of his thought and his conversion as we review the associated documents, the next of which, chronologically, is his major work constituting a theory for Anglicanism.

THE ECCLESIOLOGICAL TRACK:
Document 4 —
Lectures on the Prophetical Office of the Church viewed relatively to Romanism and Popular Protestantism[70]

THE FOCUS OF THE PROPHETICAL OFFICE IS THE JUSTIFICATION of a theory for the English *Via Media*: "Their main object [the *Lectures* into which the book was divided] is to furnish an approximation in one or two points towards a correct theory of the duties and office of the Church Catholic."[71] Protestantism is rejected outright since "It does not attempt this at all; it abandons the subject altogether."[72] A lengthy comparison of England and Rome on the subject ensues, which is essentially a question of authority in the form of the argument over infallibility: "The case stands as follows: Roman theology first professes a common ground with ourselves ... Antiquity. When we appeal to Antiquity accordingly, it shifts its ground (and) falls back on its infallibility."[73] But Newman rejects any argument from infallibility on the ground that only the united Church can so speak, and the Church has not been united since at least the eighth, and perhaps as early as the fourth, century:[74]

---

69   Ibid., 41.
70   John Henry Newman, *The Via Media*, vol. 1 (London: Longmans, Green, and Co, 1911).
71   Ibid., 7.   72   Ibid.   73   Ibid., 126.   74   Ibid., 207.

Since the Church is not now one, it is not infallible; since the one
has become in one sense the many, the full prophetical idea is not
now fulfilled; and, with the idea also is lost the full endowment
and the attribute of Infallibility in particular, supposing that
were ever included in it.[75]

Since this guarantee of infallibility has been lost, Church tradition
has been corrupted by additions to the primitive creed, under threat of
anathemas, of which Trent is the prime example.[76] Newman moves from
the argument against Rome to his model of the Church in its two offices,
the episcopal and the prophetic. Generally, these stand to each other as
reason or logic does to intuition. The episcopal tradition is the "creed"
and a "tradition . . . formally and statedly enunciated and delivered from
hand to hand."[77] The prophetic tradition interprets revelation as

> a vast system . . . consisting of a certain body of Truth, pervading
> the Church like an atmosphere, partly written, partly unwritten,
> partly the interpretation, partly the supplement of Scripture,
> partly preserved in intellectual expressions, partly latent in the
> spirit and temper of Christians; poured to and fro in closets
> and upon the housetops, in liturgies, in controversial works, in
> obscure fragments, in sermons, in popular prejudices, in local
> customs. This I call Prophetical Tradition, existing primarily in
> the bosom of the Church itself . . . of a very different kind from
> Episcopal Tradition, yet in its first origin it is equally Apostolical,
> and, viewed as a whole, equally claims our zealous maintenance.[78]

The vulnerability of such a tradition, according to Newman, led to its
corruption by the Roman Church, especially in its doctrine of infallibility.
Here Newman makes his case for the Church of England: She professes to
be the Catholic Church through her sacraments, ordinations, and liturgies,
whereas Rome is defective through its assertion of numerous non-apostolic
doctrines and devotional practices.[79] As a final rebuff to Rome's doctrine
of infallibility, Newman reverts to the principle he learned from Hawkins
a decade earlier: the Church only teaches, while Scripture proves. Thus,
tradition is subservient to Scripture, the supreme authority. Moreover,
tradition contains no truth necessary for salvation.

Bouyer has called Newman's exposition of the subject "as near the
truth as any theory ever advanced regarding the nature and meaning of

---

75 Ibid., 201.   76 Ibid., 232.   77 Ibid., 249.
78 Ibid., 250.   79 Ibid., 262–63.

Tradition."[80] But equally as important for our purposes are the various factors which Newman perceived as the causes of both corruption and fidelity, which relate to the "other track" of religious epistemology, to which Newman will switch shortly in his *Lectures on Justification*. "Truth has a force which error cannot counterfeit,"[81] the pursuit of which, a trait since his early Evangelical days, will ultimately cause his intellectual conversion. This truth, however, Newman assumes is found in the Anglican divines,[82] but what is lacking is order and system: "We have a vast inheritance, but no inventory of our treasures. All is given us in profusion; it remains for us to catalogue, sort, distribute, select, harmonize, and complete."[83] Newman thus made an act of faith in the Anglican divines, of which he will write forty years later in the *Preface to the Third Edition* of the *Prophetical Office*:

> He admitted far too easily what those divines said about the early Fathers, and what they said about Rome. . . . In the years which followed the publication of the Volume, in proportion as he read the Fathers more carefully, and used his own eyes in determining the faith and worship of their times, his confidence in the Anglican divines was more and more shaken, and at last it went altogether.[84]

What drove Newman's *Prophetical Office*, then, was his desire for truth and an uncritical faith in the Anglican divines as transmitters of that truth. A third factor was Newman's perception of the causes of the corruptions of the Prophetical tradition, a loss of love grounded in a willfulness of temper: "For a time the whole church agreed together in . . . the Tradition; but in course of years, love waxing cold and schisms abounding . . . branches developed portions of it for themselves . . . (and) they are the ruins and perversions of Primitive Tradition."[85] The truth-seeker, "If he would possess a reverent mind, he must begin by obeying. If he would cherish a generous and devoted temper, he must begin by venturing something on uncertain information. . . . He must repress his busy intellect, and forbear to scrutinize." Newman accuses both Protestantism and Rome of this failure of submissive obedience to the truth transmitted by Antiquity. Ultimately, he concludes, truth is discovered more through intuition than reason: "They do not know how they see."[86]

80 Bouyer, *Newman*, 166.   81 Newman, *The Prophetical Office*, 142.
82 Ibid., 4.   83 Ibid., 24.   84 Ibid., xxxiii.
85 Ibid., 251–52.   86 Ibid., 283.

These divergent comments lead to a conclusion consistent with our thesis: religious truth is grounded in the affectivity of love, obedience, submission, and faith, in response to a vision of the truth. However, an affective aversion can affect the intellect: "(M)en evade what they do not like. They find reasons for pleasing themselves. . . . (T)he difficulty of obedience (is) a trial of our motives."[87] Ironically, Newman was speaking of obedience to the authority of the Anglican divines. While his act of uncritical faith in the divines would result in the demise of his *Via Media* theory, his establishment of an affective base to religious knowledge, which he would develop in the *Justification* lectures, is consistent with our thesis, as is his definition of faith given near the end of the *Prophetical Office* — "submission of the reason and will towards God"[88] — and he employed the familial imagery so characteristic of his own experience; it is like the reliance of the child on the mother.[89] Submission and faith, then, are grounded in the affection of love.

However, the imagery of Newman's Church at this stage, which the 1877 *Preface to the Third Edition* bears out, contains an aesthetic flaw. By 1877, Newman's image of the prophetical office expanded to include the priestly and kingly offices, a vision of "not the Prophetical office alone and in isolation, as these Lectures virtually teach, but three offices, which are indivisible, though diverse, viz. teaching, rule, and ministry."[90] Newman's intellectual state in 1837 was accompanied by an aesthetic element similarly partial and incomplete, and a deeply affective aversion to Rome, which he characterized in extremely nasty terms, such as "perverted," a "disgrace," and holding a "monstrous" ecclesiastical theory.[91]

However, the *Prophetical Office* also included forty significant references to the principle of the universal Church, or Church unity, the very note of the Church which would shatter Newman in 1839, although he clearly overlooked its importance in 1837. Also, he made many allusions to the principle of the development of doctrine. Thus, the material from which he eventually would refashion his Church image was very much at hand, and his next conversion stage would activate them. Now, however, we will examine his document treating of religious epistemology, the other track on which Newman's mind was operating in 1838.

---

87 Ibid., 261–62.　　88 Ibid., 257.　　89 Ibid., 257–58.
90 Ibid., xl.　　91 Ibid., 41, 44, 49.

THE RELIGIOUS EPISTEMOLOGY TRACK:
Document 2 —
The Lectures on Justification

ALTHOUGH NEWMAN WROTE THAT HE HAD CONTEMPLATED
the subject of the *Lectures on Justification* even before his work on the
Arians,[92] it was an immediate "controversial brush with the vehemently
Protestant *Christian Observer*" which pushed him into action.[93] This work
is considered of "inestimable importance"[94] and a "pioneering classic of
ecumenical theology."[95] Newman's theme is the compatibility of Christian
doctrine and justifying faith, a synthesis he perceived in the *Via Media's*
position between the extremes of Protestantism and Rome. Thus, he saw
the solution to the Church problem as essentially grounded in religious
epistemology, such as the nature and cause of faith, righteousness, and
justifying faith. Each of the three Church communities is distinguished
by its commitment to differing principles on these topics.

The Protestant position of justification by faith alone is rejected as
"erroneous,"[96] and the Roman position of justification by obedience is
rejected as "defective."[97] The former is rejected because it "exercises its gift
without the exercise or even the presence of love[98]. . . . It justifies, then,
as *apprehending* Christ, which is its essence;"[99] and the latter is rejected
because it is "incomplete — truth, but not the whole truth; viz., that
justification consists in love, or sanctity, or obedience, or 'renewal of the
Holy Ghost.'"[100] Conversion is an essential issue in this dilemma: "It is
affirmed that, since man fell, he has lain under one great need. . . . (H)e
needs a new birth unto righteousness."[101] This is accomplished by God
"creating in us new wills and new powers for the observance of it[102]
(and) converting that which is by nature an occasion of condemnation
into an instrument of acceptance."[103] But contrasted with the Protestant "apprehensive" view, "Righteousness then is a *Law in the Heart*,"[104]
a conversion which, from another perspective, means that "Gospel righteousness is obedience to the Law of God, wrought in us by the Holy

92 John Henry Newman, *The Letters and Diaries*, vol. VI, ed. Gerard Tracey (Oxford:
Clarendon Press, 1984), 212.
93 Henry Chadwick, "The Lectures on Justification," in *Newman After a Hundred
Years*, ed. Ian Ker and Alan G. Hill (Oxford: Clarendon Press, 1990), 288.
94 Bouyer, *Newman*, 171.   95 Ker, *John Henry Newman: A Biography*, 157.
96 John Henry Newman, *Lectures on the Doctrine of Justification*, 3rd ed. (London:
Rivingtons, 1890), 2.   97 Ibid.   98 Ibid., 29.
99 Ibid., 16.   100 Ibid., 30.   101 Ibid., 32.
102 Ibid., 34.   103 Ibid., 35.   104 Ibid., 42.

Ghost."[105] This conversion is the effect of the power of grace: "the justifying grace of God effects what it declares."[106] What grace effects is the change of heart[107] which makes obedience gracious, unlike the obedience of unregenerate man.[108] Therefore, justification and renewal, or conversion, "are practically convertible terms."[109] Thus, works are a "cooperation" and "concurrent cause" of ratifying the imputation of grace. Justification is "a Word having a work for its complement[110]. . . . That is, the word will rightly stand either for imputation or for sanctification."[111]

Thus, Newman establishes the ground of justification as neither faith alone nor obedience, but the deeper causal fact of the inward presence of grace which effects first an affective change (of heart) and then a moral change (obedience). In the process, Newman also rejects two methodological approaches. The Protestant position is grounded in an excessive private judgment subjecting Scripture to antecedent principles, recalling the same methodological error Newman perceived in his brother Charles's presumptions, and similar to the "heretical temper" of the Arians. Another methodological error is to speak of justification in terms of "intellectual conceptions" or "efforts of reason." Newman suggests instead an imaginative-aesthetic model "as the profile of full face in a picture."[112] Here Newman takes the Lectures to a level which could be described as mystical, a quality which Bouyer noted in that they "paved the way for all the most fruitful developments that were to proceed from the twentieth-century theology of the Mystical Body."[113] This turn to the mystical-imaginative-aesthetic begins in the sixth lecture on "The Gift of Righteousness." Grounding his work in Paul, Newman identifies justification with the reception of the Divine Presence within us: "In Him we live, and move and have our being."[114] But further, that "Divine Presence vouchsafed to us . . . is specially said to be the presence of Christ . . . in some mysterious manner bestowed upon us[115] . . . (which is) the absorbing vision of a present, indwelling God."[116] Thus, justification is interpersonal encounter with God, which achieves forgiveness, inspires faith, and causes obedience.[117] It is therefore also ongoing[118] and open to increase (or decrease, as the case may be) by means of both obedience and the sacraments, which intensify the Presence within.[119] This Divine Presence is

---

105 Ibid., 44.   106 Ibid., 79.   107 Ibid., 88.   108 Ibid., 91.
109 Ibid., 88.   110 Ibid., 98.   111 Ibid., 99.   112 Ibid., 121.
113 Bouyer, Newman, 172.   114 Newman, Lectures on Justification, 145.
115 Ibid., 148.   116 Ibid., 190.   117 Ibid., 149.   118 Ibid., 101.
119 Ibid., 152.

said to be transferred to us, and our visible manifestation of it is called "glory," a radiance of the Indwelling, which effects sanctification through moral conversion.[120] Further, it is our cooperation which is the condition of the continued Presence within us.[121]

Having resolved that justification is the Presence of Christ within us manifested in newness of heart and conduct, indicating that conversion is wrought by grace producing affective and moral change, Newman then considers the relationship of faith to justification. Beginning again from "a text, which approaches as nearly as any statement in Scripture to a formal definition — 'Faith is the substance of things hoped for, the evidence of things not seen,'"[122] Newman draws out the nature of justifying faith as a perception of heavenly things through an intuitive trust in the divine truth of revelation.[123] Faith is not always religious. It is human before it is God-centered.[124] But faith has the requirement of a "softened heart": "Something more than trust is involved in justifying faith; in other words, it is the trust of a renewed or loving heart."[125] Thus, faith is conditioned by affectivity.

Faith also has an epistemological dimension. Through the Indwelling and obedience, it promotes knowledge of the supernatural.[126] This is nothing short of the Apostolic method of conversion: an appeal to the heart through the beauty of holiness.[127] In this way faith is also said to give direction.[128] With affectivity as the ground, "so love is the modelling and harmonizing principle on which justifying faith depends, and in which it exists and acts."[129]

Faith also involves the element of the will, as it includes submission to the rule of works grounded in the temper of charity.[130] Here, in his twelfth lecture on "Faith Viewed Relatively to Rites and Works," Newman synthesizes Paul and James on the principles of faith and works, discrediting the Protestant methodological error of "faith only" as consistent with the Arian error of logic: "faith only" does not exclude works if they are an essential element of faith. This was like the Arian error of saying "Christ is not God, because the Father is called the 'Only God.'"[131]

Ultimately, faith has an imaginative dimension which introduces perhaps the best concluding summary of the *Lectures*:

> It is faith developed . . . as an image . . . the beginning of that which is eternal, the operation of the Indwelling Power which acts

---

120 Ibid., 178.   121 Ibid., 184.   122 Ibid., 252.   123 Ibid., 253.

124 Ibid.   125 Ibid., 257.   126 Ibid., 267.   127 Ibid., 269–71.

128 Ibid., 273.   129 Ibid., 266.   130 Ibid., 274.   131 Ibid., 276.

from within us outwards and round about us . . . so intimately
with our will as to be in a true sense one with it [and] runs over
into our thoughts, desires, feelings . . . and works, combines
them all together into one, makes the whole man its one instrument. . . . Such is faith, springing up out of . . . love . . . existing
indeed in feelings but passing on into acts, into victories . . . over
self, being the power of the will over the whole soul for Christ's
sake, constraining the reason to accept mysteries, the heart to
acquiesce in suffering, the hand to work . . . the voice to bear
witness . . . (T)hey are all instances of self-command, arising from
Faith seeing the invisible world, and Love choosing it.[132]

Here we find Newman harmonizing the various elements and their
accompaniments of conversion: the aesthetic image, the Indwelling Presence, and the invisible world and its mysteries; the affective heart, feelings,
and the power of love; the intellect; the duty of acts and works; the will
and desires; unconditionality for Christ's sake; and the conviction of
witness. Most important, however, is that the divine gift is the cause of
faith which sees, and of love which chooses what is seen. The Gift-giver
is ultimately the ground of our power of choosing Him in the end.

Newman concludes this lecture with a brief, systematic statement: "We
are justified by grace, which is given through Sacraments, impetrated by
faith, manifested in works."[133] Therein we have the source of the gift,
the means of response, the response, and its expression.

At numerous points throughout this work Newman states that the Articles are consistent with his Scriptural and historical analyses from Antiquity,
and, since his object is to discredit the Protestant doctrine of justification
by faith alone, he is generally favorable toward Rome. In this respect and
others, Lectures offers a distinct and relevant contrast to the Prophetical Office.
While the primary focus of the latter was ecclesiological with doctrine a
subordinate theme, Lectures reverses that priority. This contrast supports
the view that the two works indicate the "double track" on which Newman
was working. Furthermore, this duality is also evidence of the dissonance
which we have seen throughout this study, best documented by the many
significant footnotes Newman added to the 1877 edition to the Prophetical
Office, reversing, criticizing, or rescinding his original positions on at least
thirty-seven important points. This is in sharp contrast to his 1874 Preface
to the Third Edition of the Lectures, wherein he states, "Unless the Author
held in substance in 1874 what he published in 1838, he would not at this

---

132   Ibid., 302–3.   133   Ibid., 303.

time be reprinting what he wrote as an Anglican; certainly not with so little added by way of safeguard."[134] *Lectures* contains thirteen significant footnotes, nine of which are elaborations of points and only four of which are corrections.[135] A conclusion of this analysis is that there existed a consistency in Newman's insights regarding faith and religious epistemology that was lacking in his ecclesiological theory. Perhaps another striking piece of evidence of this conflict comes from Newman's own allusion in the *Lectures* to the unconscious dimension of righteousness. In Lecture VI on "The Gift of Righteousness," Newman speaks of infant baptism: "For as God dwelt secretly in His material Temple, ever hallowing it, yet only in season giving sensible evidences of what was there, so may He be present with their souls, rescuing them from Satan, and imparting new powers, manifesting new objects, and suggesting new thoughts and desires, without their being conscious, or others witnesses, of his work."[136] Thus, grace can work its wonders without, or prior to, the conscious knowledge of the recipient, and here we find the trace of that element which will ultimately convert Newman's intellect: the principle of development. In this lecture it is implied in faith, and eventually we will see Newman discovering it as a principle of doctrine as his two tracks converge. However, their merger is yet years away.

Newman returned to the University pulpit in early 1839, after an absence of more than six years, to deliver three sermons on faith, which had also been the focus of three of his thirteen *Lectures on Justification*. A review of these documents will conclude our first stage of Newman's intellectual conversion, which was characterized by an uncritical, assumed faith in the Anglican divines that resulted in a partial, skewed, ecclesiastical image, but which was countered by the presence of an insight into the nature of faith that sets up Newman's ensuing conflict.

THE RELIGIOUS EPISTEMOLOGY TRACK:
Documents 3, 4, and 5 —
The Oxford University Sermons of 1839: Numbers X, XI, and XII

THESE THREE SERMONS WERE ALL DELIVERED IN EARLY 1839 and show influences of the *Lectures*. The first, entitled "Faith and Reason, Contrasted as Habits of Mind,"[137] was preached on January 6 and generally

---

134 Ibid., ix.
135 Ibid., Elaborations: 2, 31, 73, 154, 198, 201, 226, 343, 348–49. Corrections: 101, 186, 190, 236.
136 Ibid., 152.   137 Newman, *Fifteen Sermons*, 176–201.

describes what faith is and how it works: an original principle, independent of,[138] and thus not dependent upon, reason.[139] As we have seen in the *Lectures*, it is the first fruit of grace,[140] and it resides in the heart, the home of grace.[141] Reason merely critiques, but does not create, faith.[142] However, they have an important reciprocal relationship: "Reason may be the judge, without being the origin, of faith . . . (and) Faith may be justified by Reason, without making use of it."[143] The crucial difference between the two lies in their operation: "(H)ow is it conformable to Reason to accept evidence less than Reason requires?" Faith, in contrast to reason, "is mainly swayed by antecedent considerations . . . . Reason, by direct and definite proof."[144] Newman again quotes the Pauline definition of faith, commenting that "its desire is its main evidence . . . . This is . . . why Faith seems . . . so irrational."[145] This desire is nothing short of Newman's ongoing theme of temper: "But a man *is* responsible for his faith, because he is responsible for his likes and dislikes, his hopes and opinions, on all of which his faith depends."[146] Thus, one's affectivity is a matter of moral responsibility, since one's affective disposition grounds one's expectations, hopes, and desires (antecedent probabilities), and consequently one's faith. And if faith is from grace, a "supernatural principle," so is affectivity: "(T)hese are feelings not natural to fallen man, and they come only of supernatural grace; and these are the feelings which make us think evidence sufficient, which falls short of a proof in itself. The natural man has no heart for the promises of the Gospel."[147] But if "faith is an instrument of knowledge and action,"[148] what is this knowledge? It is Newman's lifelong motivating principle, truth, and thus Newman concludes the sermon with a synthesis of mind and heart: "For is this not the error . . . of the world, to think itself a judge of Religious Truth without preparation of heart?"[149] As was detailed previously from Newman's early life, affectivity always grounded his trust and faith in others, from home to school and friends. As he says in this sermon, faith "simply accepts testimony."[150] It was this very principle of religious epistemology which led Newman, in our first chapter analysis, from the experience of love to the act of faith, but it is also the violation of that principle which caused the dissonance between his own analysis of faith—his intellectual element—and his own act of faith—regarding the Churches. For in that same paragraph as the previous quotation, he

---

138 Ibid., 182–83.   139 Ibid., 184–85.   140 Ibid., 176.
141 Ibid., 177.   142 Ibid., 183.   143 Ibid., 184.
144 Ibid., 187.   145 Ibid., 190.   146 Ibid., 192.
147 Ibid., 193.   148 Ibid., 179.   149 Ibid., 198.
150 Ibid., 180.

identifies the source of testimony: "Faith cometh by hearing, and hearing by the word of God."[151] When it came to the nature of the Church, Newman placed his faith in the word of the Anglican divines, which was human testimony, rather than in revelation, or divine testimony, a fact which he acknowledged in the *Apologia*.[152]

Newman's next *University Sermon* was given one week later on January 13 and "approach(es) the question (of faith) phenomenologically."[153] Entitled "The Nature of Faith in Relation to Reason,"[154] it affirmed the affective ground of faith, and that "testimony is the only method . . . by which the next world can be revealed to us."[155] But Newman takes his analysis further in two respects: first, in the assertion that faith is an act of reason, since all knowledge is based upon some form of assumption,[156] and secondly, the quest for religious truth and knowledge is essentially a test of our love.[157] Thus, affectivity grounds not only faith but also knowledge, and since faith is also an act of reason, affectivity also grounds reason. A third point Newman makes is that affectivity is the ground of our vision of God:

> Even though the feelings which prompt us to see God in all things, and to recognize supernatural works in matters of the world, mislead us at times, though they make us trust in evidence which we ought not to admit, and partially incur with justice the imputation of credulity, yet a Faith which generously apprehends Eternal Truth, though at times it degenerates into superstition, is far better than that cold, sceptical, critical tone of mind which has no inward sense of an overruling, ever-present Providence.[158]

About four months later, on May 21, Newman delivered his third *University Sermon* of the period on faith, "Love, the Safeguard of Faith Against Superstition,"[159] in which he takes his exploration of faith a step deeper. Acknowledging that faith requires a criterion or "safeguard" to prevent abuses such as superstition and fanaticism, Newman attributes this function to affectivity:

> The safeguard of faith is a right state of heart. This it is that gives it birth; it also disciplines it. . . . It is Love which forms it

151 Ibid.   152 Newman, *Apologia*, 186.
153 Avery Dulles, "From Images to Truth: Newman on Revelation and Faith," *Theological Studies* 51 (1990): 262.   154 Newman, *Fifteen Sermons*, 202–21.
155 Ibid., 214.   156 Ibid., 206, 214–15.   157 Ibid., 215.
158 Ibid., 220.   159 Ibid., 222–50.

out of the rude chaos, into an image of Christ; or, in scholastic language, justifying Faith, whether in pagan, Jew, or Christian, is *fides formata charitate.*[160]

Thus it is the "new life," or conversion, "which leads the soul to Christ."[161] Here Newman employs a familiar familial metaphor: the child trusts his or her parents not because of proofs but rather "from the instinct of affection. . . . We *believe* because we *love.*"[162] We believe because we discern the cause of our own feelings, which is He who loves us, and the recognition of Him causes us to love reciprocally, and then believe. In this sense, believing is the manifestation of that which we have already perceived as the Object of our love. Again, affirming the affective ground of morality and the intellect, "I say, the principle of Love, acting not by way of inquiry or argument, but spontaneously and as an instinct, will cause the mind to recoil from cruelty, impurity, and the assumption of divine power."[163] Newman summarizes the interrelationship of faith, intellect, and moral disposition (temper):

> Right faith is the faith of a right mind. Faith is an intellectual act; right faith is an intellectual act, done in a certain moral disposition. Faith is an act of Reason, viz. a reasoning upon presumptions; right faith is a reasoning upon holy, devout, and enlightened presumptions[164]. . . . (H)oliness, dutifulness, or love, however we word it, and not Reason, is the eye of Faith,[165] the discriminating principle.[166]

A distinction is to be made, however, about what this love is: "By love in these texts he does not mean the theological virtue of charity, which presupposes faith, but a devout inclination toward the source and goal of heavenly life."[167]

---

160 Ibid., 234.   161 Ibid., 235.   162 Ibid., 236.

163 Ibid., 240–41.   164 Ibid., 239.

165 Pierre Rousselot's work *The Eyes of Faith* (New York: Fordham University Press, 1990) has much in common with Newman's analysis of faith and with our hypothesis and analysis of Newman's conversion experiences. In the Introduction to that work, John M. McDermott hails it as "the most penetrating and influential analysis of the act of faith in modern theology" (2). "By orienting the intellectual affirmation to God Rousselot understood the intellect as a dynamism toward the True and the Good. Thereby he overturned the basis of the traditional distinction between intellect and will in terms of their formal objects, the true and the good. Knowing and loving henceforth influence each other intimately" (16).

166 Newman, *Fifteen Sermons*, 238.   167 Ibid.; Dulles, *From Images to Truth*, 263.

Newman closes this sermon with a description of faith which has functions, effects, and elements similar to our conversion hypothesis, which have been italicized in the following quotation: "Such . . . is real Faith: a presumption . . . a *reaching forward* . . . a *movement* . . . kept in the narrow path . . . by . . . *dutifulness* . . . which . . . judges it . . . an *intellectual* act . . . and it takes its character from the *moral* state of the agent. . . . It is perfected by *obedience*. . . . (T)he *direction* it gains from *Love*." Finally, the will, so crucial to conversion, is the issue. Conforming the will to God's revealed will is the ultimate criterion: "Faith leads the mind to communion with the invisible God; its attempts at approaching and pleasing Him are acceptable or not, according as they are or are not self-willed; and they are self-willed when they are irrespective of God's revealed will."[168]

These three *University Sermons*, then, witness Newman's deepening thought about the nature of religious faith, formally begun earlier in the *Lectures on Justification*. As an extension of that work, they contain the development of a religious epistemology which is comprehensive, accounting for the functions not only of grace but of the various dimensions of man's nature — affectivity, reason, will, and imagination — as all aspects relate to the principle of action.

However, as developed as was Newman's theological theory of faith, it contrasted sharply on several counts with his ecclesiological theory of the *Via Media* elaborated in the *Prophetical Office*. The former was obviously the product of Newman's own theological reflection, whereas the latter was largely assumed from the Anglican divines. Secondly, these reflections on faith were essentially free of the anti-Roman bias with which Newman's ecclesiastical outlook had been "stained" since youth, which was yet an element of his Church prejudice. The result is that we find Newman, in the spring of 1839, exhibiting an intellectual dissonance fueled on the one hand by an affective aversion to Rome, which in itself contained an ambivalence, as we have seen, and on the other, by an uncritical faith in the Anglican divines. This intellectual dissonance existed between reflections on faith on the one hand and Church on the other. Newman himself confirms this dual focus and tension, which supports our "two track theory" of his conversion development during this intellectual phase: "(A)t the end of 1835 or beginning of 1836, I had the whole state of the question before me, on which, to my mind, the decision between the Churches depended. . . . (I)n my view the controversy . . . turned upon the Faith and the Church."[169] The ultimate result of this period is an aesthetic

---

168   Newman, *Fifteen Sermons*, 242.   169   Newman, *Apologia*, 111.

flaw, Newman's vision of the *Via Media*, which could rightfully be called an uncritical image grounded in an uncritical faith supplemented by an affective aversion, which succinctly describes this first stage of Newman's intellectual conversion. This development of Newman's "ecclesiological track" parallels but contrasts with the development of his "religious epistemological track" regarding faith, and this dialectic tension leads us to the second stage of this period, which begins with the clash of imagery that will shatter Newman's uncritical image of the *Via Media*. But it is important to note that the inspiration which drove Newman's insights in the *Lectures on Justification* and the *University Sermons* was the enduring principle he had learned as a young convert: the pursuit of truth. This pursuit is borne out in the second stage of Newman's intellectual conversion, the clash of images.

STAGE TWO:
The Clash of Images

THE UNCRITICAL VERSUS THE REVEALED IMAGES:
The Via Media *versus* Securus Judicat Orbis Terrarum, 1839–1841

THIS PERIOD BEGINS WITH TWO EVENTS, EXPRESSED IN THREE significant documents, and closes with several more significant events. The first two events in the summer and fall of 1839 begin a period of crisis for Newman as his *Via Media* theory is "pulverized" by Catholic imagery. As a result, Newman authors three major documents within a year. He delivers two *University Sermons* continuing the development of religious epistemology, but now he incorporates the relationship of doctrines into that process, prompted by his doubts about the *Via Media*. Between these sermons, he also writes what would be the last *Tracts for the Times*, his controversial number 90, as an investigation into the Articles of the Church of England, thus continuing his ecclesiological track. However, the spring and summer of 1841 witnessed pivotal events in Newman's conversion. In April 1841, Newman became acquainted with Dr. Charles Russell, an Irish Catholic priest eleven years his junior, a relationship which would have a monumental effect, as we have noted: "He had, perhaps, more to do with my conversion than anyone else."[170] Russell's personal relationship with Newman, grounded in affectivity, would become the catalyst for Newman's intellectual, and then ultimately his unconditional, conversion, or submission, to Rome. But in addition to this relationship, which appears to have influenced Newman's second *University Sermon* of this period, Newman

---

170   Newman, *Apologia*, 178.

would suffer "three blows" just after the relationship with Russell began which would fatally damage his faith in the Anglican Church. As Russell's influence extends into the next phase of Newman's conversion, it will continue to affect Newman right up to the eve of his Roman conversion, when he writes Russell on that very night to inform him of his conversion. This we will examine in the next period of Newman's conversion, along with other major influences, but here we focus on the second stage of Newman's intellectual conversion dealing with the clash of ecclesiastical images.

Newman wrote to acquaintances in July, 1839: "I am able [in] the long vacation to return to my own line of reading . . . suspended since the long vacation of /35 [1835] — the controversies of the first centuries. I hope to master the Nestorian and Eutychian controversies in the course of the Vacation,"[171] and "My immediate subject is the 5th century controversies on the Incarnation."[172] Newman recounts in a third letter, dated July 12, a significant fact in light of later developments: "Two things are very remarkable at Chalcedon — the great power of the pope (as great as he claims now almost), and the marvellous interference of civil power, as great almost as in our kings."[173] Thus, Newman had discovered at this early date in history a church principle which he had long attacked as contrary to Antiquity. Then

> It was during this course of reading that for the first time a doubt came upon me of the tenableness of Anglicanism. . . . (B)y the end of August I was seriously alarmed. . . . My stronghold was Antiquity; now here, in the middle of the fifth century, I found, as it seemed to me, Christendom of the sixteenth and the nineteenth centuries reflected. I saw my face in that mirror, and I was a Monophysite. The Church of the *Via Media* was in the position of the Oriental communion, Rome was where she is now, and the Protestants were the Eutychians.[174]

And then, as his letter above about the papacy indicated,

> (It was) difficult to condemn the Popes of the sixteenth century, without condemning the Popes of the fifth. The drama of religion, and the combat of truth and error, were ever one and the same. . . . (T)here was an awful similitude. . . . The shadow of the fifth century was on the sixteenth. It was like a spirit rising

---

171 Newman, *Letters and Diaries*, vol. VII, ed. Gerard Tracey (Oxford: Clarendon Press, 1995), 106.

172 Ibid., 110.   173 Ibid., 105.   174 Ibid., 114.

from the troubled waters of the old world, within the shape and lineaments of the new.[175]

What is most noteworthy about these passages is that they indicate that Newman was changed not merely by intellectual research, although that is obviously a factor, but even more so by an analogical imagination resulting from that study.[176] Newman saw a new image of the Church, the old within the new. But why was this any different from the image of the Anglican as the new, with Antiquity the old? An even more confirmatory image occurred the very next month. On September 19, Robert Williams called Newman's attention to an article in the *Dublin Review* by Wiseman attacking the Church of England as schismatic. Notably, Newman had read the article and missed the shattering imagery, for Wiseman had referenced Augustine's overarching principle of ecclesiastical validation: "*Securus judicat orbis terrarum.*" In a passage which Ian Ker calls not only one of the most dramatic and powerful in all of Newman's writings but also a note of Newman's "deconversion,"[177] Newman admits the words

> had escaped my observation. . . . They gave a cogency to the Article, which had escaped me at first. They decided ecclesiastical questions on a simpler rule than Antiquity. . . . (H)ere then Antiquity was deciding against itself. What a light was thereby thrown upon every controversy in the Church! . . . (T)he deliberate judgment, in which the whole Church at length rests and acquiesces, is an infallible prescription and a final sentence against such portions of it as protest and secede. . . . (T)he words of St. Augustine struck me with a power which I had never felt from any words before. . . . (B)y those great words . . . the theory of the *Via Media* was absolutely pulverized.[178]

175 Ibid.

176 Gerard Magill comments, "Newman's use of the imagination in his theological method complements [David] Tracy's analogical imagination by weaving together the three characteristics of discernment. . . . These dynamic, holistic, and subjective characteristics . . . clarify the epistemological function of the imagination in Newman's works, and thereby they illumine Tracy's strategy for comprehending claims to meaning and truth in theology." Magill, "Moral Imagination in Theological Method and Church Tradition: John Henry Newman," *Theological Studies* 53 (1992): 473–74.

177 Ker, *John Henry Newman: A Biography*, 182–83. Ker does not explain this interpretation.

178 Newman, *Apologia*, 115–16. Again, the axiom is found in Augustine, *Contra Epistolam Parmeniani*, iii.3. Newman translated it as "The universal Church is in its judgments secure of truth" (*Ess.* ii. 101).

Newman's letters from this period confirm his alarm, as he wrote first to Frederick Rogers and then S. F. Wood that very September:

> I have had the first real hit from Romanism. . . . Dr. Wiseman's Article . . . has given me a stomach-ache. . . . It certainly does come upon me that we are not at the bottom of things[179]. . . . At this moment we have sprung a leak. . . . (B)ut I do not deny that it requires considering and has a claim upon us for an answer.[180]

During the same period he wrote to Pusey: "Since I read Dr. W's article I have desponded much."[181] And to his old school friend Bowden, he confided: "As to Dr. Wiseman's article . . . It made a very great impression here — and . . . it made me for a while very uncomfortable in my own mind."[182] But Newman was also sure of how he would approach the dilemma:

> I think I should never make up my mind to any overt act towards Rome, without giving up two or three years as a time of religious preparation towards forming a judgment. And . . . I should not even then act, without having the sanction of one or two persons whom I most looked up to and trusted.[183]

Characteristically, affectivity and reflection would be brought to bear on the dilemma, and the former would come from a most unexpected source, the Roman Catholic Russell. To return to the imagery, Newman described the effect of this insight in imaginative terms as the

> shadow of a hand upon the wall . . . a ghost. . . . The heavens had opened and closed again. The thought for the moment had been, 'The Church of Rome will be found right after all,' and then it vanished. My old convictions remained as before . . . and at length the vivid impression upon my imagination faded away.[184]

But it would not fade without significant effect. Newman characteristically felt the impact on both his mind and his morality: "I had to determine its logical value, and its bearing on my duty."[185] Though the urgency of the impression faded, the mark was left, only to resurface in 1841. It was in fact this article by Wiseman challenging the Apostolic succession of the Church of England which motivated Newman to write the documents of this period, two on his "religious epistemology track" and one on his "ecclesiological track."

---

179 Newman, *Letters and Diaries*, vol. VII, 154. 180 Ibid., 156.
181 Ibid., 214. 182 Ibid., 241. 183 Ibid., 180.
184 Ibid., 116. 185 Ibid.

NEWMAN'S RELIGIOUS EPISTEMOLOGY TRACK:
Document 6 —
University Sermon XIII: "Implicit and Explicit Reason"

ON JUNE 29, 1840, NEWMAN DELIVERED HIS THIRTEENTH UNI-
versity *Sermon*, distinguished by several themes: (1) The effects of the *securus
judicat orbis terrarum* imagery; (2) the damage to his intellectual confidence
revealed in several self-critical statements; and (3) a reflection on the relationship of faith, reason, doctrine, and the Churches or, in other words,
the beginning of an intellectual synthesis. The crucial epistemological
advance which Newman makes is the nature of doctrine as a product of
the human mind. Therefore, to understand the assent of the mind, which
is incremental and thus developmental,[186] is to understand the nature
of doctrine.

Newman alludes to the nature of his sermon as a corrective for assumptions, and thus errors, of reason: the "science of Evidences" cannot grasp
the "recondite reasons" which motivate belief, "since it cannot analyze
and exhibit these momentous reasons," and "leads the student to mistake what are but secondary points in debate, as if they were the most
essential."[187] No doubt exists that he is criticizing his own oversight of
the Augustinian maxim:

> As to the difficulty of detecting and expressing the real reasons on
> which we believe, let this be considered — how very differently an
> argument strikes the mind at one time and another, according to
> its particular state, or the accident of the moment. At one time it is
> weak and unmeaning — at another, it is nothing short of demon-
> stration. We take up a book at one time, and see nothing in it; at
> another, it is full of weighty remarks and precious thoughts.[188]

And this leads Newman to the ecclesiastical dilemma which the *securus
judicat orbis terrarum* imagery posed:

> Such, for instance, are the following . . . that there must be an
> infallible Head of the Church on earth; or that the Roman Church,
> extending into all lands, is the Catholic Church; or that a Church,
> which is Catholic abroad, cannot be schismatical in England.[189]

---

186 Avery Dulles perceives these qualities in Newman's own conversion: "His
conversion was therefore not a repudiation but an affirmation of the past; it was
continuous, progressive, and incremental." Dulles, "Newman, Conversion, and
Ecumenism," *Theological Studies* 51 (1990): 723.
187 Newman, *Fifteen Sermons*, 272.   188 Ibid., 271.   189 Ibid., 272.

Thus, the cause and underlying focus of the sermon leads to an exploration of "reason implicit or explicit, (and) staked out the ground for what was afterwards to become the *Grammar of Assent*."[190] The reasonings of faith are latent and implicit:[191] recondite, à priori reasons (not in the logical sense) determine assent.[192] Using the metaphorical imagery of painting to conception, Newman compares the attempt to represent the act of belief and its subjects to the mind's artistic vision: "(W)e shall surely understand the difficulty, or rather the impossibility, of representing . . . that substance and that exactness in detail in which consists its likeness to the original."[193] When it comes to religion, upon reflection beliefs are expressed as doctrines. In other words, implicit reasoning, through the work of the intellect, becomes explicit in the form of doctrine. However, implicit reasoning in religion, or faith, "is complete without this reflective faculty, which . . . often does interfere with it."[194] Doctrines, then, are but "symbols of the real grounds."[195] Then Newman makes an analogy which is pivotal. Doctrinal statements may seem inconsistent when contrasted, just as do pictures of the same person at different times in life. However, the inconsistency is resolved when the principle of development is understood as inherent — both in man and, most importantly, in doctrines as the product of man's mind. We find in this sermon the beginning of an intellectual change by which Newman was now investigating doctrinal development as perhaps the natural extension of an innate mental process. Doctrine itself, however, was a subordinate theme to the process which produces them. Thus, the nature of reason and its relationship to faith is the primary theme, but we find here the seed of Newman's reflections about the nature of doctrine, which will become the primary focus of his fifteenth *University Sermon* and then the *Essay on the Development of Christian Doctrine* during his final conversion phase. It is important to note that this intellectual development was fostered by the aesthetic conflict of images — the *Via Media* versus Augustine's *securus judicat orbis terrarum*, a clash which Newman's intellect did not perceive initially, even though the *securus judicat* principle was recognized in his *Prophetical Office*. Thus, we have intellect moved by image; an uncritical image, taken on faith in its human authors, which clashes with the revealed image, producing a significant intellectual change in Newman.

This sermon was written during Newman's work on *Tract 90*, which he published six months later. We now move on to examine the impact of the *securus judicat* imagery on that aspect of Newman's ecclesiological track.

---

190 Bouyer, *Newman*, 186.   191 Newman, *Fifteen Sermons*, 277.

192 Ibid., 272.   193 Ibid., 267.   194 Ibid., 277.

195 Ibid., 275.

THE ECCLESIOLOGICAL TRACK:
Document 5—
Tract 90: Remarks on Certain Passages in the Thirty-Nine Articles,
February 27, 1841[196]

NEWMAN STATES THAT HE HAD CONSIDERED A WORK ON THE
Articles since the time of his tutorship,[197] and by 1841, with his doctrinal
views substantially changed, he was moved to action by problems with the
Via Media theory as well as decreased aversion to Rome. He also felt that the
respective Roman and Anglican creeds were "obscured . . . by . . . 'Popery'
and 'Protestantism,'" and he sought to minimize the differences.[198] The
thesis of Newman's essay on the Articles contained three tenets: (1) The
Articles do not oppose Catholic teaching; (2) They only partially oppose
Roman dogma; and (3) They primarily oppose the dominant errors of
Rome,[199] that is, the non-dogmatic, corrupt practices. Newman draws several conclusions. First, reminiscent of the distinction he first learned from
Hawkins, Newman asserts that according to the Articles, while scripture
contains the content of faith, it is the Church, or rather tradition, which
expands and enforces it.[200] However, the Articles do not address the crucial
issues of authority and method of judgment. Secondly, the Articles (number
xi) affirm that justification is by faith alone, and Newman reiterates his
argument from the Justification lectures: "(N)ewness of heart is the sine qua
non life of it . . . . Faith working by love is the seed of divine graces."[201]
Thirdly, Newman expounds notes of the true Church (Article xix), three
of which are essential: "a congregation of faithful men in which the pure
Word of God is preached, and the Sacraments be duly ministered."[202]
Thus, community, gospel, and sacraments are marks of the true Church.
But most notably Newman denies universality as a requisite note at this
time: "Whether intercommunion with the whole be necessary to each part
of it . . . (is) not expressly treated of in the Articles."[203] Fourthly, Newman details the Anglican objections contained in the Articles to Roman
devotional corruptions (Article xxii), sacramental differences (Article xxv),
including especially Transubstantiation, and the problem of the Papacy
(Article xxxviii), as Newman declares that the doctrine is not Apostolic:

---

196   John Henry Newman, "Remarks on Certain Passages in the Thirty-Nine Articles,
1841," The Via Media of the Anglican Church, vol. ii (London, Longmans, Green and
Co, 1908), 259–356.
197   Newman, Apologia, 84.   198   Ibid., 85.   199   Ibid.
200   Newman, "Remarks on Certain Passages in the Thirty-Nine Articles," The Via
Media of the Anglican Church, vol. ii, 275–76.
201   Ibid., 283.   202   Ibid., 288.   203   Ibid., 289–90.

> There is nothing in the Apostolic system which gives an authority to the Pope over the Church. . . . It is altogether an ecclesiastical arrangement, not a point *de fide*, but of expedience, custom, or piety, which cannot be claimed as if the Pope *ought* to have it.[204]

But Newman's conclusions admitted a much greater degree of potential agreement between the Churches, a view which was perceived as Romanizing: "The Articles . . . leav(ing) open large questions . . . state broadly extreme truths, and are silent about their adjustment."[205] However, Newman thought that his *Tract* firmly established the fact that the Articles were indeed Catholic and in continuity with Apostolic tradition, and thus rebutted Wiseman's attack. But many Anglicans saw it as very favorable to Rome because of the doctrinal continuity which it indicated between the two Churches. Actually, Newman pointed out the important historical fact that the Articles were written prior to the Council of Trent, and therefore, since the doctrinal decrees of that Council had not yet been promulgated, the Articles were not, and could not have been, written in opposition to Tridentine doctrines, but were clearly aimed at Roman devotional corruptions.

However, Newman's problems with the notes of unity and authority kept him within the bounds of the Anglican communion. His intellect may have been plunged into doubt through the imagery of the *securus judicat*, but his work on the Articles led him to believe that the Anglican Church was justified without intercommunion and that an internal reform could remedy the situation. Added to this was his lingering affective aversion to Rome, especially what he perceived as its unapostolic principle of authority.

The negative response to *Tract 90* was fast and furious, in response to which Newman wrote a lengthy public letter, a common technique of the time, to Dr. R. W. Jelf[206] in an attempt to mollify his opponents. Newman condemned Roman abuses,[207] especially infallibility, which he perceived as the root of all trouble: "If there is one doctrine more than another which characterizes the present Church of Rome, and on which all its obnoxious tenets depend, it is the doctrine of its infallibility."[208] Newman made clear his belief "of the impossibility of any approach of the English toward the Roman Church."[209] He protested that his interpretation that the Articles leave questions open provided grounds for effecting conversions to the

---

204   Ibid., 342.   205   Ibid., 345.

206   John Henry Newman, "A Letter Addressed to the Rev. R. W. Jelf in Explanation of the Ninetieth Tract," *The Via Media of the Anglican Church*, vol. ii, 365–93.

207   Ibid., 368.   208   Ibid., 376.   209   Ibid., 389.

Anglican Church, rather than grounds for the English Church to move toward Rome. Except for the Creed, "a great diversity in doctrine"[210] is confirmed by the Anglican divines. Thus, Newman perceived his insight of a flexibility in the Articles as a strength rather than a weakness for the Church of England. But perhaps the most important ecclesiastical note Newman struck in the letter was his perception that man's religiosity is fundamentally affective, and the Church of England must so appeal to it, since this is the very core of Rome's strength:

> There is at this moment a great progress of the religious mind of our Church to something deeper and truer than satisfied the last century. . . . The age is moving toward something, and most unhappily the one religious communion . . . in possession of this something, is the Church of Rome. She alone . . . has given free scope to the feelings of awe, mystery, tenderness, reverence, devotedness, and other feelings which may be especially called Catholic.[211]

Thus, the feelings toward Rome which Newman perceived during his Mediterranean journey, and to a degree felt himself, are the grounds of ecclesiastical attraction. This affectivity was also then the ground of faith and the core of religious experience, as here we see Newman's two tracks beginning to converge. That same month, March 1841, Newman wrote to his bishop[212] in response to the latter's concern over the disruption caused by Tract 90. Newman protested that the Tract did not display "a leaning towards Roman Catholic error."[213] Rather, as he had indicated to Jelf, he "had observed what a very powerful source of attraction the Church of Rome possessed in her devotional Services, and he wished, judiciously or not, to remove it by claiming it for ourselves."[214] Thus, Newman's intent was to appropriate the hold which Rome had on man's affections through devotional services. Newman maintained that even though Rome may be a true apostolic Church, while "this system I have called Romanism or Popery . . . exists . . . we can have no peace with that Church. . . . (W)e cannot, without a sin, sacrifice truth to peace,"[215] again affirming one of his lifelong motivations. But most importantly, Newman indicated a change of strategy in his search for notes of the true Church. His confidence

---

210   Ibid., 380.   211   Ibid., 386.

212   John Henry Newman, "A Letter Addressed to the Right Reverend Father in God, Richard, Lord Bishop of Oxford, on the occasion of the Ninetieth Tract," The Via Media of the Anglican Church, vol. ii, 395–424.

213   Ibid., 399.   214   Ibid., 402.   215   Ibid., 412.

in the Church of England having been shaken, he now switched his key note of the true church to that of sanctity: "Whatever be a religious body's . . . doctrines — whatever its worship — if it has but the life of holiness within it, this . . . will take care of itself. . . . (S)anctity is the great note of the Church."[216] Of all the possible signs of the true apostolic Church, Newman felt most confident that the possession of sanctity, and the capacity to produce it, validated the Church of England. *Tract 90* had substantiated a doctrinal continuity between the Churches, so that was no longer a significant point of difference to Newman. By means of the note of sanctity he believed he could make a case against Rome: "Instead then of speaking of errors in doctrine, I was driven, by my state of mind, to . . . the ground which I felt to be good against her . . . the moral ground."[217]

Despite the storm of protest over *Tract 90*, Newman managed to prevent it from being condemned by the authorities. He refused to back down on his conclusion that "the Articles were tolerant, not only of what I called 'Catholic teaching,' but of much that was 'Roman.'"[218]

An important note here is the intellectual dimension of Newman's research. The evidence, or the truth, was that the churches of England and Rome were not insurmountably opposed on doctrine, and in fact just the opposite. Therefore, if the Church of England moved against this fact, it would be moving against truth. For the moment, the Church authorities did not do so. But Newman perceived what he thought was a stronger argument for Anglican independence, its note of sanctity in comparison to the "simply secular and political" conduct of Rome, as exemplified by such activities as those of the Irish Catholic O'Connell, who was endorsed by Rome.[219] Newman believed he had a formula, albeit tenuous, which could justify the autonomy of the Church of England while acknowledging the doctrinal agreements with her sister, but not superior, Church at Rome. Newman's formula would last but a few months, when "between July and November, I received three blows which broke me."[220] However, just prior to these incidents, perhaps the most important event affecting Newman's intellectual conversion occurred in 1841. The Irish priest Dr. Charles Russell had read *Tract 90* and wrote to Newman with basically one theme, and it was intellectual: that Newman misunderstood both Catholic doctrine and practice. The correspondence between them began on April 8, 1841, just weeks after *Tract 90* was published, and their ensuing relationship would be the primary cause of Newman's investigations

---

216 Ibid., 422.   217 Newman, *Apologia*, 120–21.
218 Ibid., 89.   219 Ibid., 121.   220 Ibid., 133.

into Roman doctrine and devotional practices and would thus start in motion a process which would culminate in Newman's intellectual conversion. Before we examine both the "three blows" which would push Newman over the edge in respect to the Church of England, as well as his simultaneous relationship with Russell, let us examine the importance of Russell's impact in the early days of their relationship, beginning in the spring of 1841.

DR. CHARLES RUSSELL:
The Affective Influence on Newman's Religious Intellect

RUSSELL AND NEWMAN EXCHANGED SIX LETTERS IN THE BRIEF period between April 8 and May 5, 1841, each writing three.[221] Several facts of this correspondence are significant. First and foremost was Russell's temperament. He wrote respectfully, even apologetically, and expressed great regard for Newman and the Movement. His tone is that of a generous-hearted individual, and Newman, always impressed by people of affection, was thus disposed to the intellectual themes of Russell's letters. Russell contended that Newman was incorrect in many of his assumptions about Roman doctrine and practice. Regarding Transubstantiation he wrote, "Rest assured . . . that you have completely misconceived us."[222] Newman replied that he actually was aware of Russell's objections, but that "my object in it (*Tract 90*) was not to defend you, but to exonerate our Articles from what is traditionally imputed to them. The Articles merely condemn a certain extreme view of it (Transubstantiation) which some persons or party [?] in your Church have put forward." Then Newman went on to rebuke Roman practices: "O that you would reform your worship . . . the extreme honours paid to St. Mary and the Saints, your traditionary view of indulgences, and the veneration . . . to Images."[223] Russell replied that he was consoled that the issue regarding doctrine had been resolved but that Newman was equally in error regarding Roman practices: "If you knew us well . . . your fears of our 'traditionary system' would disappear." Then Russell made a key point sure to impress Newman: "Every Hymn has its doxology. . . . (E)very Prayer terminates by assigning the merits of our Lord as the ground of its petitions."[224] Thus, Roman devotions were in fact Christ-centered, as Newman himself would insist they be. Newman's reply is an indication that he clung to his affective aversion

---

221   John Henry Newman, *Correspondence of John Henry Newman with John Keble and Others, 1839–1845* (London: Longmans, Green, and Co, 1917), 118–29.
222   Ibid., 121.   223   Ibid., 122–23.   224   Ibid., 125.

toward Rome as he assumed from the mere fact of the Reformation that there had to be "some very grave errors on the side of Rome."[225] Russell responded that "there is much significance in this contrast" between the Churches of England and Rome, that "the danger of lapsing from Anglicanism into Protestantism . . . is fearfully greater than that of falling . . . from the doctrines of the Council of Trent into superstition or idolatry." Russell, who was striking chords all too familiar to Newman, closed the letter with two very important points. First, he appealed to the Roman note of Catholicity: "With us, Catholicism is the rule, and these extremes (devotions, etc.) if they existed, would be but accidental exceptions; while with you, until of late years even the shadow of Catholicism had been unknown for an entire century," a statement which had the unmistakable ring of Augustine's axiom. Secondly, Russell closed the letter with an appeal to the intellect to disabuse Newman's misgivings: "that secondary and traditionary system among us, which seems to haunt you . . . has no existence in fact . . . . (H)ad you the same sources (and God will give them to your prayers) of information, you would believe with me that your fears are groundless."[226] As their relationship continued, this would indeed be the case. But Newman replied to this letter rather stiffly that if Russell thought a "jump" to Rome were immanent, that was "a fatal mistake." Then Newman closed with a telling statement that, though his affections toward Rome were growing, his intellect, having been previously deceived, was not as positive: "That my *sympathies* have grown towards the religion of Rome I do not deny; that my *reasons* for *shunning* her communion have lessened or altered would be difficult perhaps to prove. And I wish to go by reason, not by feeling."[227] This final sentence, taken out of context, can easily be mistaken to mean that Newman mistrusted his feelings, which is not accurate.[228] In context, we see that he means that feelings *alone* would

---

225 Newman, *Apologia*, 174.

226 Newman, *Correspondence of John Henry Newman with John Keble and Others, 1839–1845*, 128–29.   227 Newman, *Apologia*, 175.

228 Terrence Merrigan offers an example of such cleavage of affectivity and intellect: "The realisation of Newman's determination to go by reason, not imagination, and to bow only to arguments, not sympathies . . . is also . . . important testimony to the place of intellection in his religious development." Merrigan, "Newman's Progress toward Rome: A Psychological Consideration of his Conversion to Catholicism," *The Downside Review* 104 (April 1986): 95–112. It is suggested by both our hypothesis and our analysis of Newman's conversion experiences that the two elements of intellect and affectivity interact, in the conversion process, in a simultaneous and reciprocally influential way, much as Rousselot noted. Merrigan's quote above implies the difficulty in describing this complex relationship.

not be sufficient grounds to move closer to Rome. He already possessed some of those feelings, especially after *Tract 90*. But having been intellectually deceived by the Anglican divines after placing his faith in them, he was not about to make any such decision again on an assumption or on feelings *alone* without intellectual validation. In this respect Newman was indicating the need for *both* affective and intellectual validation before he could make such a major commitment. At this stage Newman's intellect was in turmoil, and that conflict was promoted by the intellectual influence and challenge of Russell, wrought through his affection for Newman: "I can scarcely account, even to myself, for the strangely powerful impulse by which I am drawn towards yourself, personally a stranger in all except your admirable writings."[229]

This flurry of correspondence transpired between *Tract 90*, published on February 27, 1841, and Newman's fourteenth *University Sermon*, to which we now turn for further evidence of Newman's developing religious epistemology, especially with the added impact of Russell's influence.

THE RELIGIOUS EPISTEMOLOGY TRACK:
Document 7 —
University Sermon XIV:
"Wisdom, *as Contrasted with Faith and Bigotry*"[230]

ACCORDING TO IAN KER, THIS SERMON CONTAINS THE "GENESIS of the *Idea of a University*,"[231] and contrasts the nature of mind in three of its dimensions: faith, wisdom, and bigotry. To understand this sermon, we begin at the end. The purpose of knowledge is to know the whole counsel of God.[232] Knowing is a function of the mind, and its objective is nothing short of the last major issue raised by Russell to Newman, catholicity, on which Newman here reflects: "True catholicity is commensurate with the wants of the human mind."[233] This statement indicates an important intellectual change in Newman, since he only recently insisted that Church unity was not required, but now he asserts a common, natural religious end as the mind's objective. This knowledge of the whole is wisdom, and it is at once affective, aesthetic, intellectual, imaginative, and moral: "Wisdom is the clear, calm, accurate vision, and comprehension of the whole course, the whole work of God."[234] But this knowledge begins with the required elementary grace of

229 Newman, *Correspondence of John Henry Newman with John Keble and Others, 1839–1845*, 119.   230 Newman, *Fifteen Sermons*, 278–311.
231 Ker, *John Henry Newman: A Biography*, 264.
232 Newman, *Fifteen Sermons*, 311.   233 Ibid., 310.   234 Ibid., 293.

faith.[235] The acquisition of knowledge enlarges the mind, and thus religion, theology, and conversion, all forms of enlargement, lead to a deeper, more comprehensive sense:[236] "Uneducated persons . . . on their turning to God (and) regulating their hearts, reforming their conduct, and studying the inspired Word . . . seem to become, in point of intellect, different beings from what they were before."[237] In the field of religion, Newman returns to his constant source for the expansion of the mind: "Bishop Butler's *Analogy* . . . enlarge(s) the mind itself which is put in possession of (it),"[238] as Newman knew from experience. Butler's work leads to an even deeper aspect of knowledge: "It is the knowledge, not only of things, but of their mutual relations . . . this enlargement (of mind) creates in the comparison of the subjects of knowledge one with another . . . a comprehensive mind . . . (and) implies a connected view of the old with the new; an insight into the bearing and influence of each part upon every other; without which there is no whole, and would be no centre."[239] The contrast of the three states of mind, then, are thus: wisdom applies adequate principles to things, bigotry applies narrow or inadequate principles, and faith maintains principles without applying and adjusting them.[240] Perhaps the most important fact regarding this sermon is that the tracks of Newman's ecclesiological and religious epistemological developments were growing ever closer. The former track, moving closer to Rome through the *Tract 90* research and then especially the influence of Russell, begins to intersect with the latter as faith develops into wisdom, and then this development is reflected in dogmatism, an ecclesiological function: "What is invidiously called dogmatism and system . . . is necessary to the human mind; we cannot reason, feel, or act without it,"[241] and again,

> Faith . . . is necessarily a principle of mental growth. . . . As the world around varies, so varies also, not the principles of the doctrine of Christ, but the outward shape and colour which they assume. . . . Faith alone is able to accept it as one and the same under all its forms. And thus Faith is ever the means of learning something new.[242]

Finally, in this last excerpt from the sermon, Newman begins to synthesize Antiquity, Catholicism, the intellectual influence of Butler, and his own reflections on religious epistemology as they affect doctrine:

---

235   Ibid., 279.   236   Ibid., 284–85.   237   Ibid., 285.
238   Ibid., 286.   239   Ibid., 287.   240   Ibid., 297.
241   Ibid.   242   Ibid., 303.

> In the foregoing observations I have . . . been showing . . . what
> is the true office . . . of Reason which may best be described by
> the name of systematizing . . . in comparing, adjusting, con-
> necting, explaining facts and doctrines ascertained. Such a use
> of Reason is Philosophy (and) . . . the reason of Newton . . . and
> the reason of Butler; and the reason of those ancient Catholic
> divines . . . Athanasius, Augustine, Aquinas.[243]

The differences between the tracks of religious epistemology and ecclesiology were clearly narrowing, and Charles Russell had a significant influence on that process. However, Newman was shortly to suffer "three blows"
between July and November 1841, just months after the sermon above,
and they conclude the second stage of Newman's intellectual conversion.

THE EVENTS OF 1841:
The "Three Blows" to Newman's Intellect

IN THE APOLOGIA NEWMAN NOTES THESE THREE EVENTS. THE
first was the reappearance of the ghost of 1839 during Newman's research
into the life of Athanasius, ironic in the sense that this Church Father was
a major focus of Newman's study of the Arian heresy, and now he was
the catalyst for Newman's image of the Church of England as schismatic,
as Newman's imagination, triggered by reflection, reproduced the analogical imagery of 1839:

> I saw clearly, in the history of Arianism, the pure Arians were the
> Protestants, the semi-Arians were the Anglicans, and that Rome
> now was what it was then. The truth lay, not with the *Via Media*,
> but with what was called the extreme party.[244]

Then while in the "misery of this unsettlement,"[245] the second blow
hit as the bishops began to condemn *Tract 90*. Convinced of the truth of
the Tract's conclusion that the Articles admitted of a catholic interpretation, Newman saw in the bishops' act the potential end: "If the view
were silenced, I could not remain in the Church."[246] In short, the Church
of England would be denying the truth of its own Anglican divines, an
intellectual error of such magnitude that it would drive Newman out
of that Church. That potential end became realized when the third and
final blow hit shortly thereafter — the creation of a multidenominational
foreign bishopric.

---

243 Ibid., 294–95.   244 Newman, *Apologia*, 134.   245 Ibid.
246 Ibid.

> The idea was to construct out of such stray Protestants as might
> be living in Palestine, converted Jews, and any minor oriental
> sects . . . a third great communion (in addition to the French-
> Catholic and the Russian-Orthodox) under the protection of
> England and Prussia[247]. . . . Our Church seems fast protestantis-
> ing itself[248]. . . . It will be the most fearful event for the Church
> of England since her separation from Rome.[249]

In October of 1843 Parliament authorized the establishment of a Jerusalem bishopric under English control but multidenominational. This
action would bring to fruition Newman's worst fears about the *Via
Media*, since it would "prove all I hold a mere theory and illusion — a
paper theology which facts contradict."[250] Newman drafted a formal
protest to Bishop Bagot and the archbishop of Canterbury, claiming that
the bishopric would be a recognition of heresy and an admission of
heretics to the Church without recantation, effectively destroying the
Church's ground as a branch of the Catholic Church. "This was the third
blow, which finally shattered my faith in the Anglican Church. . . . Such
acts . . . led me to the gravest suspicion that since the 16th century, it had
never been a Church all along[251]. . . . It brought me on to the beginning
of the end."[252] With his previous recognition of the *Via Media* image
as uncritical, and now as also unapostolic, Newman was faced with the
additional fact of the ascending imagery of Rome as the seat of Augustine's note of the true Church, *securus judicat orbis terrarum*. Charles Russell,
as we shall see, was the catalyst for the continued development of that
image. At this point Newman was in a kind of ecclesiastical limbo, "a sort
of theological 'no-man's land.'"[253] The Church of England was increasingly proving itself, in Newman's eyes, to have been not a true Church
at all. "From the end of 1841, I was on my death bed in the Anglican
Church."[254] Newman's ecclesiastical dilemma required an intellectual
solution, and into this crisis stepped Russell. As noted earlier, Newman
had stated that "he had, perhaps, more to do with my conversion than
anyone else."[255] We will now examine what caused Newman to make
such a momentous statement.

---

247   Newman, *Correspondence of John Henry Newman with John Keble and Others,*
1839–1841, 146.   248   Ibid., 147.   249   Ibid., 156.
250   Ibid., 157.   251   Newman, *Apologia*, 137.   252   Ibid., 140.
253   Merrigan, "Newman's Progress toward Rome," 103.
254   Newman, *Apologia*, 141.   255   Ibid., 178.

STAGE THREE:
The Affective Ground of
Newman's Intellectual Conversion

PERHAPS THE MOST HELPFUL INSIGHTS REGARDING THE effects of Russell on Newman's conversion come from Henry Tristram, editor of Newman's *Autobiographical Writings*. Other than his article on the subject and Newman's brief but impressive reference to Russell in the *Apologia*, this relationship has not received the prominence it deserves as is the case with Newman's relationship with his brother Charles, which generated the important body of correspondence and theological themes almost twenty years earlier, especially the function of temper or affective disposition in respect to the intellect and the act of faith.

We have previously noted the exchange of six letters in the spring of 1841 when Russell engaged Newman over the latter's misconceptions about both Roman doctrine and practice, "the beginning of one of the most important correspondences in Newman's life."[256] On June 2, 1841, Russell sent Newman another letter informing him of his work on "the autograph of the *Systema Theologicum* of Leibniz.... I shall take the liberty of sending you a copy."[257] There is no record of any other exchange until more than a year later when, on October 31, 1842, Russell sent Newman a volume of sermons of St. Alphonsus Liguori "as a specimen of our popular teaching; and perhaps there never was a writer who spoke more strongly upon the prerogatives of our Blessed Lady than St. Alphonsus."[258] Newman sent a thankful reply on November 22, but indicated that even if he changed his position on devotions, it "would have 'no necessary tendency' to undermine his allegiance to the English Church."[259] On December 5 and 10 they again exchanged correspondence, and in the last letter Newman expressed his affection for Russell's gift of the sermons, and for the gift-giver himself: "I shall be much obliged for your intended present, both for its own sake, and as given me by a person, who has written to me in so kind a spirit. I assure you it was a disappointment to me to find there was so little chance of your coming to Oxford."[260]

Thus, between April 1841 and December 10, 1842, Russell and Newman exchanged at least eleven letters, all dealing with topics about Rome which deeply troubled Newman, with Russell painstakingly explaining,

---

256 Michael Ffinch, *Newman: Toward the Second Spring* (San Francisco: Ignatius Press, 1992), 113.

257 Tristram, "Dr. Russell and Newman's Conversion," 195.

258 Ibid. 259 Ibid., 195. 260 Ibid., 196.

correcting, and proving to Newman, through the devotional materials he supplied, that Newman's assumptions were essentially unfounded. As a consequence, we see the first major effect of Russell when Newman took "a significant step, perhaps as a result of his influence, by publishing anonymously, although the identity of the writer was never in doubt, in February, 1843, a *Retractation of Anti-Catholic Statements* dated, be it noted, 12 December, 1842, two days after his last letter to Russell."[261] Newman's *Retractation* statements went as far back as anti-Roman declarations made in 1833 and up to 1837, including those in such works as *Arians*, the *Prophetical Office*, and *Tracts* 15, 20, and 38.[262] In closing the statement, Newman summarized both the causes of these now-retracted statements and his personal ecclesiastical dilemma as well. Commenting on how he could attack "a communion so ancient, so wide-spreading, so fruitful in Saints," Newman attributed it to two factors: his faith in the Anglican divines and "an impetuous temper, a hope of approving myself to persons I respect, and a wish to repel the charge of Romanism."[263] Thus, his uncritical faith in the Anglican divines and his affective disposition against Rome, which was so inbred, grounded his anti-Roman sentiments. But his retractations, a negation of negatives, did not effect a positive resolution of the ecclesiastical issue. Rome may not have been the Antichrist he had once imagined, but that fact alone could not move Newman to Rome: "Admissions such as these involve no retractation of what I have written in defense of Anglican doctrine . . . that the Anglican doctrine is the strongest, nay the only possible antagonist of their system. If Rome is to be withstood, this can be done in no other way."[264]

It is especially important to note that here Newman writes of his *conviction* regarding Anglicanism. We have seen earlier that the sense of this word for Newman is more on the order of a belief rather than a formally logical position. At this stage Newman *wanted* to retain his old beliefs, though the arguments and the logic against Rome in the negative sense were diminishing, primarily due to Russell's influence on both Newman's affections and intellect. But the removal of negations was certainly not strong enough to convert Newman's intellect. This would require positive factors, and over the next several months Newman himself would provide them. Just eight weeks after he authored his *Retractation*, he preached his

---

261   Ibid., 196.
262   Newman, "Retractation of Anti-Catholic Statements," *The Via Media of the Anglican Church*, vol. ii, 425–33.   263   Newman, *Apologia*, 184.
264   Newman, "Retractation of Anti-Catholic Statements," 433.

fifteenth *University Sermon*, the "last and most brilliant" of the series.[265] Here we find evidence that the two tracks of ecclesiology and epistemology meet. Not only does this document commence the beginning of a synthesis for Newman which would eventually resolve his dilemma, but his diary indicates that during this period, between December 1842 and May 1843, Newman's intellectual conversion had in fact been accomplished in the sense that he now *knew* the truth of the Church issue, evidence of which we will now examine.

THE INTERSECTION OF THE TRACKS:
University Sermon XV:
"The Theory of Developments in Religious Doctrine"[266]

NEWMAN CONFIRMS OUR CONTENTION THAT THE TWO TRACKS meet in this sermon, delivered on February 2, 1843: "It is my purpose . . . to investigate the connection between Faith and Dogmatic confession, as far as relates to the sacred doctrines."[267] Ironically, the devotions to Mary, which Newman had so long opposed, are the examples he uses to illustrate his theory, since Mary symbolizes both the "faith of the unlearned" and the reflections "of the doctors of the Church."[268] Regarding the revelation to her at the Annunciation, Mary believed and, out of its grounding in love, began to "ponder" her revelation. Drawing on Butler once again, Newman states the first tenet of his theory. Reason submits and ministers to faith,[269] and faith by impulse attempts to express its "great sight."[270] Impressions upon the mind are prior to reasoning,[271] and furthermore, regarding revelation, the mind "cannot reflect upon that idea, except piecemeal, cannot use it in its oneness and entireness, nor without resolving it into a series of aspects and relations. And in matter of fact these expressions are never equivalent to it."[272] Thus an idea and its expression are related as "widely separated parts having relations . . . and betokening a common origin."[273] This is the strictly epistemological basis of Newman's theory of development, which he then applies to the development of dogma, fusing the intellectual and the religious dimensions: dogma changes, even reverses, all the while advancing and evolving to a "completeness" of the "whole truth": "part answering to part, one, absolute, integral, indissoluble."[274] It is Newman's analysis of the nature of both dogma and its development

265 Ker, *John Henry Newman: A Biography*, 266.
266 Newman, *Fifteen Sermons*, 312–51.
267 Ibid., 319.   268 Ibid., 313.   269 Ibid., 317.
270 Ibid., 327.   271 Ibid., 334.   272 Ibid., 331–32.
273 Ibid., 316.   274 Ibid., 317.

as the meeting-place of revelation and man's perception and expression of that divine truth that leads him to his ultimate intellectual rejection of the Church of England for Rome. Dogma is the expression of the recorded truths perceived as impressions or images which arouse reflection. Thus, an aesthetic experience is at the core of dogma,[275] which promotes the intellectual reflection that develops dogma's content,[276] "till what was first an impression on the Imagination has become a system or creed in the Reason."[277] Impressions, however, may be latent and unconscious, and thus "the birth of an idea, the development, in explicit form,"[278] is the intellectual continuation and evolution of that aesthetic experience. The importance of the image plays a primary role in the perception and expression of dogma, and also is related to moral as well as intellectual judgment, since even the "temporary obscuration of some master vision" produces a state in which "nothing seems true, or good, or right . . . . When Faith seems a name, and duty a mockery, and all endeavours to do right, absurd and hopeless."[279] Newman was speaking from personal experience. He states in the *Apologia* that, during the late 1830s and into the 1840s, the period we are currently examining, "It was my portion for whole years to remain without any satisfactory basis for my religious profession, in a state of moral sickness, neither able to acquiesce in Anglicanism, nor able to go to Rome. But I bore it, till in course of time my way was made clear to me."[280] This is a most meaningful disclosure for our study regarding the interaction of our conversion elements. It seems that Newman's internal dissonance was traceable to the lack of a "master vision," a Church image, which would both satisfy his intellect and direct his moral sense. It is precisely this aesthetic dimension, the conflict of images as examined in this chapter, which drove Newman's intellectual conversion.

Returning to the process of development in Newman's sermon, grace is the ultimate means by which ideas of the Transcendent make their way between God and man,[281] so that "there may be a certain correspondence between the idea, though earthly, and its heavenly archetype, such, that that idea belongs to the archetype."[282] Images, then, allow an approximation to truth.[283] Thus, revelation is a graced idea, or, in

---

275 Commenting on the relationship of intellect and imagination in Newman, John Coulson states that "the development of doctrine, as Newman conceives it, is, in fact, a prime example of growth in imaginative responsiveness." Coulson, "Belief and Imagination," *The Downside Review* 90 (January 1972): 13.

276 Newman, *Fifteen Sermons*, 320.   277 Ibid., 329.   278 Ibid., 321.

279 Ibid., 322.   280 Newman, *Apologia*, 75.

281 Newman, *Fifteen Sermons*, 339.   282 Ibid., 340.   283 Ibid.

Avery Dulles's interpretation of this passage, "Revelation in its essential nature is not a fact or a doctrine but a real, living idea."[284] Newman harmonized vision, dogma, development, and idea: "As God is one, so the impression which He gives of Himself is one.... (I)t is the vision of an object.... One Individual Being.... (A)ll our attempts to delineate our Impression of Him go to bring out one idea ... in its separate aspects."[285] Newman appeared to make his intellectual break with Anglicanism when he stated that opponents to development perceive harmony as discord, see no connection between "inward religious belief and scientific expositions" (faith and reason, or impression, idea, and dogma), and end in "reducing creeds to the number of private opinions, which, if individuals will hold for themselves, at least they have no right to impose upon others."[286] By such actions, objective truth is denied.

In closing the sermon, Newman relates affectivity to revelation which, as the "outpourings of eternal harmony... from some higher sphere," produce "those mysterious stirrings of heart, and keen emotions, and strong yearnings after we know not what, and awful impressions from we know not whence."[287] Thus, revelation grounds both our affectivity and our imagination: "We have an instinct within us, impelling us, we have external necessity forcing us."[288] And what is the end of these drives? Here Newman employs a telling analogy: "They are echoes from Home."[289] Thus, nothing greater can express the relationship of man to God than the very ground from which all of Newman's religious instincts developed, the loving affectivity of home. The "echoes" of revelation are but a calling home to the source of being and affectivity.

The great error, on the other hand, is the subversion of revelation by reason, "the ambition of being wiser than what is written; of employing the Reason ... in impugning it."[290] Reason, rather, should be "content to be

---

284   Dulles, "From Images to Truth," 260.   285   Newman, *Fifteen Sermons*, 330.
286   Ibid., 319.   287   Ibid., 346–47.   288   Ibid., 349.
289   Ibid., 347. See also Robert C. Christie, "Echoes from Home: The Personalist Ground of Newman's Ecclesiology: Affection as the Key to Newman's Intellectual Conversion," in Robert C. Christie, ed., *Saint John Henry Newman: Preserving and Promulgating His Legacy* (Newcastle Upon Tyne: Cambridge Scholars Publishing, 2019), 129–63. This article explores the interrelatedness of our conversion elements in this stage of Newman's conversion, including Russell as the affective ground of Newman's intellectual conversion. For another perspective on the theme of home in Newman, see Donald Graham, "Newman's View of the Church as a Home: Ecclesiology and Anthropology in a Pastoral Context," *Saint John Henry Newman: Preserving and Promulgating His Legacy* (Newcastle Upon Tyne: Cambridge Scholars Publishing, 2019), 110–28.
290   Ibid., 351.

a little child, and to follow where Faith guides it." Here Newman employs yet another familial analogy to indicate that reason is properly subservient to a higher, loving authority. Newman concludes by subordinating reason "to the obedience of Faith," and "in dutiful submission to His will."[291] It is this note of submission which provides the transition to the final stage of Newman's conversion. It appears clear that this sermon marks Newman's intellectual break with the Church of England. Aidan Nichols provides an interpretation of the development of Newman's thought at this time.[292] But it would take almost two more years of personal struggle before he could submit to Rome, which is the focus of our final chapter.

But to return to a major influence on Newman's development, this sermon culminated a period of further research by Newman on Catholic devotional materials obtained from Russell. Henry Tristram concluded that the following diary notes from the same time period as the sermon "reveal the direction in which his mind was moving, obviously in consequence of Dr. Russell's representations":[293]

> What are the Roman doctrines of the Invocation of Saints, &c., but vivid realizations of truths which we profess to believe as well as R. Catholics?
>
> March 18, 1843
>
> Are not the doctrines of purgatory, saint-worship, &c., but the realizations, or vivid representations, of the feelings and ideas which the primitive principles involve?
>
> April 7, 1843[294]

---

291 Ibid.

292 "This sermon continues a line of thought worked out in five homilies on the relation of faith and reason preached before Oxford University between 1839 and 1841 (which we have examined above). . . . Newman had drawn a distinction between . . . 'implicit' and 'explicit' reason. Implicit reason is the spontaneous interpretation of experience. Explicit reason is the analysis of this spontaneous operation into formal procedures of induction and deduction. . . . Newman proposed that implicit reason is the more fundamental, because it considers the evidence for a conclusion in terms of an entire experiential field or flow. In this total experiential field many considerations occur to the mind which are lost to view when explicit reason takes over. . . . Newman applies these ideas to revelation (and) illustrates his thesis by doctrines that emerged *after* the patristic period. . . . (W)ith this sermon Newman abandoned the main argument against the Roman Church in the *Prophetical Office*, namely, that many of its doctrines were incredible since post-patristic in formulation." Aidan Nichols, *From Newman to Congar: The Idea of Doctrinal Development from the Victorians to the Second Vatican Council*, (Edinburgh: T&T Clark, 1990), 40–41.

293 Henry Tristram, "Dr. Russell and Newman's Conversion," 197.   294 Ibid.

Newman had concluded in the last sermon that, returning to the influence of the *securus judicat* imagery of Augustine that had haunted him since 1839, "one thing alone has to be impressed on us by Scripture, the catholic idea," which influences the "moral character, and . . . the whole man."[295] Thus we now turn to Newman's final struggle with submission to that idea in the form of Rome. Confirming his separation from the Church of England and his conversion to intellectual truth, Newman wrote to Keble that "I consider the Roman Catholic Communion to be the Church of the Apostles. . . . I am very far more sure that England is in schism, than that the Roman additions to the Primitive Creed may not be developments, arising out of a keen and vivid realizing of the Divine Depositum of Faith."[296]

Based on the above evidence, Newman's intellectual conversion occurred during early 1843, and was in large part due to the affective quality of his relationship with Dr. Russell, which Henry Tristram affirmed.[297] Before moving on to the consequences of that conversion and its further development, let us compare this period of Newman's conversion with our conversion hypothesis.

CONCLUSION:
Newman's Intellectual Conversion and Our Conversion Hypothesis

OUR THESIS SEEKS EVIDENCE OF FIVE MAJOR CONVERSION ELE-ments: the aesthetic, affective, moral, intellectual, and unconditional. Evidence of the fifth element surfaces in Newman's final conversion stage, which we will examine in the next chapter. During the period we have just analyzed, we find the presence of the first four elements, and we find they interacted in a process which appears consistent with other aspects of our hypothesis: it is developmental, including the seven aspects of this principle, especially those of simultaneity, complementarity, and reciprocity. It is directed, by evidence of a primacy of type, by the intellectual element, and it indicates a dimension of aesthetic mediation through the importance of imagery and the imagination. The four early *Tracts* of the period contain these four elements, which are revealed through the "dual track" method of analysis employed to examine Newman's developing thought on faith and Church during this ten-year phase. We found a

---

295   Newman, *Fifteen Sermons*, 336–37.   296   Newman, *Apologia*, 190.
297   Tristram, "Dr. Russell and Newman's Conversion," 199.

deep-seated affective aversion to Rome and an intellectually uncritical faith in the Anglican divines which produced a flawed aesthetic ecclesiastical image, the *Via Media*. Morally, Newman's commitment to truth grounds the entire period and process. The "dual track" became more apparent in 1837 and 1838 with Newman's *Prophetical Office* and *Lectures on Justification*. Here we found in the former a development of the justification of his ecclesiastical image, the *Via Media*, albeit aesthetically flawed, as his 1877 *Preface to the Third Edition* detailed.

Newman's position against infallibility is most revealing since it indicates the self-willed, anti-submissive temper driving Newman at the time. The *Lectures on Justification*, on the other hand, regarding the nature of faith, justification, and conversion, as well as the three *University Sermons* of 1839 indicate Newman's insightful perception of the interpersonalist nature of these experiences through the Indwelling of the Spirit and the primacy of the heart in the perception of the Image of Christ. Thus the affective element grounds the aesthetic. We believe because we love. But a significant contrast is that of Newman's static ecclesiological theory with his developmental theory of religious epistemology. The *Via Media* which opposed Roman developments was a static image of the Church, whereas Newman's analysis of faith was just the opposite, a living, dynamic relationship. This contrast is most sharply drawn by June of 1839 with the completion of the third *University Sermon* of that year on faith. Thus, perhaps this dissonance between the Church image driven by negative affectivity and the interpersonalist nature of religious faith actually anticipates both the impact which the *securus judicat orbis terrarum* image had on Newman and the appearances of the "ghost" of schism during his intellectual research. Here we again find the interaction of aesthetic images, affectivity, and intellectual reflection. This conflict takes the specific form of the argument over infallibility. Newman rejected Rome's claim to this principle of doctrine on the grounds that it requires the universal Church as its condition, and without the Anglican and Protestant branches in union with Rome, there could obviously be no universality of judgment and thus no infallibility, according to this logic. Up until the impact of the *securus judicat* imagery, Newman had overlooked the circular reasoning of his argument. Church separation does not of itself defeat the condition, especially if the schism is attributable to the willfulness of the separating party. This clash of Church theory and doctrine began to synthesize through Newman's religious epistemology as he began to develop it in his thirteenth *University Sermon* in 1840. Here we find insights of the principles which would ultimately ground Newman's theory of doctrinal development: doctrine operates on the same principle as its creator, the mind. As the latter develops, such as in the notion of faith, so does doctrine. Doctrine is the result of reflection upon faith reasoning, which is always assumptive, supra-rational, and an act of trust.[298] Newman's theories on Church and faith evolve from contrast to convergence, an intellectual change wrought by the aesthetic imagery of the *securus judicat* and his resultant reflection. Another product of that aesthetic element was Newman's *Tract 90*, his intellectual reflection upon this dilemma. Newman's research confirmed that his Church theory could not be sustained. A notable insight by Newman is that affections are essential elements of religion (*University Sermon* XIII) and this, as he wrote Bishop Bagot in defense of *Tract 90*, was the contention of his tract — to appropriate for the Church of England religious devotions which would appeal to the heart. Thus, by the time of *Tract 90* Newman was beginning to synthesize the issues of Church and faith in the affections as their base. Newman's intellectual argument against Rome also was collapsing, and he realized it was grounded on an intellectual error rooted in his uncritical faith in the Anglican divines, an affective act which produced an unreal image. By early 1841, the affective, aesthetic, and intellectual elements all interacted to bring Newman to a point of serious doubt, tending toward crisis.

It was at this point in 1841 that his relationship with Charles Russell began, and it had a profound intellectual effect, but just as importantly it was grounded in affectivity, as Henry Tristram detailed. A note here, not discussed earlier, should be made of events in Newman's personal life which may have had a bearing on his receptivity to Russell. In 1836, Newman suffered two major personal losses. Once again his personal correspondence provides the best insight into the profound effect of these

---

298   Thomas K. Carr, in his study of Newman's religious epistemology (*Newman and Gadamer: Toward a Hermeneutics of Religious Knowledge* [Atlanta: Scholars Press, 1996], 160–61), offers a valuable reference on the interrelationship of faith, trust, and the imagination, following John Coulson: "As Coulson writes, 'Because faith, however conceived, is a spontaneous act, and because spontaneity . . . presupposes trust, without trust there can be no faith. To allow imagination to diffuse and dissipate where there is initially no acceptance of someone or something as trustworthy, is to risk inevitable disintegration and dissociation . . . probabilities fail to converge into certitude; the leap of faith falls short'" (*Religious Imagination* [Oxford: Clarendon Press, 1981], 76). Carr continues, "Coulson's description shows imagination to be dependent upon a prior act of trust, which then expresses itself in the believer who strives to complete the 'ambiguous' and empirically unverifiable knowledge of God through the experimental working-out of his or her beliefs in the day-to-day 'performance' of them."

events on Newman. In February, Hurrell Froude died from his long illness, and on May 17 Newman's mother died suddenly. It might fairly be said that he lost the two most influential people in his life within months. Newman had always admired both Froude's intellect and style, and his openness to Rome softened Newman in that regard. Newman confirmed his indebtedness in a letter to Froude just four weeks before he died: "I have got all my best things from Keble and you.... You and Keble are the philosophers and I the rhetorician." [299]

The day of Froude's death, he wrote a friend:

> I have this day heard tidings sadder to me on the whole than I ever can hear — i.e. more intimately and permanently trying, Froude's death. I never can have such a loss, for no one is there else in the whole world but he whom I could look forward to as a contabernalis for my whole life. [300]

The following day he wrote to another:

> I can never have a greater loss, looking on for the whole of life.... I cannot describe what I owe to him as regards the intellectual principles of religion and morals.... Yet every thing was so bright and beautiful about him, that to think of him must always be a comfort. [301]

To his sister Jemima he wrote, "I would say something of dear Froude, if I could get myself — but I cannot — it is too great a grief." [302] To his longtime friend Maria Giberne he wrote:

> As to dear Froude ... it is a loss such as I can never have again. I love to think and muse upon one who had the most angelic mind of any person I ever fell in with — the most unearthly, the most gifted.... I feel the longer I live, the more I shall miss him. [303]

There exists a clear link between Newman's affection for Froude, his exposure to Roman devotional practices, and his conversion. Upon Froude's death, Newman was invited to select a book from Froude's library. Upon discovering that Butler's *Analogy*, his first choice, was already taken, Newman was advised to select the Roman Breviary "which Hurrell had had with him at Barbadoes. Accordingly, I took it, studied it, wrote my Tract from it, and have it on my table in constant use till this day." [304]

---

299 Newman, *Letters and Diaries*, vol. V, ed. Thomas Gornall (Oxford: Clarendon Press, 1981), 225.   300 Ibid., 247.   301 Ibid., 249.
302 Ibid., 261.   303 Ibid., 263.   304 Newman, *Apologia*, 82.

Just three months later, on June 24, Newman issued his *Tract 75*, "On the Roman Breviary as embodying the Substance of the Devotional Services of the Catholic Church." It was to this *Tract* that Newman referred in his letter to Bishop Bagot in 1841 during the controversy over *Tract 90*, when Newman noted the claim which Rome had upon the affections due to such devotional practices as the Breviary, causing him "to admit the real excellences, and to dwell upon the antiquity of the Roman ritual."[305] Thus, Newman's deep affection for Froude, which endured long after his death, disposed Newman to his Roman tendencies, leading Newman to the conclusion that at least some Roman devotions were of significant value for the cultivation of the religious affections. Again, we find the interplay of affectivity and intellect in Newman's conversion process.

Yet another grievous blow occurred less than three months after Froude's death, and without warning. To his Aunt Elizabeth he wrote on May 16, 1836: "A change took place in my Mother yesterday. . . . If it be God's will to take my dear Mother, most bitter as will be the loss to me, the acutest I can conceive."[306] The same day he wrote to Pusey, "I am in very great affliction — My mother is pronounced past recovery."[307] The very next day Mrs. Newman died, and Newman wrote to his Aunt Elizabeth in images recalling the reality of the invisible world and the unreality of the phenomenal world, similar to his experience following his sister Mary's death: "My dearest Mother is taken from us. . . . Every thing is strange in this world — every thing mysterious. Nothing but sure faith can bring us through."[308] To his friend Bowden he wrote:

> The most overpowering event it is to me — my dear Mother's death. I did not know of her danger till the day before yesterday — she died yesterday. It is indeed a most bitter affliction, but . . . it will make me look forward more earnestly for the day of Christ's coming to end this troublesome world, and bring her back.[309]

And lastly, he wrote to another friend, "This is so bitter an affliction to both Harriett and me, that unless we knew Christ was coming, I do not know we should bear it."[310]

These deep personal losses in 1836 caused a spiritual development in Newman,[311] compounded by insights into the characters of others close to

---

305 Newman, "A Letter to Richard, Lord Bishop of Oxford," *The Via Media of the Anglican Church*, vol. ii, 415.   306 Ibid., 298.   307 Ibid.
308 Ibid., 299.   309 Ibid.   310 Ibid., 300.
311 Vincent Blehl interprets these events as occasioning a change in Newman: "In 1836 there is evidence of a clear development in Newman's spiritual life. The change

Newman: "Pusey's . . . inability to see things from any point of view but his own" and Keble's possessing "a mind that was always dependent upon others."[312] This made them poor candidates to assist Newman during his crisis. It was this void of personal influence which Russell seems to have filled. Russell was both affectionate and intellectually well-grounded, traits which opened and then influenced Newman, as had happened frequently in the past. From home to Mayers to Whately to Hawkins to Froude and then to Russell, this pattern repeats itself, so that we witness the interaction of these two conversion elements again in the Russell relationship: affectivity and intellect.

From his own statements in the *Apologia*, as well as the supporting documentation of their correspondence and the devotional materials which Russell provided, Newman realized in late 1842 that he had been in intellectual error regarding Rome, as his *Retractation* statement substantiates. Then just two months after his retraction Newman preached *University Sermon* XV on "The Theory of Developments in Religious Doctrine," indicating that his two tracks, the ecclesiological and the religious epistemological, had met. Faith, doctrine, the nature of the human mind, and its ecclesiological import were synthesized in a vision at once affective, intellectual, and aesthetic. The same month as the sermon, Newman wrote an article recanting his belief regarding Roman corruptions.[313] Newman *knew* the truth intellectually, but his final problem was that he could not yet trust again, having previously been so painfully deceived by the Anglican divines. Thus, Newman's final step of conversion was one of faith and the submission inherent in that act. Newman confirms that though the changes of his religious opinions of this period were concluded in late 1843, it took him two years to finally submit to Rome. Newman had to convert from a lifelong habit of Anglican independent judgment and a personally reasoned truth to the submission of "one's will and intellect to a divinely accredited organ or oracle of religious truth."[314] This was the clash represented by the aesthetic images, the *Via Media* and the universal Church, one human and one divine. From Newman's reflections on this aesthetic-intellectual conflict, he was brought to the affective and moral precipice of faith, all of which converged on the question of his submission

---

is occasioned by the death of his close friend Hurrell Froude, the death of his mother, and the marriages of his two sisters." Blehl, "John Henry Newman's Conversion of 1845: A Fresh Approach," *Milltown Studies*, no. 37 (Spring, 1996): 25.

312   Bouyer, *Newman*, 220–21.   313   Ibid., 229.

314   Avery Dulles, "Newman: The Anatomy of a Conversion," in *Newman and Conversion*, ed. Ian Ker (Edinburgh: T&T Clark Ltd., 1997), 34.

to Rome. This is the focus of our final chapter in Newman's conversion. However, during this period, from 1833 to 1843, we clearly see the four elements of conversion, the affective, aesthetic, intellectual, and lastly the moral challenge of decision, interacting in a process consistent with our conversion hypothesis, with a primacy of the intellectual element, which therefore gives its name to this period of Newman's conversion. We now move on to examine the final phase of Newman's conversion to Rome, from 1843 to 1845, for evidence of the unconditional element in that process.

CHAPTER FIVE

Newman's Unconditional Conversion 1843–1845

INTRODUCTION

WE NOW MOVE ON TO THE CONSEQUENCES AND DEVELOPMENTS of Newman's intellectual conversion of early 1843. Three stages occur prior to what we term his unconditional conversion in 1845. First, the continuing influence of Dr. Russell provided both the affective ground and the intellectual momentum by exposing Newman to Roman devotions. Secondly, as an apparent result of these factors, Newman's discovery and practice of the *Spiritual Exercises* of St. Ignatius had a profound impact, which he noted in the *Apologia*.[1] Thirdly, Newman's final major document of this period, *An Essay on the Development of Christian Doctrine*, provided the intellectual assurance Newman required to validate his belief and feelings before he could once again make a major act of faith.

This interaction of intellect with affection and the "ghost" of the aesthetic image of the revealed Church combined to move Newman into the final challenge in his conversion process. This was actually a question of faith in both its affective and intellectual dimensions, which Newman himself described. After he resigned as vicar of St. Mary's on September 18, 1843, because of his waning faith in the Anglican communion, he wrote:

> I had one final advance of mind to accomplish, and one final step to take. . . . That further advance of mind was . . . to be . . . able honestly to say that I was *certain* of the conclusions at which I had already arrived. That further step, imperative when such certitude was attained, was my *submission* to the Catholic Church.[2]

This two-year process Newman could not have completed any sooner "with any true conviction of mind or certitude."[3] Newman's language is quite relevant in that it correlates aspects of his conversion with those of

---

1 Newman, *Apologia*, 180.   2 Newman, *Apologia*, 195.   3 Ibid.

our hypothesis: certainty, imperative submission, conviction. Because he had come to see and understand Rome as the one true Church, he had the moral obligation to *do* what he *knew*: submit to the revealed word in the image of the universal Church, the *securus judicat orbis terrarum*. In November of 1844, Newman summarized the history of his doubts from 1839 and linked them to his moral responsibility to act on his intellectual insight:

> The one single over-powering feeling is that our Church is in schism — and that there is no salvation in it *for one who is convinced of this.* . . . If I once am absolutely convinced that our Church is in schism, there is, according to the doctrine (I believe) of every age, no safety for me in it.[4]

The only possible release from this obligation is for those in "invincible ignorance, not to those who . . . discern what the real state of the Church is."[5] This was Newman's state of mind "between the autumns of 1843 and 1845."[6] We now examine the three major stages of that period for evidence of the nature of his final conversion movement.

STAGE ONE:
Dr. Charles Russell, *Continued*

HIS AFFECTIVE AND INTELLECTUAL INFLUENCES ON NEWMAN'S UNCONDITIONAL CONVERSION

IN HIS LETTER OF NOVEMBER 22, 1842, NEWMAN EXTENDED an invitation to Dr. Russell to visit him in Oxford, should the possibility arise. Russell did so on August 1, 1843.[7] This was Russell's only visit, as Russell later corrected Newman's *Apologia* account to the contrary.[8] In the *Apologia* Newman described the affective influence of Russell: "He was always gentle, mild, unobtrusive, uncontroversial. He let me alone."[9] Russell, as previously noted, had sent Newman Catholic devotional materials which caused Newman to alter his intellectual stance regarding Roman "corruptions." In early 1844, Russell sent him another volume of St. Alphonsus's sermons and Catechetical Instructions, along with a "packet of little books" representative of common Italian devotions, "identical

---

4   Newman, *Correspondence of John Henry Newman with John Keble and Others, 1839–1845*, 345–46.   5   Ibid.   6   Newman, *Apologia*, 195.
7   Tristram, "Dr. Russell and Newman's Conversion," 196.
8   Newman, *Apologia*, 347.   9   Ibid., 179.

with those referred to by Newman in the (Essay on) Development."[10] A portion of these books were Marian devotions, which were, as we have seen, a particular focus of Newman's criticism. However, after examining them, he concluded that these devotions were no longer guilty of "interfering with that incommunicable and awful relation which exists between the creature and the Creator."[11] Thus, Russell's influence was both affective and intellectual. But a third effect, a combination of these two elements, was perhaps Russell's major contribution to Newman's development and ultimate conversion. That was the exposure of Newman, apparently through his relationship with Russell, to the *Spiritual Exercises of St. Ignatius*. Newman's use of the *Exercises*, which is recorded in his diary, in the *Apologia*, and in his final major work of the period, his *Essay on Development*, linked together many of the factors involved in Newman's final, unconditional conversion. We now examine the influence of those *Exercises* on Newman's conversion.

STAGE TWO:
The *Spiritual Exercises of St. Ignatius* and Newman's Unconditional Conversion

THE *EXERCISES* WERE A MAJOR CAUSE OF NEWMAN'S EVENTUAL decision and act of conversion to Rome. It further appears that Newman was exposed to the *Exercises* either as a direct result of the devotional materials received from Russell or at least as an indirect result of his being opened up to researching Catholic devotional practices in general. This contention is supported by the connection between the sermons of St. Alphonsus with their Marian devotional content and the *Exercises*. In the *Apologia* Newman discusses them together as if from the same source, although this is not specifically stated, but neither is any other source referenced.[12] Two extremely significant facts emerge from this account. First, through the devotional literature and then especially the *Exercises*, Newman was led to understand the true nature of Catholic belief in the primacy of an affective relationship with God: "Only this I know full well, and I did not know then, that the Catholic Church allows no image . . . to come between the soul and its Creator. It is face to face, 'solus cum solo,'"[13] a reference strikingly similar to the phrase which described Newman's first conversion in 1816: "Nunquàm minus solus, quàm cùm

---

10 Tristram, "Dr. Russell and Newman's Conversion," 197.
11 Ibid., 198. 12 Newman, *Apologia*, 180. 13 Ibid., 179.

solus."[14] The difference is that this state of affectivity was now directed by much superior intellectual, imaginative, and aesthetic elements in comparison to those of 1816. But his affectivity, impressed with the "stain on the imagination" against Rome from decades earlier, resisted the lead of his intellect. Newman's struggle to control his will, the battle between self-will and God's will, is borne out by his diary entries during two specific Ignatian retreats he made in 1843. A review of these entries, along with the insights of several commentaries on the *Exercises*, is the source of evidence for this stage of Newman's conversion. "For here again," Newman remarked about the *Exercises*, "the soul was 'sola cum solo.'"[15] In April 1843, Newman made a six-day Lenten retreat, and then another five-day Advent retreat in December. Newman specifically listed the *Exercises* he performed: The End of Man, On Sin, On Death and Judgment, On Tepidity, On the Two Standards, On the Presence of Christ, and On the Expectation of Christ.

Newman's reflections during the first retreat disclose several relevant themes, the most noteworthy of which were his problems with willfulness and self-centeredness, which even extended into his reflection on his work in the Movement: "If disobedience is *against nature*, I am, in the sight of Angels, like some odious *monster.* . . . I have acted hardly ever for God's glory. . . . My motive in all my exertions during the last ten years, has been the pleasure of energizing intellectually. . . . How little I have used my gifts in God's service. . . . Self-love (has) been my motive, and that possibly is *the* sovereign sin in my heart."[16] Newman closed his reflection on this *Exercise* on the End of Man with an acknowledgment of his spiritual need, which was surrender to God: "At the end I solemnly gave myself up to God to do what he would with me — to make me what he would — to put what he would upon me,"[17] a theme he reiterated in the following *Exercise*: "Also I renewed my surrender of myself in all things to God, to do what he would with me at any cost."[18] In this entry, most interestingly, he also noted this related thought: "Various great trials struck at me . . . (one of which was) having to join the Church of Rome."

The second day saw a repetition of the theme of willfulness: "I cautioned myself against acts of willful impetuosity or obstinacy," and the third day contained a repeat of his lament over self-centeredness in the Movement: "Taking the ecclesiastical movement of the last 10 years as a whole, it has not

---

14 Merrigan, "*Numquàm minus solus, quàm cùm solus* — Newman's first Conversion: Its Significance for his Life and Thought," *The Downside Review* 103 (April 1985): 112.
15 Newman, *Apologia*, 180.   16 Newman, *Autobiographical Writings*, 223.
17 Ibid.   18 Ibid., 224.

in any sense been performed (on my part) with a pure intention towards God."[19] On the fourth day the ecclesiastical and submission themes return:

> I was led on to meditate on the fortunes of the Church at present, and especially in England, and on my own duties regarding it.... I prayed that in all I did, I might have before my eyes the example of Christ's subjection to his parents. This picture of Christ's subjection seemed to me a very striking one, and likely to be affecting.[20]

Here we find the interaction of imagination, affectivity, and will. On the fifth day, Newman again confessed his willfulness in the form of attachment to fame and envy: "I seem unwilling to say, 'Give me utter obscurity'; partly for a hankering after posthumous fame, partly from a dislike that others should do the work of God in the world, and not I."[21] Newman closed the fifth day with a reference to "St. Alphonso," indicating Russell's influence.

The second retreat's diary notes disclose a similar theme of willfulness. On the first day Newman again prayed for the grace to submit his will to God. Then contemplating his end, he makes a very relevant reference: "Chief thoughts 1. That I am created *here* and *now* ... surely not for myself. 2. how God in time past has chastened me & guided me. E.g. in 1816, 1827 – 28. Is it to be for nothing?"[22] Newman's identification of these dates as pivotal for him coincides with our proposed alignment of his major conversions: 1816, the first, and religious, conversion to God, and 1827 – 1828, his second, and moral, to the Church.[23] He closes the first day with an acknowledgment of his sins, of which a primary one is "selfcentered thoughts."[24] On the final day Newman prayed for "obedience to Christ and a reliance on His power and grace to bring me through."[25]

---

19 Ibid., 226.   20 Ibid., 227.   21 Ibid.   22 Ibid., 229.

23 Notably, Bouyer (*Newman*, 196) references Newman's 1845 conversion to Rome as "this second conversion of his, which we may call his conversion to the Church." Bouyer also cites the primacy of the intellectual element in this process characterized by "an even greater independence of view, an even completer intellectual autonomy than characterized by his first conversion, to God." Our thesis agrees with Bouyer's analysis but with an added distinction. What might be distinguished as Newman's *general* Church conversion commenced in 1827–1828 and came to fruition in 1833. Then began Newman's intellectual conversion, or search for the true Church, which culminated in 1843, followed by his act of unconditional conversion to the *Catholic* Church, a distinction within his Church conversion, or a further development thereof.

24 Newman, *Autobiographical Writings*, 230.   25 Ibid., 233.

In sum, these retreats disclose Newman's confronting willfulness, self-love, disobedience, self-centered intellectualism, and attachment to worldly fame, but seeking the grace to surrender his will in obedience to God. The most significant extra-personal theme is his concern over the state of the English Church. It seems fair to say that these diary entries represent a microcosm of the forces and themes of this two-year period. But to understand better what Newman was experiencing let us now look at the nature of the *Exercises* in respect to our study.

THE NATURE OF THE *SPIRITUAL EXERCISES* IN RELATION TO NEWMAN'S CONVERSION

IN RESPECT TO THE EXERCISES, ROBERT GLEASON'S INTRODUC-tion to the *Exercises* indicates numerous points relevant to Newman's conversion experience. The meditation On the Two Standards, which Newman noted as one of the most effective for him, "is aimed at a decision which the exercitant is to make: the following of Christ in service to the Church."[26] Newman's reflections indicate a preoccupation with this subject. Another meditation, On the Three Modes of Humility, is focused on "subjection to God,"[27] Newman's primary concern during the retreats and throughout this phase of his conversion. This "conquest of self-love through love of Christ" is the theme of two major *Exercises* which Newman recorded, the Two Standards and the Kingdom. Submission of the will is linked to the love of Christ, which is produced by moving the affections by means of "forming of pictures in the imagination."[28] From the very design of the *Exercises*, and as Newman recounted them, intellectual, moral, aesthetic, and affective elements interact to foster "service of the Church through complete conformity to the will of God."[29] The success of the *Exercises*, however, is essentially dependent upon that fundamental predisposition or temper, which Gleason terms "fundamental attitude,"[30] embedded in the Principle and Foundation at the outset of the *Exercises*. "The purpose of these *Exercises* is to help the exercitant to conquer himself."[31] Another commentator on the *Exercises*, George Ganss, translates this state of "indifference" as the disposition "to desire and choose only that which is more conducive to the end for which we are created."[32] As

---

26   Robert W. Gleason, Introduction to *The Spiritual Exercises of St. Ignatius*, trans. Anthony Mottola (New York: Doubleday, 1964), 15.

27   Ibid.   28   Ibid., 25.   29   Ibid., 21.   30   Ibid., 16.

31   Ibid., 47.

32   George E. Ganss, *The Spiritual Exercises of St. Ignatius: A Translation and Commentary*, (St. Louis: The Institute of Jesuit Sources, 1992), 32.

we have seen throughout this study, such predisposition is the ground of all future development or lack thereof.

The *Exercises*, then, function to change one's disposition to promote conversion: "*Fundamental attitudes* underlying the faults and failures (are) discovered and altered. The soul in itself is in readiness for a *metanoia*, a new conversion."[33]

An examination of the *Exercises* themselves reveals this basic structure and purpose. A particular image or picture is suggested as the focus of meditation, and after an imaginative reflection upon the vision, one is moved "to deeper emotions by means of (the) will."[34] The exercitant moves to a decision of "amending and reforming one's life and state,"[35] an ultimate objective of the *Exercises*. This decision or "election" is produced through successive meditations on the "Consideration of the States of Life."[36] Here important imagery is employed to facilitate the process:

> (T)he example which Christ our Lord has already given us for the first state of life [is] the observance of the commandments, in the meditation on His obedience to His parents. We have also considered the example that He gave us for the second state of life, that of evangelical perfection, when He remained in the temple, leaving His foster father and His Mother according to nature, that He might devote Himself entirely to the service of His heavenly Father. We will begin now to contemplate His life, and at the same time, to investigate and to ask in what kind of life or state His Divine Majesty wishes to make use of us.[37]

It is notable that Jesus's example of obedience to his parents is the particular imagery employed to create the vision of the first state of life which, as we have seen, particularly struck Newman. In addition to the importance of obedience, or submission, as the foundation for the question of a direction of one's life, it is noteworthy that Newman made particular reference in his diary to this specific imagery, reinforcing the contention that loving familial relationships were of primary significance in his development.

Hugo Rahner offers two major insights on the *Exercises* which support our thesis, especially in relation to the nature of Newman's conversion

---

33 Gleason, Introduction to *The Spiritual Exercises of St. Ignatius*, 28.

34 Ganss, *The Spiritual Exercises*, 41.

35 Gleason, Introduction to *The Spiritual Exercises of St. Ignatius*, 87.

36 Ibid., 75–87.   37 Ibid., 75.

experience. First, the Exercises indicate the presence of the five conversion elements and their developmental process. First there is the relationship, and even the grounding, of knowledge in the aesthetic dimension, beginning with the experience of Ignatius himself:

> These [religious] visions strengthened him greatly... and produced such a firmness of faith in him that ever after he often thought to himself, "If he had no knowledge of these mysteries of our holy religion from the Scriptures, he would still be ready and resolved to die for them, for no other reason than that he had beheld them in these visions."[38]

Rahner holds that these visions provided "an insight into the relationships among all the divine mysteries."[39] Vision and insight ultimately have an affective ground for Ignatius:

> And this leads directly to the heart of the theology of the Spiritual Exercises.... "The love which moves me and makes me choose something has to descend from above, from the love of God; so that he who makes the choice must first of all feel (sienta) within himself that this love, be it greater or less, which he has for the object of his choice is for his creator and Lord alone."[40]

Christological imagery is the means "by which the exercitant makes the life of Christ existentially present in his mind and heart and then, in the light of this, sets about ordering his own life."[41]

This reciprocal relationship of mind and heart is most evident in the Exercises' Application of the Senses, "a simple yet sublime way of making conceivable what is beyond conceiving....[42] The Application of the Senses [functions in a way] that [a] small earthly thing conveyed by word, image or gesture suddenly presents itself to us as the whole — God, both hidden and disclosed. The whole is apprehended in the movement of the spiritual senses towards the object seen, heard, and touched.... Everything which is perceived in [sic] seen as coming from God."[43] Affectivity and intellect coalesce in the moral dimension of the Exercises. Doing begets

---

38 J. F. X. O'Conor, The Autobiography of St. Ignatius Loyola (New York, 1900), 25 in Hugo Rahner, The Spirituality of St. Ignatius Loyola, trans. Francis John Smith (Westminster: The Newman Press, 1953), 88–89.

39 H. Rahner, The Spirituality of St. Ignatius, 89.

40 H. Rahner, Ignatius the Theologian, trans. Michael Barry (London: Geoffrey Chapman, 1968), 7, citing Monumenta Ignatiana II.

41 Ibid., 101–2.   42 Ibid., 189.   43 Ibid., 209–10.

knowing: "The *Exercises* are *to be made.* . . . They are not a book."[44] Citing the Jesuit commentator Torres, Rahner emphasizes this point: "Only he who has passed through the profound and sweet experience will be able to understand fully the meaning of the *Spiritual Exercises* and at the same time come to recognize the harmony existing between its teachings and that of the Gospels and the Fathers of the Church."[45]

In addition to facilitating the harmonization of the four elements of conversion, the *Exercises* culminate in the fifth element, unconditional surrender, which is the core of the election in the *Exercises*. The election, however, requires a solid intellectual ground for maximum effect: "It will be impossible to understand and especially to guide the election, the masterpiece of the *Spiritual Exercises*, without deep theological study."[46] Notably, Newman was in such a state of intellectual reflection when he made the *Exercises*, and thus we find a correlation between Rahner's analysis, Newman's experience, and our conversion hypothesis: the exercitant moves toward an election through a reflective or intellectual stage. This promotes what Rahner calls the "basic rule of the *Exercises* concerning the surrender of self-love and one's own will and interests."[47] The election is "the very heart of the *Spiritual Exercises*. The 'supernatural decision'. . . when the exercitant comes to see the will of God for his own life."[48] Rahner culminates his description of the election with the very element which completes our conversion hypothesis, "*unconditional service*"[49] (italics added).

Secondly, the performance of the *Exercises* gives evidence of a "two track" method involving the exercitant and the Church, correlating with our analysis of Newman's theological method. Following the Ignatian commentator Nadal, Rahner states, "It is Nadal who best describes this theology arising from the tension between interiority and the visible Church. . . . 'Ignatius began to probe deeply into his soul. . . . The Lord gave him a sublime understanding and very lively feelings . . . in regard to the divine mysteries and the Church.' Ignatius here discovered the connection between his own spiritual battle and the Church," and eventually he "subordinated all mysticism to this visible organization."[50] As an example of this principle, he subjected the *Exercises* to the dogmatic control of the Church.[51] This principle is incorporated into the *Exercises* through the

---

44 H. Rahner, *The Spirituality of St. Ignatius*, 91.
45 Ibid.   46 Ibid., 96.   47 Ibid., 95.
48 H. Rahner, *Ignatius the Theologian*, 230.   49 Ibid., 237.
50 Ibid., 218.   51 H. Rahner, *The Spirituality of St. Ignatius*, 89.

election made therein. This decision should likewise be subordinate to the "certification and guarantee" of the Church.[52] Rahner synthesizes the two tracks, much as did our analysis of Newman's theological method: "In these rules the grace of personal experience (*unctio*) and technique (*traditio*) have so coalesced as to become inseparable."[53] As Rahner notes, Ignatius himself synthesized these same two dimensions due to his "sudden insight into the connection between the mysteries of our Faith and of our Church."[54]

Thus, Rahner's analysis helps us to understand better Newman's experience during his approach to an unconditional conversion, one which harmonized the four major elements of conversion while synthesizing the theological tracks of faith, or religious epistemology, and ecclesiology, since the *Exercises* "exercise a tremendous power and influence upon the internal conversion of our souls."[55]

Karl Rahner, commenting on the two major *Exercises* of the Kingdom of Christ and the Two Standards, notes the degree of submission required: "We should surrender ourselves to this Lord unconditionally,"[56] and commenting on the degrees of humility, he states that one "is completely subject to the unconditional disposition of God." It is this challenge of unconditional commitment which characterized Newman's final two years, and the importance which he placed on the *Exercises* in the development of his final stage confirms that he was indeed involved in this struggle of submission of his will. From the conflict with his father over his early evangelical spirit, to the dispute with Hawkins over the Oriel tuition, to his "dark night of the soul" in Sicily, to his self-centered conduct during the Movement, and finally to the struggle of his intellect and will over the decision to submit to what he knew to be the one true Church, willfulness against the will of God characterized Newman's conversion journey. It was brought to a head between 1843 and 1845 because the other elements of affectivity, aesthetic, and intellect were all moving toward a coalescence. They required, however, harmonization which would at last resolve the dissonance which Newman had felt for so long. As his will began to change, evidenced by the diary entries on the *Exercises*, he approached that state of conversion which harmonized all its elements. "Then I had nothing more to learn; what still remained for my conversion, was, not further change

---

52   H. Rahner, *Ignatius the Theologian*, 231.
53   H. Rahner, *The Spirituality of St. Ignatius*, 96.
54   Ibid., 94.   55   Ibid., 92.
56   Karl Rahner, *Spiritual Exercises*, trans. Kenneth Baker (New York: Herder and Herder, 1965), 188.

of opinion, but to change opinion itself into the clearness and firmness of intellectual conviction."[57] Newman here described his final movement as the challenge of faith, "the necessity of passing beyond private judgment and of submitting one's will and intellect to a divinely accredited organ or oracle of religious truth."[58] In sum, the *Exercises* led to a harmonization of the intellect, affections, and imagination by converting the will to an unconditional submission to God's will, expressed in a decisive act of faith. For Newman, this would be his unconditional conversion to Rome.

To return to the possible link between Russell and Newman's acquaintance with the *Exercises*, Newman mentioned them in a letter as early as February 1843, and between then and June of that year, three more letters contain references to the *Exercises* and another to the Jesuits.[59] Given that Russell had sent Newman devotional material as early as October, 1842, and that they were of sufficient import to affect Newman's *Retractation* statement and his fifteenth *University Sermon*, such literature was apparently either the direct or indirect source of Newman's introduction or reference to the *Exercises*. The timeframe from early November 1842, when he first received the materials from Russell, and the first mention of the *Exercises* in his letter of February 1843, makes this quite possible, if not likely, since Newman had virtually no other acquaintance with Catholics or Catholic devotional literature.

It is most important to note that Newman's *Apologia* account of the effects of the *Exercises* indicates a further conversion of the imagination in the form of a new perception: an analogy of the Roman devotions to the affection for loved ones. Neither "are inconsistent with that supreme homage of the heart to the Unseen."[60] Again an act of the analogical imagination began to resolve Newman's difficulty with devotions. Newman began to see that, just as human affectivity through the love of others complements the love of God, so can religious devotional affectivity function likewise. Thus, this aesthetic element was accompanied by the realization of an affective element. "The command (of the *Exercises*) practically enforced was, 'My son, give Me thy heart.'"[61] An even greater aesthetic element emerged as Newman perceived that the devotions were therefore part of a

---

57 Newman, *Apologia*, 183.

58 Avery Dulles, "Newman: The Anatomy of a Conversion," *Newman and Conversion*, 34.

59 Daniel Patrick Huang, "The Spiritual Exercises and the Conversion of John Henry Newman," *America* 29 (July 1995): 25–27.

60 Newman, *Apologia*, 180.   61 Ibid.

much more elaborate scheme: "The harmony of the whole, however, is of course what it was. It is unfair then to take one Roman idea, that of the Blessed Virgin, out of what may be called its context."[62] These affective and aesthetic elements produced an intellectual insight:

> I saw that the principle of development . . . was in itself a remarkable philosophical phenomenon, giving a character to the whole course of Christian thought. . . . It served as a sort of test, which the Anglican could not exhibit, that modern Rome was in truth ancient Antioch, Alexandria, and Constantinople.[63]

This insight led Newman to explore the nature of an "idea" in the mind, the basis of the *Essay on Development*, to which we now turn. But the facts indicate that the *Exercises* promoted an aesthetic, affective, moral, and intellectual development in Newman, all converging on his final unconditional conversion.

STAGE THREE:
An *Essay on the Development of Christian Doctrine*[64] and Newman's Unconditional Conversion

THE PREVIOUS TWO STAGES BROUGHT NEWMAN TO HIS ULTI-mate challenge, submission to Rome:

> My difficulty was this: I had been deceived greatly once; how could I be sure that I was not deceived a second time? . . . How could I ever again have confidence in myself? . . . To be certain is to know that one knows; what inward test had I, that I should not change again, after that I had become a Catholic? . . . So, at the end of 1844, I came to the resolution of writing an Essay on Doctrinal Development; and then, if, at the end of it, my convictions in favour of the Roman Church were not weaker, of taking the necessary steps for admission to her fold.[65]

Newman's language is telling. By his wording, "if not weaker," he indicates that in late 1844 his mind was intellectually "convinced" regarding Rome, consistent with our analysis of his intellectual conversion. What he lacked until late 1845 was that step beyond intellectual certainty — faith.

---

62   Ibid., 180–81.   63   Ibid., 182.
64   John Henry Newman, *An Essay on the Development of Christian Doctrine* (Westminster: Christian Classics, 1988).   65   Newman, *Apologia*, 205–6.

The *Essay* was "an hypothesis to account for a difficulty."[66] The hypothesis was the intellectual justification for Newman's difficulty of faith and his related problem of submission. The priority of faith and will at this stage of Newman's conversion is important lest the intellectual work of the *Essay* overshadow the fact that Newman's intellect required the foundation of faith and will during this period. Intellect provided direction, but the necessary ground of action, of movement and change, was faith and will. Newman had perceived this priority of faith over reflection in his thirteenth *University Sermon* almost five years earlier:

> I have been engaged in proving the following points: that the reasonings and opinions which are involved in the act of Faith are latent and implicit; that the mind reflecting on itself is able to bring them out into some definite and methodical form; that Faith, however, is complete without this reflective faculty, which, in matter of fact, often does interfere with it, and must be used cautiously.[67]

Religion, he further states in the same sermon, is seated in the affections, according to Scripture.[68] The *Essay*, then, was written to give explicit form to Newman's faith, which was necessary because of the previous deception of that faith.

The *Essay* is distinguished by several facts: (1) Intellectually, it synthesizes the two tracks of faith and Church on which Newman had been developing his thought, especially the primacy of faith over reason in the initial acceptance of doctrine; (2) In terms of submission and obedience, it recounts Newman's experience with the *Spiritual Exercises*. This fact links the influence of Russell and the devotions to the final movement in Newman's conversion, and it indicates that it was primarily a matter of faith and will, strengthened by intellect; (3) He elucidates the "great law of development" which underlies both the nature of the human mind and the plan of Providence in revelation, which leads to the principle of doctrinal development and, by extension, to the doctrine of infallibility, which validates Rome as the true, constantly developing Church; (4) Newman constructs an overarching analogy of person to Church, or individual to institution, based on the "great law of development," and thus of faith (personal) to doctrine (Church or institutional)[69]; (5) Aesthetically, this is borne out by the very

---

66   Newman, *An Essay on Development*, 30.   67   Newman, *Fifteen Sermons*, 276–77.
68   Ibid., 262.
69   As Avery Dulles states, "We may say that Newman experienced in himself something analogous to the cumulative process that he attributed to the whole Church in his famous *Essay on the Development of Christian Doctrine*." Dulles, "Newman,

first and primary note or test of true development which Newman asserts in the *Essay*: preservation of type, or the maintenance of the original idea of Christianity; one, catholic. This note supersedes even that of apostolic succession and validates Rome over the separated Church of England. Newman leaves no doubt about the aesthetic quality of this note: a "symbol" of the true Church as "everywhere one."[70] The primacy of this aesthetic note is evident in that Newman dedicated almost as much discussion to this one note (115 pages) as he did to the other six notes combined (122 pages). It is this note that Ian Ker claims as "the cause of Newman's conversion."[71] (6) Lastly, Newman brings forth three significant sources from his previous work which significantly influence the *Essay*, demonstrating also the consistency of his development. First, the image of the Church as *securus judicat orbis terrarum*, integral to his first and primary note of true development, is referenced twenty times. Secondly, Joseph Butler, his lifelong guide, is referenced on six occasions to substantiate various significant positions. Thirdly, Newman brings forward and synthesizes the work of the *University Sermons* on faith, reason, and development.

To understand fully Newman's intellectual synthesis in this work, we will examine the meeting of the two tracks of ecclesiology and religious epistemology by means of the "great law of development." This will include a review of his overarching analogy of the development of mind to that of Church doctrine which leads to the apprehension of the aesthetic image of the one true apostolic Church at Rome. Then in closing we will examine the references to the *Spiritual Exercises* in the *Essay*, as well as Newman's correspondence on the very eve of his submission to Rome for evidence of the unconditional element in his conversion.

THE INTELLECTUAL ELEMENT IN
NEWMAN'S UNCONDITIONAL CONVERSION:
The Analogy of Development and the Synthesis of Faith and Church, Mind and Doctrine, and Epistemology and Ecclesiology

EPISTEMOLOGY GROUNDS NEWMAN'S METHOD IN THE DEVELopment of his theory. First, there is the nature of the mind, a perspective stemming from his final *University Sermon* on the mind's "piecemeal" nature of perception: an idea "is commensurate with the sum total of its possible aspects."[72] The many aspects, then, "are capable of coalition . . . into the

---

Conversion, and Ecumenism," *Theological Studies* 51 (1990): 723.

70   Newman, *An Essay on Development*, 262.

71   Ker, *John Henry Newman: A Biography*, 310.

72   Newman, *An Essay on Development*, 34.

object" to which they belong. Through confusion, conflict, modification, expansion, and combination, "the idea to which these various aspects belong, will be to each mind separately what at first it was only to all together.... This process ... (which) I call its development ... is carried on through and by means of communities of men."[73] Knowledge, then, is gradual, piecemeal, and communally transmissive:

> It is characteristic of our minds...[that] whole objects do not create in the intellect whole ideas, but are ... thrown into a series, into a number of statements, and with more or less exactness approximating, as they accumulate, to a perfect image. There is no other way of learning or of teaching. We cannot teach except by aspects or views, which are not identical with the thing itself which we are teaching.[74]

This process is one of spontaneous, gradual growth and "comes of its own innate power of expansion within the mind."[75] The aesthetic nature of an idea is also borne out: an "idea (is) its complete image, as seen in a combination of diversified objects."[76] Christianity is an idea,[77] and as such is subject to the previous development. However, it is also "a revelation, which comes to us as a revelation, as a whole, objectively, and with a profession of infallibility."[78] Newman traces this development from revelation to impression to idea to doctrine: "As God is one, so the impression which He gives us of Himself is one.... It is the vision of an Object.... Religious men ... have an idea or vision of the Blessed Trinity in Unity."[79] It is thus God's intention that doctrine be developmental—"There is a plan of things"[80]—but therefore "some rule is necessary for arranging and authenticating these various expressions and results of Christian doctrine."[81] This is the infallible power of deciding the truth of theological and ethical statements.[82] The principles of development of doctrine and that of infallibility meet in the example of the fourth century. Here both the doctrine of the "same substance" of the First and Second Persons of the Trinity and the power to decide that issue coalesced. Thus, Papal supremacy was itself a form of doctrinal development.[83] Then Newman

---

73 Ibid., 35, 37–38.   74 Ibid., 55.   75 Ibid., 73.   76 Ibid., 38.
77 Ibid., 56.   78 Ibid., 53.   79 Ibid.   80 Ibid., 75.
81 Ibid., 77.   82 Ibid., 79.

83 Ibid., 142–44, 154. Newman's assertion of the existence of the principle of papal supremacy in the ancient Church is an extension of the principle of development, "a theory to reconcile what is and what is not recorded about it; and, which is the principal point, a theory to connect the words and acts of the Ante-Nicene Church with that

provides the final link in the chain joining the religious epistemology of faith and the ecclesiological issue of doctrine: "We do not in the first instance exercise our reason upon opinions which are received, but our faith. We do not begin with doubting; we take them on trust, and we put them on trial.... We prove them by using them."[84] Faith and doctrine, then, are inseparable, and faith requires submission, in this instance to the Church. Also, if Catholicity is *the* note of true development, then the Roman Church, and not the Church of England, meets that test.[85] It is unity, and not apostolic succession, which is the foremost note of the true Church.[86] The ghost of 1839, which reappeared in 1841, was now seen as a real, living idea grasped in the image of the one Church.

Heresy, on the other hand, is characterized by a refusal to submit. It is that temper of self-will which Newman perceived to be at the root of all unbelief, and which he had grasped beginning in the exchanges with his brother Charles, through his Arian studies, and which plagued his own personality. It was a refusal to submit to the principle of God's own Being imbued into the world, as St. Clement of Alexandria best expressed it for Newman: "'Whereas there is one God and one Lord,' says St. Clement, 'therefore also that which is the highest in esteem is praised on the score of being sole, as after the pattern of the One Principle.... In substance then, and in idea, and in first principle, and in pre-eminence, we call the ancient Catholic Church sole.'"[87] However, this introduced an understanding of the Church as a kingdom rather than a family.[88] Thus, the monarchical principle is a defining element of the Church as an exponent of revelation. As God is sovereign, so is His temporal locus, and a sovereign requires submission by definition. Failure to submit to the authority of the Church, then, is the ecclesiastical form of a violation of the inherent nature of the relationship between God and man. It was this "temper" which fueled the great heresies of Antiquity beginning with the principle of the literal interpretation of Scripture by Theodore, who embodied the principle that man's self-centered reception of revelation can subvert God's transmission. Theodore was the teacher of Nestorius, and this principle of self-will made its way through the ancient world until it was passed on to Paul of Samosata, and then to Arius, and eventually to Eutyches in the Monophysite controversy, which had such an

---

antecedent probability of a monarchical principle in the Divine Scheme, and that actual exemplification of it in the fourth century, which forms their presumptive interpretation."
84 Ibid., 101.   85 Ibid., 169.   86 Ibid., 265–66.
87 Ibid., 257.   88 Ibid., 252.

impact on Newman. Eutyches' great sin was nothing less than his refusal of unconditional submission: "Eutyches . . . refuse(d) an unconditional assent to the Councils and Fathers."[89] But the question remains how this requirement of unconditional submission affected his own conversion, now that Newman had apparently resolved the issue of an intellectual basis for the case in favor of Rome. For that we turn to the final movement of his conversion in his references to the *Exercises* contained in the *Essay*, as well as the revelations of his conversion eve correspondence.

THE *EXERCISES* IN THE *ESSAY* AND NEWMAN'S CONVERSION EVE CORRESPONDENCE

NEWMAN MAKES NUMEROUS REFERENCES IN THE ESSAY TO THE Jesuits and, toward the end, as he was nearing his conversion, to the *Spiritual Exercises*. In his chapter on the fourth note of a true development, logical sequence, Newman traces the development from Scripture of the doctrines regarding baptism, penance, satisfaction, purgatory, and ultimately monastic rule: "In no aspect of the Divine system do we see more striking developments than in the successive fortunes of Monachism."[90] Newman credits the Jesuits with bringing into "singular prominence" a principle of Monachism previously underdeveloped, which is the key to unconditional conversion: obedience.

> It was reserved for modern times to furnish the perfect illustration of this virtue. . . . The great Society . . . has been still more distinguished than any other Order before it for the rule of obedience. . . . It may be fairly questioned, whether, in an intellectual age, when freedom both of thought and of action is so dearly prized, a greater penance can be devised for the soldier of Christ than the absolute surrender of judgment and will to the command of another.[91]

---

89   Ibid., 303. These issues are reflected in the contemporary discussions about the Second Vatican Council, in the competing and conflicting interpretations of it as either a "'hermeneutic of discontinuity and rupture' or 'the hermeneutic of reform', of renewal in the continuity of the one subject-Church which the Lord has given to us. She is a subject which increases in time and develops, yet always remains the same." Pope Benedict XVI, "Christmas Address to the Roman Curia" (22 December 2005). Pope Francis endorsed the hermeneutic of continuity in his letter of 19 November 2013 to Cardinal Walter Brandmüller. All quoted in Ian Ker, *Newman on Vatican II* (Oxford: Oxford University Press, 2014), 40. "In his *Essay on the Development of Christian Doctrine*, Newman makes exactly the same point." Ibid.   90   Ibid., 395.
91   Ibid., 398–99.

In this intertwining of intellect and submission of the will, we find
evidence from Newman himself that his insights required action and
obedience to that authority which was, convincingly to him, the one
and only true Church. On the eve of his conversion Newman wrote to
many of his friends. These letters, at what was perhaps the most intense
moment of a very intense life, reveal some of his innermost thoughts, and
they are relevant to our study. To one he wrote confirming the elements
of submission and affectivity, along with the objective nature of truth.
He intended "to submit myself to what seemed an external call. Also, I
suppose the departure of others has had something to do with it, for
when they went, it was as if I were losing my own bowels."[92] To another
he wrote of the moral element in his action: "And since I had all along
been obliged to act from my own sense of right, I was not sorry that
an external call, as it might seem, should come."[93] And to another, he
linked the call to obedience: "I was not sorry for what seemed an external
call to which I would show obedience."[94] To another he makes a most
important remark for our purposes regarding the relationship of faith
to intellect, with references to penance and contrition: "May I have only
one tenth part as much faith as I have intellectual conviction, where the
truth lies! . . . My heart is so hard . . . that I have been quite frightened
lest I should not have faith and contrition enough to gain the benefit of
the sacraments. Perhaps faith and reason are incompatible in one person,
or nearly so."[95] Here we find Newman indicating that his final need
was for faith in order to move beyond the limits of his intellect. Interestingly, the recipient of this last letter replied, indicating the aesthetic
element in Newman's action: "If I saw the truth distinctly, as you do, I
should follow your example."[96] This truth was the recurring reference to
Rome in many of Newman's letters that night as "the one and only true
fold of the Redeemer."[97] Lastly, in another revelatory passage, Newman

---

92 Newman, *Letters and Diaries*, vol. XI, ed. Charles S. Dessain (Oxford: Clarendon
Press, 1993), 3.   93 Ibid., 5.   94 Ibid., 7.
95 Ibid., 12.   96 Ibid.
97 Ibid., 8–12. Stanley L. Jaki calls attention to these references to Rome in the
correspondence, leading to a new terminology for Newman's ecclesiology: "Among
the recipients were Faber, Manning, Pusey, Church, Woodgate, Allies, and Dodsworth.
Each of these found in the letter written to him the phrase, 'One True Fold'. . . which
revealed the innermost recesses of his powerful mind by repeating that he was about to
be received 'into the One True Fold'. . . . Details of the guidance he gave to prospective
converts constitute what may be called Newman's existential ecclesiology. . . . For
Newman . . . one had to recognize in Rome the only True Fold, no matter what

described the character of the Passionist priest Father Dominic Barberi, from whom he would seek admission to the Roman communion, as "a shrewd, clever man, but as unaffected and simple as a child; and most singularly kind in his thoughts of religious persons in his communion. I wish all persons were as charitable as I know him to be."[98] It was not to the likes of an intellectual or an influential statesman, such as a Wiseman, to whom Newman turned at this moment, but to one whom he perceived as, above all, simple, kind, and charitable, or in a word, affectionate. In the final analysis, no matter how high the intellect soared, for Newman it had to be grounded in the affections.

Among the more than thirty people to whom Newman wrote that night of October 8, 1845, was Charles Russell: "You have felt that interest in me, that you will be glad to know that I am expecting this evening Father Dominic the Passionist, whom I shall ask to admit me into the bosom of the Catholic Church."[99] In the expression of "gladness," we find one of the few happy comments in all of the correspondence of that evening, and it was directed to Russell. So instrumental in Newman's conversion, he would remain a lifelong friend.[100] Aside from Russell, the only other Catholic to whom Newman wrote that evening was the convert John Moore Capes, founder of the *Rambler*.[101]

There is one final note of irony regarding the date of Newman's conversion. His diary of October 8, 1845, reads: "Father Dominic came at night. I began my confession to him."[102] Just months earlier while writing the *Essay*, Newman noted this very date as a momentous occasion in ancient Church history related to the issue of papal supremacy, infallibility, and schism. Quoting Fleury on Pope Leo I and the Council of Chalcedon, Leo "had obtained from the most blessed Peter and head of the Apostles . . . authority to defend the truth for the peace of the Church . . . (and) rescued the East from a grave heresy. The Council met on the 8th of October, 451, and was attended by the largest number of Bishops of any Council before or since."[103]

In this Anglican deathbed correspondence we find the primary aspects of submission and obedience, which are the marks of unconditional conversion, linked with the intellectual, moral, aesthetic, and affective elements,

---

the price . . . which he articulated nowhere more concretely than in his letters to prospective converts." *Newman's Challenge* (Grand Rapids: Wm. B. Eerdmans Publishing Co, 2000), 79, 81–82, 84.

99   Newman, *Letters and Diaries*, vol. XI, 9.

101   Ibid., 309, 335.   102   Ibid., 4.

98   Ibid., 5.

100   Ibid., n. 2.

103   Ibid., 308.

all of which are harmonized in this final orchestration. In the *Apologia* Newman noted the unconditional nature of conversion: "I profess my own absolute submission to its claims,"[104] the chief of which is "a power, possessed of infallibility in religious teaching . . . for smiting hard and throwing back the immense energy of the aggressive, capricious, untrustworthy intellect."[105] To submit to the doctrine of infallibility is an act of "right faith," as is consent to any doctrine. Heart, will, mind, and imagination coalesce in an act of unconditional submission to the "oracle of revealed truth." Thus, it was in this step beyond intellectual certainty, when Newman unconditionally submitted his will to the Church of Rome by acquiescing to its truth-claims, that he brought to a close the final stage of his conversion to Rome. As these facts bear out, Newman's final stage was one of faith development and the decision to trust again, befittingly called his unconditional conversion.

CONCLUSION CHAPTER FIVE:
Newman's Unconditional Conversion and Our Conversion Hypothesis

WE EXAMINED THREE STAGES IN NEWMAN'S FINAL CONVERSION movement: the continuing influence of Russell, the impact of the *Spiritual Exercises*, and the insights of *An Essay on the Development of Christian Doctrine*. In this concluding stage of his conversion, we find evidence to support a final element described as unconditional, wherein, as stated in our hypothesis, "Conversion consists of five primary elements (modes or types): the *aesthetic*, the *affective*, the *moral*, and the *intellectual*. A fifth mode is now suggested, designated as the *unconditional*, as the state of fully integrated conversion, which is attained when the following three developments occur and exist simultaneously: the four modes function in harmony, the five major functions of conversion are realized (vision of the Transcendent Other, change of heart, knowledge of being loved, faith, and reciprocal forgiveness), and the three major effects of conversion are attained (ongoing experience of the Transcendent Other, sacramental insight and experience, and obedience)."[106]

We found the affective element present from the beginning in Newman's relationship with Russell, the influence of the conversions of his close friends, and even in the character of the priest who was to receive him into the Roman communion. But human affections are only religious

---

104 Newman, *Apologia*, 224.   105 Ibid., 220.   106 See page 42.

if they are extensions of affection for God. Thus, it was one influence of the *Spiritual Exercises* that it fostered such a feeling in Newman, which he expressed as the command, "My son, give Me thy heart." A further influence of the *Exercises* was a correction or development of the aesthetic element, from the "partial" or "out of context" previous interpretation of Roman doctrinal "corruptions" to the concept of a "whole," and the correlative intellectual insight that a principle of development is inherent in all human ideas. These two elements, the intellectual and the aesthetic, are operative in Newman's further development of the doctrine of infallibility, which leads to a perception and identification of the Ancient and modern Churches in the most fundamental note or idea of Christianity: one, or catholic. A further development of the aesthetic dimension is wrought through the imagination, facilitated by the *Exercises*, which envisioned the obedient Christ as the model of man, who is also the absolutely good and therefore the absolutely true, and, by their union and expression in creation, the absolutely beautiful, or, in other words, the One Being of God.

However, knowing is not doing. It remained for Newman to complete in act and in heart what he apprehended in reason as the truth and in imagination as the beautiful. As Newman had said, since he perceived and felt the weight of the truth, he was beyond the excuse of invincible ignorance, and thus he believed that his very salvation hung in the balance. His ecclesiastical decision, then, was of an ultimate moral character. In the final analysis, his decision was a matter of will, submission, trust, and faith. Such is the revelation of his conversion eve correspondence from which, as stated earlier, we learn more about his state of mind than from any formal treatise. In making the decision and committing the act of conversion, Newman attained the fifth element of conversion, the unconditional, when affection is directed to God by overcoming self-will in loving obedience to the Church, the intellectual and the aesthetic elements perceive and understand the image and nature of Christ and the nature of the Roman Church as the oracle of divine truth with the mark of infallibility, and those feelings of the affections and insights of the intellect and the imagination are galvanized in the moral act of concrete submission to that truth. In Newman's conversion experiences we find the presence of all five elements of our conversion hypothesis: affective, aesthetic, moral, intellectual, and unconditional.[107] In addition, from

---

107 D. A. Drennan, *Privilege of Intellect: Conscience and Wisdom in Newman's Narrative* (Scranton: University of Scranton Press, 2013), 133: "This complemental similitude of Newman's heart and mind amalgamated his commitment of devotion with

the evidence herein presented, these elements also operate according to the process and function described in that hypothesis, with the attendant source of grace and effects stated therein. We now turn to the conclusions of our study in light of this analysis of Newman's conversion experiences and the assertions of our conversion hypothesis.

---

learning, to faith and understanding, and bonded his sense of moral action with intellectual accomplishment. Here, indeed . . . is Newman's sense of connections and interconnectedness, which so pervades his enlarging approach to human experience."

The Logic of Conversion

THE HARMONY OF HEART, WILL, MIND, AND IMAGINATION IN JOHN HENRY NEWMAN

TO COMPLETE OUR STUDY, WE OFFER A SUMMARY OF THE results of our research followed by insights from other commentators on Newman and conversion.

In Part I, Chapter One, analyzing the period up through 1824, we concluded that Newman's early home life and its loving human relationships, along with its religious influences, formed the basis for all of his subsequent development. As James Fowler noted, during this period, relationships with our first caregivers, our first experiences of mutuality, influence our affections, intuition, and imagination as pre-images of God.[1] It was from this foundation that Newman developed faith in others, which led him to accept the intellectual influence of those for whom he felt affection. In 1816, when he experienced his first conversion, it was substantially due to his affectionate relationship with Walter Mayers, and as a result he embraced Mayers's evangelicalism. We found in that first conversion the first four elements of our hypothesis: the affective, the aesthetic, the moral, and the intellectual. The affective and the aesthetic dominated this period as Newman formed an image of the God-man relationship in very personal terms, which also produced a redirection of his affections to God: *Numquàm minus solus, quàm cùm solus* ("Never less alone than when alone"). According to our hypothesis, given the primacy of these elements, this constituted a religious conversion. The intellectual and moral elements, though present, were clearly subordinate. In short, head followed heart, as experience rather than reflection dominated Newman's thinking. Thus, his first conversion caused him to accept much too uncritically the tenets of evangelicalism along with Mayers's friendship. This produced a dissonance which earned his father's admonition, resulting in serious reflection by Newman in the first significant clash at home.

---

1 See Fowler, Fowler, *Stages of Faith*, 37, 39 – 41, 49.

Newman's writings of the period indicate several major factors at work: a religious intuition shaped by an instinctive anticipation or grasp of interpersonal faith and relationship, obviously the effects of his early home life, coupled with the intellectual principles of evangelicalism. Here he began to reflect on issues which would be of lasting concern to him: the nature of justification, regeneration, sanctification, the nature of the God-man relationship, the nature of faith, and the principle of analogy in relation to the nature of intellectual method, especially as influenced by willful temperament. However, these first documents were significantly pro-evangelical, although his home-bred religious intuition, with a very different sense of faith and interpersonal relationship between God and man, shows through, indicative of a dissonance.

In the early 1820s, Newman came under the influence of the liberals of Oxford, notably Richard Whately and Edward Hawkins. Again due to the affection they showed for him, he was easily led to adopt their rationalistic methodology, even though it was at the other end of the spectrum from the emotionalism of evangelicalism. The head again followed the heart. But in late 1824, Newman suffered his first great loss when his father died. One major result was his assumption of responsibility, in response to his mother's pleas, for the spiritual direction of his younger brother Charles, which resulted in his most significant intellectual development of the period, the series of letters with Charles on the nature of belief. A major element of the Newman corpus, although generally overlooked in Newman studies, this correspondence reveals Newman's discovery of the principle of willful temper, or antecedent bias, at the root of unbelief. Newman's religious intuition saw in this self-centered affectivity the ground which corrupts intellectual method. Most importantly, it affirmed the principle that intellect is grounded in the affections.

Chapter Two analyzed the period from late 1824 through 1827, the second half of Newman's first conversion phase, "religious" in that it was dominated by affectivity directed to God and a vision of that personal relationship, elements which form the foundation of each subsequent stage, but which change as a result of interaction with other conversion elements. In this period we found three major interpersonal experiences, each of which had a significant effect on Newman's developing intellect. In 1824 Newman accepted the curacy of St. Stephen's Church, where he immediately became involved in the spiritual life of his parishioners. From these experiences we discovered a second series of documents generally overlooked in Newman studies, his record of what we termed personal case histories. These provide invaluable insight about some of the actual causes of his transition from evangelicalism to the mainstream Church of England. From his first-hand experiences of visiting his very ill or dying parishioners, he was led to conclude that the evangelical hard-line "either-or" concept of regeneration was "unreal." This led him back to his intuitive feelings about the nature of relationship. We also find that the death of his father at the beginning of his curacy marked a shift in disposition toward his parishioners. He became more understanding and compassionate, less admonishing.

The second major personal influence was that of Edward Hawkins. Again greatly influenced by the affection which Hawkins had shown him, Newman gradually accepted Hawkins's insights on the importance of tradition, apostolic succession, and the "neither so good, nor so bad" concept of human nature, as opposed to evangelicalism's "either-or." Newman's parish experience bore out Hawkins's insights.

Intellectually, these influences produced a major development in Newman's theology. In his sermons of 1825, Newman developed his thinking along two major tracks which became characteristic of his theological method: religious epistemology, or faith, on the one hand, and ecclesiology on the other. In his series of sermons on faith he made a notable advance in his exposition of the nature of faith as an interpersonal, relational dynamic, affectively grounded, but with both implicit and explicit intellectual dimensions. In this sense religious faith operates primarily through intuition as an aesthetic or imaginative vision of personal relationship with the Transcendent Other. This experience is also affective in that it is grounded in a conversion of the heart, and it is moral in that it expresses itself in the performance of good works. Newman also preached a series of sermons on the nature of the God-man relationship in the ecclesiastical setting, concluding that justification occurs in baptism, even through the surrogate faith of the sponsor. This marked a clear divergence from evangelical theology. In two other significant sermons, he posits affectivity, or the heart, as the ground of religious knowledge and thus the foundation for conversion and obedience. On his ecclesiological track, he preached a series of sermons on the Church, which was now gaining prominence in his theology as a direct result of the influence of Whately and Hawkins.

In 1825 Newman also read Joseph Butler's *Analogy*, arguably the most influential single work affecting his theological development. Butler's principles of analogy and sacramentality confirmed Newman's previous insights, and we began to see their influence in his series of sermons on the Church.

Newman's major theological document of the period, however, is his essay on the *Miracles of Scripture*. This work has its genesis in his correspondence with Charles on the nature of belief, wherein he put to Charles a lengthy series of questions about the nature of miracles and the ground for their acceptance or rejection. Newman's personal experience with Charles on the subject helped him to formulate his theology. In this essay, his first actual extended theological work, he again traces the issue to an affective base: faith or trust in the credibility of the witness is the criterion for the acceptance of a miracle. Thus, the interpersonal dynamics of relationship, or faith in an "other," is the key to understanding and accepting revelation. Newman also indicated the importance of the intellectual ability to distinguish the natural from the supernatural, a further development of his religious epistemology track. Thus, faith, witness, and innate perceptual ability provide the ground for conversion, or belief in miracles. With this document Newman achieved his first significant intellectual synthesis, combining the influences of not only personal experience but theological reflection as well.

In two major sermons preached in 1826, Newman asserted the interpersonalist nature of Christianity and the importance of sanctification, or holiness, in the development of man's relationship with God. Here Newman introduced the deeply interpersonal, even mystical, notion of the Divine Indwelling at the heart of this relationship. As interpersonalist, Christianity is in essence relational and affective.

By 1827, we see a decisive shift which indicated Newman's approaching moral conversion from privatized to communal religion, or from evangelicalism to the mainstream Church of England. In a sermon on the Church, he espoused its social nature and the unity of its visible and invisible dimensions. Then his paper on infant baptism formalized his break with evangelicalism as he confirmed his previous position that the sacrament is the moment of regeneration. The influence of Butler is unmistakable in both documents, and Newman's aesthetic ecclesiastical vision highlighted its interpersonalist, affective nature.

The third and final major personal experience of the period was the sudden death of his young sister, Mary. This tragedy took his awareness of the sacramental nature of existence to new heights, and it rescued him from the brink of liberal rationalism. The nature of the visible world as but a veil for the real invisible world made a very deep impression on him. It was at this time that Newman began a transition of moral conversion to a more interpersonal form of religion. The axiom which characterized his first conversion, *numquàm minus solus, quàm cùm solus (never less alone than when alone)*, wherein the privatized, self-absorbed one-to-one relationship with God sufficed, no longer could support Newman's growing sense of the interpersonalist nature of existence and man's relationship with God. In summary, the period from 1816 through 1827 was one of religious conversion. The affective and aesthetic elements were primary, impacting Newman's intellectual and moral development. Through personal experiences, intellectual influences, and reflection, he gradually moved to a higher plane by 1828, that of a moral conversion to the Church characterized by his new vision of the "right" locus of the God-man relationship in the visible world.

The subject of Part II, Newman's period of moral conversion from 1828 through mid-1833, was characterized by his increasing commitment to the Church of England. Here we found two major and related personal experiences which reveal a major defect in Newman's affectivity, which will haunt his conversion journey through 1845. This was his own willfulness of temper and his resultant problem with submission and obedience to authority. His dispute with Hawkins over the nature of the Oriel tutor position was symptomatic of a far deeper spiritual problem, but it also somewhat explained why he felt comfortable within the Church of England, with its ample room for private judgment: more interpersonal than evangelicalism, but not authoritarian. During his Mediterranean journey in 1833, he interpreted his severe illness in Sicily as punishment for his own willfulness toward Hawkins in a harrowing realization that he suffered from the same spiritual flaw which he had perceived in Charles, in the self-centered spirit of the heretics of his Arian study, which he had just completed, and a disposition which ran counter to his own intellectual theology of faith. He believed that he resolved the crisis by a commitment to both a personal submission to God's will and a reformation of the Church of England. However, at this time he had not yet grasped, as he later would, that the Church of England was the ecclesiastical form of individual willfulness, the realization of which characterized his next conversion phase.

During his Mediterranean sojourn he also was exposed significantly to the Church of Rome for the first time, and the experience had lasting, though ambivalent, effects. On the one hand, he felt the Roman devotional practices were indications of intellectual corruptions, while on the other he was deeply moved — affectively and aesthetically — by Roman liturgies and especially the effect which he perceived they had on the affections of Catholics. However, his meetings with the Catholic Dr. Wiseman in Rome convinced him that Rome's requirement of submission of personal judgment to Church authority made any relationship with Rome impossible, an indication of the willfulness he would soon confront in Sicily.

His theology of the period, developed prior to his Mediterranean confrontation with willfulness, Roman liturgical affectivity, and authority, indicates significant advances. First, his liturgy sermon series is a second significant intellectual synthesis of his tracks of religious epistemology and ecclesiology. This sermon series offers valuable evidence that Newman's theological insights were extremely advanced as his intellect began to make major strides in development during this period. From one perspective it could be said that his burgeoning intellect was beginning to outpace his affective development.

These liturgy sermons synthesize the personal experiences of faith, hope, and charity in the communal experience of the Church, and it is the liturgy which both communicates doctrine through its aesthetic dimension and which also promotes the expression of religious affection. Newman's discovery of the virtue of concord, an Athanasian trait which harmonizes the elements of our conversion hypothesis, is the ultimate objective of the liturgy. Newman's insights regarding liturgy undoubtedly set the stage for the influence of the Roman liturgies.

His major theological work of the period, and perhaps his most seminal document, was *The Arians of the Fourth Century*. Here in his study of the ecclesiastical and doctrinal controversies of the ancient Church he saw a parallel threat to his own time from a similar principle (or temper) of rationalism. He found at the very core of the heretical mind the same principle about which he contended with Charles, a self-centered willfulness which recognizes no external authority. This affective defect causes an aesthetic defect by forming an inaccurate image not only of the God-man relationship but even of the nature of God himself. This flawed perception results in intellectual error in the resultant dogmatic expressions which are grounded in this flawed vision. Ultimately, he found in the Alexandrian Church and its leader, Athanasius, that very virtue of concord which was the master Christian virtue espoused by his sermons on the liturgy. However, even though his theological research discovered again the principle of willful temper at the root of heresy, he was apparently not conscious of the extent to which he himself exhibited the same trait, at least until his Sicilian experience.

In summary, this period of Newman's moral conversion was characterized by a change from the privatized religion of evangelicalism to the more interpersonalist Church of England as the manifestation of the invisible world in the visible. This element of moral decision dominated this period, culminating in the axiom he employed to express his reformer's zeal returning from his Mediterranean experiences: *Exoriare, aliquis!* ("Arise, avenger!"). This moral element, or decision as to the right ecclesiastical expression in the world, was produced by a change in aesthetic perception of a new image of relationship. Intellectually, through his liturgy sermons and *Arians*, he established the ground for the Church of England as the legitimate heir to the ancient Church. However, though he ultimately realized the affective dissonance within himself in Sicily, he did not yet realize that this dissonance also determined his ecclesiastical convictions and program, a fact which came to the forefront in his next conversion phase. But we can conclude that the first four elements of our conversion hypothesis were present and operative during this phase, dominated by the moral element.

In Part III, Chapter Four we examined Newman's intellectual conversion from 1833 through 1843. During this period Newman made his most significant development of the two tracks of religious epistemology and ecclesiology. On the one hand, through *Tracts for the Times*, the *Oxford University Sermons*, and the *Lectures on Justification*, he continued to sharpen his religious epistemology. The *Lectures on Justification* achieved a major advance by attributing justification to the presence of the Indwelling Spirit which both changes the heart and promotes the moral effect of obedience. During this period he was also developing his ecclesiological track which culminated in the *Prophetical Office* where he constructed an intellectual basis for his ecclesiological theory of the *Via Media*. This theory was, however, fatally flawed by Newman's uncritical faith in the principles of the Anglican divines. In the *University Sermons* he asserted that faith is both an act of reason and grounded in affectivity. In *University Sermon* XIII we found him beginning to join the two tracks as he combined both epistemological and ecclesiological themes in fashioning an epistemological basis for doctrine by contrasting the imaginative, intuitive dimension of implicit reason with its expression in explicit reason.

Newman discovered the error in his ecclesiological theory in 1839 through his own analogical imagination, and he recognized the possibility that the Church of England might in fact be schismatic. His research for *Tract* 90 convinced him that his interpretation of the Anglican divines was woefully incorrect in regard to Rome, and he believed that the two communions were much more doctrinally compatible that he had realized. However, Anglican authorities rejected his intellectual insights.

This was an extraordinary period dominated by intellectual and aesthetic development, but in early 1841, just after the publication of *Tract 90*, a major affective influence was introduced in the person of Dr. Charles Russell. The Catholic Russell, in respectful, affectionate ways, corrected Newman's understanding of Roman doctrine and devotions, laying the groundwork for Newman's theory of development of doctrines. When Newman grasped the significance of Augustine's maxim *securus judicat orbis terrarum* ("The universal Church is in its judgments secure of truth") in September of 1841, this aesthetic image of Church unity as the definitive note of the true Church was the decisive blow to Newman's Anglicanism. These intellectual, aesthetic, and affective influences led Newman to compose his *University Sermon* XIV with an additional insight of religious epistemology: the perception of the principle of catholicity as consistent with the objective of the human mind. After a period of reflection, and heavily influenced by Russell, Newman published a statement retracting many of his criticisms of Rome and shortly thereafter he preached his final *University Sermon* XV on the theory of developments in religious doctrine. Here the tracks of religious epistemology and ecclesiology were synthesized, and Newman reached the point of intellectual conversion when he recognized the Roman Church as the true apostolic heir to the ancient Church. Most importantly, this development was brought about through Russell's affective and intellectual influence, coupled with Newman's aesthetic insight into the relationship between epistemology and doctrine as the expression of perceived truth.

However, even though he attained an intellectual conversion in early 1843 when he knew Rome to be the one true Church, Newman made no move to act on his insight for almost two years. He had one last hurdle to overcome, the willfulness which characterized so much of his behavior for more than twenty-five years. Newman's practice of the *Spiritual Exercises*, most likely an effect of the influence of Russell, was extremely instrumental in aiding Newman's ultimate conversion decision. Our analysis of the *Exercises* indicated that they contained the spiritual antidote for Newman's willfulness. Coincidentally, the *Exercises* affect all five elements of our conversion hypothesis. Employing aesthetic imagery of the life and person of Christ, insight is developed and the affections are aroused. Ultimately, they promote decision or election about one's state of life through discernment of, and subordination to, God's will. *Unconditional* is the term found repeatedly among commentators to describe the nature of the commitment required by the *Exercises*. It took Newman almost two years to develop the spiritual capacity for such a decision and action. Newman himself attested to the influence of the *Exercises* by his discussion of them in the *Essay on the Development of Doctrine*, his intellectual focus during this period. Our research supports this final challenge of submission as a distinct element in Newman's final movement toward Rome, and it indicates Newman's serious emotional dilemma. The added element of the unconditional gives existential efficacy to the affective, aesthetic, moral, and intellectual elements that precede the act of submission.

As noted at the conclusion of the previous chapter, our hypothesis stated that unconditional conversion is conceived to be that state of fully integrated conversion which is attained when the following three developments occur and exist simultaneously: the four elements function in harmony, the five major functions of conversion are realized, and the three major effects are attained. In actual experience, they all function simultaneously.

In respect to the five major functions, we find them operative in Newman's submission to Rome: a vision of the Transcendent Other, change of heart, knowledge of being loved, faith, and reciprocal forgiveness. With the exception of reciprocal forgiveness, these factors were essentially present even prior to his Roman conversion. However, his conversion eve confession indicates a change in this direction.

Regarding the three effects, again we find two essentially present prior to his final conversion: ongoing experience of the Transcendent Other and sacramental insight and experience. The final effect, obedience, is accomplished in the act of submission.

Lastly, the four elements are brought into harmony: the affective, the aesthetic, the moral, and the intellectual were brought into a reciprocal and complementary relationship, and to this extent Newman could be said to have attained the very virtue, concord, which he discovered in Athanasius, and about which he wrote in his liturgy sermon series. It should be made clear again that throughout this study the four elements are often described separately, as each tends dominate at any given time, but in actual experience they all function simultaneously. Perhaps a helpful image to describe these interactions is that of a kaleidoscope, wherein the movement of every piece affects all others, and in the process creating a new image, a new vision.

Several commentators offer evidence which supports various aspects of our thesis. Addressing Newman's "so-called first conversion," Vincent Blehl agreed that this "was really not a first commencement" but (as Newman said in the *Apologia*) a "returning" and "renewing" of principles *already* felt (emphasis Blehl's).[2] Terrence Merrigan also analyzed Newman in the light of Jungian categories, concluding that he was "an introverted thinking type with a particular intuitive gift."[3] In his article "Newman: Anatomy of a Conversion," Avery Dulles noted three conversions. Writing of the first, "He seems to have relied on his own spiritual intuitions, the personal example of convinced believers, and the logical coherence between biblical and ecclesiastical teaching."[4] Newman's movement from evangelicalism to the mainstream Church of England, though "not commonly" considered so, is nonetheless a "second conversion."[5] Newman's third conversion was a combination of intellectual discernment but "beyond this conclusion a further step was necessary — that of actual submission."[6] As Blehl noted, "In 1843 Newman was already convinced of the development of Christian doctrine."[7] Our analysis is consistent with these, but we suggest a distinction between Newman's intellectual conversion and his prolonged quandary over submission. In addition, Dulles sees certain "structural features" common to many conversions:

> The heart and the imagination supply the antecedent probability that normally enters into the process of discernment. . . . Newman can teach us the necessity of passing beyond private judgment and of submitting one's will and intellect to a duly accredited organ or oracle of religious truth. . . . As Newman clearly saw. . . [this is] requisite for faith, in the theological sense of the term.[8]

In this statement we find two facts supportive of our thesis. First, all of the elements of our conversion hypothesis are present, or described in similar terms: heart, imagination, discernment, and intellect, and submission of will. Second, in the relationship of faith to the Church, we also find a synthesis of the two tracks of religious epistemology and ecclesiology, our assertion of the nature of Newman's theological method.

Dulles also references Emilie Griffin's work on conversion especially in respect to the final stage of Newman's movement: "First, there is the Desire or longing; second, the Dialectic, or argumentative, reasoning

---

2   Blehl, "John Henry Newman's Conversion of 1845: A Fresh Approach," 21.
3   Merrigan, "Numquàm minus solus," 102.
4   Dulles, "Newman: Anatomy of a Conversion," in *Newman and Conversion*, 26.
5   Ibid., 28.   6   Ibid., 33.
7   Blehl, "John Henry Newman's Conversion of 1845: A Fresh Approach," 28.
8   Dulles, "Newman: Anatomy of a Conversion," 34.

phase; third, the Struggle or crisis; and finally the Surrender."[9] Dulles notes that "it would not be hard to identify all these stages in each of Newman's conversions."[10] Not only does this indicate the presence of our conversion elements, but it also implies the developmental principles of the process which we also specified in our hypothesis.

In regard to the intellectual element of Newman's conversion, Merrigan addresses "the logic of Newman's conversion." Merrigan's analysis helps to synthesize the multi-dimensional nature of conversion expressed in our thesis. "The *Essay on Development* represents Newman's attempt to verify, and to give intellectual coherence to, the persistent 'intuition' that the primitive Catholic Church was preserved in, and represented by, Rome, not Canterbury."[11] Merrigan closes his article with a statement confirming the presence of our elements in Newman's experience: "Newman's evolutionary theory of development . . . is also a further testimony to his sense of the totality of the thinking, feeling, willing, and imaging being that man is, as well as a confirmation of his sensibility for the complex character of human experience."[12] The subtitle of our thesis offers another perspective on these elements: "The Harmony of Heart, Mind, Will, and Imagination."

A final commentator holds that "in his mature thought Newman emphasises the importance of the image of Christ as the means of conversion. In doing so he stresses the significance of the imagination in religious conversion. Indeed Newman underlines that the presentation of religious faith should appeal to the whole person (and not just the intellect)."[13]

In closing this study we may call attention to three points that recommend themselves for further study and action. First, as matter for theological research, the numerous significant documents of the Newman corpus that are generally overlooked or underappreciated are worthy of further research. Rich in content and stemming from the earlier periods of his development, they offer the possibility of deeper insights into

---

9   Emilie Griffin, *Turning: Reflections on the Experience of Conversion* (Garden City: Doubleday and Co, 1980), 29.

10   Dulles, "Newman: Anatomy of a Conversion," 36, n. 43.

11   Merrigan, "Newman's Progress Towards Rome: A Psychological Consideration of His Conversion to Catholicism," 105.

12   Ibid., 108.

13   Michael Culhane, "Conversion in Newman's Theology," *Christliche Heiligkeit als Lehrer und Praxis nach John Henry Newman* (Sigmaringendorf: Regio-Verlag Glock u. Lutz, 1988), 195.

Newman's fascinating conversion experiences. Second, the relationship of personal faith development to the Church is also fruitful ground for exploration. These two tracks of Newman's personal development and theological method were the most problematic aspect of Newman's conversion journey, because therein was the dilemma of submission. The question of submission, of subordinating self-will and personal judgment to a higher authority, is at least as relevant today as it was in Newman's time. This tension plagued Newman throughout his entire conversion pilgrimage, and it underlies many contemporary problems between the Church and secular society today.[14] Further study of Newman's successful resolution of this dilemma, and his subsequent experiences within the Roman community in this light, could perhaps expand the grounds of dialogue on this fundamental issue of authority versus personal judgment. A third related and final aspect for further beneficial study is the nature of penance and forgiveness, in its interpersonal and sacramental dimensions. This existential dilemma was at the heart of Newman's problem of submission, and it is likewise at the heart of the spiritual crisis in society today. The very lack of a sense of the need both to be forgiven and to forgive defines this crisis, which is also reflected in the declining emphasis on the sacrament of penance in recent decades. Further study of the dynamics of repentance and forgiveness in the context of Newman's conversion trials may prove very beneficial in that respect, since being forgiven by God and forgiving others as we have been forgiven is certainly one of the defining aspects of Christian revelation. Newman himself reflected on the dynamics of this experience, stressing our conversion element of the unconditional:

> The most noble repentance (if a fallen being can be noble in
> his fall), the most decorous conduct in a conscious sinner, is

---

14　Robert Barron is a Church leader exhorting us to fight for the Church today that has been wracked by scandal, by beginning with ourselves, very much in the spirit of the Newman of action. Words are a call to conversion: "75% of us regularly stay away from Mass (91). . . . We . . . have been derelict in our obligation to proclaim Christ and to make membership in his Church appealing to a culture grown skeptical and secularist. . . . Catholics more or less track with the secularist consensus. . . . (W)e all have to become holier ourselves (92). . . . (A)bove all, we need saints (97). . . . Fight by raising your voice in protest . . . by writing a letter of complaint . . . by insisting that protocols be followed (101) . . . by your very holiness of life. . . . Perhaps the best way to be a disciple of Jesus right now is to stay and fight for his Church (102)" Barron, *Letter to a Suffering Church. A Bishop Speaks on the Sexual Abuse Crisis* (Park Ridge: Word on Fire, 2019).

an *unconditional surrender* of himself to God — not a bargaining about terms, not a scheming (so to call it) to be received back again, but an instant *surrender* of himself in the first instance. Without knowing what will become of him, whether God will spare or not, merely with so much hope in his heart as not utterly to despair of pardon, still not looking merely to *pardon as an end*, but rather looking to the claims of the Benefactor whom he has offended, and smitten with shame, and the sense of his ingratitude, he must *surrender himself* to his lawful Sovereign. . . . God, indeed, meets us on our way with the tokens of His favour, and so He bears up human faith, which else would sink under the apprehension of meeting the Most High God; still, for our repentance to be Christian, there must be in it that generous temper of self-surrender, the acknowledgment that we are unworthy to be called any more His sons, the abstinence from all ambitious hopes of sitting on His right hand or His left, and the willingness to bear the heavy yoke of bond-servants, if He should put it upon us. . . . This, I say, is Christian repentance.[15]

If, as we have contended, the imagery of Jesus is the key to moving the affections and the intellect to a conversion in submission to God's will and love, there is no better model for us than that of a dying Jesus who, at the height of his agony, could be yet so moved as to ask that his murderers be forgiven: "Father, forgive them; for they know not what they do" (Lk. 23:34).

---

15   Newman, *PPS*, III, 7, "Christian Repentance," 96–98 (Nov. 20, 1831).

BIBLIOGRAPHY

Barron, Robert. *Letter to a Suffering Church: A Bishop Speaks on the Sexual Abuse Crisis.* Park Ridge: Word on Fire, 2019.

Beaumont, Keith. *Blessed John Henry Newman: Theologian and Spiritual Guide for Our Times.* London: The Incorporated Truth Society, 2010.

Biemer, Günter. *Newman on Tradition.* New York: Herder and Herder, 1967

Blehl, Vincent. "John Henry Newman's Conversion of 1845: A Fresh Approach." *Milltown Studies*, no. 37. Spring 1996, 18–30.

Bouyer, Louis. *Newman: An Intellectual and Spiritual Biography.* New York: Meridian Books, 1960.

Braxton, Edward K. *The Wisdom Community.* Ramsey: Paulist Press, 1980.

Brent, Allen. "Newman's Moral Conversion." *The Downside Review* 104. April 1986, 79–94.

Butler, Joseph. *The Analogy of Religion Natural and Revealed, to the Constitution and Course of Nature*, 15th ed. New York: Mark H. Newman, 1843.

Carr, Thomas. *Newman and Gadamer: Toward a Hermeneutics of Religious Knowledge.* Atlanta: Scholars Press, 1996.

Chadwick, Henry. "The Lectures on Justification" in *Newman After a Hundred Years*, edited by Ian Ker and Alan G. Hill. Oxford: Clarendon Press, 1990, 287–308.

Christie, Robert C., editor. *Saint John Henry Newman: Preserving and Promulgating His Legacy.* Newcastle Upon Tyne: Cambridge Scholars Publishing, 2019.

Conn, Walter. *Christian Conversion.* Mahwah: Paulist Press, 1986.

Coulson, John. "Belief and Imagination." *The Downside Review* 90. January 1972, 1–14.

_____. *Religious Imagination.* Oxford: Clarendon Press, 1981.

Crowe, Frederick. E. *Lonergan.* Collegeville: The Liturgical Press, 1992.

Curran, Charles. "Christian Conversion in the Writings of Bernard Lonergan." In *Foundations in Theology.* Edited by Philip McShane. Notre Dame: University of Notre Dame Press, 1972, 41–59.

Doran, Robert M. *Theology and the Dialectics of History.* Toronto: University of Toronto Press, 1990.

_____. *Psychic Conversion and Theological Foundations.* Chico: Scholars Press, 1981.

_____. *Theological Foundations.* Vol. 2. Milwaukee: Marquette University Press, 1994.

Drennan, D. A. *Privilege of Intellect. Conscience and Wisdom in Newman's Narrative.* Scranton: University of Scranton Press, 2013.

Dulles, Avery. *Newman.* New York: Continuum, 2002.

_____. *The Assurance of Things Hoped For.* New York: Oxford University Press, 1994.

_____. "From Images to Truth: Newman on Revelation and Faith." *Theological Studies* 51. 1990, 252–67.

_____. "Newman: The Anatomy of a Conversion." *Newman and Conversion.* Edited by Ian Ker. Edinburgh: T & T Clark, 1997, 21-36.

_____. "Newman, Conversion, and Ecumenism." *Theological Studies* 51. 1990, 717–31.

Egan, Philip A. "Lonergan on Newman's Conversion." *The Heythrop Journal* 37:4. October 1996, 437–55.

Ffinch, Michael. *Newman: Toward the Second Spring*. San Francisco: Ignatius Press, 1992.

Fowler, James. *Stages of Faith*. San Francisco: Harper, 1981.

Gelpi, Donald. "Religious Conversion: A New Way of Being." In *The Human Experience of Conversion*. Edited by Francis A. Eigo. Villanova: Villanova University Press, 1987, 175–202.

Gilley, Sheridan. *Newman and His Age*. Westminster: Christian Classics, 1990.

Gleason, Robert. Introduction to *The Spiritual Exercises of St. Ignatius*. Translated by Anthony Mottola. New York: Doubleday, 1964.

Ganss, George E. *The Spiritual Exercises of St. Ignatius: A Translation and Commentary*. St. Louis: The Institute of Jesuit Sources, 1992.

Haughton, Rosemary. *The Transformation of Man*. New York: Paulist Press, 1967.

_____. *Love*. Baltimore: Penguin, 1971.

Häring, Bernard. *This Time of Salvation*. New York: Herder and Herder, 1966.

_____. *A Sacramental Spirituality*. New York: Sheed and Ward, 1962.

_____. *Shalom: Peace*. New York: Farrar, Straus, and Giroux, 1967.

_____. *Free and Faithful in Christ*. Vol. 1. New York: The Seabury Press, 1978.

Huang, Daniel Patrick. "The Spiritual Exercises and the Conversion of John Henry Newman." *America*. 29 July 1995, 25–27.

Jackson, F. J. Foakes. *Anglican Church Principles*. New York: The Macmillan Company, 1924.

Jaki, Stanley L. *Newman's Challenge*. Grand Rapids: William B. Eerdmans Publishing Co, 2000.

Ker, Ian. *John Henry Newman: A Biography*. New York: Oxford University Press, 1988.

_____. *Healing the Wound of Humanity: The Spirituality of John Henry Newman*. London: Darton, Longman and Todd, Ltd, 1993.

_____. *Newman and the Fullness of Christianity*. Edinburgh: T & T Clark, 1993.

_____. *Newman the Theologian*. Notre Dame: University of Notre Dame Press, 1990.

_____. *Newman on Vatican II*. Oxford: Oxford University Press, 2014.

_____. *Newman and Conversion*. Edinburgh: T&T Clark Ltd, 1997.

Lynch, William. *Images of Faith*. Notre Dame: University of Notre Dame Press, 1973.

Magill, Gerald. "Moral Imagination in Theological Method and Church Tradition: John Henry Newman." *Theological Studies* 53. 1992: 451–75.

Merrigan, Terrence. "Newman's Progress Toward Rome: A Psychological Consideration of his Conversion to Catholicism." *The Downside Review* 104. April 1986: 95–112.

_____. "*Numquàm minus solus, quàm cùm solus* — Newman's first Conversion: Its

Significance for his Life and Thought." *The Downside Review* 103. April 1985: 99–116.

Middleton, R. D. *Newman at Oxford*. New York: Oxford University Press, 1950.

Moleski, Martin. *Personal Catholicism. The Theological Epistemologies of John Henry Newman and Michael Polanyi*. Washington: The Catholic University of America Press, 2000.

Newman, John Henry. *Apologia pro Vita Sua*. Edited by Ian Ker. London: Penguin Books, 1994.

_____. *The Arians of the Fourth Century*. London: Basil, Montague, Pickering, 1876.

_____. *Autobiographical Writings*. Edited by Henry Tristram. New York: Sheed and Ward, 1956.

_____. *Correspondence of John Henry Newman with John Keble and Others, 1839–1845*. London: Longmans, Green, and Co, 1917.

_____. *An Essay in Aid of A Grammar of Assent*. Westminster: Christian Classics, 1973.

_____. *An Essay on the Development of Christian Doctrine*. Westminster: Christian Classics, 1968.

_____. *Essays Critical and Historical*. Vol. I. London: Longmans, Green, and Co, 1895.

_____. *Fifteen Sermons Preached Before the University of Oxford*. London: Rivingtons, 1872.

_____. *Lectures on the Doctrine of Justification*. 3rd ed. London: Rivingtons, 1890.

_____. "A Letter Addressed to the Right Reverend Father in God, Richard, Lord Bishop of Oxford, on the occasion of the Ninetieth Tract." *The Via Media of the Anglican Church*. Vol. ii. London: Longmans, Green, and Co, 395–424.

_____. "A Letter Addressed to the Rev. R.W. Jelf in Explanation of the Ninetieth Tract." *The Via Media of the Anglican Church*. Vol. ii. London: Longmans, Green, and Co, 1908, 365–93.

_____. *Letters and Diaries of John Henry Newman*. Vol. I. Edited. Ian Ker and Thomas Gornall. Oxford: Clarendon Press, 1978.

_____. *Letters and Diaries*. Vol. II. Edited by Ian Ker and Thomas Gornall. Oxford: Clarendon Press, 1978.

_____. *Letters and Diaries*, Vol. III. Edited by Ian Ker and Thomas Gornall. Oxford: Clarendon Press, 1979.

_____. *Letters and Diaries*, Vol. IV. Edited by Ian Ker and Thomas Gornall. Oxford: Clarendon Press, 1980.

_____. *Letters and Diaries*. Vol. V. Edited by Thomas Gornall. Oxford: Clarendon Press, 1981.

_____. *Letters and Diaries*. Vol. VI. Edited by Gerard Tracey. Oxford: Clarendon Press, 1984.

_____. *Letters and Diaries*. Vol. VII. Edited by Gerard Tracey. Oxford: Clarendon Press, 1995.

_____. *Letters and Diaries*. Vol. XI. Edited by Charles S. Dessain. Oxford: Clarendon

Press, 1993.

———. *The Life of Apollonius Tyanaeus: with a Comparison between the Miracles of Scripture and those related Elsewhere as regards their respective Object, Nature, and Evidence.* No publication data.

———. *List of Works Written and Edited by His Eminence Cardinal Newman, in the Library of Sir William H. Cope, Bast., at Bramshill.* Unpublished, 1885.

———. *Parochial and Plain Sermons.* Vol. ii. London: Longmans, Green, and Co, 1908.

———. *Parochial and Plain Sermons.* Vol. vi. London: Longmans, Green, and Co, 1908.

———. *Parochial and Plain Sermons.* Vol. viii. London: Longmans, Green, and Co, 1908.

———. *Philosophical Notebook.* No publication data. Cited in Nicholas Lash. Introduction to *An Essay in Aid of A Grammar of Assent.* Notre Dame: University of Notre Dame Press, 1979.

———. "Remarks on Certain Passages in the Thirty-Nine Articles, 1841." *The Via Media of the Anglican Church.* Vol. ii. London: Longmans, Green and Co, 1908, 259–356.

———. "Retractation of Anti-Catholic Statements." *The Via Media of the Anglican Church.* Vol. ii. London: Longmans, Green, and Co, 1908, 425–33.

———. *The Via Media of the Anglican Church.* Vol. ii. London: Longmans, Green and Co, 1908.

Nichols, Aidan. *From Newman to Congar. The Idea of Doctrinal Development from the Victorians to the Second Vatican Council.* Edinburgh: T&T Clark Ltd, 1990.

O'Conor, J. F. X. *The Autobiography of St. Ignatius Loyola.* New York: Publisher Unknown, 1900. Cited in Hugo Rahner. *The Spirituality of St. Ignatius Loyola.* Translated by Francis John Smith. Westminster: The Newman Press, 1953.

Rahner, Hugo. *Ignatius the Theologian.* Translated by Michael Barry. London: Geoffrey Chapman, 1968.

———. *The Spirituality of St. Ignatius Loyola.* Translated by Francis John Smith. Westminster: The Newman Press, 1953.

Rahner, Karl. *Spiritual Exercises.* Translated by Kenneth Baker. New York: Herder and Herder, 1965.

Rousselot, Pierre. *The Eyes of Faith.* New York: Fordham University Press, 1990.

Smith, Jean. "Newman and Sicily." *The Downside Review.* April 1989: 155–82.

Tristram, Henry. "Dr. Russell and Newman's Conversion." *The Irish Ecclesiastical Record* lxvi. September 1945: 189–200.

Tyrrell, Bernard. "Affective Conversion: A New Way of Feeling." In *The Human Experience of Conversion.* Edited by Francis Eigo. Villanova: Villanova University Press, 1987.

———. *Christotherapy.* Mahwah: Paulist Press, 1975.

———. *Christointegration.* Mahwah: Paulist Press, 1989.

———. "Affective Conversion: A New Way of Feeling." In *The Human Experience of*

Conversion. Edited by Francis Eigo. Villanova: Villanova University Press, 1987.

Velez, Juan. *Holiness in a Secular Age: The Witness of Cardinal Newman.* New York: Scepter Press, 2017.

von Balthasar, Hans urs. "Seeing the Form." *The Glory of the Lord.* Vol. 2. San Francisco: Ignatius Press, 1989.

_____. "Theology and Aesthetic," *Communio* 8. Spring 1981: 62–71.

Walsh, John, Colin Hayden, and Stephen Taylor, eds. *The Church of England, c. 1689–1833.* Cambridge: Cambridge University Press, 1993.

Wilthy, Donald A. "John Henry Newman and Dr. Charles Lloyd." *The Downside Review.* October 1993: 235–50.

INDEX

liberal, forces, 253, influence, 78, influences, developing, 81, insurgents, 251

liberalism, 48, 50, 67, 75, 78–79, 153–55, 157, 233, 238, 249, contemporary religious, 207, 221, defined, 48, in religion, 48

liberalistic theory, 78

liberality, false, 184

liberalizing, 75, influences, 153, tendencies, 147

liberal-rational influence, 117

liberals, 207, 238, 252, 326, contemporary religious, 205, of Oxford, 326

Liberia Spithover, 48

liberty, 56, 196, 290, false, 78

Liddy, Richard L., 10

life and, conduct, 123, death, 80, person of Christ, 332

lifelong, encounter, 249, friend, 321, influence, 142, 199, motivations, 282, reality, 249, theme for Newman, 249

life of, Athanasius, 288, Christ, 310, holiness, 283, love, 57

light, and beauty, 230, radiating, 32

limits of reason-based method, 95

literary structure, 77, 80

"Little Gidding," 47

Littlemore, 32

Liturgical Press, 33, 39, 339

liturgy, 166, 184–88, 190–93, 196–97, 225–26, 236, 254–56, 262, 330, southern, 235, [and affection, 184]

liturgy-engendered faith to love, 191

liturgy's appeal, 187

liturgy series, 190, 198

liturgy sermons, 210–11, 220, 222, 225, 240, 330–31

liturgy sermon series, 184–85, 330, 333

liturgy's promotion of faith, 191

living power of faith and love, 199

Lk 23:34, 337

Llandaff, bishop of, Edward Copleston, 160

Lloyd, Charles, 110–11, 113–18, 120, 343

Locke, John, 45

locus, characteristic, 192, primary, 128, of religious intuition, 155, right, 161, 329, temporal, 318

logic, deductive, 92, roles of, and moral feeling, 87, syllogistic, 45–46, 140

logical, cogency of faith, 142, coherence, 334, result, 74, sense, 95, 279, sequence, 319

logic of, conversion, 332–36, 340, 342, of faith, 83, 89, of invisible grace, 250, Newman's conversion, 335, to Rome, 302, theological tracts, 111

London, 47, 50–51, 55, 61, 254, 259, 261, 265, 280, 284, 339–42

Lonergan, Bernard J., 1–12, 14–21, 24–25, 26, 36–39, 339, and Conn, 20, 24

Lonergan on, conversion, 36, Newman's conversion, 39, 340

Lonergan framework, 23, school, 1

Lonergan's affection, 39, analysis, 2, Aristotelian-based anthropology, 3, concept of conversion, 39, conversion theology, 2, 7, 10, 14, critique of developmental process, 12, description of horizon, 8, development, 39, horizon, 29, intentionality analysis, 15, intentions, 10, mode of religious conversion, 36, pattern, 24, schema, 9, sense, 10–11, theology, 9, theory of intentionality, 17, work, 9, 20

Longmans, Green, and Co., 81, 129, 156, 238, 254, 259, 261, 280, 284, 340–42

Lord Bishop of Oxford, 282, 300, 341

Lord's, divinity, 216, economy, 200, judgment, 229, Supper, 228, loss, great, 107, first great, 326

Loss and Gain, 80–81, 107, 246

loss of fatherly love, 81, of love, 263

love, abstract, 223, act of, in response to, 8, act of, 13, 129, condescending, 197, defined, 223, description of Christian love, 197, faith which worketh by, 123, filial, 249, fraternal, flooding, 7–8, 89, free gift of, 124, habitual, 192, human, 41, little, 232, merciful, 27, mutual, 137, product of, 97, radiating, 149, religious, 7, 14, religious matters, 2, self-donating, 125, social, 224, souls, source of love and stability, 48, true, xv, 223, unmerited, 138, waxing cold, 263, working by, 63

love and, affections, 35, compassion, 37, experience, 130, power, 130, power of Christ, 130, loved, 9, 13, 37, 41

love of, Christ, 26, 47, 308, God, 11, 57, 93, 157, 310, 313

O

ABOUT THE AUTHOR

ROBERT C. CHRISTIE is past President of the Saint John Henry Newman Association, serving on its board of directors for more than twenty years. He was also editor of the Association's newsletter during that period. He has authored numerous articles, book chapters, and a stage play about Newman, titled *Echoes from Home*. His work focuses particularly on Newman's conversion experiences and interpersonal relationships, and how they informed his theological and spiritual insights. Formerly Senior Professor of Philosophy and Religion at DeVry University in North Brunswick, New Jersey, he has also taught theology at numerous Roman Catholic colleges and universities, including Seton Hall and Saint Peter's. He is the former Executive Director of the National Institute of Newman Studies and a founding member of that Institute's Board of Trustees, and the former editor-in-chief of the Institute's publication, the *Newman Studies Journal*. His doctoral dissertation was a study of Newman's conversions, under the direction of Newman scholar Avery Cardinal Dulles. He also has twenty-five years' experience in professional theatre, which he has employed as a major tool in communicating the legacy of Saint John Henry Newman. Recently, he has edited and published two collections of essays, *Saint John Henry Newman: Preserving and Promulgating His Legacy* (2019), and *The Relevance of Newman in a Post-Christian World* (2021), with Keith Beaumont.